GW01279223

MONASH

Act of the State Parliament of Victoria founding the University — 1958

University opens to students under Vice-Chancellor Louis Matheson — 1961

number of students reaches 10 384 in seven faculties (32 per cent women) — 1970

number of students reaches 14 096 (43 per cent women) — 1980

the McNeill committee of Council proposes a more corporate leadership — 1985

John Dawkins issues the Commonwealth Green Paper on higher education — 1987

mergers with Chisholm and Gippsland Institutes — 1990

merger with the Pharmacy College, first off-shore graduations — 1991

number of students reaches 34 920 in ten faculties (50 per cent women) — 1992

Monash International established as a University-controlled company — 1994

Berwick campus opens: combined courses with TAFE — 1995

number of students reaches 41 543 (54 per cent women), 5795 international students — 1996

Monash Malaysia opens — 1998

Remaking the University
MONASH
Simon Marginson

ALLEN & UNWIN

Copyright © Monash University, 2000

All rights reserved. No part of this book may be reproduced or transmitted in any form or by any means, electronic or mechanical, including photocopying, recording or by any information storage and retrieval system, without prior permission in writing from the publisher.

First published in 2000
Allen & Unwin
9 Atchison Street
St Leonards NSW 1590
Australia
Phone: (61 2) 8425 0100
Fax: (61 2) 9906 2218
E-mail: frontdesk@allen-unwin.com.au
Web: http://www.allen-unwin.com.au

National Library of Australia
Cataloguing-in-Publication entry:

Marginson, Simon.
    Monash: remaking the university.

    Includes index.
    ISBN 1 86508 268 6.

    1. Monash University—History. 2. Universities and colleges—
    Victoria—Melbourne—History. I. Title

378.9451

Set in 10/14 pt Fairfield by DOCUPRO, Sydney
Printed and bound by Brown Prior Anderson Pty Ltd, Burwood, Vic.

In memory of a great Monash historian, Geoffrey Serle (1922–1998)

Contents

Tables and figure	viii
Foreword	ix
Preface	xiii
1. Beginnings	1
2. Clayton in steady state	22
3. The 'Unified National System'	48
4. Strategic management and cultural change	69
5. Monash merges	97
6. Gone global	135
7. Greater Monash	161
8. The arts	185
9. Learning, teaching, research	198
Afterword	249
Endnotes	251
Index	273

Tables and figure

Tables

1.1	Student numbers by sex, Monash University, 1961–76	11
1.2	Equivalent full-time students by faculty, 1962–76	12
2.1	Students in higher education, 1975–87, selected years	24
2.2	Student numbers by sex, Monash University, 1976–88	30
2.3	Equivalent full-time students by faculty, 1976–86	31
3.1	Enrolments in Australian higher education, 1987–96	57
3.2	Consolidation of institutions in Victoria, 1987–94	61
5.1	Staff Association of Monash University plebiscite, August 1989	107
5.2	Engineering and Science enrolments by campus, 1995	121
5.3	Computing enrolments by campus, 1995	122
5.4	Arts, Education, Law, Medicine, Nursing and Pharmacy enrolments by campus, 1995	125
5.5	Student load in Business and Economics, 1990–96	128
5.6	Business and Economics enrolments by campus, 1995	130
5.7	Enrolments at Monash by campus, 1990–96	132
6.1	Declining costs of global transport and communications, 1970–90	138
6.2	International students at Monash, 1987–97	144
6.3	Monash international students, 1996, country of origin	148
7.1	Monash students by sex, 1988–97	162
7.2	Student load by faculty, 1986–97	163
7.3	Sources of income, Monash University, 1995	175
7.4	Sources of the income of each faculty, 1995	176
9.1	The 20 schools providing the largest number of school-leavers to Monash University, 1991 and 1995	209
9.2	Research publications and research grants per head, 1993: six universities compared	219
9.3	Expenditure on research, Engineering, 1991–97	231

Figure

9.1	Job vacancies registered at the Monash University Student Employment and Career Service, 1980–96	204

Foreword

'Only in a new university.' My attention was first drawn to Monash in 1965 as the place where the study of Asia was about to reach the largest number of undergraduates in Australia. At the time, I was visiting the Australian National University (ANU) as one of its first Asian Fellows. Monash had just graduated its first students but was already distinguished by its striking willingness to innovate. Asian studies was still in its infancy in Australia and very much a Cinderella in the old universities. Only a new university could really push at the edges of what was allowable in the culture of the day as the ANU had started to do a decade and a half earlier. But the ANU had done so mainly in the postgraduate area. What Monash did was to take Asian studies into the heartland of the arts and social sciences disciplines, offering challenging choices to a wider school-leaving cohort. In this way, it gave a new generation of Victorian undergraduates an opportunity that had not been available for their earlier counterparts during the past century of higher education in Australia.

How does a new university differ from a university that does new things? Even the oldest universities are supposed to be able to do new things from time to time, especially if they can reach out to new frontiers of knowledge. I thought I knew what newness meant, having been a freshman at the new University of Malaya, Singapore when it was established in 1949 and a new staff member when the university established its Kuala Lumpur campus. But, in comparison with Monash, neither was quite as new. The first had been a merger of two colleges and started with staff and students who were already there. The other was no doubt the first in a new country, one that was launched to nation-build where no nation existed, but it was nevertheless more like an extension of a pre-existing campus that had been transplanted to a new site. In any case, both were markedly copies of metropolitan universities in England. Only when I experienced the newness of Monash did I see the difference.

The difference can be compared with that between late industrialising countries and earlier ones. We know what Germany and Japan were able to do when they set out to catch up with Britain. The world is still amazed at what the United States has been able to do as it passed everybody else by the second half of this century. The lateness forced countries to hurry. The newness enabled them not only to learn from earlier mistakes and do things differently, but also to try to do totally new things. With a university, the former task raised its profile among its peers, but the latter challenge was what Monash has come to take up. It has taken a whole generation after its first Vice-Chancellor, Louis Matheson, to get there. This book, *Monash: Remaking the University*, sets out to show how and why the university braved so many new challenges during its less than forty years.

Monash might well have started with a blank sheet. But the authorities who wanted it in the late 1950s saw no need to reinvent the wheel, and all the guardians of higher education would have allowed was perhaps a different make and size of wheel. And since the original wheel was already in Melbourne, the best that could be expected was a more colourful imitation. This has been the fate of new universities for so long that such a fate would have been taken for granted. Catching up was all that could be hoped for, and one would marvel if it could catch up fast, even though the new kid would always be seen as an ambitious second best.

Since my first visit to Monash in 1965 and during my 18 years at the ANU until my departure for the University of Hong Kong in 1986, I have seen many new universities in Australia. After 1986, I came to see more new ones in Hong Kong. Many of them have indeed done remarkably well. One of them, the Hong Kong University of Science and Technology, also built up from scratch, reminded me very much of the early Monash of the Matheson years. Challenging the older universities, it was also daring to innovate, and looked far and wide for brighter and better models. Like Monash, it achieved renown quickly at a time when funding was not a problem. It was another example of what can be done in good times.

But what distinguishes Monash today is that its 'remaking' was done in what universities would call financially troubled, even bad, times. Simon Marginson has outlined that complex and testing process in great detail and I do not need to go into it here. Monash had already won its well-deserved place as an innovative institution in almost every one of its faculties. Many of them had achieved this reputation without abandoning the quality in teaching and research that universities all strive for. In addition, Monash had been receiving large numbers of students from Malaysia, Indonesia and Singapore earlier than other universities. But Monash still saw opportunities to do better in the fiercely competitive atmosphere of the late 1980s.

In the midst of much uncertainty for the established universities, Monash did not stay defensively with its upper crust peers but sought to expand its outreach in several directions at once. It expanded its local base in Victoria at a spectacular rate and, in so doing, moved the markers that tradition had long prescribed. At the same time, it explored opportunities all over East and Southeast Asia. The decision to locate its first offshore campus in Malaysia was a particularly bold one at the time. That experience has now led Monash further afield. In its latest mission statement, *Leading the Way: Monash 2020*, the plan is to go global, with campuses in every continent. Thus Australian students would be able to break out from their end of the world and choose to seek commonalities among a wide variety of cultural and political systems. Also students from the original homelands of the multiple communities of Australians new and old would have access to the country's most variegated kind of university. There are testing times ahead for Monash to remake itself again.

Will the new university of 1961 now become 'a new kind of university'? That is perhaps not the right question. Many universities claim to be new kinds of universities. The bigger challenge for Monash is whether its efforts to produce a new kind of university will make a difference. The real question may be: where will Monash fit in when the many new kinds of universities are lined up to be counted? How will it serve the widest range of needs ever identified in education history? There are not only the many levels of imaginary league tables that officials, academics and journalists have been trying to construct, but also the varieties of institutions that are shaping to serve specific and practical needs. Perhaps these latter will not qualify as universities for a while yet, but with new technology and the changing public purposes devised for higher education and training, it will be increasingly difficult to insist that these would never become universities. The story here of the remaking of Monash must give us pause when we seek to define the future of universities. It may not be outlining a frontier in knowledge, but might it not be seen as mapping another frontier in university building?

Professor Wang Gungwu
East Asian Institute
National University of Singapore,
former Vice-Chancellor
University of Hong Kong

Preface

The decade after 1984 was a period of accelerating change in Australian higher education. Individual universities remade themselves, and the higher education system was transformed. No university experienced greater change than did Monash University, where the spirit of the times found its most concentrated form.

This book is the story of the remaking of Monash, amid the larger story of the remaking of the Australian university as a social institution. In only five years Monash more than doubled in size and greatly expanded its role and reach. It became perhaps the best-known Australian university in East and Southeast Asia. One campus at Clayton in the mid-eastern suburbs of Melbourne became six. Mergers brought sites at Parkville, Caulfield, Peninsula and Gippsland, a new campus sprang up at Berwick and off-shore activities began. Business enterprises, corporate leaders, new marketing images and new technologies appeared and disappeared at a bewildering rate. Long-standing processes of research, teaching and scholarship continued, but the setting around them was moving and changing. Monash became a byword for making and seizing opportunities in a more volatile university environment. For the first time in its history it was a university with a distinctive model of itself—a new kind of university with global reach, one that other universities watched and imitated.

This was the second great period of growth and change in Monash's history. The first was the decade after the signing of the *Monash University Act* in 1958, when a world-class teaching and research university developed from nothing (chapter 1). The achievement was remarkable, based in a rare combination of academic talent and administrative acumen, yet the strategies of the 1960s were not marked by organisational innovation. Rather, the new Monash took existing models of a good university and made them better, developing not unlike its older counterpart at the University of Melbourne. Not until the 1980s and 90s—and not without strains and tensions—did Monash strike out alone.

As a history of the recent past, this book focuses on the years 1984–96. Its starting assumption is that the remaking of Monash can be understood only in the governmental, economic, cultural and educational context of the times. Many university histories treat their subject as a kind of private institutional biography, as if universities can be separated from the larger social realm that nurtures them. It is a methodological stance grounded in a certain idea of what the university should be, the notion of it as a place apart from the bustle of life. But I am convinced that this period in the history of the institution we call 'the university' is now over, and the remaking of Monash is one sign that it has passed. This is above all a story of larger engagement, and of the manner in which the inner and outer worlds acted on each other. Correspondingly, the mode of storytelling is that of public history.[1] While subject to academic conventions of research and narration, the book was prepared outside a university history department and designed to be read by a larger 'public' than an academic one. Interested as it is in scholarship and research, in the University's internal systems and cultures and self-identity, it was also written with an eye on the implications of the story for public policy and corporate precedent.

'History depends on evidence and is shaped by ideas. History is always a contest between imagination and evidence', remarked one historian in a newspaper article as the book's construction was beginning,[2] and in the case of recent history the 'contest' takes a particular form. On the one hand, there is the opportunity to make sense of the present. On the other, it is more difficult to secure the distance necessary for historical judgements about larger trends. Recency also dictated the methodologies used. Here again there were pros and cons. Compared with other university histories published in Australia while I was writing this one,[3] the time span of the main part of this study is somewhat shorter and relatively recent. Correspondingly, the book has made a greater use of interviews, with less dependence on documents and papers. The late Cliff Bellamy, Monash's founding Dean of Computing and Information Science, remarked in June 1996 during the course of my interview with him that 'what's on paper and in the archives of any organisation is only a small part of the story'.[4] With librarianship and archives within the domain of his large new faculty, Bellamy was in a good position to judge; and perhaps this is more valid in a time of rapid organisational change, when formal decisions often mark the completion of initiatives rather than their gestation. When memories are still fresh the interview mode really comes into its own. Minutes of meetings seem to miss much of the flavour, while revealing personal papers are still largely inaccessible. Interviews also have their downside as a source of record, for interviewees tend to read events of the immediate past in terms of their present interests and activities. Here a range of interviews provides a check, while archival records can be used to correct and verify the data provided by interviewees, particularly the details of time and place. I am indebted to the quality of Monash's own archives, which are a treasure trove of wonders for someone wanting to know the University, and for the fine professional assistance

I received from Archives and Records Officer Ann Mitchell and Archivist Jan Getson.

This book was prepared amid an endless whirl of personal change, a small mirror to the times it talks about: graduations, publications, orations, travel, relocations at work and home. It was exciting, though I sometimes craved stability and quiet (are these things gone from us?). Most important was the birth of Ana Rosa. As ever, I was very fortunate in my partner, Melba. Reading Braudel's *The Mediterranean* was a stimulating beginning to the object of study. In the long drives to Clayton and back I drew much from ABC Radio National (long live!), from audio recordings of Jonathon Swift's *Gulliver's travels*—I hope that I resisted the impulse to discover its personages scattered across the University—from Schubert's three posthumous piano sonatas, and from the great keyboard concertos of Mozart and Bach, in which so much of our mentality is brought to life.

I am grateful to Elizabeth Morrison for fine research assistance, especially in relation to chapters 2 and 4, and for the work of Isabelle Normand on the IVF program and on the arts (chapters 8 and 9). Bridget Nettelbeck and Daryl Dellora conducted specialist interviews. Arthur O'Neil of the University of New England generously shared chronologies of the merger period from his own research. The project was overseen by Elizabeth Anderson in its first 15 months and carried to completion by Peter Darvall. I owe much to both of them, to their ideas and their patience, not to mention their sharp judgement and differing senses of humour. Liz was the originator of the book. Peter's feel for the University was the mainstay in the writing phase. Peter Spearritt and Marian Quartly were at the heart of things from the start, and Peter provided facilities at the National Centre for Australian Studies. Peter Darvall, Peter Spearritt and John Duncan read all or part of the penultimate manuscript. Gay Baldwin and Liz Anderson commented on earlier versions. I am grateful also to Paul Ramler who chaired the Council Committee, and to Bill Melbourne. Warm thanks to John Iremonger and Rowena Lennox at Allen & Unwin. I was also sustained by Trish Holt at the NCAS, and Diana Appo and Angela Bailey in the University Offices were unfailingly helpful. It was a pleasure to work with everyone connected with this project.

Thanks go to my former colleagues at the University of Melbourne's Centre for the Study of Higher Education for tolerating my long absences, and to Michael Tan who was patient during the sometimes difficult Monash–Melbourne contract negotiations. When eight of the nine chapters were completed, I transferred my employment from Melbourne to the Monash Faculty of Education, for reasons unconnected with the project. I am glad that I did not move earlier, because this is a book that an insider would have found difficult to write. Given that I am now a Monash staff member—also that this was a commissioned history of a university not averse to manufacturing its own image—it is important to record that all who were asked gave information freely, and at no time was I treated with less than the courtesy due an independent historian. Though consultation often enabled me to improve the accuracy of the work, drafts were never tampered with. Warts-and-all, the story remained intact. Consequently, while I was aided by many and learned from more, I bear sole responsibility for the interpretations herein.

Simon Marginson
October 1999

Beginnings

1

A vigorous offensive is in the long run cheaper than a timorous defensive.
John Monash, *The Australian victories in France in 1918*,
Hutchinson, London, 1920, pp 289–90

The name before the University: John Monash

Monash University was founded by an Act of the Victorian Parliament in 1958, and under Vice-Chancellor Louis Matheson it opened to the first students in March 1961. The new university was the second in the State of Victoria, after the University of Melbourne, the tenth university in Australia and the first one named after a person rather than a city or a State. The person chosen was an Australian and a Melburnian: John Monash (1865–1931). The name 'Monash' was first suggested by two chemists, John Swan of CSIRO and R.G. Gillis of the Defence Standards Laboratories, in 1956. Swan later became a Professor, Dean and finally Pro-Vice-Chancellor of the new university.[1]

Some institutions named after famous men or women bear little relation to the lives or characters of their namesakes, whose exploits are in any case largely forgotten. Not so with Monash University. John Monash's achievements were grounded in the educated virtues, and there were significant resonances between the life and work of Monash the person and the kind of institution that the University was to become.

Monash was an engineer and part-time citizen soldier who became one of the leading generals of the First World War, the founding manager of the State Electricity Commission, Australia's first doctor of engineering, part-time Vice-Chancellor of the University of Melbourne, president of the Australasian Association for the Advancement of Science, business leader, doyen of Melbourne's Jewish community, patron of many causes and associations. In the

John Swan. Professor of Chemistry, Dean of Science (1976–84) and Pro-Vice-Chancellor. Along with R.G. Gillis, Swan first suggested the name 'Monash'.

1920s Monash was regarded as the greatest living Australian.[2] When he died in 1931, overworked and exhausted, 300 000 people lined the streets to his funeral.

John Monash's life is chronicled in Geoffrey Serle's *John Monash: a biography* (1982). He graduated from the University of Melbourne with his first degree, a Bachelor of Civil Engineering with high second-class honours and the *Argus* prize, on 4 April 1891, took out a Masters degree on the basis of his final honours, and graduated in Arts and Law in 1895. His first post after graduation was at the Harbor Trust, where he designed a swing-bridge over the Maribyrnong river in the west of Melbourne, and roads and drains at Victoria Dock. After being retrenched during the severe depression of the 1890s he founded a private engineering practice with J.T. Noble Anderson (1894–1905),[3] subsequently going it alone. The early years were difficult, but Monash secured the right to exploit the patents for the use of reinforced concrete in bridge and building construction, a new technique then opposed by much of the engineering profession. The Reinforced Concrete Company was the basis of his success and prosperity after 1906. Over the next decade it was responsible for extensions to the Melbourne Town Hall, Collins House, and many bridges, offices and other private and public constructions.

After the First World War he became the founding general manager and chairman of commissioners of the State Electricity Commission of Victoria (1920–31), which opened up the brown coal deposits of the La Trobe Valley, 'a task of great public importance, difficulty and attractiveness to an engineer'.[4] It was the age of universal electrification. Monash applied German processing techniques in a climate still hostile to all things German, overcame a crisis caused by the unexpectedly high moisture content of the brown coal, and provided Victorian industry and households with their first reliable source of cheap and abundant power. Serle concludes that at the State Electricity Commission 'the creativity, loyalty and affection he inspired seem to have few or no parallels in any other large Australian corporation. . . . a champion who saw the S.E.C. through to an unusual position of public pride and acclaim for a state instrumentality'.[5] Later, La Trobe Valley power created the conditions for the foundation of the Gippsland Institute of Advanced Education at Churchill, which became Monash Gippsland.

Monash's role on the Western front in France in 1916–18 created his reputation. In that senseless and terrible war, which he loathed[6] but prosecuted with exemplary effectiveness, Monash rose to Lieutenant-General, the leading Australian and one of 20 corps commanders in the British Army under Field Marshall Douglas Haig and the five army commanders. His combat achievements at Hamel and Mont St Quentin, and his contribution to the British army's advance before Amiens on 8 August in what was probably the decisive battle of the war,[7] marked him out. Monash's capacities for organisation and the avoidance of mistakes contrasted with the British high command, whose reliance on valour and discipline without much regard for technical factors underwrote slaughter on an unprecedented scale. Monash's generalship earned him such high praise that at the end of the war there was talk of elevating him to commander-in-chief of the British army. This was probably out of reach, but Serle estimates that if the war had gone on for another year Monash would have become an army commander.

The British military historian Basil Liddell Hart stated that Monash demonstrated 'probably the greatest capacity to command in modern war among all who held command'.[8] His strengths as a general were the strengths of the engineer as manager. He planned meticulously, deployed technology effectively and maximised the human resources at his disposal:

> I had formed the theory that the true role of the Infantry was not to expend itself upon heroic physical effort, nor to wither away under merciless machine-gun fire, nor to impale itself on hostile bayonets, nor to tear itself to pieces in hostile entanglements . . . but, on the contrary, to advance under the maximum possible protection of the maximum possible array of mechanical resources, in the form of guns, machine guns, tanks, mortars and aeroplanes; to advance with as little impediment as possible; to be relieved as far as possible of the obligation to *fight* their way forward; to march, resolutely, regardless of the din and tumult of battle, to the appointed goal; and there to hold and defend the territory gained; and to gather in the form of prisoners, guns and stores, the fruits of victory.[9]

John Monash. Bust of John Monash in the ground floor of the University Offices at Clayton. More than once the bust was the target of student protests.

The First World War hardened some people to suffering and death. Yet in others it produced its opposite: a new sensitivity to the value of life, and the passionate desire for a better world for all. Monash came out of the experience more caring, more tolerant and more appreciative of ordinary folk. He set aside the notion of life as survival of the fittest. He 'became much more inclined to devote himself, after the war, to serving the people'.[10] The great general returned from managing the demobilisation of the Australian army in France to be a builder of public infrastructure, an educator, an advocate for science, a lover of music and literature. On becoming a Knight Grand Cross of the Order of

St Michael and St George, Monash chose a Latin motto for his crest of arms which read 'For war and the arts'. (In Australian higher education in the 1990s, when world war was a distant memory but corporate economic competition, war by another means, was becoming the norm, a vice-chancellor might almost have chosen the same motto.) Monash became a great public servant who saw no tension between his public service and his business career, except conflicts of time and energy. His enemies attacked his administration of the State Electricity Commission as 'state socialist', and so the great public corporations might appear to a later, more market-driven age. But in reality Monash was not of the political left but the centre, albeit bolder than most. His outlook anticipated the Keynesian notion of the mixed economy, which was to flourish in the institution-building period following the Second World War, when the University was founded, 30 years after his death. Like the universities of the future were to do, he worked across both the private and the public sectors, and he saw their roles not as antagonistic but as complementary. In 1923, providing advice for young people on the threshold of their careers, he urged that:

> Adopt as your fundamental creed that you will equip yourself for life, not solely for your own benefit, but for the benefit of the whole community.[11]

He shared with the Monash University-to-be a respect for science and its applications to industry, a love of learning and scholarship, an awareness of the international dimension, a spirit of active engagement with society, a willingness to try new approaches, and an outlook that was modernist, flexible and relatively democratic. He loved learning and kept doing it. He was fluent in German and French, competent in Latin, a Hebrew scholar and an active musician all his life. He was both educator and populist. (Monash was the first Chairman of Directors of Luna Park Ltd, which opened in 1912. He did not always pick the popular mood. His advice that the oval shape of the Melbourne Cricket Ground should be reduced to a circle was not well received!)

One suspects that Monash would have welcomed the later emergence of mass higher education. Certainly he identified strongly with universities and their broad social mission. As a student in 1883 he helped found the Union at the University of Melbourne and was notably active in student affairs, sometimes to the detriment of his studies. In 1902, campaigning for more government money for the university, he put the issues squarely: 'Shall we raise fees, and make higher education only a rich man's ambition, or shall we practically shut down the schools?'. The lack of government support was a scandal, he argued.[12] In 1909–12 he was the second President of the University Club, in 1911 President of the Graduate Union; and in 1912 he joined the University Council. After the war he was elected part-time Vice-Chancellor in 1923—armed with his military reputation he immediately secured a 50 per cent increase in the university's government funding—and from March 1925 served as acting chancellor for 12 months. 'The University is about as difficult to manage—if not more so—than an army', he remarked.[13] No doubt his successors would concur. Monash urged that students should acquire a broad general education and opposed early specialisation, though here he was less successful. In science, he lobbied the Commonwealth government to establish the Council for Scientific and Industrial Research, which later became the CSIRO, with one of its main sites next to Monash University at Clayton.

In many respects Monash was ahead of his time. In an age that was openly racist—Serle records that one of Monash's admirers in the army in France praised him as 'one of the whitest men God ever put breath into'[14]—Monash mostly rejected ethnic, religious and class-based prejudices, and his own success was a striking response to the anti-semitism that still lingered at all levels. He wavered sometimes on ethnicity, and like most of his male contemporaries he was largely blind to women's rights. In an age when the Australian middle class was imbued with the class consciousness of the Britain from which the new nation had sprung (1901), Monash was a nationalist and a meritocrat. He associated Australia with equal opportunity and the career open to the talents, in which nothing was more important than hard work and concentrated will. Monash was utterly confident of the capacity of the organised intellect to solve technological and social problems through scientifically based innovations, and believed in the capacity of Australians working in their own institutions to create something better. He was passionate about progress and absorbed in the power of the self-managed will, the centred self, while conservative in values. His was the *persona* of the institutional pioneer-manager:

> He achieved greatness, essentially as an administrator, by cultivating to a super-pitch of excellence the ordinary talents and virtues: a retentive memory, energy and capacity for hard work, concentration, orderliness, common sense, power of logical analysis, attention to detail, fine judgement.[15]

Monash trained himself, and he encouraged autonomy in others; he 'led and did not drive'. 'The subordinate should not be hampered by too precise or detailed instructions, but is to be encouraged to act according to local circumstances', he stated.[16]

John Monash would have been much at home in the pioneering days of Monash University in the 1960s. Though stronger on centralisation than devolution and a grand planner in the high modern manner, he would have found plenty of scope in the more complex settings of the 1990s. One suspects that the University's assumption of a larger educational role and its determination to link itself to industry and commerce (thereby bringing two parts of his own life more closely together), and its reforging of itself as a national institution within a globalising world, would all have greatly appealed to him.

Foundation of the University

What then led the State of Victoria, with the support of the Commonwealth government, to establish a large new university at Clayton in John Monash's name 27 years after his death? The story of the first making of the University, told elsewhere,[17] will be touched on only briefly here. Nevertheless, the early years were remarkable. The two decades from 1955 to 1975 saw the greatest educational expansion in Australia's history. Here the foundation of new universities was the outcome of profound changes in economy, government, society and knowledge.[18] Monash was the first and in conventional terms the most successful of all of the universities that were established at this time.

A decade of economic growth, technological revolution in industry and growing social programs underpinned the expansion of white-collar, technical and professional jobs, especially in the services and professions most dependent on formal credentialling. At the same time, after World War Two and the devastating lesson of Hiroshima, science and technology were seen as the source of future national competitiveness in which economic and military aspects were blended. The launch of the first Soviet unmanned spacecraft (the Sputnik) in 1957 raised the competitive stakes in science education. The growing demand for university-trained people, coupled with the broadening of prosperity and consumption that typified the 1950s in Australia,[19] were matched by rising aspirations for higher education. University was becoming *the* tool of self-improvement—the avenue to upward social mobility and the cultural sensibilities and aesthetic experiences once confined to pockets of the *bourgeoisie*. The number of students staying on to the later years of school began to grow, and from 1956 onwards applications for higher education rose sharply.

The existing Australian universities, such as the University of Melbourne which was founded a century before in 1853, were small and comfortable enclaves of professional training and elite culture. They defined themselves as one remove from government and industry and 'a place apart' from the more plebeian society around them.[20] These universities now began to feel the pressures created by the emphasis on science and technology, government-driven modernisation strategies, and growing student demand. It was no longer possible to take all comers in every course. In 1956 the University of Melbourne introduced a quota in the first year of the medical course, and the University of Sydney soon followed. Other courses then became subject to quota. Pressure for new universities grew, together with pressure for Commonwealth government intervention. In December 1956 Prime Minister Menzies invited the Chairman of the University Grants Committee in Britain, Sir Keith Murray, to chair a review of university education in Australia that was to establish the basis for national policy-making, national funding and administration, making possible the modernisation of higher education within an expanding national system.

The Murray committee reported in September 1957. 'The most urgent demand which is made of the universities of to-day is for the provision of sufficient graduates', it stated. 'The post-war community calls for more and more graduates of an increasing variety of kinds . . . doctors, dentists, lawyers, economists, ministers of religion, teachers, scientists, engineers, agriculturalists, veterinary scientists, technologists, administrators, and many others'. (There was no mention of managers, economists, accountants and financiers, who were to be the targets of growth strategies in the 1980s.) In Victoria there was 'strong ground' for the creation of a second university in Melbourne. It could not be expected that the University of Melbourne, which had 7908 students in 1957, would be able to grow much beyond 12 000. This would not be enough. While Melbourne's engineering school was able to expand in the basic engineering fields there were also needs for training and research in 'a wide variety of chemical and engineering technologies. These can only be provided in a second university'.[21]

The Murray committee did more than legitimise an expansion in the number of universities. It established a new kind of relationship between universities, public need and government as interpreter of public need, which was to mark the university at Clayton and those that followed as different from Melbourne and the other first-wave universities in Australia. Monash was to be more of a creature of government and its modernising strategies, and of the mass educational participation that was a part of those strategies, and less of a 'place apart'. This did not compromise the academic character of the new universities or signify that they were not autonomous. Rather, it meant that the nature of their autonomy was more closely implicated in public policy. Thirty years later, this difference was to show itself in Monash's positive response to the Dawkins' reforms to higher education (chapters 3 and 4) at a time when Melbourne considered opting out of the national system of higher education altogether. The Murray committee put the new, reciprocal relationship between universities and government thus:

> The days when universities could live in a world apart, if ever they truly existed, are long since over. No independent nation in the modern age can maintain a civilised way of life unless it is well served by its universities; and no university nowadays can succeed in its double aim of higher education and the pursuit of knowledge without the good-will

and support of the Government of the country. Governments are therefore bound to give to universities what assistance they need to perform their proper functions; but in their turn universities are bound to be vigilant to see that they give the services to the community that are required by the necessities of the age.[22]

Nevertheless, the question of *how* to serve the community remained somewhat unsettled, and in the planning of the new university there was a tension between a science/technology focus and a more general academic foundation.[23] There was long-standing support for a technological emphasis. In 1941 representatives of the University of Melbourne and the Melbourne Technical College had discussed the possible mutual creation of a faculty of Technology. In 1946 the Victorian government had decided to establish a Victorian Institute of Technology, based on the Melbourne Technical College (later the Royal Melbourne Institute of Technology, RMIT), but in 1947 a change of minister stalled the proposal.[24] In 1956 the State government's Ramsay committee recommended the creation of a university of technology, like the NSW University of Technology (later the University of NSW), which had been formed from Sydney Technical College in 1949. The Victorian government's submission to the Murray committee was prepared by the director of technical education, and reflected this thinking. Nevertheless, the growth pressure on the University of Melbourne was such that a second multi-faculty institution was becoming inevitable, despite lobbying by the Melbourne Technical College.[25] So the Murray committee saw it. Requirements for arts and commerce graduates were growing as fast as requirements for scientists and engineers. The committee argued that not only would applied sciences thrive better in association with pure science, but a further association with the arts, social sciences and humanities would help to broaden the technological outlook.

Yet the glowing vision of a technological university, powered by dreams about the role of science and vaguer notions of synergy with industry, was persistent. The University was named after an engineer. In the passage of the *Monash University Act* in April 1958, the State Minister for Education stated that Monash would 'take care first of the study of the application of science to industry'. He appointed Robert Blackwood—the general manager of the manufacturing firm Dunlop, and a former Dean of Engineering at the University of Melbourne (1947)—its first Chancellor. On the 26-member interim council, nine were from business, and the majority from education had scientific qualifications. That council appointed a first Vice-Chancellor, Matheson, who had served as Professor of Civil Engineering at Melbourne (1947–50), and subsequently held a chair at Manchester.

The Act specified that courses in applied science and technology, science and engineering would open first, and the interim council settled on Science,

Engineering and Medicine, with Arts, Commerce, Applied Science, Education and Law to follow. In the outcome the AUC forced the addition of Arts and Commerce to the first group. This was direct national intervention in the shaping of the University, brokered as part of a compromise between an interim council and State government (intent on early opening by 1960 or 1961) and a Commonwealth wanting to delay the opening of Monash until the Murray committee's preferred date of 1964. The result was to further accelerate the already rapid formation of Monash, while ensuring it was a general university from the start—though perhaps, notwithstanding the claims of Law, it was the sciences and science and technology-based professions in Engineering and Medicine that became Monash Clayton's greatest strength. To that extent the original vision of a science and technology-based university survived.

The site of the new university occasioned much debate. The interim council considered and rejected arguments in favour of a country rather than a city location, though perhaps the Clayton site was another compromise, for it was 20 kilometres southwest of the city centre. The argument for the site was that according to the demographic planners, the southeast was the epicentre of Melbourne's future population. Monash might eventually enrol 12 000 students, it was reckoned, and the interim council was granted 115 hectares, of which 15 were allocated to the CSIRO. This allowed plenty of room for both buildings and parkland.

The choice of the Clayton site was an important decision. Thirteen other sites were examined by the interim council, and the alternatives that were rejected included the site of Kew Mental Hospital and the Caulfield racecourse.[26] Earlier possibilities included the site of Pentridge Prison at Coburg and the Jolimont railway yards. Caulfield might have been less expansive, but in retrospect it seems the better choice than Clayton. People do not cluster in the epicentre of abstract models but where transport lines are leading, and where other social institutions are located. In 1986 the historian and Dean of Arts Professor John Legge remarked that if Caulfield had been chosen Monash might not have been the 'nine-to-five university' that Clayton became. Public transport would have been better and students would have walked out of the university into the busy Dandenong and Glenferrie Roads. Hotels, coffee shops and restaurants—and later bookshops and theatres—would have multiplied to service a growing and international clientele, the University would have been alive at night and Monash's staff would not have had to journey to Lygon Street in Carlton, Brunswick Street in Fitzroy and Acland Street in St Kilda to live the life of the cafe intellectual.[27] Only the 'Nott' (the Nottinghill Hotel in

Robert Blackwood. Engineer, business leader, author and the University's first Chancellor (1958–68).

Ferntree Gully Road just north of the campus) provided an off-site meeting point in Clayton. Monash Clayton was to become a cultural centre for the surrounding suburbs, but those suburbs did not respond in kind. If Clayton the suburb was expected to develop its own cosmopolitan ambience and institutions, at the end of the 20th century, 40 years after the foundation of Monash, there was no sign of this happening as yet.

Located where it was, Monash Clayton might easily have become a 'place apart' like one of the older universities. The result was that it had to work even harder to engage with the metropolis, until the expansion strategies of the late 1980s took the university to Parkville, Caulfield, and the central business district. In this context, the Monash Clayton merger with Chisholm at Caulfield might be seen as correcting an old error, reinserting the University closer to the inner suburbs of the city.

The University's colours and coat of arms also occasioned much debate: 'Amateurs of heraldry—who proved to be numerous—came up with many different blazons' (Matheson). The final design pleased the advocates of John Monash's coat of arms: it incorporated his sword and wreath, joining these to the nationalist symbol of the stars of the Southern Cross and the open book as the symbol of learning. The irrepressible foundation Biology Professor Jock Marshall, at the centre of every argument, nominated the University's colours of turquoise and white and the Italian motto *Ancora Imparo*, 'I continue to learn'. The sentiment was generally approved at the time,[28] but three decades later the official motto became overshadowed by a marketing slogan, 'Monash: Australia's international university'; and a corporate logo with new colours had partly displaced the coat of arms (chapter 7).

The first professors were appointed in 1960 and had only a few months to organise staff, library holdings, equipment, laboratories and lecturing facilities, and to plan their courses. Administrative staff were housed in the Vice-Chancellor's spare rooms, even his garage. The master plan was entrusted to Bates, Smart and McCutcheon, advised by members of the staff of the faculty of Architecture at the University of Melbourne. Construction began with parts of what later became the Science faculty. The heavy clay soil of Clayton was turned into a sea of mud, and for a long time gumboots were an essential item. Somehow the University was sufficiently ready for its official opening in the science courtyard by the Liberal Premier of Victoria, Sir Henry Bolte, on 11 March 1961. Bolte was later to be made an honorary Doctor of Laws (1967). The weather was fine. Matheson reports that before the ceremony he and his wife completed the sweeping up that had been abandoned at 2 am the night before by the exhausted cleaners.[29]

On 13 March, the first 363 students arrived and teaching began.

TABLE 1.1   STUDENT NUMBERS BY SEX, MONASH UNIVERSITY, 1961–76

	Women	Men	Persons
1961	92	271	363
1962	227	571	798
1963	481	1109	1590
1964	854	2069	2923
1965	1307	2976	4283
1966	1823	4101	5924
1967	2173	4947	7120
1968	2597	5869	8466
1969	2956	6586	9542
1970	3333	7051	10 384
1971	3635	7399	11 034
1972	3958	7680	11 638
1973	4175	7972	12 147
1974	4628	8209	12 837
1975	5001	8248	13 249
1976	5326	8425	13 751

Source: Monash University statistics.

The early years

The pace of growth in the early years was astounding. Student numbers doubled each year in 1962, 1963 and 1964, doubled again in the next two years to 1966 and almost doubled again in the next five years, reaching 11 034 in 1971. The total reached 13 751 in 1976 (see Table 1.1), almost 2000 ahead of the starting target, after which it plateaued until the mid-1980s. Students were relatively young and most of them were full-time. In keeping with the times, especially in Engineering and Science, the early student body was also masculinist, with two men for every one woman.

Arts with Deans Bill Scott and then Guy Manton was always the largest faculty, followed by Science with Marshall and Kevin Westfold, and Economics and Politics, later divided between Business and Arts, with Donald Cochrane. Education and Law began in 1964 with the former headmaster of Scotch College (Richard Selby-Smith) and a University of Melbourne law professor (David Derham) as founding deans. Medicine, led by Rod Andrew, grew steadily. It was ironic, given the imaginings about a university of technology, that despite the able deanship of Ken Hunt the growth of Engineering fell short of projections. Matheson comments that 'the original diagnosis of need was not well based and rested more on hope than on realistic analysis'. By 1975, 57.5 per cent of all students were enrolled in Arts, Law and Economics and Politics, 36.8 per cent in Science, Medicine and Engineering, and 5.7 per cent (half the

TABLE 1.2   EQUIVALENT FULL-TIME STUDENTS BY FACULTY, 1962–1976*

	Arts	Science	Eco/Pol.	Medicine	Engin.	Education	Law	Total
1962	304	224	172	70	9	0	0	779
1963	563	388	336	177	42	0	0	1506
1964	1046	710	538	292	118	29	73	2806
1965	1352	912	775	440	171	116	150	3916
1966	1804	1366	1048	612	304	204	235	5573
1967	2117	1680	1238	818	416	381	376	7026
1968	2298	1939	1536	927	512	442	530	8184
1969	2483	2146	1783	1044	619	601	593	9269
1970	2569	2317	1961	1147	722	638	654	10 008
1971	2630	2536	1937	1233	801	755	639	10 531
1972	2814	2585	2110	1253	998	713	807	11 280
1973	2906	2636	2192	1306	1092	974	877	11 983
1974	2931	2696	2057	1521	1055	1071	861	12 192
1975	2969	2703	2242	1502	950	1171	1024	12 563
1976	3078	2869	2358	1484	890	1216	1143	13 008

* Equivalent full-time students, not actual enrolments. Part-time students count less than one unit.

Source: Monash University statistics.

planned level) in Education (Table 1.2).[30] Monash did not create faculties in Architecture, Dentistry, Veterinary Science and Agricultural Science, but left these to Melbourne.[31]

Despite its rate of growth Monash could not accept all applicants, and in 1968 quotas were imposed. By then a third Victorian university, La Trobe, was being established at Bundoora to the northeast of the city. The advanced education sector, including Caulfield Institute of Technology, later to form part of Chisholm, was also expanding. There seemed no end to the demand for tertiary places.

The 1960s at Monash were an exciting time. The site was changing daily. Many of the professors were younger than the norm and the University was small enough to permit informality and a high level of staff–student contact, enhanced by tutorials, which were a recent innovation in Australia. Staff and students were pioneers, the rawness and newness were all about them; there was an energetic and self-confident air. A distinct Monash style emerged, with 'a fair admixture of brashness' (Legge) and the ability to respond quickly and effectively, solve problems and get things done. When Terry Hore, later to become Director of the Higher Education Research Unit, arrived at Monash in 1968 he found the Education faculty 'a very exciting place to be'. Louis Waller found the same in Law, where Derham thoroughly reworked the Melbourne curriculum, and small-group teaching and skills development enabled a stronger pedagogy.[32]

There were also limits to the academic and organisational creativity. In the structure of disciplines, the ordering of faculties and the use of the department as the main building block, and even small-group teaching, the University was following established models. Some of the new universities that followed were to take more radical approaches. La Trobe used schools in place of faculties, and Murdoch (Western Australia) and Griffith (Queensland) completely reworked discipline boundaries. At Monash the decision to combine Economics and Politics varied from the Melbourne pattern, but had British antecedents. The opportunity for cross-disciplinary innovations, special centres or foundation years to provide a better general education, was not taken. In these respects Matheson later compared Monash unfavourably to the University of Sussex, which began at the same time.[33] Those modest experiments that were attempted tended to falter. At first students were required to cross the science/humanities frontier for at least one subject, but neither students nor staff liked this, and it was dropped. Plans for a Monash College, whereby students would be prepared for the school–university transition, faded. At Clayton an uncommon enthusiasm was harnessed to the conventional vision of the university.

Perhaps the very speed of the foundation dictated the adoption of established norms, and the new university was competing with another university whose approach was dominant in the city. The conservatising effect of Melbourne was locked in by the Monash Act itself. Section 5 (c) prescribed that 'the standard for graduation in the University shall be at least as high as prevails in the University of Melbourne'. Although Monash was always more nationalist and modernist than Melbourne, and in some respects more democratic, the Act directly precluded educational approaches that were substantially different from Melbourne's. It must be stated that Melbourne was no perfect example—no model university at the time. Many Monash staff regarded Melbourne as academically complacent, if not downright antiquated and outmoded; and Melbourne underwent a sclerotic crisis in 1964 and 1965 before modernising its administrative and financial systems in the second half of the decade. There was talk of a Royal Commission. Government officials, and Melbourne staff, made unflattering comparisons with the administrative effectiveness of the young Monash.[34] Yet that young Monash found itself always looking over its institutional shoulder at Melbourne, and it was a habit that proved hard to break. For its part Melbourne was often sceptical about Monash, and in Medicine it was bothered and often hostile to the new faculty, despite the need for more doctors. Monash 'had to claw its way into an unsympathetic world—especially in medicine' (Matheson). Plans for a major teaching hospital located at or near Monash were long frustrated, while Melbourne's medical faculty secured a grand new building and the creation of enough new staff positions to restrain the Monash challenge.[35]

In management and governance Matheson created a distinct structure within

Sir James Adam Louis Matheson, Vice-Chancellor 1960–76

I am still learning

Born in 1912, Louis Matheson studied at Manchester University, where he ultimately took the Beyer Chair in Engineering (1950–59) following a stint as a civil engineer (1933–38), a lectureship at the University of Birmingham (from 1938) and a first postwar appointment as an engineering professor at the University of Melbourne, where he helped to modernise the curriculum (1946–50). His appointment to Monash was not the sum of his public contribution. He was a member of the interim council of the University of Papua Nuigini (1965–68), chaired the council of the Papua Nuigini University of Technology from 1966, and was Chancellor from 1973 to 1975, active in the Institute of Engineers of Australia, the CSIRO and the Association of Commonwealth Universities, and was appointed to both the Ramsay committee on the Development of Tertiary Education in Victoria (1961–63) and the sensitive Royal Commission into the failure of the Kings Street Bridge, which collapsed with loss of life (1962–63). On retirement Matheson chaired the Australian Scientific and Technical Council and the planning and finance committee of the Victorian Schools Commission, among a succession of posts.

In this active career the young university was closest to his heart. Matheson's *Still learning* (1980) is a readable story of the early years, told in self-deprecating style. Commenting on the tiring round of city functions and engagements to which a Vice-Chancellor was compelled, he noted nevertheless that 'it was often possible to have a word with a minister, or some other influential person. In fact I used to think that I did more good for Monash by drinking my way round town than by sitting in my office trying to run the place'. Today that might read as if his performance was impaired by alcohol, but Matheson could scarcely have been a better Vice-Chancellor. In his modest account his sense of focus and his utter absence of pretension show through. Looking back, it was 'the thrilling sense of adventure' in the early days that he remembered best. Though the long-term goals were always clear, 'the steps by which we might get there were much more obscure'. Leadership was not so much a plan as a process of serial problem-solving. 'Take one day at a time', the second Chancellor, Sir Douglas Menzies (1968–74), had put it; 'I am still learning', stated the words of the University motto. 'Taken together the two precepts served me well', concluded the founding Vice-Chancellor.[36]

The builder for the times. Louis Matheson, Vice-Chancellor (1960–76).

established practices, one that served the University well during the early years and survived them to become thoroughly entrenched. The main feature of the Matheson structure, a variation from the Melbourne pattern but one with British forebears, was full-time non-rotating deans with a relatively high level of financial and operational autonomy. The powerful deanship facilitated the 'sleeves-up' building of each faculty, while at the same time the Vice-Chancellor used the Committee of Deans as a principal advisory body in broader university affairs. In the 1960s the deans almost seemed to run the University, discussing all appointments in each other's faculties and reviewing major items before the Professorial Board and the Council. Later, the pressure of business weakened the proactive capacity of the deans in university government, but each faculty retained its strong and separate educational identity. Fortress faculties with distinctive cultures and powerful deans became permanent, cementing the orthodox academic structures with which the University began. In this framework cultural clashes across faculty boundaries were not always easy to resolve, for example when Science and Medicine found themselves in radical disagreement over pass rates.[37]

In another variation from the Melbourne pattern the Vice-Chancellor was made the chair of the Professorial Board, and the advocate of the Board at the Council. This and the character of the Committee of Deans established Matheson's role as the deans' leader rather than their manager. Though this aspect of the vice-chancellorship changed in later years, the powerful deanship was to survive all efforts to modify it.

In financing, the Registrar (later Comptroller) Frank Johnson secured agreement for a formula-based distribution between faculties of the government funds that comprised virtually all the University's income. A small fund from other sources was distributed at the Vice-Chancellor's discretion, enabling innovations and rescue operations: 'Very often Johnson would advise giving a supplicant half of what he asked on the grounds that if his project was so very important he would surely be able to find the other half from his own resources' (Matheson).[38] Thus, from the beginning, educational devolution was joined to the partial devolution of budgetary responsibilities.

The more thoroughgoing innovations were in buildings and grounds, where

Leading and managing. (L–R) Frank Johnson (Registrar 1960–65 and Comptroller 1965–80), Jim Butchardt (Registrar 1965–86) and Louis Matheson.

transforming modernism and local pride were given full expression. There were no sandstone buildings or church-based colleges at Clayton. Historian John Rickard notes that the tone of Monash was aggressively secular modernist from the start.[39] The Council established an interdenominational religious centre rather than separate places of worship—an approach unusual in Australian universities—as if to say that through the scientific eye all religions were the same. The buildings were mostly practical, sometimes monotonous, sometimes beautiful (as with the religious centre and the Leonard French window at the end of the Blackwood Hall), and sometimes touched by an unreflective grandiose typical of 1960s institutional architecture. The spectacular example of the last quality was the Menzies Building (see box).

The gardens and plantings were a happier combination of science, nature and university. At the insistence of Marshall, and consistent with the nationalism at the core of the University, only native planting was undertaken. Native trees and shrubs ensured in turn that native birds would find a home. Not everything that was planted took to the Clayton clay, and native planting was not to everyone's taste, but in the outcome Monash's botanical ornamentation was original and memorable. It helped establish a distinctive Australian university ambience, one that was replicated at Newcastle, Griffith at Nathan, La Trobe and other campuses.

The University consolidates

Even before its growth was complete the University was a household word in Melbourne and was well known to higher education circles in Australia and abroad. It was not the University's verve and growth, or its record in research and teaching, that secured this broad reputation—it was the student protest and student power of the 1967–72 period, which took a particularly striking form at Clayton. The dramatic collisions between the expanding modernist university and the largest student meetings seen in Australia catapulted Monash into the headlines. Much against his will, Matheson found himself drawn into symbolic politics of the era, posed against student leader Albert Langer in the popular mind. 'Administration building occupied again!', 'Students to send aid to communists!', 'Who is running Monash?', screamed the headlines.

The roots of the worldwide movement for student power at the end of the long postwar boom lay in the accumulating effects of mass education, full employment, rising aspirations, the celebration of and rejection of popular consumerism, the counterculture, the Vietnam War, the conscription of young men to fight in the war, the campaigns against racism and, later, the second wave of feminism in the early 1970s. In the student activism of that time, a generation of people shared novel experiences which had a profound and lasting impact on their political and aesthetic sensibilities. In this context the story of student power at Monash is rich and important and should be told, but it will not be told here. It is enough to state that, while the disturbances of Monash's normal functions were brief and episodic, the effects on the culture and reputation of Monash lasted into the 1980s. 'The troubles' cost the University support in powerful sections of Melbourne society. Hostility was meted out indiscriminately to students, staff and university leaders. Among students there was continuing Left and Labor Party activism, and sometimes activism of the Right, though the scale and intensity of 1967–72 did not return.

Student activism at Monash became so spectacular that it seemed to crowd everything else off the stage. Yet in the early 1970s Monash had much to be proud of in the more conventional sense. It had arrived as an institution. In a decade it had become one of the biggest universities in Australia. The planned growth was complete, though it was becoming evident that postgraduate courses and enrolments needed further development. There was a strong presence of international students from Malaysia, Hong Kong, Thailand and other countries who had been recruited via the Colombo Plan. Research in the science-based disciplines was well established. Engineering was a strong faculty. Medicine and Law provided successful alternative approaches to Melbourne, characterised by a spirit of innovation, an emphasis on good-quality teaching and on relations with the professions. Medicine approached the prestige of the Melbourne faculty, and in the eyes of some in the legal profession Monash Law was moving ahead.

Louis Waller, a staff member in Law for a third of a century and Dean in 1969–70, argues that the key to Monash's early development was 'the people'. If the deans were important, it was the Vice-Chancellor who was central to the success of the University. The anecdotal and written evidence about Matheson is consistent. He was in office for 16 years (1960–76). Student power notwithstanding, few vice-chancellors have been as uniformly well regarded by their contemporaries, or so successful in achieving their stated aims. If the times favoured a builder—the flow of Commonwealth funding was to be less generous after 1976—Matheson was the builder for the times. He used the available resources to create systems and structures of lasting value. He was especially skilful in adjusting his role as the scale of the University changed. His contemporaries state that Matheson had both a strong overview and a grasp of detail, he was open and flexible, he made feasible planning decisions and good appointments, encouraging a broad range of scholarly strengths to emerge; and he knew when to hold back and leave the initiative to others, and when to hold a position for the right candidate. 'A good vacancy is better than a bad appointment' was one of his oft-repeated aphorisms. In reviewing the period Matheson himself emphasised the work of Johnson, and also that of

The Menzies Building

The Menzies Building housed (and still houses) the Clayton-based faculties of Arts and Economics, and was built in three stages commencing in 1962, 1968 and 1973. 'A tall and massive building was thought to be necessary to give some relief from the predominantly two-storey scale of the other buildings', stated Matheson. 'An attractive, well-proportioned and clean-cut structure, it dominates the University and is a prominent landmark in the southeastern metropolitan area', stated Blackwood. At the time the 'Ming Wing', as it was nicknamed,[40] was claimed as the largest building in Australia. At its completion the northern wing of the building was 125 metres long, the roof was over 50 metres above the ground and the building was serviced by two lifts and 18 escalators. Composed of suspended concrete floor slabs

The Menzies Building. 'Monash will have the most beautiful campus in Australia.' (*Financial Review*, 1964)

supported by a system of vertical structural mullions which also formed the external façade, it had a total floor area of 33 150 square metres and could house upwards of 2000 people. It foreshadowed a conception of Monash that never quite developed, that of a core of high-rise buildings surrounded by grasslands and park: a high-rise metropolis in a suburban botanical landscape. In the original plan for Menzies there were to be two parallel slabs like the first, with 50 metres between them at ground level.

On its first erection many people at Monash felt immense pride in the Menzies Building. It seemed right for the time. Commentators praised it. The *Financial Review* predicted in 1964 that 'Monash will have the most beautiful campus in Australia'.[41] By the late 1960s doubts were emerging. Blackwood proclaimed it 'a thoroughly satisfactory teaching building', but admitted that 'experience has revealed some minor defects in its design'.[42] The building made the people in it feel small and weak, little dots of agency, amid a gigantic structure that seemed to rob them of the capacity for self-assertion. The rooms were like cells, all measured to exactly the same size as specified by the Tertiary Education Commission; the earlier conception of common rooms creating educational community between different departments was lost. The thousands of small windows honeycombing the exterior walls completed the feel of an insect colony. Built to show the human domination of nature, the planners of the 'Ming Wing' found that the elements were not so easily suppressed. In a classical ecological parable about modernism, the building inadvertently focused the force of nature against people:

> The Menzies Building is functionally quite satisfactory and the escalators, serving no less than nine floors, have effectively solved the problem of vertical transport. What was not realised when the building was being planned was that such a large obstacle would have a profound effect on the wind pattern at ground level. On days when a strong north wind is blowing it is difficult to get down the steps on the way to the library; automatic sliding doors had to be installed to replace the original swing doors so that one could get in and out without danger.[43]

The wind effects of a second 'Ming Wing' 50 metres away and parallel to the first can only be imagined. The south wing that was built instead was tacked on without the provision of additional vertical transport. Later, the Johns and Waygood department-store-style escalators began to break down, partly isolating the upper floors. The decor faded and the space ran out. 'The crowded classes, dirty windows, smelly toilets and stalled escalators in the Ming Wing are not quite life threatening', wrote a later Dean of Arts, Marian Quartly, 'but they have worked to strangle pedagogic growth and innovation'.[44]

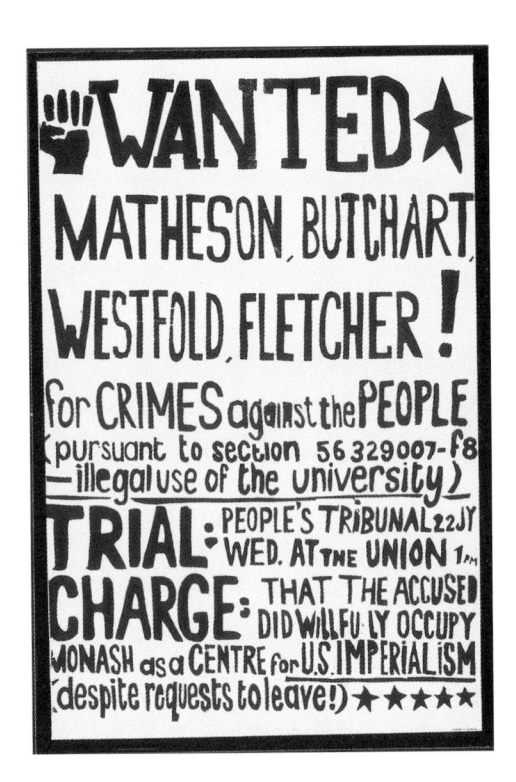

A world turned upside down. Late 1960s student power catapulted Monash into the headlines.

Jim Butchardt as Assistant Registrar and Registrar, noting that the contribution of non-academic administrators tends to be unrecognised.[45]

The 1960s was the golden age of Australian universities. The need for university education was widely recognised, while traditional scholarly authority remained largely unchallenged. Academic staff were younger than in the succeeding generations, and good postgraduates found many opportunities. Whole fields of knowledge were being built in Australia for the first time. Physics and Chemistry were flourishing, and this underpinned a greatly expanded program of basic scientific research, regarded as a public good and subject only to peer review and academic autonomy, while supporting developments in more applied fields such as Engineering and Medicine as well. Academics could believe that they were contributing to society without feeling direct pressure to engage more actively or respond to detailed accountability requirements. There was little need to sell services or otherwise raise private funds. Competition with other universities was driven by the dynamics of prestige rather than economics. The pressure created by growth is easier to bear when that growth is well financed by government. In the 1960s staffing ratios were generous by later standards, and performance was largely a matter of self-motivation.

An environment ideal for scholarship and research, encouraging as it did a process of self-determined innovation, did have its downside. According to Bob Williams (Dean of Law from 1988), when he began teaching at Monash not all university staff worked hard:

> When I came here in 1972, people used to disappear to play tennis at lunchtime. That is fine—they still do—but in those days they didn't come back. People used to play bridge: you would see two tables of bridge in the staff club that would go all afternoon. People accepted this as the norm. Those who quaffed their coffee quickly and headed off to the library were OK, there were people like that in the University, but they didn't set the tone of the place.[46]

Still, if the load was not evenly spread this serves to highlight the achievements of those who did the main pioneering work.

After the mid-1970s, at the end of the growth period, in a less favourable fiscal climate and amid the downturn in student activism, Monash settled into a period of consolidation. Inevitably—with the young staff appointed during the

1960s now ageing, and less opportunity for new appointments—there was some hardening of the arteries. Changes of all kinds were slower than before, except in relation to gender: there was a sharp rise in the proportion of women students. The more routine pressures of research innovation continued, and administrators became more creative in the face of tightening public resources, but in the decade after 1975 the early momentum was largely dormant. Nevertheless, the qualities that enabled Monash to build itself from nothing in a hurry were to be called on again when the next great transformation occurred, in the late 1980s: responsiveness to government and public need, openness to the outside world and the global realm, speed of reaction, the capacity for structural and cultural change, and the creation of modernisations with lasting value.

2 Clayton in steady state

> It has become abundantly clear that, since 1975, a quite fundamental change has occurred and that we are now in a new era in which there is little prospect for growth for some years. Monash has entered a condition which is nowadays termed 'the steady state'. After investing a great deal of intellectual capital and effort in establishing courses and systems, we no longer enjoy the stimulus of rapid growth and fresh beginnings. The challenge ahead will be to initiate and adapt, despite having fewer resources. Like all established institutions, we must strive not to become set in our ways.
>
> Professor Ray Martin, Vice-Chancellor, *Report of the Council 1977*, Monash University, p. 2

A quiet time

The decade after 1975 was a quiet time in Australian higher education, between two periods of growth and dramatic change. In a university sector dominated by the Commonwealth government, the policy settings and funding settings scarcely altered. The role of institutions was more or less constant, and in the full-grown universities such as Monash there was no significant growth in student numbers. The main trend was the slow accumulation of cost pressures in a tightening fiscal environment.

The international recession of the mid-1970s signalled the end of the long postwar economic boom and the collapse of the Keynesian strategies of economic management that had sustained the expansion of spending on the universities. The Liberal–National Party government under Prime Minister Malcolm Fraser came to power in December 1975 intending to restrain the growth of public spending; and while the Labor government elected in March 1983 in another recession began with a mildly expansionary welfare policy, at first it made little change to education programs.[1] But the old claims that public investment in education augmented economic growth and created a more equal society no longer enjoyed government support. Following neoliberal economists such as Milton Friedman it began to be argued that, because university students were socially advantaged, public spending on higher education was a regressive transfer from working-class taxpayers to middle-class student beneficiaries—notwithstanding the opening up of the universities that public funding and free education had facilitated.[2]

Despite the new fragility of markets, a greater faith in market solutions was emerging. On 6 October 1981 Monash was host to the British Conservative Prime Minister Margaret Thatcher, two years into her first term in office. 'I believe in the essential importance of *personal* responsibility; in *personal* free choice; and I disagree fundamentally with those who seek to replace that personal freedom with the presumed superior wisdom of the state', Thatcher declared.[3] Already her government had implemented large cuts in the public funding of British universities, forcing greater dependence on industry funding and overseas marketing. Monash University's own Centre of Policy Studies under Michael Porter helped to catalyse the economic politics of small government and small tax in education and other sectors. 'Australia's tertiary education sector is highly protected and over-regulated', declared Porter in 1984. Instead of allocating more public funding, the government should turn higher education into a demand-side market of fee-charging institutions. Competition and market incentives would shake up the universities, improving their performance.[4]

These arguments were gaining ground in the economic departments in Canberra. Yet the Fraser government was unsuccessful in its attempts at market reform in higher education. It planned to legislate for fees for second and higher degrees in 1976 and again in 1981, but on both occasions was defeated by nationwide student protests. 'User charges' were not reintroduced until Labor did so in 1987, except for international students, who from 1980 were required to pay a visa charge. The outcome was that from 1976 to 1986 policy on the funding and provision of higher education remained frozen. The policy framework that emerged from the postwar boom—national funding, free education for everyone qualified to enter, a planned division of labour and shared funding between institutions—enjoyed strong support inside and outside the universities, restraining the Commonwealth from introducing the more marketised system it now wanted. At the same time, the government was no longer willing to finance

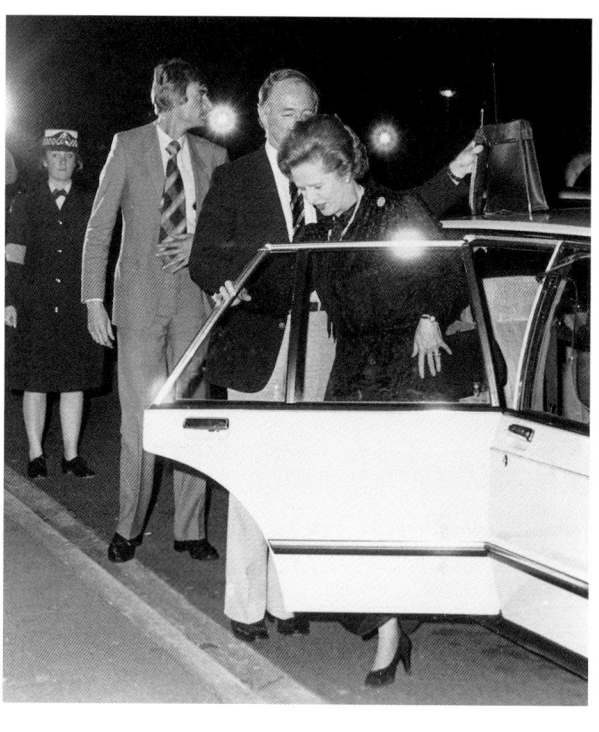

Harbinger of a harsher age. British Prime Minister Margaret Thatcher arrives to speak at Monash in the evening of 6 October 1981. Thatcher's message was about smaller government and larger markets, foreshadowing the reduction of federal funding per head and growing dependence on private funding that were to transform Australian universities.

TABLE 2.1 STUDENTS IN HIGHER EDUCATION, 1975–87, SELECTED YEARS

	Universities	Colleges of advanced education	All higher education	Women students as a proportion of all students
1975	147 754	125 383	273 137	40.1%
1983	168 639	179 893	348 532	46.3%
1987	180 803	212 931	393 734	50.1%

Sources: CTEC 1986,[10] pp 282–3; Anderson and Vervoorn 1983,[11] pp 21, 49, 57.

the expansionary logic of the boom, or even to compensate universities in full for the rising costs of a static system. There was a policy hiatus.

What the Fraser government did achieve was a ceiling on public costs. It restrained both the supply of higher education and the demand for it. It supported little growth in university places,[5] slowed growth in the colleges of advanced education (CAEs), and cut annual spending on building works to less than half.[6] The proportion of full-time undergraduate students receiving financial assistance from the States or Commonwealth dropped from two-thirds in 1976 to just over one-third in 1982.[7] Meanwhile, the Commonwealth encouraged the growth of TAFE, where student places were one-third the cost of higher education and were largely funded by the States. After 1975 and 1982 the proportion of 15–19-year-olds in TAFE rose sharply, while participation in higher education declined, especially among young men.[8] The growth in higher education was largely sustained by mature-age students, especially women. Between 1975 and 1981, the number of students aged over 30 years jumped from 41 416 to 85 854.[9]

In the late 1970s conferences were held under titles such as 'Higher education in the aftermath of expansion', and 'Academia becalmed', images with particular resonance in universities such as Monash. In *A new era for tertiary education* (1980), Terry Hore, Director of Monash's Higher Education Advisory and Research Unit (HEARU), noted a 'decreasing public confidence in the tertiary system'. Some potential students saw 'few benefits in pursuing a tertiary qualification', while some employers believed that 'the education provided is irrelevant to the task at hand'.[12] In *Learning and earning* (1982), the Commonwealth Tertiary Education Commission (CTEC) expressed serious concern about a 'retreat from education'. If so, this 'retreat' was in part the product of official policies themselves, and the CTEC missed the implications of the growth in female school retention and in women as a proportion of higher education students (see Table 2.1).[13]

At the same time the universities were experiencing growing difficulties with funding. Under Fraser, between 1975 and 1983, the student load in higher education grew by 12.2 per cent but public funding of higher education fell slightly,[14] so that public spending per student declined. In institutions such as Monash where no growth was taking place there was no scope for economies of scale, and the unit cost of staffing was rising, because the 'bulge' of academics recruited in 1960–75 was moving up the incremental and promotional scales. Opportunities for young academics were in steep decline. The CTEC warned that standards were at risk. The Federation of Australian University Staff Associations (FAUSA), representing academic staff, used the term 'crisis'. Monash University's submissions to the Commonwealth voiced similar concerns. In 1982 the University sustained a cut of $1.1 million in recurrent funding and a further $0.2 million in 1983.[15] There was little flexibility. Almost 98 per cent of the operating budget was from Canberra, and more than four-fifths was tied up in staffing costs. In total University earnings contributed only $1.5 million.

'Only essential academic vacancies have been filled', the 1983 Monash submission to CTEC's Universities Council stated, and 'promotion prospects of continuing staff have been much reduced'. At 13.9 students per staff Monash had 'the highest student–staff ratio in Australia'.[16] Libraries were also in difficulty. In March 1983 the floating of the dollar raised the cost of international publications, cutting library resources further. The University librarian cancelled 245 periodicals. Council agreed to double library fines to $1 per day from June, despite bitter attacks from *Lots Wife* (the student newspaper). In March 1984 the Vice-Chancellor noted that 'some of the buildings are showing signs of poor repair' and that extensions to Science and the new multidisciplinary building housing the University Gallery were partly being financed from the University's own resources. A total of $1.5 million was allocated to the multidisciplinary building, including $0.5 million from the Friends of Russell Drysdale, the Australian artist. The construction of the Queen Victoria Medical Centre in Clayton (later the Monash Medical Centre), due for completion in late 1986 and jointly funded by State and Commonwealth, was being jeopardised by a delay in the approval of Commonwealth funds: 'The State Government intends to build the university component only in shell form until a commitment from the Commonwealth is obtained'.[17]

Politics of funding. Delegates from the Staff Association of Monash University meet with Noel Dunbar (centre) from the Australian Universities Council.

Campaigning for access. Labor's Minister for Education, Susan Ryan (1983–87), focused on educational opportunities for women and students from poorer families. Monash was not receptive to suggestions that selection procedures might be changed.

In the last full year of Fraser government in 1982 there were signs of a more positive education policy, with an increase in secondary student allowances to encourage retention at school; and the election of a Labor government in 1983 raised hopes of better things in the universities. Labor's first Minister for Education was Senator Susan Ryan. She left the system settings undisturbed, declaring that fees would not be introduced and that the dividing line between the CAEs and the universities (the binary system) would be preserved into the 1990s. Within those settings she called on universities to become more engaged with industry and more accessible to students from underrepresented social groups, including women in non-traditional courses such as Engineering. She also supported a modest rise in total student numbers, though this fell short of demand.[18] Monash did not share in this growth, however. After the 1983 election Ryan confirmed CTEC's earlier advice that the University would be expected to *reduce* its effective full-time student load to 12 800, a fall of 2.4 per cent, in 1984.[19]

Despite this, in mid-1983 Monash Vice-Chancellor Ray Martin expressed the guarded hope that fiscal relief was ahead and 1984 would be the last of the 'difficult years'.[20] But Labor continued the Fraser pattern of funding at a constant level. The 1986/87 allocation of $2097 million was below the allocation for 1976/77, 10 years before.[21] Monash was bound to be further squeezed. On 9 July 1984 Martin told Council the government was not confronting the effects of deteriorating student ratios and library funding. This was evident: the real question was what options this left for the University.

Many staff simply hoped the old environment would return. Monash had always been a creature of Commonwealth funding. Reflecting on his work, Matheson remarked that, while vice-chancellors and presidents of American private universities spent much of their time and energy in fund-raising, 'I found this utterly beyond me'.[22] Yet Labor was now arguing that universities should move closer to the corporate sector and develop greater economic utility in research. The 1983 budget introduced 50 postdoctoral fellowships in industry. Monash, located near BHP's Melbourne research laboratories, Telecom's national laboratories, and six divisions of the application-focused CSIRO, was better placed than most universities to develop income from industry. In 1983 the Monash University Foundation was created by Council with the responsibility for attracting and earning funds 'from a wide range of sources' that could be used for university purposes in the most efficient and productive way.[23] But it was difficult to change the culture of the University—difficult to imagine private funding on a large scale. At the July 1984 Council meeting the Vice-Chancellor agreed with Engineering Dean Lance Endersbee that while some faculties could raise private monies, the government's proposition was 'worrying and unrealistic in all but a few specialised cases'.[24]

Monash in the Martin years

The University Council chose a scholarly British peer to succeed Matheson, Lord John Vaizey, the Head of Social Sciences at Brunel University in Middlesex, England. However, when Vaizey began to demand special favours and arrangements—rumour had it that these included a $150 000 Vice-Chancellor's house to compensate Vaizey for leaving his existing residence, to which he was much attached, and the job of chief art critic on a Melbourne newspaper for his wife, who held such a post on the *Sunday Times*—the colonials jacked up. When phone calls and letters from Vaizey indicated that he was unhappy with Monash and was inclined to stay at home, on 18 September 1975 the Chancellor, Sir Richard Eggleston, solved the problem all round by sending the Vice-Chancellor-designate a telegram announcing that the University had accepted his resignation:

Richard Eggleston. Chancellor (1975–83) in the chair when Vice-Chancellor-designate Lord John Vaizey developed cold feet in 1975.

> YOUR CABLE RECEIVED STOP WE NOTE AND ACCEPT YOUR RENUNCIATION OF APPOINTMENT ACCEPTED BY YOU STOP WILL RESERVE FURTHER COMMENT UNTIL RECEIPT OF YOUR LETTER

'Eggleston's finest hour' took a place in Monash folklore. A new vice-chancellor now had to be appointed, with the inevitable delay, and the founding Dean of Arts and Pro-Vice-Chancellor Bill Scott agreed to be interim Vice-Chancellor until the arrival of Ray Martin. Scott stayed as an influential Deputy Vice-Chancellor under Martin until retiring in 1981.

In people, there was still much continuity with the early days. Johnson stepped down as Comptroller in 1980 but Butchardt continued as Registrar until Martin's last year in 1986. The founding Dean of Ecops, Donald Cochrane, retired in 1981. Many of the professors appointed in the first half of the 1960s were still at Monash in 1984: West in Inorganic Chemistry, who became Pro-Vice-Chancellor in 1976; Legge, who took the first History chair and became Dean of Arts in 1980; Schofield in Anatomy, who became Dean of Medicine in 1977; Bornstein, the first Professor of Biochemistry; Canny in Botany, Potter in Chemical Engineering, Brown, the founding head of Chemistry, Skinner in Indonesian and Malay, Finch in Mathematical Statistics, Wood in Obstetrics and Gynaecology, Nairn in Pathology, Davis in Politics, and Preston in Pure Maths. Yet the environment had changed. In the 29 March

1985 graduation address at the close of his career at Monash, it seemed to Bornstein that the Commonwealth had 'lost interest in the development of universities and hence, probably Australia'. The 'old anti-intellectualism' was back, he stated, as was manifest in the growing financial pressures on the University. Still, he added, 'if indeed Monash is a university in the tradition of Bologna, Paris, Oxford, Cambridge, Uppsala, Heidelberg, Leyden, Harvard, Yale, and many others, then . . . those of us who began it in 1960–61 have succeeded in our aims'.[25]

Monash's second full-term leader came from outside. Ray Martin was a distinguished research scientist in Inorganic Chemistry, author or joint author of 150 articles, reviews and papers in scientific journals and books, and the winner of a series of scholarships, medals and prizes. Educated at the University of Melbourne and with a PhD and DSc from Cambridge, he worked in industry before taking a professorial chair at the University of Melbourne and later the Australian National University in Canberra. Martin's tenure coincided precisely with the steady-state period in both national policy and the history of Monash—a time in which underlying tensions gradually accumulated, building a momentum for change that was apparent only after the Vice-Chancellor had stepped down. Martin faced a different set of problems from those Matheson had dealt with, and approached them in a more low-key manner, consistent with the quieter time and with his own more placid and measured personality. He left the impression that he would have been happy to remain in the laboratory, and took an executive post only out of a sense of duty and the conventions of career.

At the end of his first year in 1977, Martin noted that though Monash was standing still in funding terms its commitment to academic excellence would be maintained: 'In the remarkably short time since its creation, Monash has achieved an outstanding reputation (especially overseas) for the quality of its scientific and scholarly work . . . Excellence in scholarship and a deep sense of commitment to Monash are qualities that will be needed' in the difficult times ahead.[26] He was to return repeatedly to these themes throughout his

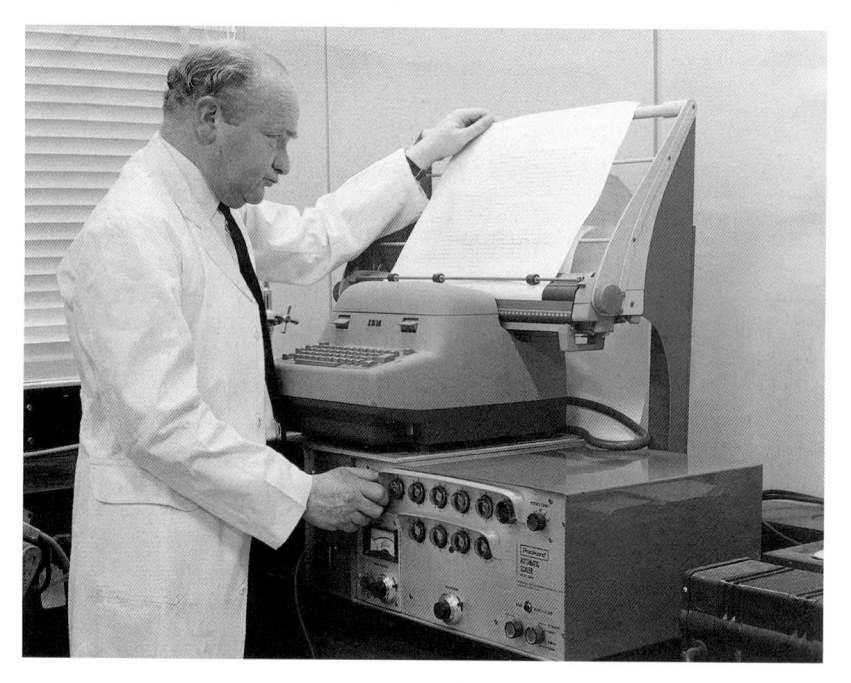

Joe Bornstein. Professor of Biochemistry (1961–83): 'If Monash is a university in the tradition of Bologna, Paris, Oxford, Cambridge . . . those of us who began it in 1960–61 have succeeded in our aims.'

Raymond Leslie Martin AO, Vice-Chancellor 1977–87

A quiet man in steady state

Born in 1926, Ray Martin attended North Sydney Boys High School and Melbourne's Scotch College before studying Chemistry at the Universities of Melbourne and Cambridge. He amassed scholarships and prizes, earning a great reputation in the discipline and three doctoral degrees, from Cambridge (PhD, ScD) and the Australian National University (DSc). Martin lectured in Inorganic Chemistry at the University of NSW in the 1950s, and after working as a research manager at ICI from 1960 to 1962 accepted a chair at the University of Melbourne at the age of 36 years, staying at that University until 1972. He subsequently became Dean of the Research School of Chemistry in the Institute of Advanced Studies at ANU, the post he held until his arrival at Monash in 1977.

Along the way the future vice-chancellor was a visiting scientist in the Bell Telephone Laboratories in New Jersey in 1967, a Visiting Professor at Columbia University in 1972, and a former President of the Royal Australian Chemical Institute (1968). Martin had a Cambridge blue in lawn tennis and was interested in the arts: he served on the council of the Victorian College of the Arts (President 1992–95) and as a director of Heide Park and Art Gallery after his retirement. His quiet, sombre vice-chancellorship contrasted sharply with the pioneering leadership of Matheson that preceded him, and Logan's adventurous and entrepreneurial regime that followed. Yet it must be stated that, like the *personae* of Matheson and Logan, the qualities exhibited by Martin were uncannily matched to the context of his office. The years 1977–86 were the quiet time in Australian higher education. Faced with the end of growth in public funds, Martin saw his mission as being to safeguard Monash's academic standing in a difficult period. His approach was collegial rather than managerial, focused on preservation and consolidation rather than change.

After stepping down in 1987 Martin took a Monash professorship in Chemistry until retirement in 1991; he also chaired the Australian Science and Technology Council (ASTEC) in the Prime Minister's Department in Canberra (1988–92).

Monash in steady state. Ray Martin was the University's second full-term Vice-Chancellor (1977–87) after Bill Scott (1976–77) filled the gap left by Vaizey's withdrawal.

tenure. 'Research is the very lifeblood of the University', he declared in 1986.[27] 'Research' mostly meant natural sciences, Engineering and Medicine. Under Martin the publicly funded science departments were in especially high standing, and central to the University's image of itself.

There was little change in the size of the student body during the Martin years. The total number of students fell slightly and then rose to 3.4 per cent above the 1976 mark in 1982 before falling again in 1983–85 (see Table 2.2).

Within the steady-state student body there were shifts and changes. In the decade after 1976 the number of students in Arts, Science and Economics and Politics (Ecops) fluctuated but changed little overall. Engineering and Medicine grew, Law was constant and Education declined. The University's efforts to expand the Science proportion of enrolments were unsuccessful (see Table 2.3). The main change was the sharp rise in female students, which from 1976 to 1986 grew by one-quarter while male student numbers declined: by 1986 almost half of all students were women. Enrolments in higher degrees rose from 1692 to 2379 while undergraduate numbers fell. The part-time share of enrolment rose in the second half of the 1970s to one-third in 1980, before starting to fall again: the trend back to full-time study resulted in another rise in costs within a static budget.

Monash had stabilised as the fifth-largest university in Australia. With 13 819 students in 1983 it was behind only Sydney with 18 404, Queensland with 17 948, NSW 17 787 and Melbourne 15 708. Monash had almost as many higher-degree students as Melbourne, but much fewer in science-based fields, and fewer staff overall. For example, there were 201 central administrative staff at Monash compared with 342 at Melbourne, though similar numbers of administrators in the faculties, reflecting Monash's decentralised character.[28]

TABLE 2.2 STUDENT NUMBERS BY SEX, MONASH UNIVERSITY, 1976–88

	Women	*Men*	*Persons*	*% women*
1976	5326	8425	13 751	38.7
1977	5334	8216	13 550	39.4
1978	5551	8147	13 698	40.5
1979	5800	8110	13 910	41.7
1980	6066	8030	14 096	43.0
1981	6264	7897	14 161	44.3
1982	6438	7783	14 221	45.3
1983	6402	7417	13 819	46.3
1984	6450	7359	13 809	46.7
1985	6474	7112	13 586	47.7
1986	6655	7184	13 839	48.0
1987	6766	7237	14 003	48.3
1988	7305	7463	14 768	49.5

Source: Monash University statistics.

TABLE 2.3   EQUIVALENT FULL-TIME STUDENTS* BY FACULTY, 1976–86

	Arts	Science	Eco/Pol.	Medicine	Engin.	Education	Law	Total
1976	3078	2839	2358	1484	890	1216	1143	13 008
1977	3026	2562	2342	1531	917	1168	1147	12 693
1978	3029	2560	2356	1501	883	1231	1168	12 727
1979	3004	2612	2374	1509	897	1266	1201	12 863
1980	3030	2667	2379	1585	840	1238	1236	12 975
1981	3105	2640	2472	1682	871	1140	1241	13 214
1982	3104	2681	2446	1747	969	1158	1280	13 447
1983	2902	2765	2293	1710	1042	1103	1231	13 111
1984	2888	2740	2290	1767	1135	1065	1198	13 148
1985	2836	2692	2242	1731	1093	1090	1158	12 902
1986	2959	2645	2428	1753	1114	1098	1111	13 168

* Equivalent full-time students, not actual enrolments. Part-time students count less than one unit.

Source: Monash University statistics. These data have been compiled on a different basis from those in Table 7.2, in which double-counting is eliminated.

In 1984 *The Australian* published an article on 'How to choose your university'. Sydney, NSW, Melbourne, Monash, Queensland, Adelaide and WA universities comprised its 'big seven', while the ANU was stated to have a special role in research. Monash was identified as a leader in Medicine and Law, had 'a very strong BA with geography as a speciality', and strengths in Southeast Asian studies, Chemistry, Physics and Computing. Library facilities were 'better than most'. 'Monash has built a solid reputation across all disciplines', stated *The Australian*, though it had 'failed to topple Melbourne as the State's most prestigious university'. While these judgements were based on word-of-mouth rather than objective indicators, they indicated Monash's contemporary standing.[29]

The prestige of Monash had been maintained. This was the achievement of the Martin years, and their limit. In the face of what the Vice-Chancellor saw as distractions from the core academic mission, occasioned by rising costs and the growth in regulatory paperwork,[30] there was a gritting of the teeth, a determination to hold and preserve, rather than to expand, create and win. The administrative mood was containment. People who experienced both the Martin years and those that followed later described it as a period notable for what did *not* happen. It was 'pretty quiet' (Mal Logan, later Vice-Chancellor); 'a very quiet phase' (Bill Melbourne, Engineering); 'a very unexciting period' (Robert Porter, Medicine).[31] It was 'a time of consolidation' that was marred by resentment towards young staff and new ideas (Endersbee, Engineering). No doubt these judgements are coloured by retrospect. Martin and his contemporaries were bound by the ambiguities and uncertainties of their time. They had no idea that the criteria for judging the success of universities and their leaders were about to change, and that institutional innovation would again become essential.

In the longer term, Martin's commitment to the academic values associated with strong universities functioned as a vital investment for Monash. It created a built-in corrective against any wavering of mission and decline in standards during the expansion and mergers of 1988–92, when the central university leadership was fixed on goals other than research. At the same time, more than a commitment to research and scholarly excellence was needed. An environment conducive to good research, teaching and professional preparation could not be maintained by standing still. In the later Martin years the University was able to identify some of the solutions to its difficulties, such as more strategic leadership (see chapter 4), more active relations with industry, greater private funding, and the fostering of an alumni, but Monash had yet to acquire the capacity to carry those solutions through. A greater impetus was required than was evident in the Martin years, whether that impetus was external, internal or both together.

Martin told one newspaper that Monash was 'pretty conservative'.[32] A student who interviewed the Vice-Chancellor for *Lots Wife* in early 1986 found that 'he said absolutely nothing and took two hours to say it'.[33] Perhaps Martin wanted to shake the persistent after-image of Monash as a hotbed of student power, but the refashioning of Monash as 'conservative' had other implications. A conservative identity might have suited Cambridge and Melbourne, where Martin had been educated, but created a serious strategic impasse for Monash. While Monash had developed conventional disciplines and a traditional approach to scholarship—and in this respect was not so much 'the first of the new universities' as 'the last of the old', a catchphrase used by Monash people to distinguish the University from La Trobe and Deakin[34]—the earlier Monash had balanced its orthodoxy with newness, growth and an electrifying vigour. If the University was to focus *solely* on tradition, failing to differentiate itself from 'old' universities such as Melbourne, it was bound to suffer in the comparison with them. All had longer histories and reputations and larger alumni. The cessation of growth had placed Monash at a particular disadvantage, from which the government showed no sign of wanting to rescue it; but to make a virtue of that disadvantage was unwise, for it reinforced the effect.

At times Martin himself wavered on how to play it. Monash 'still retains its vigour and freshness but alas, no longer its youth', he stated in the 1984 annual report. Two years later it seemed Monash was becoming younger. It was 'enjoying the benefits of youthful adulthood', as the Vice-Chancellor put it. Yet there was more truth in this reversion than it might seem. Universities do not experience the same life cycle as the individuals that inhabit them. In the end, they outlast every one of those individuals, and from time to time they are capable of renewing themselves. The way out of the strategic impasse was for Monash to transform itself as an institution, determining its own expansion and fashioning an educational mission and an identity that would differentiate it from its comparators.

Administration, education and research

With the achievement of the planned institutional size, the character of the administration slowly changed. Until 1971 Matheson had managed without any deputies. John Swan became the first part-time Pro-Vice-Chancellor (1971–75), followed by Bill Scott (1972–76), Kevin Westfold (1976), Bruce West (1976–82) and Mal Logan (1983–85), all drawn from the Science and Arts faculties. They deputised for the Vice-Chancellor at university committees and functions, reflecting an expansion in the size and number of executive responsibilities. More significant was Scott's tenure as the first Deputy Vice-Chancellor (1976–81), followed by Kevin Westfold (1982–86) and Mal Logan (1985–87). The Deputy Vice-Chancellors became full-time, the first extension of the central academic leadership whose growth was to be a striking feature of later years. Correspondingly, the role of the Committee of Deans in general university affairs declined, although several deans in concert could usually block unwanted changes.

This is not to say that a collegial university was suddenly replaced by a centrally managed one. In a sense the University was more conventionally collegial than before. Having grown to maturity, it found itself running on a largely devolved basis, in the manner of most of the older universities in Australia (except in times of financial crisis) and consistent with both Martin's inclinations and the strength of the faculties. Reflecting on his time as a Pro-Vice-Chancellor and Deputy Vice-Chancellor, Logan stated that:

> We weren't really involved in policy making in the University as a whole. In fact, we hardly ever talked about policy in those days . . . The main arena where we did talk about policy issues was the Committee of Deans, which has always been a very powerful committee at Monash, but they weren't long term policy issues, they were short term questions, such as 'what do we do with the staff association, bit of trouble there, how do we handle it?' It was a question of 'how do you solve problems?' rather than 'what is the strategy?'.[35]

At the same time, the Council was becoming more significant again in University affairs. The Monash Chancellor never played an executive role, but the successive Vice-Chancellors relied on the capacity of their Chancellors to manage the mood of the governing body. Sir Douglas Menzies (1968–74) was succeeded by Sir Richard Eggleston (1975–83). 'He never interfered with the day-to-day running of the University, although he was always available for consultation', said Council member and chair of the Finance Committee Sir James McNeill, the Managing Director of BHP, on Eggleston's retirement. 'Sir Richard will be remembered by most members for his warmth, wit and wisdom and a seemingly endless repertoire of anecdotes'.[36] Eggleston was followed by Sir George Lush (1983–92), a justice of the Victorian Supreme Court since 1966. A less formal leader for a less formal time, Lush was to preside over the most important Council meetings since the early days, and the appointment of the next generation of leaders.

On becoming Chancellor Lush told the *Monash Reporter* that his role was to listen and to help the Vice-Chancellor do his job.[37] But the Council took seriously its duty to oversee the executive arm of the University. As the 1980s proceeded it became more active in long-term issues, perhaps because of the University's difficulties and the vacuum in executive-led planning. At the second Council meeting of 1985 it established a small commmittee, chaired by McNeill, to review the structure and character of senior leadership. Its proposals were to help shape the University for the next decade (see chapter 4).

The faculties went on as before. The selection of Endersbee in Engineering (1976), Bob Baxt in Law (1980) and Peter Fensham in Education (1982) ensured that the deanship would remain powerful, though Fensham was more collectivist than the others, in the manner of state education. Teaching and research programs were largely still dominated by the professors, who were nearly all men. When Jean Whyte was chosen as foundation professor in the Graduate School of Librarianship in 1975 she was one of only five women with chairs. The others were Maureen Brunt in Economics, appointed in 1966, Enid Campbell in Law (1967), Mollie Holman in a personal chair in Physiology (1970), and Marie Neale who was a research professor in Education (1970). At the time this placed Monash in the forefront of the slow trend to gender equality, but there was far to go.

Ron Brown. Professor of Chemistry (1960–96): a major force in perhaps the most successful research department.

There were stirrings at sub-professorial level, with a more democratic mood in some departments, especially in Arts, and an emerging industrial culture.

FAUSA took its case for registration as an industrial union to the High Court, and gradually accustomed its members to affiliation with the peak union council, the ACTU. The Staff Association was a player in University affairs. More stringent funding, the slowing of promotion and the decline in salaries relative to other professionals and to US academics since the mid-1970s strengthened the trend to industrial relations. When the Federal Cabinet announced in January 1983 that, to increase administrative 'flexibility', universities would be required to maintain a ceiling on tenure of no more than 80 per cent of academic staff, there was concern. Some argued that limitations on tenure were incompatible with academic freedom. But scarcity was forcing a greater differentiation in academic incomes. Economics and Politics Dean Gus Sinclair, appointed in 1983, noted that the decline in academic salaries made it difficult to recruit staff in business and accounting.[38] FAUSA was opposed to variations in the common salary scale determined by the Academic Salaries Tribunal, but turned a blind eye to private earnings through research, consultancy and professional services, and was soon to accept recruitment 'loadings' in certain disciplines. In 1984 in an act of symbolic egalitarianism Ryan announced that the government would penalise universities paying their vice-chancellors at above-award rates. This did little to stem the trend to market-determined remuneration.

Schofield later recalled a mini-crisis in Medicine one year when the faculty's budget was suddenly cut by $100 000,[39] but despite resource problems the faculties were mostly healthy, with strong student demand and some scope for new initiatives. There was a trend to interdisciplinary studies, for example in Law and Business, where for a time the economist Brunt worked in Law, and in various centres for research and postgraduate education, for example Human Bioethics, Molecular Biology and Medicine, Aboriginal Research, Policy Studies, Continuing Education, Southeast Asian Studies, Migrant and Intercultural Studies, Laser Studies, Law and Applied Legal Research, and the Graduate School of Environmental Science.[40] The centre structure enabled the University to respond flexibly to emerging demand. New fields of professional training were developing. In Librarianship Monash offered the first postgraduate courses and a continuing education program for the profession at large, at the time when on-line services were first becoming general to libraries. In the mid-1960s

Physics promotes itself: Sue Aylward of the Physics Department drawing office and Fred Smith (Professor of Physics 1976–91) model the Physics Society's new T-shirts.

Westfold had the foresight to support the creation of a computer centre in Science under Cliff Bellamy, though it was long left in limbo between service arm and academic department. In 1970 Bellamy was granted professorial level status and the right to attend meetings of the Professorial Board, but without the title 'Professor' or even, for a time, the right to speak. The growth of computing in the Martin years made the anomaly more obvious, though it was not until the merger with Chisholm that a faculty of Computing was created under Bellamy as Dean; he became a *bona fide* Professor only in 1990.[41]

A number of Monash staff were established as public figures, and a larger group moved in and out of the news with the ebb and flow of debate. Endersbee was constantly commenting on engineering, science policy, transport, urban planning, Asian students, unemployment and a host of other issues. Peter Singer was becoming the best-known philosopher in Australia and a world authority on animal rights. The tone of the *Monash Reporter* was almost gloating when he was asked to prepare the entry on 'Ethics' for the *Encyclopaedia Britannica*.[42] Geoffrey Serle ranked with Manning Clark and Geoffrey Blainey in narrative Australian history. Alan Fels in Administration was serving as Prices Commissioner. In 1984 Waller was appointed to head the State government's Law Reform Commission. In research the great event was the refinement and application of IVF technologies (chapter 9). The commercial arm, IVF Australia Ltd, was formed in 1985. The IVF program engendered much debate, and as head of the program Carl Wood became a well-known Monash face on television. The IVF research also triggered the formation of the Centre for Human Bioethics, to monitor scientific research in the terms of public ethics. Singer played a leading role in the new centre. It was a case of IVF thesis, CHB antithesis, with both forming part of the Monash contribution to public affairs.

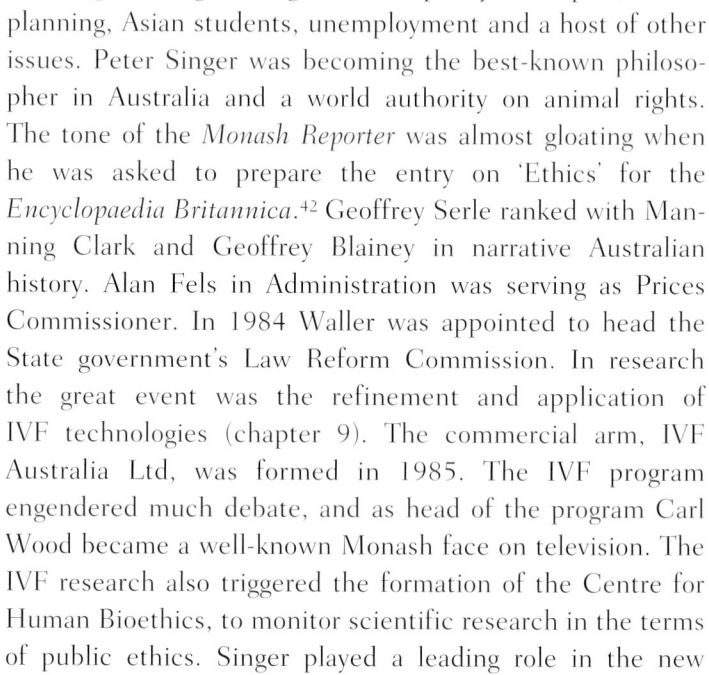

Geoffrey Serle. Author of *John Monash: a biography* (1992) and a series of major works in Australian history, Serle refused to become a professor, regarding himself as scholar rather than administrator.

By no means all significant research received public recognition or was reported in University publications. The promotion of certain kinds of applied research helped to sustain the image of Monash as a university that was practical, relevant and socially useful. In November 1984 the *Monash Reporter* summarised a range of projects. The Monash Centre for Migrant Studies had surveyed the western suburbs of Melbourne and found widespread English language problems. The IVF team had achieved a world scientific and ethical first with the birth of a child from a donated ovum. Researchers at the Baker Institute had made progress on the relationship between dietary fats and atherosclerosis, the thickening and hardening of the arterial wall associated with coronary heart disease. A Monash zoologist had helped to discover three new kinds of plankton in the Antarctic.[43] Sometimes the publicity was negative. In 1984 the Victorian Farmers' and Graziers' Association took exception to a Centre of Policy Studies report on the costs and benefits of irrigation; there were angry public meetings in the country, and National Party motions in State Parliament.

Support for research rested on the operating funds of the University and project grants from Commonwealth research-funding agencies. The main project-based sources were the Australian Research Grants Council (ARGC) and the National Health and Medical Research Council (NHMRC). In 1983 Monash received 8.4 per cent of the nation's Australian Research Grants Council funding.[44] About half of Monash's total ARGC and NHMRC funding went to Medicine, which in 1984 received $2.3 million from the NHMRC, $0.3 million from the ARGC and $2.5 million from other sources, including private sources. Little private money was flowing to Science, but in the summer of 1983–84 Martin, together with Brown of Chemistry, visited universities in North America and the UK to examine ways of developing research relations with private companies. In November 1984 Council received the report *Technology transfer and Monash University*, in which they proposed a Monash Office of Innovation and Liaison. The 'small number' of staff developing potentially commercialisable technology needed legal and organisational help to bring it to product stage. A science park might be beneficial, with the potential to generate future income through rental and a share in licensed inventions.[45] Later in the month the Labor government announced that if re-elected it would introduce a 150 per cent tax concession for industry research and development, a measure that was bound to boost the potential for industry financing of university research.

The faculty best attuned to these developments was not Science but Engineering. Endersbee had been a professional engineer rather than an academic. He graduated in 1949, working on the Snowy Mountains Scheme and then as Project Design Engineer for the Tasmanian Hydroelectric Commission, where he accumulated an international reputation in civil engineering. In November 1975, following the deliberations of a Council selection committee, he was invited by Matheson to accept the position of Dean of the Monash faculty, and began four months later with a charter to look for additional sources of income to compensate for the slowdown in Commonwealth funding. Under Endersbee (1976–88), the faculty was successful in raising corporate funding, and this led to tensions in a University still premised on public service-style annual funding. With each rise in private money the University reduced the centrally determined allocation to Engineering, on the grounds that the faculty was partly self-supporting. Endersbee argues that part of proper Engineering's funding entitlement was siphoned into Science, and that Engineering was expected to self-finance not just research activities but some of its undergraduate teaching, which was strongly resented in the faculty.[46]

David Kemp. Professor of Politics (1979–90) and later a Liberal–National Party Minister for Education, Training and Youth Affairs.

These were signs of the future. In Engineering there were other initiatives that foreshadowed the larger changes to come to the whole University in the late 1980s and 90s. The faculty created a strong coursework Masters program, improving relations with the profession. It introduced double-degree programs which proved to be popular, for example Science–Engineering, and Engineering–Arts with majors in German and Japanese. At the same time, like Medicine and Science, it continued to perform very well in research.

With its orientation to forging external relationships, Engineering also developed a set of glossy promotional brochures. More slowly, the rest of the University was becoming more communication-conscious. In 1984 the 'media release' replaced the traditional 'press release' issued from the Vice-Chancellor's office; the electronic media had been officially recognised. In a graduation address in May, History's Graeme Davison stated that the University was opening itself to indigenous and international students, and by developing recurrent education for its alumni was moving it closer to business and the professions.[47] There had been various community services for some time. Physics provided a popular program of free lectures for year 12 students. Concerts, theatre and exhibitions were often very well attended. The Monash-Oakleigh Legal Service began operating in August 1983: like the Springvale and Fitzroy services it was staffed by the faculty of Law, and final-year students worked there as part of the Professional Practice course. Funding was shared by local councils, the faculty, the University and the Legal Aid Commission.[48]

But there was a limited interest in the international realm. Academics continued to visit, train, conference and spend their study leave in the English-speaking world and sometimes Europe, but the tone of the University's discussion of itself was insular by comparison with what was to come. The reference points were British, American and Australian. There was little interest in Asia, except in specialised fields, such as the Japanese Study Centre opened by the Victorian Premier John Cain on 28 February 1984. Judging by student general meetings (SGMs) and *Lots Wife*, active students were more prepared to embrace diversity than was the University. Proceedings of the Professorial Board's Standing Committee on Overseas Academic Relations were slow. Rarely were all four members of the committee present, sometimes only two. Protracted negotiations with China's Nanjing University eventually led to an agreement on staff and student exchange, but Australia–USSR talks came to little, as did the discussions with the small private Doshisha University of Kyoto in Japan. The committee seemed more at ease in presiding over the routine exchange agreement with the University of California.

At the graduation on 11 April 1984 Sinclair gave the Occasional Address. 'The emergence of Asia as a major centre of economic growth is a development of great importance for Australia', he argued. The Commonwealth government—

and Monash graduates themselves—ought to be thinking about avenues for cooperation in Asian countries. As yet there was little echo inside the University.

The student mix

After 1979 demand for entry grew and there was a rise in the minimum year 12 scores required. Other institutions were absorbing the growth in student numbers in Victoria. The combination of a static enrolment and Monash's prestige made the University more exclusive, enrolling a growing proportion of the top group of year 12 students. In Engineering the level of the lowest year 12 score needed for entry to the faculty (the 'cut-off score') rose dramatically, from 226 in 1976 to 282 in 1982.[49]

Academic performance tends to correlate with social background.[50] There are individual exceptions to this generalisation but, taken overall, to the extent that a university becomes more academically exclusive it tends to become more socially exclusive as well. The trend created a potential collision with the Labor government elected in 1983. Speaking to the national council meeting of FAUSA in Brisbane, Ryan urged that universities should raise the proportion of students drawn from underrepresented groups. There was an 'entrenched systematic bias' in university selection that favoured affluent students, she stated at Monash in September 1984. Different selection methods could be used. For example, nurses should be able to complete Medicine without doing the full six-year course. Their training and experience placed them 'far in advance of other first year students'.[51] There was unease at Monash and other established universities, which were determined to retain traditional controls over student selection. The Vice-Chancellor stated in the 1984 annual report that, in the face of pressure for broader educational access, steps would be taken to ensure that Monash entrants were adequately prepared.

Monash felt itself vulnerable for, as HEARU's regular studies of the first-year intake showed, the student body was relatively middle-class. Hore and West found that, in 1982, 63 per cent of undergraduates were from families with fathers in professional, technical, administrative or managerial occupations, though only 22 per cent of the male Victorian workforce was in these occupations. From 1970 to 1982 this social unrepresentativeness of the Monash intake had grown. The role of government high schools in university entrance had declined, from 52 per cent of the intake in 1975 to 46 per cent in 1982. It fell again to 43 per cent in 1984. Non-Catholic private schools were strongly overrepresented.

Nevertheless, Ryan confined herself to rhetorical exhortation, making no move to intervene directly in selection policy. She offered extra funding to universities that designed projects intended to improve access to the disadvantaged, and on 13 August 1984 Acting Vice-Chancellor Westfold told Council that Monash would receive an additional $250 000 by this route. Despite these projects the further survey by HEARU in 1986 indicated no improvement in the social composition of the first-year intake.[52] In the absence of an expansion in intake, the trend to more competitive selection favoured students from schools and families best equipped to compete.

The politics of symbolic egalitarianism did not work well when the Minister was running counter to the social trends. She was more successful in relation to gender where the trend was to equality. But Monash responded only slowly to the groundswell. In mid-1984 Gay Baldwin was appointed as a 12-month Research Fellow in Equal Opportunity, with a brief to make recommendations on employment issues, and at the November meeting the Council approved amendments to the University regulations to install gender-neutral language. The harder issue was childcare. The two government-funded centres at Clayton had insufficient places, and cost was a problem for some parents. At the December 1982 Council, Martin stated that it would be premature to take action until the results of the Australian Vice-Chancellors' Committee (AVCC) survey of needs was in and national policy was known. Staff representative Martin Sullivan urged that in the meantime Council should take action. He proposed an ad-hoc committee. In its 1983 election platform the ALP promised an extra $20 million for campus childcare. The inaugural meeting of the Council's Childcare Review Committee took place on 24 February, but left no minutes. The second meeting in July noted that it was a long-standing view of Council that University funds should not be used to subsidise special groups. However, an ex-gratia payment was made to the Monash Student Creche Cooperative from non-recurrent sources: the Monash Community Family Cooperative protested at this differential treatment.

In 1984 a survey at enrolment found 2911 students with dependants. In April CTEC announced that childcare was an important factor in governing access to education; the Council Committee met in June and agreed in principle to further funding support for childcare, but in August it found there was little pressing financial need. More investigation was needed. The Council was still awaiting the committee's full report in early 1985.[53]

More promising was the creation of the Monash Orientation Scheme for Aborigines (MOSA). Monash had been committed to the education of indigenous people from the early 1960s, when Marshall agitated successfully for a small number of scholarships. In November 1982 the Professorial Board received the MOSA prospectus. The objectives were to 'accelerate access by Aboriginal people to university qualifications, thereby increasing Aboriginal

Slow to change. In 1984, more than a decade after the second wave of feminism arrived in Australia, Gay Baldwin was chosen as a Research Fellow in Equal Opportunity, the first appointment designed to address gender-based issues.

participation in the professions, public service, management and community leadership, and contribute to aboriginal self-management'.[54] The goal was a full year's preparation for university study. The first director was Isaac Brown. The first group of students, drawn from all mainland States and Territories, were aged between 21 and 30 years. The curriculum incorporated English, History, Anthropology and Sociology, plus a numeracy course, and was designed as preparation for Law and Arts.[55]

It was a sign of the insular times that the debate about international education in 1983–85 concerned not how to build better global relations but how to restrict the number of international students. Here Endersbee played a leading role. He argued repeatedly that international students were displacing qualified Australian citizens from entry to Monash, a claim that gained more credibility as the number of international students increased at the same time as the cut-off scores for entry rose. Endersbee carried the faculty with him, and in December 1982 the proposal for a quota of 80 international students within a total enrolment of 300 students in first-year Engineering was agreed by Council. There was debate on both the Professorial Board and Council, where minorities were strongly opposed to discrimination on national grounds, which was seen as racist or as strengthening racism. International students campaigned against the University's decision in *Lots Wife*. In response Endersbee stated that he was 'proud' of Asian students in Engineering; the issue was the need to provide opportunities to domestic students. He was not a racist but a 'realist'.[56]

Similar arguments were taking place throughout Australia. The Vice-Chancellors' Committee supported quotas, but was opposed by FAUSA and, with most international students drawn from Malaysia, Singapore, Hong Kong and Thailand, overseas student leaders warned that cuts in the intake would jeopardise Australia–Asia relations. Speaking at Monash in May 1983, Ryan indicated this was a primary concern: 'The new Government was keen to develop a closer relationship with our Asian neighbours and play a more constructive role in the region'. The issue could not be reduced simply to quotas.[57] The debate at Monash became more heated. On 4 August, 1300 students at a general meeting passed a resolution declaring that Endersbee had used 'extreme racist and nationalist arguments to support the continuance of sub-quotas'. The Professorial Board carried a motion to suspend quotas,[58] and on 26 October the University did so. By then the government had established two committees with a brief to examine the future of the subsidised scheme that supported international students. This enabled Monash to postpone further decision on local quotas. The matter was best left to the government, stated Martin in the 1983 annual report.

In 1984 there were 1912 international students enrolled at Monash, 13.8 per cent of the total enrolment. The two government reports disagreed with each other. The Goldring report plumped for a continuation of the subsidised scheme, with more generous quotas, while the Jackson report urged the government to open a full-fee market for international students that was additional to the funded student load. The Jackson strategy had the potential to circumvent the problem of quotas, providing open access to international students with the capacity to pay without reducing the places available to domestic students. Ultimately this approach was taken (see chapter 6), though many of the opponents of quotas were unhappy with a 'user-pays' approach, and concern about standards was unresolved. In the meantime, Monash needed a policy for 1985. The Board and Council adopted a limit of 25–30 per cent on the bachelor level intake in Engineering.

Student life in the early 1980s

Despite national quotas, the student body was becoming more cosmopolitan. The European migration of the 1950s and 60s and the Asian immigration of the 1970s and 80s contributed, along with international students. HEARU found that from 1970 to 1984 the proportion of first-year students who were Australian-born fell from 84 to 68 per cent, and the Asian-born proportion rose from 5 to 20 per cent. Second-generation Greek and Italian migrants had also increased dramatically. In Economics and Politics, 31 per cent of students were from Malaysia. In Engineering 39 per cent were born in Australia and 54 per cent in Asia, many from migrant families unaffected by Endersbee's quota. A new Monash was emerging. It was also a more career-minded and vocationally focused student body, responding to the growth of unemployment and the rise of market ideology in public life.

Older and more solipsistic aspects of student life continued. The University banned 'Farm Week' after public complaints in 1984; it was alleged that students had interfered with Princes Highway and Wellington Road traffic, damaged vehicles, 'terrorised' a learner-driver, disrupted lectures by 'invasions of hooded hooligans hurling eggs, flour and water indiscriminately at staff and students', 'splattered with eggs' a disabled student in a wheelchair, and invaded an evening lecture by 'throwing horse manure'. It seemed that a disproportionate number of the targets were women.[59] As in most Western universities there was a drinking culture, and a 'dope' (marijuana) culture centred on the Small Caf in the Union until it was raided by the police in 1984 (see box). Kevin Brianton, who edited *Lots Wife* with Anita Bahree in 1984, later recalled his early days as a Monash student:

> The Monash culture I was in was very very enjoyable. We had a gymnasium, and we had squash courts and the Small Caf and the Nott. We had lots of parties and lots of drinking and we had a good time. I

remember that on orientation day there would be sixty clubs competing for your membership. Anything you wanted to do and as cheap as anything. If you wanted to do skydiving you could go and do it . . . The culture of young people having fun. When someone jumped off the Ming wing you knew that they weren't all having fun, that there were some people under enormous pressure.[60]

Student life was not always easy. The dark undertone of any large student community, suicides, were rarely discussed. The University modified upper-floor windows and sealed the access to roofs, but the problem continued. The porters were issued with tarpaulins to cover the bodies of those who jumped. The Monash Association of Students (MAS) had an agreement with the University not to publicise the issue, to discourage imitation, but this buried the problem so that it became more difficult to tackle the relevant environmental factors. There was a marked rise in the use of student counselling services in 1983.[61]

Doug Ellis. The Sports Centre was later to be named after the long-standing director of the Monash Sports and Recreation Association.

> It was a bland place. I had expected it to be more vigorous. It was unfriendly. You could feel totally lost. It was alienating. For example, the enrolment procedures—they were so hard to follow, and stressful. Layout was a factor. Everything was so dispersed—Physics there, then Engineering, Medicine, Law . . . and that awful Ming Wing. And not much assistance.[62]

But each year most students found their way through the large modern University, some because of their courses and the friends they found there, some because of their involvement in clubs and activities, and others through student politics and student media. Conservative political groups played a rather greater role than before. From the mid-1960s to the early 70s the issues were the Vietnam war and military conscription, apartheid in South Africa, and student power and the University's discipline statutes. In 1973 and 1974 there were campaigns on course content and assessment.[63] There were still students in the early 1980s who chose Monash because it once housed such figures as Albert Langer and the swashbuckling 1960s editor of *Lots Wife*, Peter Steedman, who became the Labor member for the local seat of Casey in 1983.[64] Peter Wade later recalled that in 1985 when he told friends in business that he was going to work as Comptroller at Monash, they said 'That's where that bloke Langer was, wasn't he? What's it like out there now?'.[65] The radical past was a fading memory; the radical present was more low-key.

At the beginning of the 1980s student activists to the left of the ALP were still a significant political presence, even though they no longer decided the

University's public reputation. In 1983, under Craig Silva and Lyn Winzer, *Lots Wife* focused on indigenous rights, environmental activism, welfare and education, and international issues such as East Timor. On the Middle East the radical left took a pro-Palestinian position, to the chagrin of local Zionist groups. Racism was a continuing issue, with the conflict over international student quotas, and when New Zealand Prime Minister Robert Muldoon gave the Sir Robert Menzies Lecture on 21 June 1984, five students were arrested in a demonstration against his decision to tolerate an All Black rugby tour of South Africa despite the international boycott.[66] The radicals sometimes controlled the Monash Association of Students, sometimes did not. In 1982 the ALP students won and acted as a moderating force. A then-member of that MAS Administrative Executive recalled later that:

About right, too.
Stuart Roth's cartoons were a feature of *Lots Wife*.

> We had an understanding with Mal Logan, the Pro Vice-Chancellor. If demonstrations were proposed at an SGM [Student General Meeting] we would advise Logan to . . . ahh . . . lock certain doors. Mal Logan was very approachable. But I had the impression that he was on the outer with the other university authorities.[67]

In September 1984 there was a swing to the right with the landslide election of 'The Cure' ticket, Debbie Blashki and Carmella Ben-Simon, in the first full direct election for *Lots Wife* editors. (Previous editors were appointed by the MAS Publications Committee.) 'The Cure' was supported by the Monash Jewish Students Society, the ALP right and some Liberal students. Using posters in 12 different languages 'in order to tap into the diversity of the culture' (Blashki), it defeated both the ALP and the 'Left Press' teams. 'The ghost of Monash Union's radical past was exorcised last week', declared *Lots Wife*. The statement turned out to be prophetic. After 1984 the activist Left declined. Nick Economou, active in Monash student affairs 1981–86 and later a politics lecturer, recalled that in student elections the title 'left' became 'a killer'.[68] Facing a hostile Publications Committee, Blashki and Ben-Simon did not have an easy time, but their glossy 1985 *Lots Wife* with $40 000 in advertising from Swatch, full-colour covers, cultural themes and emphasis on reader access[69] was popular. For her part, Blashki saw 'The Cure' not as the nemesis of Monash radicalism but as its inheritor, in the form of a radicalism expressed as modernist culture, not revolutionary politics:

> I loved Monash culture. There were twenty people working non stop in *Lots Wife* with us and there was this constant partying, and brainstorming. Thrashing out political ideas, thrashing out changes. We were

being paid to do this, there was a sense of responsibility but there was also a sense of exploring new avenues . . . we weren't conservative and bogged down, we were aware of the 1960s, and worshipped that whole era. That culture was very strong—it was our whole life. By the next year I think it had begun to become a bit more conservative.[70]

For much of 1982–84, relations between the Union and the University Council were strained because of a dispute over the Sports and Recreation activities of the Union. In August 1982 Council received a submission from the President of Sports and Recreation asking for a separate body, following a decade of disputes with the Union leadership. Council set up an inquiry, conducted by Mr Justice Tadgell, which recommended divorce.[71] Union Board student representatives and *Lots Wife* opposed the report, and campaigned against Politics Professor David Kemp,[72] the Chair of the Union Board who was committed to the Council position. Though the Union Board passed a motion of no confidence in Kemp[73] he retained the support of the Vice-Chancellor, and in 1985 the separation of Sports and Recreation from the Union was put into effect. Another problem was transport. There were recurrent tensions over parking fees and permits; and much incredulity at the January 1984 findings of a joint Monash University–Ministry of Transport survey which concluded that 'students attending Monash University had no major transport problems, despite the commonly held belief that the university is poorly served by public transport'.[74] The absence of adequate public transport was too big an issue for the University to address.

An account of meetings and papers scarcely captures the flavour of Monash in the first half of the 1980s for every individual student who was there: the small tales of essays late and lab reports; of changing images and careers, courses and ideas; of things same, and things different; of cars and clothes and love and friendship. Student stars rose, fell, and rose again. In February 1983 *New Idea* reported that Arts student Louise Pago was playing Margery Carson in Network Ten's *Carson's Law*. A 30-year-old MA student, Robert Burrowes,

Monash mind-power. In 1986 the University chess team took out the Victorian Chess Association's A-Grade title. L–R: Guy West, Matthew Drummond, Ross Thomas and Murray Smith.

The Small Caf and the Wholefoods Restaurant

Feed the head: the Union as a place apart

In the heyday of the student counterculture the Union building was a zone in its own right, with its own informal rules. The style of politics had little to do with Parliament House in Spring Street, and there were activities not generally tolerated in the outside world. One was drug-taking, mostly 'soft' drugs such as marijuana ('pot', later 'weed' and 'dope'). The dimly lit Small Caf was the place for smoking marijuana—sometimes the smell wafted throughout the building—and operated as an ongoing drug market. 'There were garbage bags of marijuana', one student of the time recalls: 'We used to buy in bulk from Monash and distribute from home as a cooperative'.[75]

On 27 July 1984 at 12.30 pm the Small Caf was raided by a squad of uniformed and plain clothes police. There was a scuffle in which chairs were overturned, and nine people were arrested, eight of whom were charged, five with trafficking and possession of cannabis. Only one was an enrolled Monash student. The police also seized three bags containing 'Buddha sticks' and $1000 in cash. The raid followed complaints from parents about the ready availability of drugs. Afterwards, more than 1000 students at a special general meeting of the Monash Association of Students condemned the raid as a breach of university autonomy, and 200 people demonstrated outside Cheltenham police station, where those arrested were held. However, Chief Superintendant Bill Goodings of Cheltenham stated that detectives had the power to enter the Monash grounds and arrest students. 'They are exactly the same as other people in the community', he said.[76]

So it proved. *Lots Wife* denounced the 'drug bust' and some desultory trafficking resumed, but the Small Caf never recovered its status as a place immune from outside rules. In the memories of those active in the Union at the time the July 1984 police raid stands out, one of those events with greater meaning than its intrinsic character suggests. It was followed soon after by the victory of 'The Cure' team in the election for *Lots Wife* editor. While radical left politics did not altogether disappear, and could still be stimulated by external events, the internal dynamics of the Union changed. After 1984 the desire for a separated student culture was more modestly expressed. It was activities such as the Union's Wholefoods Restaurant, a vegetarian food bar run by Helen Clarke and David Sibley, staffed by volunteers, egalitarian and non-commercial and packed with hungry students, that inherited the tradition. The Union's student politicians shifted their perpetual meetings into the Wholefoods Restaurant.[77]

refused to vote because elections were 'irrelevant'. He also refused to pay the $4 fine and $15 in costs, and was jailed in early 1984.[78] Late that year Monash Science graduate Vivian Burden became the first national Caltex Woman

Graduate of the Year for her fourth-year research with John Bradshaw in Psychology on the neurophysiological development of normal children. She planned to take her doctorate at Cambridge Medical Research Centre, extending the work to dyslexic children.[79]

Little did anyone know that there would soon to be almost three times as many such Monash stories. 'There is little expectation—in the immediate future—of further physical growth in terms of buildings or of student numbers—we long ago fulfilled the limits envisaged by our founding fathers', stated Martin in 1986. The Dean of Arts, J.D. Legge, light-heartedly tagged the 1960s notion of a Monash with 30 000 or 40 000 students as 'megalomania'. He did not realise that such a madness was soon to descend on the University.[80]

3 The 'Unified National System'

> The political and economic imperatives which we all have to confront have made explicit the tension which has always been implicit in the relationship between higher education institutions and governments.
>
> John Dawkins, Commonwealth Minister for Employment, Education and Training, 'Address' in Grant Harman and Lyn Meek, *Australian higher education reconstructed?*, University of New England, Armidale, 1988, p. 15

The University and the market

In 1853 in *The idea of a university*, Newman argued that the formation of the intellect was an end in itself. The university should not be weighed and judged according to exterior purposes; it should be measured only by its own objectives. 'For what has its *end* in itself, has its *use* in itself also', he stated.[1] Newman's vision of the university as a world of its own was subverted by two alternative models: the research university emerging in 19th century Germany and the mass teaching university of the 20th century United States. Nevertheless, *The idea of a university* retained its standing in the scholarly traditions of the English-speaking world, in which preservation of knowledge was seen as being as important as its creation, and there were invisible barriers to direct interference by the state or market forces.

Even in government-founded universities such as Monash, which was never fashioned to be a cloistered place apart from the real world, Newman's idea that a university could be judged only by itself retained a certain standing within the academic culture. The claim for university autonomy was also a demand for academic monopoly over knowledge, and the more separable was the field of academic work from other fields of knowledge and from graduate employment and the practical applications of research, the closer it came to Newman's vision. At Monash the most Newmanesque faculties were Arts and Science, though even there some good scholars and researchers were notably engaged with the world.

By the mid-1980s this imagined landscape of the Anglo-Australian university, which had long seemed fixed, was starting to move under the feet of its practitioners. Ideas about the economic benefits of higher education which had carried such force in the 1960s were starting to come back onto the government policy agenda, and this time they had implications for the internal workings of the universities, for the systems of management and financing, and for the nature of academic work itself. In the discipline of economics, according to the new 'endogenous growth' theories, education was key to economic competitiveness. Education provided people and industries with the capacity to deal with technological change and economic pressure. Again, in theories of best practice in management, Harvard's Michael Porter saw education as crucial to the capacity of individual firms and to national prosperity. In a globalising world, in which capital and materials were highly mobile, the educational qualities of the population were more fixed and were one of the elements of competitive advantage.[2] In the mid-1980s these perspectives were taken up by the 'club' of First World nations, the Organisation for Economic Cooperation and Development (OECD), which mounted a sustained and often brilliant argument for a renewed emphasis on the role of education and research. This policy position began to inform the thinking of OECD member governments, including the Labor government under Bob Hawke in Australia. The OECD argument was that higher education and science-based research were *the* cutting edge of industrial innovation and the capacity of a nation to respond and change in the face of international competition.[3] Later, the argument shifted slightly to encompass the role of information technology as well.

For the universities the policy argument was double-edged. Under other circumstances, the notion that higher education was at the core of national interest might have promised to provide a more generous funding regimen and better opportunities for academics to do the work they wanted to do. But the OECD policy position had been developed in an era of 'small government', when state financing was being withdrawn and government-dependent institutions were being privatised, or at least expected to generate part of their resources for themselves—and the OECD argued that changes were needed in education and research, to ensure the economic benefits that it imagined. This meant creating closer relationships between education and government and education and industry, and the importation of many of the requirements and the methods of business and industry into the inner workings of universities themselves. Policies to modernise and develop education and research became policies to re-engineer education. The old separations between universities and government, and universities and market, were breaking down. Suddenly, the Newmanesque vision of the university had become an obstacle to be removed.

'For what has its end in itself, has its use in itself also'.

J.H. Newman's 1853 idea that a university could be measured and judged only by *itself*, even to the extent of refusing to justify its activities in terms of particular social utilities, had strong support in certain academic circles. But by the middle of the 1980s external governmental and economic pressures were becoming difficult to resist.

One implication of these policy changes was that the higher education system would need to expand. The OECD stated that higher education had moved from the preparation of social leaders ('elite education') to the education of technical and professional elites ('mass education'), and was now entering a new phase of 'universal education' in which more than 50 per cent of the population would be prepared for 'life in advanced industrial societies, characterised by rapid social and technological change'.[4] The OECD's ideal systems were those of the USA and Japan, where high participation was joined to a mixed private/public funding system. Whereas Australian higher education was almost 90 per cent government-funded, in the USA half the total costs were met by user payments and alumni and corporate donations. The implication of the OECD argument was that, by partly relying on market mechanisms, a nation could maintain 'elite' Ivy League excellence alongside cheap accessible 'universal' institutions, at the price of downward variations in quality, and organisational and cultural change within universities. Downward variations in quality were attractive to governments, for these reduced the demands on the public budget.

In research, there was a new policy emphasis on entrepreneurial science. In the USA in 1980, ownership of patents generated in federally funded research was transferred from government to the universities, turning the latter into corporate players with the potential for huge earnings from commercial applications. Programs for government–industry–university collaboration, the Science Foundation's (NSF) Cooperative Research Centers and Engineering Research Centers, were created. These developments fragmented postwar science policy. The argument had been that, because autonomous basic research conducted in the universities generated a vast range of potential applications, and because these applications could not be foreseen before scientific curiosity was put to work, researchers should shape their own research programs. The new argument was that technologies created by academic science provided the basis for successive breakthroughs in production, efficiency and international competitiveness. Competitive pressure dictated that applications had to be shaped in advance.[5] Competitive funding mechanisms could be used to drive greater efficiency and industry synergy, albeit at some cost to academic independence. In *Higher education: a new framework* (1987), the British government urged that scientists and technologists form a common intellectual culture spanning the university–industry divide. Basic research should become more 'strategic', scientists should engage with industry, commercial research organisations should be set up alongside academic departments: 'No track record of distinguished work justifies funding for an indefinite future. Major projects need to be generously supported but given a strictly limited life'.[6] Science and technology were central to industry, but industry was being installed at the core of academic science. Its rhythms of boom and bust were becoming part of the universities, in the patterns of research funding and the fluctuating demand for research graduates. It all spelt trouble for the old open-ended research programs—not only in science-based disciplines but in all disciplines, for the rules governing research in science tended to shape research policy and management as a whole.

These research policy models emerged at a time when the Australian government was unusually receptive. Australian exports were dominated by primary production. In 1984/85, a total of 89 per cent of all export revenue was earned by mining, processed metals and agricultural commodities, with less than 6 per cent derived from machines and equipment. Services exports were negligible.[7] In the mid-1980s there was a sudden decline in the trading prices of primary commodities, triggering a severe balance of payments crisis and a run on the dollar. On 14 May 1986 the Commonwealth Treasurer, Paul Keating, warned that Australia was in danger of becoming a 'banana republic' if the trends continued. There was a sea change in official thinking. Industry policies became focused on the manufacture and export of technology-intensive goods, on the development of international trade in services in order to boost the trading position, and on the fostering of a 'productive culture', a term popularised by Industry Minister John Button. As the government saw it, to compete in high-skill production it was necessary to strengthen 'human capital', research-based industrial innovation, and the capacity to respond to technological change. This slotted Australia into the OECD policy agenda. As the government stated in 1987:

John Button. The Commonwealth Minister for Industry was a key player in the developing relations between universities and industry. A friend of Monash's Mal Logan, he also became one of the links between the University and government.

The nature and magnitude of the changes required cannot be predicted with any precision. What is important is the flexibility to capitalise on new opportunities as they arise and to accept the need for continuing change and adjustment, largely determined by international forces. A well-educated workforce is a key source of such flexibility . . . as the prime source of higher-level skills for the labour market, the higher education system has a critical role to play in restructuring the Australian economy.[8]

First, participation in education would need to increase. Second, because Australian research in the universities was strong, but research in industry by world standards was weak,[9] as the government saw it the university laboratories should be hired out as research laboratories for industry. Third, if international education was reconstructed on a market basis, education could contribute to services exports. Universities were at the heart of future national development, but to play this role they would have to be prised open. Government reform of the universities became focused on removing the 'barriers' that blocked institutions from 'responding to changing demands and circumstances'—especially the demands of industry and government itself.[10]

The Business-Higher Education Round Table, formed in November 1990 to bring university vice-chancellors together with the chief executive officers of major companies, stated that universities should be autonomous, 'but at the same time they must also be responsible and accountable to both their immediate stakeholders and the nation'; the business community had a 'legitimate responsibility' to ensure that appropriate skills were taught.[11] For 'immediate stakeholders' read business and industry. This simple statement, made with the consent of the vice-chancellors, signified a great change. For the first time business firms were interested in changing the character of the universities, and they had the support of the government, a coalition of external forces that was hard to resist. One effect was that, in the late 1980s, business models of organisation rapidly gained ground, both in government thinking about the universities and in the thinking of the universities about themselves. Increasingly, it was assumed that to manage resources effectively and to achieve targeted economic objectives universities would need to draw their tools from the corporate kitbag: the modelling of competitive position, periodic management restructure, financial standardisation and control, corporate-style devolution of responsibility within the framework of central surveillance and control, 'bottom-line' economic incentives, mergers and take-overs, product diversification, and the creation of new market opportunities. Business Studies faculties were comfortable with this. The older disciplines were not. A new language and a new set of values were entering the academic lexicon.

The Dawkins reforms

The first sign of a new reform agenda was on 5 July 1985, when Susan Ryan issued guidelines to regulate the provision of fee-based courses in higher education, Technical and Further Education (TAFE) and schooling to international students; the first full-fee higher education students arrived in 1987 (chapter 6). In September 1986 the CTEC issued its *Review of efficiency and effectiveness in higher education*, which urged the benefits of larger institutions, more professional managers, research management strategies, institutional planning, greater flexibility in staffing, and an internal culture of self-assessment using mechanism of quality assurance. These were all pointers to the next round of policies.

Nevertheless, the CTEC sought to retard the proposals for market reform in higher education, emanating from the principal coordinating departments of Finance, Treasury, and Prime Minister and Cabinet. CTEC had little faith in the claims made for market models. 'Competition between institutions would not necessarily encourage efficiency in the use of scarce resources', it stated. It was hostile to tuition fees for domestic students and sceptical about consumer sovereignty. 'Students have imperfect knowledge of the courses available and are not sufficiently mobile to have equal access to alternative courses'. It was pessimistic about the potential size of the export market (and substantially underestimated potential earnings). With rather greater accuracy it warned that in a market 'institutions with status, principally the large city institutions, could grow at the expense of others'.[12] Many people in the higher education system agreed with CTEC, though the stronger universities could see the income potential that markets offered. Nevertheless, the critique was losing its power. CTEC itself was being displaced. Against its advice the government decided that from 1987 a Higher Education Administration Charge (HEAC) of $250 would be levied on all students. In 1987 the Australian Science and Technology Committee, located in the Department of Prime Minister and Cabinet, recommended the introduction of tuition payments, government support for private institutions, university–industry collaboration and a major growth in enrolments. With the exception of government support for private institutions, these proposals were soon to be adopted.

The conditions had been set for a major change in policy, but it needed a minister with the political will. In July 1987, soon after a Federal election at which the Hawke government was returned for a third term, Cabinet met to determine the new Ministry. Afterwards Button, who had been reappointed as Minister for Industry, put through a call to the new Monash Vice-Chancellor, Mal Logan, with whom he had been friends for some years. Button said that Cabinet believed that higher education had an important role in economic restructuring but was not performing as well as it ought. Further, the growing tensions between the universities and the CAEs needed to be addressed. It had been decided to allocate John Dawkins to an expanded Employment, Education and Training portfolio including higher education, TAFE, schools, unemployment services and the training aspects of the Industrial Relations portfolio. For the first time higher education programs were to be administered from an economic department of the Commonwealth (DEET).[13]

As Minister for Finance in 1983 and 1984, Dawkins led structural reforms of the Commonwealth bureaucracy that created a corporate-style senior executive service, subject to enhanced ministerial control. As Minister for Trade from 1984 to 1987 he spearheaded the formation of the 'Cairns group' to push for liberalisation of world trade in agriculture, and supported the development of an export industry in education. An interventionist and a market deregulator by turns, he was known as a 'potent reformer', who wanted to redesign social institutions according to his own ideas. He was a modernist, with the modern virtues of openness, universality of scale, and change for change's sake, and contemptuous of claims based on parochialism and privilege. Dawkins could be short-tempered and overbearing, and was not always effective with the media and on the broad public stage, but he had immense charm when the occasion required it, he was masterly in small groups, and he had a gift for attaching smart public servants to the government's objectives.[14] He was also well prepared. He had begun his political career in the National Union of Australian University Students, and was shadow education minister before Labor took office in 1983. It was unusual for a minister to have such deep and detailed knowledge of a new responsibility, or such a profound commitment to strategies

John Dawkins speaks at Gippsland in 1989. Arguably the most successful federal Minister for Education in Australia's history, in half a decade Dawkins completely restructured higher education. Enrolments grew by 60 per cent, the binary distinction between universities and colleges of advanced education was abolished and the number of institutions was halved via mergers. Almost the whole of the ambitious Green Paper blueprint (1987) was implemented.

of reform. This mix of qualities was to enable Dawkins to become perhaps the most effective minister who ever served in the portfolio.

Soon after Logan's telephone conversation with Button the Vice-Chancellor met Dawkins at the government offices in Treasury Place. Logan advised the new Minister to set up a quick review of the higher education sector. Logan recalls that Dawkins' response was to ask: 'Why go through that if we know most of what is wrong with the system already?'. He thought it would be better to bring together a small group of people who might provide new ideas, and would provide useful feedback. If they were to play this role it would be better if they did not all think alike, or all be Labor supporters. In this manner Dawkins drew together the group of university leaders and intellectuals, which met on several occasions between the middle and end of 1987, dubbed the 'Purple Circle'. It included two advocates of wholesale market deregulation, economist Helen Hughes, and the Vice-Chancellor of the private Bond University,

Don Watts. There were four generally sympathetic to the Dawkins policy mix, in which social democratic objectives were linked to industry modernisation and partial deregulation: Professor Don Aitkin of the ANU (who became chair of the Australian Research Council), Vice-Chancellor of the University of WA Bob Smith, the Director of Ballarat CAE Jack Barker, and Logan. Brian Smith, the Director of RMIT, cultivated a more neutral position. Dawkins' senior adviser Paul Hickey was also active in discussion. Members gave papers, in which there was more agreement on the need to 'free up' the system than on how to do it. There was also 'a lot of informal interaction on the telephone' (Logan).[15] The role of the Purple Circle is hard to assess. It did not prepare the Green Paper on higher education, which was handled by Hickey, Gregor Ramsey (later Chair of the Higher Education Council) and others, but it helped to map the boundaries of possibility of the subsequent Dawkins reforms.

Dawkins moved swiftly. In the second half of 1987 he abolished the CTEC, standing down its powerful head Hugh Hudson and splitting its functions between program administration and policy advice, which went to the expanded DEET, and policy consultation via the Higher Education Council (which played a minor role thereafter). This removed the opposition to reform within the government, split program administration from the university interest groups represented on the Council, and strengthened Ministerial control. Dawkins outlined his reform program in detail in *Higher education: a discussion paper*, the Green Paper, in December 1987, and confirmed his decisions in the White Paper of July 1988, *Higher education: a policy statement*.

The 1987/88 policy blueprint, and the reforms of 1988–92 that followed, were wide in scope. Labor greatly expanded participation in higher education. It abolished the binary distinction between universities and CAEs, so that there was only one system of universities; and it set in motion a frenetic round of mergers and upgradings to university status. It encouraged closer relations between higher education and Technical and Further Education (TAFE). In place of a publicly funded university system it created a mixed public–private funding base, and encouraged market entrepreneurialism. It deliberately intensified competition between universities. It restructured the government–university relationship, and stimulated the professionalisation of university management and internal changes to governance. It encouraged industry involvement, international relations, quality assurance procedures and technological change in administration and teaching. It reworked the research system, centralising most of the resources for research and imparting a more utilitarian bias, created research centres with emphasis on relations with industry, standardised the measures of research activity, and secured a formal research management regime inside the universities. Each of these changes had a direct and detailed impact on every university in Australia. They affected Monash more than most other universities.

TABLE 3.1 ENROLMENTS IN AUSTRALIAN HIGHER EDUCATION, 1987–96

	Total student enrolments	Proportion in higher degrees (%)	Change from previous year New enrolments (%)	Change from previous year total enrolments (%)
1987	393 734	7.1	+3.4	+1.0
1988	420 850	7.2	+9.8	+6.9
1989	441 076	7.0	+7.2	+4.8
1990	485 075	7.5	+11.2	+10.0
1991	534 538	8.3	+8.2	+10.2
1992	559 365	9.6	−3.4	+4.6
1993	575 617	10.8	+3.3	+2.9
1994	585 396	11.7	+3.6	+1.7
1995	604 177	12.3	+8.7	+3.2
1996	634 094	12.4	+6.7	+5.0

Source: DEET, Selected higher education statistics.

Growth and mergers

Dawkins argued in the Green Paper that if Australia was to reach a level comparable with other OECD countries, the number of graduates should be raised from 78 000 in 1986 to 125 000 per annum by 2001. The issue was not quite as clear-cut as he suggested. When participation in both higher education *and* TAFE were taken into account, total tertiary participation in Australia was already high in OECD terms.[16] The significance of the Dawkins-led expansion of the university sector lay as much in the upgrading of student aspirations and participation—from CAE to university, from TAFE to university, and from first degree to postgraduate education—as in bringing people to tertiary education for the first time. All the same, after a decade of the steady state, Dawkins' expansion was certainly popular. It was like lifting the lid from a pressure cooker. Rising participation in secondary education led to a spreading of aspirations for betterment via higher education.[17] Australia was in the late stages of an economic boom and the demand for graduates was rising, especially for graduates with skills in business and computing. Higher education enrolments in Australia jumped by 42 per cent in the five years after 1987. In Victoria enrolments rose from 113 314 in 1987 to 156 055 in 1992. Between 1985 and 1992 the rate of participation of 17–24-year-olds in higher education rose from 11 to 17 per cent in Victoria, and from 10 to 15 per cent in Australia as a whole (see Table 3.1). This was still not enough to contain all of the growing aspirations for university education. School-leaver student demand rose, mature-age student demand rose, and the rate of progression within courses improved. Total enrolments well exceeded the levels that

Dawkins had planned. At the peak of the growth in 1990 and 1991, *unmet* demand for higher education reached the highest levels ever recorded.[18]

The fastest-growing course areas were Nurse Education (which was transferred from hospital-based to university programs during the 1980s), Law, and Business Studies. Student numbers in Engineering and Science also grew at faster than average rates. The share of enrolments in Education declined sharply: it was a time of little demand for new teachers.[19] The proportion of women students continued to grow, reaching 53.4 per cent in 1992. Perhaps the most striking change was the rapid advance in the role of postgraduate education, especially towards the end of the growth period, in both vocational coursework Masters programs and research degrees. The number of students in higher degrees grew from 27 968 in 1987 to 53 561 in 1992, reaching 78 609 in 1996. Women increased their share of PhD enrolments from 30.7 per cent in 1987 to 39.7 per cent in 1995, and in coursework Masters went from 38.6 to 47.8 per cent of all students.[20]

Higher education funding also rose, but more slowly than enrolments. The government was sustaining a medium to large higher education system in one of the smaller public sectors in the OECD. Given that the fiscal climate remained very restrictive, it was inevitable that sooner or later the growth of public funding would cease. After 1992 the government slowed the expansion of publicly funded places and tried to redirect school-leaver aspirations to TAFE. 'There is no strong rationale to support substantial additional public investment in higher education in the short to medium term', it stated in 1994.[21] Nevertheless, the system was by then irreversibly changed. In 1941 universities recruited 2 per cent of the teenage cohort. By 1975 the figure was 15 per cent. Less than two decades later it had reached 30 per cent, and postgraduate education was becoming a mass sector.

Half a decade of rapid growth also facilitated all of the other changes that Dawkins wanted to achieve. The map of institutions was completely redrawn. In 1987 there were 19 universities and 46 CAEs in Australia, a total of 73 higher education institutions with an average size of 5312 students. By 1994 the CAEs had disappeared and there were 36 public universities, with an average size of 16 166 students. There were also two small private universities located outside Labor's 'Unified National System', the Bond University in Queensland and the University of Notre Dame Australia in WA. All established universities such as Monash survived, but mergers and growth and market-based funding together led to major changes in those institutions. Some fell on hard times.

The abolition of the CAEs was inevitable, whether by Dawkins or another minister. The binary divide was obsolete. It was breaking down, and the government wanted it to break down. Founded to provide education below degree level, by the mid-1980s all CAEs offered degree programs and some had begun doctoral programs, which caused considerable resentment in the universities. In late 1986 the Curtin Institute of Technology was given the title 'University' by the WA government, and the New South Wales Institute of Technology soon followed. Within the government, there were misgivings about the old status distinction. It reflected Newmanesque notions of a division of labour between scientists, theoreticians and decision-makers on one hand, and applied engineering and business on the other. The rationale for the binary divide had also been weakened by the commercialisation of science and by innovation at the applied research end of the pure–applied continuum, which brought the research profiles of universities and the large CAEs closer together in such fields as Engineering and the Technologies. Yet the binary divide still blocked the full movement of the CAEs into research—they remained ineligible for the majority of Commonwealth research resources—also blocking the full engagement of the universities with industry and product development.[22]

Dawkins' distinctive contribution lay not in breaking down the binary divide so much as in the new system he set in its place. In the Unified National System (UNS) all institutions were funded on a similar basis and all were eligible to take part in the range of funded research programs, now subject to competitive processes. The *quid pro quo* was that all institutions were expected to provide doctoral programs at 'international standards of performance'; to demonstrate a commitment to the full range of teaching, research and community service functions; and to provide appropriate capital facilities, qualified staff and 'comprehensive and efficient' management. They were required to endorse government policies on equity, research management, credit transfer between universities, staffing and a common academic year; and to provide data in standardised forms as required by DEET.[23] They were also required to be of sufficient size. Using a benchmark developed in 1986 by the CTEC, institutions of fewer than 2000 effective full-time students were excluded from the UNS on the grounds that per-student costs were too high. The Green Paper suggested that they be placed in State TAFE systems. Institutions needed at least 5000 EFTS to be funded for a broad teaching profile, and more than 8000 EFTS to be eligible for comprehensive research funding.[24] In conjunction with the specifications for university status, the size limits pressured medium-sized and smaller CAEs to seek larger institutions as merger partners; while universities such as Monash were provided with a one-off chance to expand in size, role and geographical spread.

A market in mergers developed. Big was unambiguously beautiful. Every institution eyed every other as a potential merger partner. There was no particular *educational* merit in size as such; around the world, there were successful universities of 2500 or fewer, and successful universities of 30 000 or more, such as the US State universities. Nevertheless, Dawkins' policy settings made mergers inevitable.[25] The oldest universities in each State could afford to turn down the opportunity for large-scale mergers, because of their inherited prestige and established range of activities, but even so most of these universities grew substantially in the next half decade. For other institutions, the attraction of mergers was irresistible, though for organisational rather than educational reasons. Enrolment growth provided the potential for additional public funding in a difficult time, and mergers offered a strengthened asset base and market reach in the longer term. For Dawkins, the mergers had other benefits. In the turmoil of restructuring, in which most of the senior management positions came up for review at one time or another, the merger round provided the opportunity to encourage accelerated cultural change in the universities, led by a new layer of corporate managers with a line into the government. In the hothouse atmosphere of the mergers, in which institutional futures were uncertain, universities—normally reluctant to change—became less dependent on their past. The government encouraged its favoured merger arrangements by providing grants from its Priority (Reserve) Fund for merger-related upgrading of facilities or staff. It also selectively deployed capital funding to assist institutional upgrading and consolidation.

The casualty of this policy framework was diversity, especially diversity of size. The benefits of single-purpose institutions in the arts or professional training were lost, though they could maintain a risky semi-autonomy inside a larger university. The intimacy of the world-class comprehensive university of 8000 was also forgone. Larger universities such as Monash were encouraged to absorb smaller units, creating a new zone of universities of 20 000–40 000 students (see Table 3.2). The government regarded large institutions as likely to be more resourceful in response to changing needs, and more competitive in the corporate sense, with a strong public image and greater drawing power in the international market. In general Dawkins preferred CAE–university mergers to CAE–CAE mergers.[26] He expected the cross-sectoral mergers to be dominated by the university side of the partnership, and that this would force the CAE staff to upgrade themselves in the academic sense. At the same time, the government hoped the vocational culture of the CAEs would help to render

The Purple Circle. Two members of Dawkins' Purple Circle of policy advisers, Mal Logan (L) and Don Watts. Watts was the Director of the Western Australian Institute of Technology, which became Curtin University of Technology in 1986, and later the first Vice-Chancellor of the private Bond University.

TABLE 3.2   CONSOLIDATION OF INSTITUTIONS IN VICTORIA, 1987–94

Institution in 1987	Student load EFTSU	Institution in 1994	Student load EFTSU
Monash University	11 812	Monash University	28 681
Chisholm IT	5 196		
Gippsland IAE	1 818		
Victorian College of Pharmacy	385		
University of Melbourne	13 853	University of Melbourne	25 041
Melbourne CAE	3 955		
Hawthorn IT	1 034		
Victorian College of the Arts	583		
La Trobe University	7 879	La Trobe University	16 918
Bendigo CAE	1 756		
Lincoln Inst. of Health Sci.			
(Wodonga IAE began 1988)	1 927		
Deakin University	3 781	Deakin University	17 190
Victoria College	5 698		
Warrnambool IAE	1 171		
Royal Melbourne IT	8 313	Royal Melbourne IT*	18 619
Phillip IT	3 977		
Footscray IT	3 581	Victoria UT*	10 306
The Western Institute	220		
Swinburne Limited	4 362	Swinburne UT*	6 859
Ballarat CAE	2 001	University of Ballarat	3 387

  * includes significant TAFE component
  CAE = College of Advanced Education; EFTSU = equivalent full-time student unit;
  IT = Institute of Technology; IAE = Institute of Advanced Education; UT = University of Technology.

Sources: Dawkins, *Higher education: a policy discussion paper*, AGPS, Canberra, 1987, pp 118–21; DEET, *Selected higher education statistics*, DEET, Canberra.

the universities more employer- and industry-conscious.[27] It also hoped that there would be reduced per-capita costs via economies of scale and rationalisation, which had happened during the round of teachers' college mergers in the early 1980s.[28] However, there were also costs in mergers—not least, the cost of upgrading the CAEs to university standards—and economies of scale could be achieved only by a major reduction in existing activities. Further, the capacity of the CAEs to 'vocationalise' merged institutions depended on the willingness of the universities to change themselves in response to the CAEs. Events were to show that neither the cost savings nor the CAE to university cross-sectoral benefits were easily achieved. To an extent, the two kinds of benefit were mutually exclusive.

Potentially, the process of merger negotiations was a free-for-all in which there was a risk that the struggle for individual institutional benefit might work against an optimum division of labour. The NSW government cut across this by enforcing a State-wide blueprint. In Victoria the government preferred to make suggestions rather than lay down the law. Its suggestions were sometimes more sensible than what actually happened. It was a strange outcome that saw the Phillip Institute of Technology at Bundoora go to RMIT rather than La Trobe, for La Trobe was just over the road. Similarly, the Rusden campus of Victoria College, located in Blackburn Road next to Monash, ended up with Deakin University; while the Pharmacy College, part of the Parkville Medical strip adjoining the University of Melbourne, found itself merging with Monash (see chapter 5). When the dust settled, it turned out that Swinburne had stayed independent, though in Dawkins' terms it was scarcely large enough. So did Ballarat, which was half the size of Swinburne.

Non-government funding

The post-1987 universities enjoyed a greater financial autonomy from government, but also carried a greater financial responsibility for their own fate. The government dropped the detailed specification of budgets and capital projects which had annoyed Matheson and Martin.[29] All funding was collapsed into one operating budget, which from 1994 included capital works. From 1990 funding was determined by the 'Relative Funding Model', a formula which varied according to discipline mix and level of study. The trade-off was the Green Paper's insistence that, to meet the growth target, a third of costs would have to be met from non-government sources.[30] In 1989 the federal Labor government introduced the Higher Education Contribution Scheme (HECS), a uniform student charge fixed at an average 20 per cent of course costs. In the first year it was $1800 per full-time student. Payment could be deferred until income reached the level of average weekly earnings. This was a 'soft' fee in its impact on students, but a fee nevertheless—legitimising other kinds of fee in what had from 1974 to 1986 been a free university system. The Green Paper urged institutions to raise money by providing full-fee places to international students, and by offering vocational postgraduate courses and professional upgrading courses on a direct-fee basis. Other avenues for non-government funding were commercial research and consultancy, and corporate and alumni donations. The government maintained the undergraduate education of domestic students as HECS-based rather than direct fee-based, in order to maximise growth and access.

In the destabilised environment of a system in the middle of mergers, the beginnings of international and postgraduate fee charging in 1985–88, the HECS in 1989, the growth of relations with industry and (not least) the continued restraint of public funding, secured the cultural changes that Dawkins wanted. Commercialisation also brought with it certain dilemmas and difficulties. Company-sponsored professorial chairs were not always filled on purely academic criteria. In industry–university research projects there could be disputes over intellectual property, and postgraduates sometimes found that the publication of their theses was suppressed. Academics varied in their attitudes to commercial funding. The strongest support was found among senior managers, and staff from Business Studies. There was much less support among academics from Arts and Science.[31] Nevertheless, universities moved quickly into the new markets, probably more quickly than the government expected. No university was quicker than Monash.

Once the dynamic was established, the continuing growth of market activity was driven by the continuing deterioration in Commonwealth financial support. Resources were being stretched more thinly and the economies of scale derived from growth were not sufficient to compensate. Between 1989 and 1994 the average number of students per academic staff member rose from 12 to 15.[32] Whereas in 1986, 87 per cent of the income of all institutions was from government sources, by 1993 this had fallen to 60 per cent. One dollar in five came from students themselves; 13 per cent of income was from the HECS, 6 per cent from international marketing, and more than 2 per cent from postgraduate and continuing education. Faculty and departmental leaders, increasingly dependent on market income not only for innovations but often for basic teaching as well, found themselves searching for any and every money-making opportunity. Sometimes these ventures were grounded in the 'idea of a university', sometimes not. In 1987 the University of Melbourne advertised in *The Age* a one-day course in 'Understanding your Dog', to be held in the Old Arts Building in the Public Lecture Theatre, at a cost of $35 per person. There was no additional charge for dogs that accompanied their owners.

New forms of governance

The reforms did not stop with funding systems, and with the size and shape of institutions, but extended also to governance. The relationship between government and institutions was reworked, while the Dawkins policies set in train a new regimen inside the universities.

In the Unified National System, government control was exercised in a manner more subtle and indirect. Throughout the OECD, governments were moving towards systems of 'steering from a distance' in higher education. Increasingly, they shaped the behaviour of institutions by using a mixture of incentives, standardised data collection, contracts and accountability requirements. Politically, incentives were more effective than sanctions, because they were much less likely to generate resistance; formally, in a system based on 'steering from a distance', universities operated as self-regulating corporate institutions. At the same time, through these changes governments and business secured an unprecedented level of influence over the 'product' of higher education.[33] The capacity of the government to achieve the effects it desired was enhanced by its strategic deployment of 'competition games' in the distribution of specific funds—competitive bidding for parcels of money, in which the successful bidders were those who best met the government's objectives. In 1992, reflecting on Monash's success in winning the bid to provide the government-funded Open Learning project for broadcast educational services, a brainchild of the Minister for Higher Education under Dawkins, Peter Baldwin, *The Australian* commented that:

> Once upon a time this kind of money for this kind of national endeavour would have been distributed across the system, with the agreement of the system, with negotiations coordinated through the Australian Vice-Chancellors' Committee, and with everyone more or less convinced that while not everyone can win, no one *really* needs to lose. This time around, it's been every campus for itself, as the system quickly recognised that the electronic university will open up a world of possibilities.[34]

In effect the universities were competing for the government's favour. Baldwin gave the bid on Open Learning to Monash, not least because the government was pleased with the University's overall management strategy and policy stance. Thus Canberra used the need for money, and the pressure of competition, to influence institutional priorities, both directly and indirectly. However, it was less successful when it tried to introduce performance-based funding, or measure the total research output of institutions. Eventually it devised a partial measure of output, in the form of the research quantum. This was used to allocate part of the funding for research support, and quickly became a de-facto indicator of research standing. In turn, this tended to shape the balance and the direction of research activities within institutions.

In the annual 'profile' negotiations which began in 1988, universities were required to provide a statement of institutional mission and objectives; details of planned teaching activities, student load and research management; and evidence of their commitment to the Commonwealth's equity policies, particularly to improving the participation of indigenous students. Agreement on the profile was necessary to continued funding. Through this process of negotiation, the government was able to secure standardised data on each institution's activities, and a broad influence over its development. Universities high in the Commonwealth's favour tended to do well in submissions for capital funding, and in competitive bidding. From mid-1987 onwards, Monash enjoyed what is called in China a *guanxi* relationship with Canberra, based on continued trust and friendly dealings.

The changes that Dawkins wanted in internal university governance were equally great. The Green and White Papers emphasised the role of a professionalised management supported by financial controls and strategic planning. 'The Government is determined to . . . increase the scope for management prerogatives to be exercised', stated Dawkins. Decision-making in faculties and academic boards, and the proceedings of governing councils, were often 'cumbersome and unnecessarily protracted'. Universities could not respond quickly at need. For the Minister, the main obstacles to reform were the collegial tradition of organisation, which derived from the notion of the university as a community of scholars; and more recent reforms to internal governance that were based on notions of democracy. Dawkins wanted a greater role for 'chief executive officers', and a reduced one for elected heads and staff and student representatives.[35] Whether it was due to the government's exhortations, or the more general pattern of change in public management, by the early 1990s a trend to more corporate forms of organisation was evident in all institutions (see chapter 4).

Research

In research the government followed the course piloted by the OECD. The aim was to shift the balance from 'pure basic research' grounded in a 'long term and independent approach', in favour of 'strategic basic research' and research applications that addressed 'national economic and social problems'.[36] It continued trends to selectivity and concentration of resources, talked up the need to manage and commercialise intellectual property, and used the profile negotiations to secure from institutions a commitment to manage research activities along these lines. It also reduced operating funds by 3 per cent and allocated the money to the newly formed Australian Research Council (ARC) for distribution on a competitive basis (the research 'clawback'). A significant part of research decision-making had been shifted from university control to central control. The ARC funded only one grant application in every five, so that good researchers were no longer guaranteed support. Continuing research became a series of projects strung together and subject to periodic accountability checks and the possible loss of monies.

Later the government created the Cooperative Research Centres, modelled on the earlier program of the same name in the USA and predicated on collaboration between the universities, CSIRO and industry.

The partial separation of funding for teaching from funding for research violated the conventional academic wisdom, which insisted on a necessary nexus between the two. The ARC Chair, Don Aitkin, became a trenchant critic of that convention.[37] However, fears that the status of research would fall, or that

The Dawkins debate comes to Monash, October 1988

'There are more wankers in the humanities faculties than in others'

On 8 October 1988, 10 months after the publication of the Green Paper on higher education and amid a raging national debate on the government's research policies, the Monash Staff Association convened a meeting to discuss those policies with Don Aitkin, who had been appointed, by the Minister for Employment, Education and Training, John Dawkins, as Chair of the Australian Research Council. About 200 staff were present. The air was tense, but Aitkin's address was received in orderly fashion and his answers to the early questions were heard in relative silence.

Then Pauline Nestor from the English Department rose to speak. The grant system was biased against academics working in the humanities, she stated. It favoured the requirements of the team research used in the science-based disciplines, rather than the individual scholarship used in Arts, and gave a high place to projects of economic utility, a criterion which the humanities could rarely meet. Why, she asked, are Arts staff being discriminated against? At that point Aitkin (whose own field was Political Science) seemed to lose patience. 'Because there are more wankers in the humanities faculties than in others', he replied. There was a hush, followed by a sharp collective intake of breath. Aitkin apologised, but the damage was done. Prejudices against the Dawkins policies had been spectacularly confirmed. Civilisation was under threat. After that the meeting became mutinous and noisy, and nothing that Aitkin could say was going to be well received.[38]

After the meeting the President of the Monash Association, Ian Rae, wrote to Dawkins to demand that Aitkin be removed from his position. Dawkins declined to follow the advice. The feelings generated that day ran long and deep. Rae remembers that years later, he was in a car with Aitkin—who was a good chair of the ARC and later a successful and popular Vice-Chancellor at the University of Canberra and a significant public figure—when he reminded him of the 1988 incident. 'You know Don', said Rae, 'I just thought your tongue ran away with you. Everybody could identify a few wankers around the place, but you were most unwise to say it in public'. Aitkin hesitated. 'Um, I suppose I was', he said.[39]

Ian Rae. Then the President of the Staff Association and later Dean of Science (1990–94), Rae chaired the Monash meeting of 8 October 1988 where Australian Research Council chair Don Aitkin found himself in acrimonious debate.

higher education would become split between research-teaching universities and teaching-only universities, were unfounded. The status attached to teaching and community service rose after 1987, but research retained its principal role in appointments and promotion—and research training, publications and (most of all) grants generated additional income for universities. Most ex-CAE staff found themselves under pressure to improve their research records.

Responses to the new policies

Dawkins' Green and White Papers were probably 'the most significant change' in higher education in Australia's history, Vice-Chancellor Mal Logan told the Council, without much exaggeration, in 1992.[40] Certainly the Dawkins policies were in the same league as the Martin and Murray reports. Whether one agreed with Dawkins' vision or not, there was no doubt about his effectiveness. In a complex, politicised sector he implemented almost every one of his many objectives as they had been enunciated. Only industry involvement fell short of expectations, primarily due to a lack of venture capital.[41]

University people varied in their responses to the new policies. Former CAE academics welcomed the lift to university status, the broader vistas opened up by the mergers, and the value that the government appeared to place on the vocational and the applied. In the pre-1986 universities, academics close to the markets in intellectual property in fields such as artificial intelligence, biomedicine or material technologies often enjoyed more resources and autonomy than before.[42] People in international marketing benefited from its rapid growth. Managers found that the Dawkins framework provided them with more scope in a number of ways, especially in merged institutions.

The government also had strong and vocal critics. For a time they predominated in the public debate. The University of Melbourne's Vice-Chancellor David Penington was one; the Director of the Research School of Social Sciences at the Australian National University, Paul Bourke, was another.[43] Often, university academics working in traditional disciplines and largely dependent on public funding found themselves with less resources and more constraints. More fundamentally, many rejected the discursive framework of the Dawkins policies, on the grounds enunciated by Newman more than a century before that university education was an end in itself, and should not be judged by its utilitarian value to economy or society.[44] There was resentment at the failure of the Green and White Papers to genuflect towards the language of scholarly tradition. This was also the question of control: to what extent should research and teaching be determined by academics, to what extent by industry and government? Even those who supported utilitarian rationales for higher education often argued universities should not be subordinated to the *short-term* requirements of government, and that the relationship should be conducted at 'arms length'.

Attitudes also varied by policy. Measures designed to secure growth and deregulation were mostly supported (though there was some opposition to the introduction of user payments). More directive interventions such as the 'clawback' of research funding were strongly opposed. Many university academics also criticised the dissolution of the binary system, and the inclusion of ex-CAE academics on the same salary and promotional scales as university academics. For the most part, after 1989 these concerns slowly faded.

The different Australian institutions responded to the dynamics of the Unified National System in varying ways, as they moved to rework their long-term size, reach and role and to establish a competitive position. Some sought mergers, some avoided them. Some entered the markets in international education and postgraduate education with more vigour than others. Some focused strongly on improving research performance. All universities changed after 1987—some more so than others. In each university the kind of change that took place was determined in the intersection between the powerful external imperatives released by the Dawkins revolution and the university's own culture and leadership.

At Monash there was a closer than usual synchronisation between the internal and external factors. Despite the doubts of many staff and the outright opposition of others, its leaders embraced the objectives and the rhetoric of the Green Paper. They made a virtue out of change. This was a product of Logan's relationship with the Minister and the policy apparatus in Canberra, which ensured that for good or ill, more than most universities, Monash would be shaped by the Dawkins policies. At the same time, Monash had gained an advantage in the more competitive environment now emerging. The benefits of *guanxi* with Canberra were hard to measure, but they were potentially immense. The Dawkins–Logan axis carried risks, but it was a once-in-a-lifetime opportunity for the University.

Strategic management and cultural change

> Geography in this context is no longer an end in itself but a means to an end. It helps us to discover the slow unfolding of structural realities and see things in the perspective of the very long term. Geography, like history, can ask many questions.
>
> Fernand Braudel, *The Mediterranean and the Mediterranean world in the age of Philip II*, translated by Sian Reynolds, HarperCollins, London, 1992, p. 1

Management and leadership

In the early 1980s the language of management moved from the boardrooms and business schools and into the general culture. There were theories of 'best practice' everywhere, such as Tom Peters and Robert Waterman's *In search of excellence* (1982), which sold more than five million copies worldwide. Firms were told that to move ahead of the pack they would need to remake themselves, and to do so again and again. This idea of perpetual self-modernisation took root in business, in other organisations influenced by business practice, and in management theory itself. As Micklethwait and Wooldridge put it in their review of the discipline: 'Management theorists have a passion for permanent revolution which would have made Trotsky or Mao Ze Dong green with envy'.[1]

An early sign of the rise of business culture was the enrolment growth in management, marketing, accounting, economics and other business courses which promised a fast track to employment and promotion. Whereas in 1972, 15 014 (14.2 per cent) of Bachelor-level university students were in Economics or Commerce, and in 1983, 62 821 (18.0 per cent) of higher education students studied Economics, Business, Management and Administration, by 1994, 122 315 higher education students (20.9 per cent) were enrolled in Business and related disciplines, with many more students in business-related courses in TAFE.[2] Despite this, Business Studies lacked credibility among many academics from other disciplines: partly because it was relatively new; partly because of the faddishness, exhortative tone and the lack of intellectual scepticism and self-criticism evident in much of the literature; partly because of the absence of rigorous empirical tests. Two-thirds of the companies singled out by Peters and Waterman in 1982 as 'excellent' subsequently experienced problems. By 1987 Peters had switched tack and was preaching 'excellence isn't'.[3] Still, management theory was not easy to dismiss. Joined to corporations or to government, it was a powerful tool for reconstruction and reform. Its findings were applied quickly, often instantaneously, in the real world, unlike those of most other disciplines. And while the field had its share of clichés and charlatans, some of its leading practitioners were more substantial.

The seminal thinker was Peter Drucker. He came to notice with *The concept of the corporation* (1946) on General Motors, which argued that the key to the company's success was decentralisation. Drucker also focused on worker motivation and creativity, treating labour as a resource rather than merely a cost. Later he developed the argument that the goods economy was being transformed into a knowledge economy, and workers were becoming 'knowledge workers'; to maximise the productivity of these workers managers needed to engage their minds, and governments and companies needed to provide better education, training and retraining. Drucker balanced these humanist precepts with tougher ideas such as 'strategic thinking' based on 'management by objectives'. In *The practice of management* (1954) he stated that firms needed an elite of general managers to determine long-term strategy and structure, and to specify more immediate objectives for specialist and local managers down the hierarchy. Plans should not become too rigid and instructions should be broad enough to permit local initiative. Drucker emphasised that leadership was more than a matter of quantifiable objectives. It was a *cultural* process. Companies were 'held together by a shared vision of the future', and it was the job of leaders to develop and implement that vision.[4] Leaders were transformers, who sought higher-order changes in attitude and performance through vision, inspiration and common understandings of the realities confronting the organisation.[5] This form of leadership was at its peak in periods of rapid change, when the primary task of leaders was the management of change itself.

In some circles the idea of a small elite of visionary manager-leaders, a kind of general staff with wings, had a compelling, quasi-military appeal. 'If nothing else, managers have always fancied themselves as an officer class. Strategy is what separates them from the sergeants' (Micklethwait and Wooldridge). Drucker's argument also fitted the trends in corporate development. Firms were looking to grow via mergers and takeovers. The typical firm was a large conglomerate with diversified activities, held together by central financial controls, plus strategic direction and a common culture that were shaped by the leadership of the firm. Successful firms were flexible firms. Enhanced central control, facilitated by information technology, was coupled with Drucker-style devolution. Local agents pursued centrally determined objectives as they saw fit, while being 'steered from the distance' by manager-leaders.[6] Increasingly, these same formulae were entering public administration. For his part, Drucker considered good management to be a universal quality and his ideas as relevant to hospitals, churches and universities as to business firms.

In the universities there was already a growing emphasis on professionalised management and corporate-style leadership, encouraged by market-based activities, and the thickening of links between universities and market corporations. In April 1984 the British Committee of Vice-Chancellors and Principals established the Jarratt Committee to report on university management systems and structures. The committee noted that:

> Vice-Chancellors will always have differences of style arising from their own personalities; yet we do discern a more fundamental change which is increasingly taking place. The tradition of Vice-Chancellors being scholars first and acting as a chairman of the Senate carrying out its

Just another business? Peter Drucker considered strategic management and leadership vision to be universal qualities, and his ideas as relevant to hospitals, churches and universities as to business firms.

will, rather than leading it strongly, is changing. The shift to the style of chief executive, bearing the responsibility for leadership and effective management of the institution, is emerging and is likely to be all the more necessary for the future.[7]

Academic leadership was seen as the pivotal point where external pressures for change were mediated, interpreted and turned into internal pressures for change. In this process institutional management itself was reconstructed, and newly empowered. Business-style organisation and language was slower to enter Australian universities, but by the late 1980s most institutions were affected and Dawkins' policies (chapter 3) accelerated the trend.

In higher education corporate reform necessarily took a distinctive form. The 'core business' was teaching, research and a complex of related functions. To succeed in the new environment institutions needed to be competitive in both the corporate sense *and* the academic sense, and to use success in one to feed the strength of the other. In other words, academic prestige, values and processes remained important. The wholesale installation of a business model and the suppression of all that was complex and different about higher education—its multiple objectives, its varied intellectual fields, its academic status hierarchy and its participative character, its decentralised and individualistic mode of creativity—was *not* the optimum strategy. The success of the university in attracting students to courses, whether publicly or privately funded, and its capacity to produce services for business, depended not only on marketing acumen but also on the intrinsic academic quality of research and teaching. The best approach was to blend features of a business model with a strategy attuned to the character and history of the university, creating a hybrid organisation. Universities such as Monash already had Druckerite knowledge workers in decentralised structures, albeit decentralised structures of a collegial academic kind. This suggested that the purpose of mainstream corporate reform was not to invent such knowledge workers from nothing, but instead to relocate the existing knowledge workers in a different cultural context, subjecting them to tighter controls in the form of strategic management, performance reporting and financial efficiency requirements.

The McNeill Committee

At its second meeting of 1985, on the motion of academic staff representative Peter Darvall (later Dean of Engineering and Deputy Vice-Chancellor), the Monash University Council formed a small committee to examine the senior leadership 'structure' of the University. The chair of the Committee was Sir James McNeill, a member of Council from August

1969 until he died in office March 1987. Despite his workload as a senior executive and head of Broken Hill Proprietary Ltd (BHP), McNeill was one of the most effective contributors to the Council in its history. He chaired the finance committee, was instrumental in the creation of the Monash Foundation (chapter 7) and influenced a succession of senior appointments. The McNeill Committee was impressed by the Jarratt report and, like Jarratt, McNeill and his colleagues focused on the managerial aspect of leadership. They noted there had been little change in the administrative structure since 1960. It had served the University well, but 'insufficient time has been devoted to future planning', a problem common in Australian universities. The 'pressure of day to day management' had taken priority: 'In our view there is a real need for the Vice-Chancellor to be able to devote more time to development and planning—focussing on the year 2000 in order to be able to define what kind of University Monash will want to be at the start of the next century'.[8] The University's leader should not be desk-bound and should spend more time in faculties and departments and in representing the university outside it.

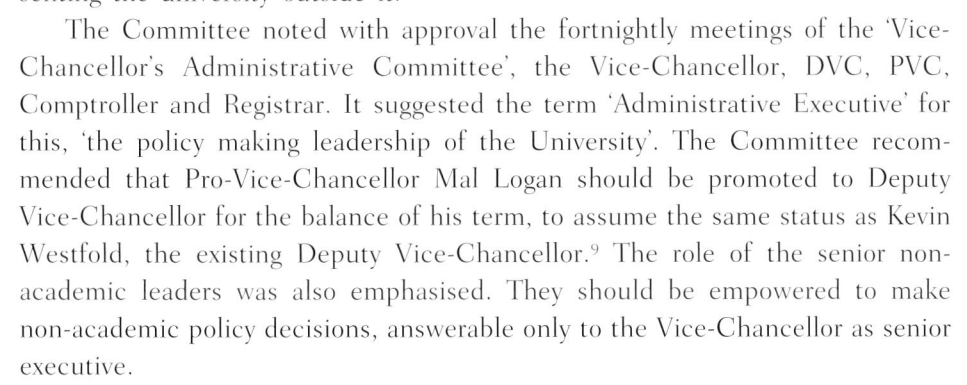

The Committee noted with approval the fortnightly meetings of the 'Vice-Chancellor's Administrative Committee', the Vice-Chancellor, DVC, PVC, Comptroller and Registrar. It suggested the term 'Administrative Executive' for this, 'the policy making leadership of the University'. The Committee recommended that Pro-Vice-Chancellor Mal Logan should be promoted to Deputy Vice-Chancellor for the balance of his term, to assume the same status as Kevin Westfold, the existing Deputy Vice-Chancellor.[9] The role of the senior non-academic leaders was also emphasised. They should be empowered to make non-academic policy decisions, answerable only to the Vice-Chancellor as senior executive.

Kevin Westfold. Professor of Mathematics and later of Astronomy, Dean of Science (1962–75), Pro-Vice-Chancellor and Deputy-Vice-Chancellor (1976, 1982–86).

> The University Community is not confined to teaching and research . . . It is a $100 million per annum institution and the Committee considers that the head(s) of the administrative divisions should fully share with their academic colleagues the responsibility for the administration of the University. Not only should this be the case but it should be seen to be the case, both in the University and in the wider community.[10]

Other issues were mentioned. General staff should have more opportunities for career development. The University needed greater capacity in risk management, and a more diversified funding base: 'Faced with financial constraint, we should aim to greatly increase our funding from non-government sources'. The Comptroller's position should be revamped as General Manager with responsibility for increasing non-government income. More could be done to build alumni support, and the commercial development of research offered rich possibilities, such as the IVF program.[11]

The turnover in the 'Administrative Executive' in 1986/1987 created favourable conditions for the implementation of the McNeill proposals. In 1985 Peter Wade transferred from the State government as the new Comptroller, replacing Len Candy,[12] and Tony Pritchard succeeded Jim Butchardt as Registrar in 1986. Kevin Westfold retired as DVC at the end of 1986. The new Vice-Chancellor took office in early 1987. Monash remade itself in the next half decade, but only because it was ready. The McNeill Committee was one reason for this. It helped to reshape the Vice-Chancellorship, from the collegial style identified by the Jarratt report and exemplified *par excellence* by Martin, to the more strategic and transformational leadership of the Logan years.

The geographer as Vice-Chancellor

In selecting Mal Logan as the Vice-Chancellor after Martin, the Council chose a person well attuned to the national and international currents that were changing higher education. Logan was a geographer who was also interested in History, Economics[13] and Public Policy, and specialised in urban planning, Third World development and global systems. In early years he was influenced by the nationalist and socialist Australian historian Ian Turner. Later he was impressed by the French geographer-historian Fernand Braudel, who analysed the interrelationship between human and natural environments, between the factor that was given and the factor that could be controlled, and who understood history in terms of everyday life. For Logan, Geography spanned the natural and social sciences, enabling a wide range of ideas to come into play; it was very useful in understanding globalisation (the growth of world systems): 'I've been interested always in how space is formed and what determines the boundaries of space. Increasingly, we now cut across national boundaries'. At the same time, Logan brought to the global sphere a national commitment. He saw the internationalisation of education as one key to developing a distinctively Australian role in the Asia-Pacific region.[14] Louis Waller described him as a 'universalist' who was also 'very very Australian', signifying a nationalist upbringing.[15]

Following teaching, lecturing and a doctoral thesis at the University of Sydney on national–international tensions in Australian manufacturing (1965), Logan became Professor of Geography and Urban and Regional Planning at the University of Wisconsin (1967–71) and Visiting Professor of Geography at the University of Ibadan in Nigeria, before taking a professorial chair at Monash in 1971. He developed a cosmopolitan curriculum vitae (see box): he was a visiting professor at four European and Asian universities and a frequent contributor at conferences and UNESCO forums; he visited China, developed an interest in Malaysia, worked at the OECD headquarters in Paris, and was one of the OECD's examiners of Japanese urban policy in 1984–86. Logan was fascinated by Japan, where economic self-interest was modified by networks of mutual support, and companies and government thought in 20- or 30-year spans.[16] With fellow geographer Maurie Daly he wrote *The brittle rim* (1989), on financial globalisation and the Asia-Pacific. Logan was also at home with business and politics, more so than most university professors appointed in the 1970s. His Labor leanings were clear: a consultant on strategy to Labor's reforming Minister of Urban and Regional Development, Tom Uren, in 1972–75, he served on a 1978 committee set up by Labor leader Bill Hayden to renovate the party's electoral fortunes, and was friendly with senior Labor figures. While this reduced his potential contribution to national affairs under a Liberal–National Party government, Labor's election in 1983 opened doors for Logan in Canberra. In August 1983 he was appointed to the Universities' Council, responsible for program administration and policy advice.[17] In 1987 he was part of John Dawkins' advisers, the 'Purple Circle' (see chapter 3).

In early 1982 Logan was asked by Martin to become a part-time Pro-Vice-Chancellor from 15 March on a 0.2 basis. The work quickly expanded and the time fraction was upgraded. Logan became Martin's 'pipeline' to the faculties and departments, feeding the Vice-Chancellor with information about what was happening in the University and from time to time representing him in problem areas. He was active in University committees as well as attending Council, the Professorial Board and the Committee of Deans; and was occasional acting DVC. The result was an extensive grounding in the workings of Monash. Logan became acquainted with all of the deans and faculties, soaking up information on the different subcultures typical of a large university and the languages and nuances of the various relations between the centre and the parts.[18]

On 25 September 1984 Martin wrote to Council stating that he did not intend to seek reappointment when his term expired in early 1987. He wanted to devote more time to academic and other pursuits, and felt that 'the interests of the University may not be best served by retaining the one person as Vice-Chancellor for more than a decade'. Council established a Search Committee to begin the process of selecting a new leader. Between February and April 1985 the position was advertised and Monash staff were asked to suggest possible candidates. Logan's name was one of those put forward, with a long list of supporting signatures. The Committee developed a set of criteria against which to measure applicants, including 'vision', a record of interaction outside universities, and a commitment to scholarship and the liberal tradition. There were 'divergent' views on the Committee concerning the role of the Vice-Chancellor's spouse and on whether this should be incorporated in selection.[19]

Malcolm Ian Logan, Vice-Chancellor 1987–96

The sheer power of education

Logan grew up in remote NSW towns, where his father taught in one-teacher schools. 'The parameters of life were relatively simple', he stated later: 'It centred around school, the Presbyterian Church and family. At the end of eighteen years of this I had formed an appreciation of just what education means to both rich and poor; the sheer power of education and its capacity to bring social change'.[20] After secondary schooling at Tamworth, Logan completed an honours degree in Geography at the University of Sydney in 1951, followed by six years in secondary teaching and at Sydney Teachers' College. He lectured in Geography at the University of Sydney in 1959–67, completing his PhD in 1965, and was Professor of Geography and of Urban and Regional Planning at the University of Wisconsin in 1967–71. He also served as a Rockefeller Foundation Visiting Professor of Geography at the University of Ibadan, Nigeria (1970–71). During the 1970s and the first half of the 80s Logan was active in World Bank, United Nations and OECD forums, attending conferences and meetings in India, Indonesia, Japan, Malaysia, Singapore, Brazil, China, France, Thailand, Taiwan and Canada; and serving as a visiting professor or scholar at the London School of Economics, the International Institute for Applied Systems Analysis in Vienna, the Hebrew University of Jerusalem and Nanyang University in Singapore. Logan worked at the OECD at its Paris headquarters during 1980–81, including a period in Urban Affairs, and was a member of the OECD Examiners of Japanese Urban Policy invited to report to the Japanese government (1984–86).

Logan was appointed by Matheson as a Professor of Geography on 5 April 1971, without advertisement, selection committee or interview. For his part Logan knew little of Monash. He accepted the job because he wanted to return to Australia, and Monash seemed 'the liveliest and brightest place' where a chair was available: 'It had warts all over it but it seemed to me to be an environment in which you could do things'.[21] He became a part-time Pro-Vice-Chancellor at Monash from 15 March 1982, upgraded to 0.5 (15 March 1983) and 0.7 (5 March 1984). As PVC, Logan

Mal Logan, Vice-Chancellor 1987–96. An uncanny capacity to read the trends in economy, government and education.

chaired the PhD and Research Committee, was a member of the Development Committee, and represented the Vice-Chancellor on the Biosafety, Parking and HEARU Committees (all of which he chaired) and the Affiliation, Buildings, Halls of Residence, Housing, Patents and Central Budgets Committees. Logan chaired the Krongold Centre, was a member of the General Library and Computer Centre Committees, and had ongoing contact with the Monash Association of Students and the Staff Association. He was made full-time Pro-Vice-Chancellor in March 1985, Deputy Vice-Chancellor in December 1985, and Vice-Chancellor in February 1987.

A member of the Universities Council (1983–86) and a Commissioner of the Victorian Tourism Commission (1983–85), Logan chaired the Victorian Committee of inquiry into the Very Fast Train Project (1989–90), served as a member of the Pacific Economic Cooperation Council from 1989, and as a director of the Committee for Melbourne (from 1990), the Business-Higher Education Round Table (1990–92) and the Docklands Authority (from 1991). His experience in Japan assisted him as a director of the Multi Function Polis Development Corporation (from 1992). He chaired the Australian Centre for Contemporary Art, was a director of the University's Playbox Theatre company, a trustee of the Committee for the Economic Development of Australia, a director of the Australian Vice-Chancellors' Committee, the Vice-Chancellors' industrial wing of the Higher Education Industrial Association, and chair of the International Development Program. In 1996 he became a Companion of the Order of Australia.

On 14 October the Committee identified a short list. It consisted of two outsiders—the Director of the Western Australian Institute of Technology Don Watts and University of Melbourne Dean of Medicine David Penington, soon to be Vice-Chancellors at Bond and Melbourne Universities respectively—and three applicants with a Monash connection: Louis Waller from Law, Logan, and former Physiology Professor Robert Porter, then head of the John Curtin School of Medical Research at the Australian National University. The choice came down to Logan or Porter. After the final interviews, on 4 December 1985 the Committee unanimously recommended Logan. The December Council agreed, also promoting him to DVC as recommended by the McNeill Committee.[22] Martin's early announcement of his departure allowed the Vice-Chancellor-designate to spend a full further year in 1986 preparing for his 10-year term of office.

Logan's ideas were more non-traditional than many of his colleagues realised. He disliked Newman's *The idea of a university*, which was to be much quoted by his counterpart and rival Penington at Melbourne. He rejected the notion that a university education might be seen as an alternative to productive, socially useful work, rather than as a preparation for it. He criticised the separations between knowledge and skill, education and training, and pure and applied research, that he saw as residues of the Newman tradition. Universities should be concerned with all of these missions—that was their strength: 'A university is uniquely able to balance a culture of curiosity with a mix of vocationally related skills'.[23]

The new Vice-Chancellor associated university education with certain 'fundamental principles', such as academic freedom and academic standards, research and scholarship, truth-seeking and objectivity, an obligation to both serve and criticise society, academic control of academic affairs; but he joined these principles to the modern and post-modern vision of the university enunciated by Clark Kerr (1963), the 'multiversity'. The concept of the multiversity 'exerted a major influence on the shape and functions of Monash', he was to tell Council in 1992. The multiversity was not premised on 'a single animating principle' but housed many purposes, and connected to 'numerous constituencies'—government, business, students, parents—that helped to shape it. It had 'many schools and departments'. It was 'in constant change because the needs of society are constantly changing'. Logan celebrated a spirit of engagement which he saw as typical of the large American state universities, such as Wisconsin where he had worked. These institutions were defined not only by their academic achievements but by their 'involvement in the community, local, national and international' and their sense of responsibility to students and other 'stakeholders'. They were 'open to all qualified young people from all walks of life'. Their objective was not 'the perpetuation of an elite class but the creation of a relatively classless society', with 'universal opportunity through education'. Logan saw academic standards less in terms of the scores that students brought to entry, more in terms of the quality of graduates at the point of exit and the 'value added' at Monash.[24]

He understood universities as a balance between the conservative and the modern that was constantly being displaced to the modern end of the equation. Universities were 'remarkably resilient and remarkably adaptable'. They survived only by periodically turning themselves into something new. The multiversity was a flexible institution, and Logan's use of the concept was also flexible. The rhetorical balances between change and conservation, between external pressures and internal identity, and between the demands of the different external constituencies, could be varied to fit the audience. On the whole, Logan emphasised the imperative of transformation. He repeatedly argued that universities could not stand still in the face of external pressures: 'State and society are more sceptical of the demands of the universities, less sympathetic to the virtues of university autonomy and more insistent that they respond rapidly to the needs of society'. Academic autonomy was a necessary part of the creative process, but to preserve academic autonomy it was necessary to (voluntarily) adjust academic work to meet external pressures. It was better 'to create our own future than to have one forced upon us', he stated. It had always been thus: 'The real strength of universities has lain in their capacity to adapt to changing environments and social demands'. Here Logan moved adroitly between the role of defender of the University in a difficult environment, and the role of an agent of change who was himself implicated in those external pressures. Like many vice-chancellors he realised that the best way of 'rearranging, restructuring and reorienting' his institution was 'by allowing those outside processes to [have an] impact on the institution'. In the process, the university whose interests he was advancing and defending was turned into a different university.[25]

'I see myself as a leader, not as a manager', with 'a sense of vision' for Monash, Logan told *The Age* in 1988. Echoing Drucker, he said that it was his role to develop 'directions' for the University. At the end of 1995 Logan remarked that 'I don't think I'm a terribly good manager at all . . . but I enjoy the big picture stuff'. He distrusted detailed plans. There was little point in meeting targets if in the meantime the imperatives had altered. Again the key quality was flexibility, the capacity to adjust to a changing context and to move quickly in response to new opportunities. The university had to become 'malleable', and its structure and budget should facilitate responsiveness. The leader's capacity to identify the right responses rested on strategic thinking, on understanding of the context and of the strengths and limitations of the institution and, most elusive, 'some understanding of what is likely to emerge down the track'.[26] Here Logan was assisted by a capacity to read trends in education, economy and government, often ahead of the hard evidence: 'He has the most marvellous smell. Sometimes it is sheer knowledge, sometimes it is kind of intuitive' (Pritchard).[27] These were not the attributes of the mystic, but of the geographer-historian-social scientist drawing on a range of disciplines, ideas and experiences. As it turned out, his interests in urban planning and world systems theory provided useful tools for reorienting a university in the late 1980s and 90s.

Logan also had sharp political skills. After the Purple Circle he continued to align himself with Labor's conception of the universities. Dawkins, he stated in 1996, 'had the long term perspective right'. Education had to be integrated with social and economic change on the national level.[28] In Logan's office political criteria tended to take priority over other merits, which had its disadvantages. Nevertheless, the political criteria were his own and not the government's (except to the extent that he shaped policy himself). Logan used a well-developed political nose to manage both Monash's relations with Canberra and consent building at Clayton.

He supported the decentralised structure he had inherited from Matheson and Martin. He supported the authority of deans within the faculties, and talked about intellectual freedom. More entrepreneur than corporate manager, Logan preferred to use incentives to shape the academic work rather than directions or compulsion. He did not like management by performance measures and accountability requirements, tending towards standardisation, which was finding favour in some universities. His personal style veered from the tough talk of the political operative to a soft-spokenness inflected with enthusiasm for the intellectual and artistic. The remote and unfailing courtesy of the Martin years was discarded. More direct, less hierarchical in interpersonal relations, Logan was also mindful of the need to consult, persuade and charm if necessary all the way through the long circuit of Monash committees and 150 professors. 'You have to be able to convince your academic colleagues of the correctness of the direction in which the University should move. And their terms are academic values', he said in 1993.[29] Monash was a participative institution. A failure to consult would generate resistance, disabling the potential for change.

Porter remarked later that the strength of the University under Logan lay in his capacity to meld different contributors in a heterogeneous culture. He had a knack for drawing on the ideas and motivations of anyone, even people he didn't like. He often delegated significant authority to relatively junior people reporting direct to him (an approach which had the not incidental effect of keeping senior colleagues off-balance). He supported the contribution of women, though one regret at the end of his term was that apart from his adviser Elizabeth Anderson there were no women in senior positions in the central administration, and Marian Quartly in Arts was the only female dean.[30] The downside of his relationships with people was that nothing was fixed. After reaching an understanding with someone, he might shift ground in response to changing events without fully consulting those concerned. Partial revision of the Chisholm-Monash understandings left Chisholm backers of the merger in a difficult position. Logan did not always support his executive colleagues 100 per cent when the going was tough. At different times, both John Hay and Ian Chubb as Deputy Vice-Chancellors ran into a wall of criticism, when they might have claimed to be on Logan's errand, to find that Logan was standing somewhat aside and preparing to deal with their critics. On big issues, personal agreements and loyalties were always subordinated to considerations of policy and power.

Not everyone who shared his reading of the factors shaping Monash shared his drive for change. Logan was an optimist. His farewell address talked about 'those small moments of hope, those shafts of sunlight in the garden, that are worth more than an eternity of dull despair'. According to the University's official objectives, Monash intended to outdo Melbourne by becoming 'the leading research university in Victoria'. Logan himself went further. 'I believe Monash has the capacity to be the best university in Australia', he stated in 1988.[31] He also thought in terms of a new model of university, and the creation of a new kind of Monash. These aims were not compatible, unless the example set by Monash could change the basis on which the 'best university' was judged. It was an ambitious program.

Strategy for the future

By establishing a single national market the Dawkins policies posed for each university the question of competitive strategy. Harvard's Michael Porter identified two sources of competitive advantage: market differentiation (superior quality), whereby customers paid for a product seen as distinctive; and production at a price cheaper than competitors.[32] These alternatives exercised the minds of leaders in higher education as elsewhere. There were other potential sources of advantage. In all markets, and the more so in newly emerging markets, the very character of the market is shaped by the behaviour of its larger players.[33] In *Competing for the future* (1994), Gary Hamel and C.K. Prahalad argue that 'the most important form of competition is the battle to create and dominate emerging opportunities'.[34] This was the Logan approach. Monash's leaders studied the markets in business and international education created by policy, and emerging opportunities in open learning and relations with TAFE, and sought to apply superior foresight, speed, size, organisation and marketing to gain 'first-mover' leverage and exploit those spheres more effectively than competitor institutions. The University set out to increase private funding and publicly funded enrolments as rapidly as possible, to maximise its clout, its capacity to determine its own destiny independent of government and other institutions. At the same time it used its standing in Canberra to secure support for a building program on six sites: Logan's ephemeral political connections were mobilised to create lasting changes.

The most important move made at this time was to develop a strategy distinctive to the University. Not all higher education institutions in the Dawkins system competed on the same basis, nor could they all profit from the same approach. The options before each institution were affected by its history, location and prestige, and its map of activities and resources. The long-established Monash instinct had been to look first of all to the University of Melbourne for advice and example. Under Martin, 'someone would get on the phone to Melbourne and check, and away we'd go' (Logan). No doubt many at Clayton took it for granted that Monash's natural competitive strategy was to strive to surpass Melbourne on the terms Melbourne had already set. For this perspective had been implicit at Monash from the beginning: the Act specified Melbourne as the University's standard (see chapters 1 and 2). But, in the more competitive environment, what was good for Melbourne was not always good for Monash. Monash's new leaders were keenly aware of this.[35]

The University of Melbourne, located just north of the central business district, enjoyed the leading reputation in the State in both professional training and research. It did not need to undertake major mergers to grow or to gain a stronger position. (Melbourne did undertake a large merger with Melbourne CAE, but that institution was already on site, and the merger amounted to stripping its assets.) It did not need to remake itself, it needed only to modernise. For Melbourne, the priorities were to corporatise administration, strengthen the underperforming faculties, expand research, step up fund-raising, and create a business school and a graduate centre. But if Monash tried to outdo Melbourne at Melbourne's game of modernisation without remaking, then Monash was likely to fail. Lacking Melbourne's location and inherited prestige, in the more competitive and partly deregulated system Monash would find itself outdone by Melbourne in industry funding and probably in research funding—perhaps even in international students. Monash would end up as a second and weaker research university of medium size, a 'little Melbourne' with declining income and prestige. As the Dean of Computing was to put it, looking back in 1996, one possible strategy was to 'aspire to be a Harvard of the South'. But such a course would be 'based on conceit and not logic', and 'the conceit would have been found to be ill founded'.[36]

Nevertheless, established universities rarely made a radical break from the past. To achieve this, the first step was to secure a mood for cultural change; the second to develop concrete proposals; the third to press forward with them when the time was right. On 17 April 1985 Logan sent a memo to Martin and Westfold, suggesting a background paper on the medium-term future. 'An excellent idea', responded Martin. One year later it began to take shape. On 22 April 1986 Logan wrote to Wade, Pritchard and Planning Officer Peter Beilby on the need for 'strategic long term planning' additional to the rolling five-year plans serviced by Beilby's Planning and Analysis Branch. In May and June Logan visited universities in Sweden and the UK, and the OECD, and he began to collect mission statements from around the world. On 20 August 1986 a joint meeting of the Development Committee of the Professorial Board and the Planning Committee of Council was held. Logan proposed a discussion paper on the development of the University, leading to a policy statement. The minutes record that 'the concept was supported with enthusiasm by the meeting'.[37] People at the meeting could not have known that Monash's traditional planning processes were about to be superseded by an executive-led strategy, in which the Development and Planning Committees would be reduced to conduits to the Board and Council respectively.

Registrar Tony Pritchard (1986–93). Logan later identified Pritchard, Peter Wade, John Hay and himself as the key group in the first stage of remaking the University.

In the mid-1980s Beilby was complaining with some justification that he was chronically underresourced in servicing the planning cycle in each faculty. The resources and functions of his office were upgraded, and at the end of 1986 Lea Swanson was appointed to assist him. On 6 March 1987 Logan again canvassed strategy and strategy planning with the Development Committee of the Board. Again the Committee was sympathetic. It agreed that Monash should be more financially independent and better promoted. There was interest in Wade's suggestion that it acquire a base in the central business district of Melbourne to facilitate contacts and teaching activities.[38] Logan advised the Committee that, while its role was central to 'the production of a dynamic plan for the University's on-going development', 'it would be useful for a small working group to be established that could maintain the planning momentum by taking charge of the actual work involved'. Thus the Planning Working Group was created, chaired by Logan and including the new DVC Ian Polmear (1987–90), formerly a professor of Materials Engineering, Wade, Alan Fels from Administration, the Vice-Chancellor's Assistant Kevin O'Connor, Beilby, and Terry Hore and Leo West from the Higher Education Research Unit. Subsequently Pritchard became involved, as did Swanson. She and O'Connor shared most of the drafting of *Strategy for the Future*.

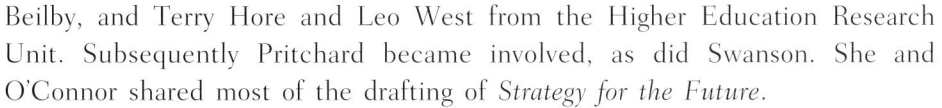

Meanwhile Logan was moving on another front. In the first half of 1987, accompanied by Hore, he attended meetings involving almost every staff member at Clayton: 'I visited every department. I listened and I talked and tried to develop a culture for change'. According to Hore, 'He made sure that people knew what he was on about'. Logan also sought feedback from each dean on faculty plans, and on 12 May he wrote to all individual Monash professors asking them to prepare a four-page document setting out the strategic strengths and weaknesses of their department. In August Logan thanked the professoriate for its contribution, remarking that it was pleasing that the need for forward planning was accepted, but disappointing that there had been few references to external factors and the potential for non-government income. Still, the main purpose had been achieved. 'A climate of self-evaluation, consultation and participation' was developing, informed by strategy considerations, Logan argued at the Development Committee on 29 May.[39] As for the strategy plan itself, that was to be generated not in the all-in process of consultation but by the Planning Working Group, Logan's chosen vehicle.

The first meeting of the Group took place on 19 May 1987. On 6 July Logan tabled a paper titled 'Some general observations'. It focused on comparative

Cause and effect: Economics Dean Gus Sinclair (1983–92) (L) with Alan Fels, Professor of Administration (1984–96). Fels helped prepare *Strategy for the future* while Sinclair became one of the 'victims' of the strategy, locked into a bitter battle for post-merger primacy with the David Syme School of Business at Caulfield.

advantage and how to achieve it. Were there outstanding staff and world-class departments? Was the location at Clayton in some sense an advantage 'or perhaps more likely, a disadvantage'? In the absence of existing advantages, the next option was to identify new advantages and move on them ahead of competitors. Southeast Asia might provide such opportunities. A more selective and focused research policy was needed. The University could make more of its teaching and its community contribution in the Arts, and might develop continuing vocational education in the city. A vigorous public relations effort could build the University's reputation and attract better undergraduates. Monash was still too introspective and complacent. 'A more entrepreneurial spirit' was needed in the faculties:

> We have to be a university where ideas are constantly flowing to the top. There are other places with more resources than we have, and if we stand still, they can always move more effectively into fields in which we already have a stake. To a very large extent we have to live on our wits.[40]

Strategy for the future was drafted, redrafted, discussed with the deans, amended by the Development Committee, circulated throughout the University for comment and redrafted again, securing general agreement.[41] It was 'warmly endorsed' by the Planning Committee of Council and 'received and endorsed with enthusiasm' by Council on 14 December 1987. This was five days after the release of the Commonwealth's Green Paper (chapter 3). At the same meeting Council received an expanded budget statement, prepared by Wade and Logan, designed to render resource allocation more transparent and to match it more closely to strategic objectives. One per cent was held back for allocation to selected new initiatives, including the Public Sector Management Institute and the Centre for European Studies.

The final text of *Strategy for the future* called for change in general terms. Compared to the corporate plans soon to be developed at the University of Melbourne, *Strategy for the future* made less of a claim for leadership in society and talked more about openness, about responding to 'the changing social, cultural and economic needs of the community'. The new policy agenda required higher participation rates, vocational relevance and new focuses on Australian Studies and Asia. Monash would explore potential mergers that were consistent with its strategy and its educational objectives. The University would need to 'compete strongly', in academic knowledge and technology, and would search and develop niche markets. The 'Western Pacific Rim' was 'an area of special interest to Monash'. Overseas marketing provided 'exceptional opportunities to increase funding and promote the university's international reputation'. Work had begun on a Monash Science and Technology Park to enhance relations with industry.

The themes were stated in general terms. The main role of *Strategy for the future* lay not in content but in process. 'It was watered down', Logan commented later: 'When we were starting to prepare the written form I got cold feet. I felt that the smart thing to do was *not* to give too much public notice of some of the things on the agenda'.[42]

Implementation of the strategy

A year later negotiations with Chisholm and Gippsland were underway; there were affiliation agreements with several other institutions, and twinning arrangements with Sunway College in Malaysia; a new Engineering building was planned, the Science Park was growing, an Office of External Relations and Alumni Affairs had been established, a more corporate image was being created. Of the $150 million University budget, $20 million came from the private sector, compared with $3 million four years before.

The University was now making its own path, and when the Act was amended a year later the decision to omit reference to Melbourne as the University's standard, erasing the legal traces of the old genuflection, required little debate (see box).

Bob Baxt, Dean of Law between 1980 and 1988, recalls the change in the atmosphere. 'Suddenly you could get things done at Monash.' When it was decided to 'take the plunge' and obtain premises in the city of Melbourne, Wade said 'Why do we want only one floor, why not take the whole bloody building?'. Later, in 1992, Stephen Matchett wrote in *The Australian* that 'for Monash life is a dash for growth and deals. Monash likes ideas that will grow, that will bring in more money and more students . . . It also wants to be ahead of the pack'. He found that 'a day with Logan and his team is a cross between a briefing at corporate headquarters and a tent revival meeting. They all believe in Monash'.[43]

At times the speed of change was reminiscent of the early days of Monash, though the hard-bitten talk about opponents of change, real or imagined, was new. Logan identified the main 'players' in the crucial first phase between 1988 and 1990—from *Strategy for the future* to the bedding down of the merger with Chisholm—as John Hay, Peter Wade, Tony Pritchard and himself. This group shaped the Monash strategy, though others were consulted, or played drafting roles. As DVC, Hay carried responsibility for negotiating and implementing some of the most difficult policies, including the merger with Chisholm and discussions with both Gippsland and Victoria College. Wade was the driver of financial and administrative reform and an important source of ideas. Pritchard also saw his role in terms of the transformation of the University. He was not the typical

Bob Baxt, Law Dean 1980–88. 'Suddenly you could get things done at Monash.'

Of apples, oranges and mandarins

The 1990 amendment: Monash University comes of age

A hard Act to follow: Monash made the official decision to stop benchmarking itself to the University of Melbourne in 1990.

When Peter Wade took up the post of Comptroller in 1985, Monash was 'in something of a cultural straightjacket'. It saw itself as the 'last of the old' universities, yet the Act had specified another old university (and its main rival) as senior, as the criterion by which Monash was judged. According to Section 5(c), 'the standard for graduation in the University should be at least as high as prevails in the University of Melbourne'. Monash was 'nervous about breaking out' (Wade), yet it was too young to outdo Melbourne on Melbourne's ground. A year later, Logan became Vice-Chancellor, and Wade found that Logan had the same view: 'He was very keen for Monash to get out and make its mark on its own, rather than trailing along in the stream of the old university'.[44]

The University's leaders realised that Monash's more individual strategy would have to become concretised in a more individual identity, and to make this stick the Monash University Act would have to be changed. In 1990 the Act was opened up to accommodate the Chisholm and Gippsland mergers, and the opportunity was taken to remove the offending words in section 5(c). Logan adopted the title 'Vice-Chancellor and President' to strengthen the University's international profile and signify a North American model. It all underlined the University's coming of age, its desire to set its own standards. As DVC Robert Pargetter put it later, the comparison was now between 'apple and orange', rather than 'orange and mandarin'. And 'that was a very important thing to do'.[45]

It was not always easy to sustain this position. The comparison with Melbourne was still made, and despite Monash's spectacular development not everyone judged it on its own terms. During the first round of Commonwealth quality assurance visits in 1993, the opening question was 'Which university do you compare yourself with?'. Logan's response was 'None'. He noted later that this did not go down well with the quality committee.[46]

'black-letter' Registrar whose brief was prudent stewardship: 'Mal wanted someone to succeed Jim Butchardt who was going to facilitate rather than block' (Pritchard). Notwithstanding internal tensions from time to time, in the face of the Board, Council, staff and outside world the leadership group was 'rock solid':

'You couldn't drive a wedge between us' (Pritchard).[47] The executive group was welded together by the heady, addictive excitement of a shared entrepreneurial mission in a conservative environment, and a glimpse of the brave new opportunities that the new period presented.

From Logan's viewpoint the timing of the release of the Green Paper in December 1987, just as he had secured an unambiguous mandate at Clayton for as yet undefined changes, was perfect. Many of Dawkins' policies were likely to be unpopular, but they confirmed Logan's arguments about external imperatives and strengthened his hand where resistance could be expected—for example in relation to growth, mergers, private income-raising, and the allocation of internal resources to support new initiatives. Logan was too close to the government to employ the stance of Penington at Melbourne, who denounced Dawkins while using the Dawkins-generated momentum for change to achieve internal objectives. Nevertheless, *Strategy for the future* ensured that the process of transformation was seen to have at least some indigenous roots, even by many academic staff disturbed by the Green Paper. Most importantly, it bought time for the Vice-Chancellor, so when staff resistance to change eventually became a factor to be reckoned with in 1991, the most important change—the merger with Chisholm—was already accomplished.

Nevertheless, at Monash important decisions could not be pushed through on a top-down basis against the deans. Baxt recalls that some deans shared Logan's reading of the imperatives, and others were uneasy or hostile. Baxt in Law and John Hay in Arts (1987–88), later to be Deputy Vice-Chancellor (1989–91), were supporters. Graeme Schofield in Medicine (1977–88) and Gus Sinclair in Economics, Commerce and Management (1983–92) had doubts. So did Endersbee in Engineering. He welcomed the emphases on private funding and relations with industry, but considered growth of little value if it undermined Monash's claim to be an elite university. Engineering should aim to be the best faculty in the field, modelling itself on Stanford rather than Wisconsin, he thought. He regretted that the absorption of the CAEs into the universities would abolish courses focused on applied technologies. Many of his colleagues in Engineering agreed, including Darvall who succeeded him as Dean (1988–94), though the dean and faculty were to apply themselves conscientiously to the merger with Chisholm engineering at Caulfield. More trenchant opposition was to come from Clayton Economics and Business (chapter 5). It was ironic that the two faculties best able to profit from the new markets were the most resistant to the costs of the Logan strategy. On the other hand, as incoming deans in 1988, Bob Williams in Law and Robert Porter in Medicine accepted the course charted by the University, though they did not always endorse the language or the policy detail. Robert Pargetter (1989–93) and Marian Quartly (1993–99) in Arts were supporters. Peter Fensham in Education (1982–88) was often critical, but his successor David Aspin (1989–93) was more sympathetic to the Vice-Chancellor's vision.[48]

Though the picture was mixed, Logan's knowledge of the faculties, skills in consultation and consensus building, and his continuing support for the Monash tradition of strong deans and autonomous faculties enabled him to bring the individual deans and the Deans Committee with him on nearly all occasions—and despite the further decline of the role of the Deans Committee in University-wide matters (see chapter 7). The Vice-Chancellor's role in the appointment of deans strengthened his position. As a succession of new deans replaced those in power in 1987, Logan found the going easier.

The support of the deans was very important at Professorial Board, later Academic Board. If the Board had accommodated the academic opponents of Logan's strategy, his reforms would have been in jeopardy. There was debate at the Board, and one close vote over the merger of the Business and Economics faculties, but the line was held. The deans and the Board knew that Logan retained the solid support of the Chancellor and the ultimate decision-making body, Council. For his part, Chancellor Sir George Lush believed that as long as a vice-chancellor retained the support of the Professorial Board, that vice-chancellor's preferred course of action should be supported as a matter of course.[49] Retaining the support of both deans/Board and Council, with each of these twin structural pillars grounded in the continuing acquiescence of the other, the consensus held, and Logan never lost the initiative or the momentum for change. It was a nearer thing than his critics knew: if one part of the support base had faltered, the others would immediately have been affected. Without skilled political management, timing and a measure of bluff, it would all have come unstuck.

Critical support. Faculty Deans Bob Williams (Law 1988–98) (L) and Bob Porter (Medicine 1989–98) (R) were key supporters of Logan's strategy, although they were not always happy with the executive group's decisions.

For their part, most of the deans moved in the entrepreneurial direction pioneered by Endersbee and now officially encouraged. 'Perhaps the most important single achievement has been the willingness of academic leaders to approach the management of their faculties and departments in a more strategic way', stated Logan in 1992, though in truth the deans scarcely had a choice but to seize every possible opportunity to enhance their resources—or, in some cases, just to maintain activities undermined by falling public funding.[50]

The executive group continued to work the lode of strategic leadership which had paid off so richly. In 1993 the University's educational objectives were amended to include 'an understanding of different cultures, both within Australia and overseas, that enriches experience and challenges assumptions'; and the community service objectives were amended to include 'to provide access to higher education to all in the community through Open Learning programs', and 'to develop more flexible pathways to the University from schools and TAFE colleges'. In 1995 the Vice-Chancellor and his office prepared a new document, *Directions for the future*. It placed still more emphasis on innovation and the international realm than *Strategy*. According to *Directions*, Monash was a 'world university', a 'more mature university with a sharper awareness of its identity and its unique place in the Australian university system', committed to the internationalisation of 'curriculum, teaching and research'; Monash 'sets the agenda, is innovative, flexible, creative, competitive and committed to getting to the front first, thereby creating its own future'. As Logan put it in 1992, there was 'a continual state of renewal inside the University as adaptation takes place',[51] just as the management textbooks advised.

There's trouble at mill: the TRAG

As the changes unfolded, the unease felt by many staff was a function not only of the pace of change, or recalcitrance in the face of demands for a broader social mission, but a product also of the strains and tensions within the strategy itself. First, Monash's leaders wanted to develop a coherent and singular image of the University in all of its spheres of operation, but they also emphasised diversity in sites and activities. Second, Monash was competing with Melbourne for the high-achieving secondary student, yet also had a commitment to broader access. High rates of growth, coupled with mergers, were bound to lower the cut-off scores for entry to at least some Monash courses. At the margin, it appeared there was a trade-off between academic reputation and access, for the public did not understand Logan's point that standards should be measured not by entry scores but by the value added at Monash. Third, much of the University's reputation still rested on the largely publicly funded research taking place in Science, Engineering and Medicine, yet the focus for development was often elsewhere. Official statements attempted to achieve a rhetorical closure between academic practices and corporate practices, and between the new Monash strategy and the emphasis on academic values and research that characterised the Martin era. The Vice-Chancellor's foreword to *Strategy for the future* stated that:

> Our responsibility now is to make certain that Monash is positioned to retain its scholastic heart and those values it shares with all great universities. At the same time Monash must take advantage of new

opportunities, and move ahead to greater excellence in all of its endeavours.[52]

Often, a generic notion of 'innovation' was used to mix images of organisational and entrepreneurial change with images of research and knowledge, as if it was all one. By 1992 Logan was arguing that 'a more enterprising and entrepreneurial approach', a client focus, and internationalisation, would in themselves enhance academic standards. The problem was not so easily solved. A corporate–academic synergy was hard work and took time to achieve. For a university to succeed as a corporation it must be academically strong, but the reciprocal relationship was not always obvious. Corporate strength did not automatically lead to good research, and in some disciplines a growing dependence on private and commercial funding had the potential to weaken areas of basic research dependent on public funding, as the Dean of Education noted in the 1987 and 1988 Annual Reports.[53] Further, though Clayton was very successful at working new avenues of research funding such as the Cooperative Research Centres (chapter 9), any merger with advanced education institutions was bound to be followed by a fall in average research funding per staff member. Until a research culture could be generalised across all campuses, Monash's reputation would decline in the eyes of those for whom research was the defining criterion of excellence. Worse, strategies such as mergers and marketing which made sense in a corporate context generated short-term costs, and these reduced the resources for building and maintaining world-class research and postgraduate supervision.

To merge and grow without meeting the financial costs was not an option. Yet a capacity in research and scholarship was at the heart of any university mission. The mergers created what Logan later called the 'soft underbelly' of Monash by weakening measured research performance.[54] More seriously, there was the danger that if Monash concentrated on growth and corporate development, and drew on the research reputation built in the Matheson and Martin years without doing much to enhance research capacity, this might lead to a longer-term decline in academic potential. Such a decline would undercut Logan's commitment to innovation (and increase his dependence on the successful but traditional Monash researchers, uneasy with his stance, who still remained). If all of the balls could be held in the air, in the long run a larger and more internationalised university would provide a stronger platform for research activity, but if so the full benefits would become apparent only in the next generation. These problems did not indicate that the strategy was wrong, but they underlined its internal difficulties. The bolder the changes at Monash, the more such difficulties were bound to be exposed. The resulting tensions were not easy to manage, especially in relation to the mergers.

Despite the extensive consultations around *Strategy for the future*, there were rumblings when its implementation began. Pritchard later remarked that unless academics are touched personally by change, and so persuaded of the need for it, they always reserve the right to resist. For most academics, loyalty to their discipline was more important than loyalty to Monash the institution. Where the two kinds of loyalty were in conflict, the academics concerned were likely to become disaffected with the University's leadership. In that case, instead of seeing the University strategy as a necessary adaptation to the Dawkins environment, their detestation of the Green Paper policies would compound their disaffection with the University. 'Growth for its own sake is ludicrous', stated one lecturer to *The Age* in October 1988: 'We're losing sight of the true purpose of a university'.[55] The strongest opposition was in Science. The pride of Monash under Martin, the faculty faced little but difficulty in the new environment. Science derived its work from Commonwealth operating funds. As many in Science saw it, to raise industry funding and to focus on international students was to veer from the faculty's core missions in fundamental research and in the education of the brightest school-leavers as the next generation of scientists.

Several Science professors expressed private reservations with the new University strategy, while some of the sub-professorial staff campaigned openly against it. In August 1989 a Staff Association plebiscite showed there was much opposition to the merger with Chisholm. Critics of the merger were not organised, and were unable to prevent its passage in May/June 1990—perhaps because they were reluctant to cooperate with the opponents of the merger at Chisholm (see chapter 5). Nevertheless, in Science a belated revolt slowly gathered ground. It began with a letter from 39 members of the Department of Chemistry to the Vice-Chancellor about budgetary problems. In research terms, Chemistry was the strongest department in the faculty, and when Chemistry's Dr Keith Murray wrote a letter to *The Age* on the same matters, there was concern in the University offices. Chemistry's stand was supported by academics in other Science departments, and the first meeting of what became the Teaching Research Action Group (TRAG) was held on 11 March 1991. At a meeting of 200 people on 10 April, speakers talked about declining academic morale and the deterioration of teaching and research at the hands of the administration. A letter of concern, circulated at Clayton, was sent to the Council: TRAG claimed that it was signed by nearly one-third of the academic staff. Meetings were held with the Dean of Science and Deputy Vice-Chancellor John Hay. The Vice-Chancellor agreed to see a TRAG deputation.

Hay and Logan were disturbed by the TRAG agitation and there was much discussion on how to deal with it. Porter and Pargetter accompanied Logan to the meeting with TRAG on 10 May 1991, Porter because 'they respected Porter as a scientist' and Pargetter because of his communication skills, as Logan and Porter later recalled.[56] Porter and Pargetter played significant roles at the meeting. There are varying interpretations of what happened, but it appears that the TRAG delegation believed that many of their concerns were taken up by the University's leaders, whereas Logan felt that he had offered a sympathetic ear without giving ground. 'I'll take it on board' summed up the Vice-Chancellor's response.

TRAG's second 'general meeting of all teaching and research staff' took place in the Alexander Theatre on 3 June. The meeting notice stated that:

> We fear that the true role of the University is being changed and high standards of teaching and research are being placed at risk. The change is reflected most of all in the corporate mode of management which is inappropriate for a University. Instead of being treated as a community of scholars we are now regarded as mere employees.

It also referred to 'severe cuts in funding', and 'a devolution of administrative tasks to faculties without a corresponding devolution of resources'. At the meeting, chaired by Malcolm Macmillan from Psychology, were 350 people. It resolved to deplore 'the general direction that the University is now taking' and condemn 'the style of management of those senior University officers who make decisions profoundly affecting University life and staff without consultation with or reference to the same staff'. One speaker, Ross Parish from Economics, expressed his regret that the motion did not 'name the villains'. Porter spoke against the motion, which was carried with only four votes against. TRAG met with an ad-hoc subcommittee of the Committee of Deans and with the Federation of Australian University Staff Associations. However, its sweeping criticisms were impossible to satisfy, except by returning to the pre-1988 University, and it had no strategy on how to deal with the post-Dawkins reality. In this all-or-nothing framework, and in the absence of support at the Academic Board or Council, it could do little except hold meetings and write letters. There was a further general meeting on 6 November 1991 in the Science Theatre, which resolved that Monash as a teaching and research university 'should not be prejudiced by entrepreneurial enterprises'. Further meetings took place in 1992. Though TRAG decided to continue in 1993, declaring its objectives as 'restoration of collegiality and the re-establishment of Monash's proper functions', the agitation was now petering out.

In the outcome, the consultations around *Strategy for the future* gained Logan enough time to steer the core policies through before the slowly emerging grassroots concern about those policies could connect with professorial unease at Board level. Nevertheless, the TRAG episode had shown that Logan's reforms could still be destabilised in the implementation phase. In 1991, following a report by a committee chaired by Enid Campbell, the Professorial Board was replaced by an Academic Board with elected faculty representatives, including some non-professorial members. The change to the Board structure was generated by the 1990 mergers, but in the outcome it helped Logan to manage consent for the changes. It brought 'alternative views' into 'the proper collegial processes inside the University' (Logan); that is, it played non-professorial interests against the traditional power of the discipline-based professoriate, thus tending to divide the potential for criticism and opposition. Each meeting of the reconstituted Board began with a lengthy vice-chancellor's report.[57]

The remaking

'Monash university identifies itself as being the largest and most comprehensive university in Australia and as being known worldwide for progressiveness, accessibility and international focus', the University trumpeted to the Committee for Quality Assurance in 1995.[58] The claim about comprehensiveness was not strictly accurate if fields of study were the measure, for Monash lacked Architecture, Agriculture and Veterinary Science. Nevertheless, it had seized the broadest role of any Australian university. Later Logan stated that he would have liked to change the curriculum structure along the lines of some American universities, by combining Sciences and Arts/Social Sciences in the undergraduate curriculum. 'But the faculty structure at Monash was too strong to even try to break' (Logan); he was not someone who confronted resistance directly, and the TRAG episode showed the barriers to educational reform. Instead, Monash diversified by accommodating the former CAE strands and distance education, and joining with TAFE.[59] The energy for reform was focused not on directly changing what was already there but on building new, more entrepreneurial structures alongside the existing ones, and attaching ever more locations and more functions so that Clayton became the semi-transformed hub of a much larger network Monash that was itself quite new. Darvall used spatial metaphors to describe the change. Under Dawkins, universities were driven by 'educational geo-politics'. At Monash there was a 'tremendous conquering of boundaries and colonisation of the territory', reaching across suburban Melbourne, Australia, and into the global sphere.[60] Open learning and distance teaching technologies were exploding the barriers of space and time. Internationalisation set out to bridge the cultural differences.

The real challenge of the times was to break the mould, to make a new and distinctive kind of university. Other universities found this difficult or

TRAG puts its foot down: the campaign by the Teaching and Research Action Group (TRAG) worried Logan, but it became apparent that TRAG had little leverage. Its stance was solely defensive and it had no alternative strategy for handling the Dawkins-defined environment. (Photo: *The Age*)

impossible to do. In the post-1987 system there was less diversity than expected. Competitive pressures and funding arrangements drove universities towards a single model, that of the comprehensive teaching and research institution. In the outcome the number of top research institutions proved to be no bigger than before; yet the small number of universities that sought another kind of mission, such as Swinburne with its commitment to niche markets, tended to struggle. Only universities with established research reputations were in a position to branch out in other directions. For them other roles could function as an addition to the research mission rather than a substitute for it. Even in the established research universities such a strategy carried risks, as TRAG was well aware. As it turned out, of the leading Australian universities only Monash was bold enough to take the risk of changing its mission and character.

Over time the University's new orientation tended to become more distinctive rather than less, a sign that it had become grounded and the risks were starting to pay off. This did not mean that Logan had achieved his ambition to make Monash the leading Australian university. Towards the end of his term Logan himself ranked Monash third, after the Universities of NSW and Melbourne.[61] As he saw it, Monash had held a position in the top eight universities in research, turned itself into a leader in internationalisation and learning at a distance, and had become the most diverse institution in the country in role and geographical spread: 'It is the multifaceted nature of Monash which must be recognised as the distinctive element' on which to build 'its greatness', he declared unabashedly in *Monash: towards 2000* in 1992. University and faculty leaders must manage Monash so as 'to ensure balance among the diverse functions', he added.[62] That was the harder part.

When Logan was retiring in 1996 it was too early to be definitive about the remaking of Monash. Despite this, there was widespread recognition that something momentous had taken place. On 25 January 1996 *The Australian* announced that Logan and Penington were its joint Australians of the year. Editor-in-Chief Paul Kelly wrote that:

> The performance of higher education institutions is fundamental to Australia's future and the national newspaper believes that Mal Logan and David Penington, each in his own way, has provided decisive leadership. They have displayed a vision and a commitment over a sustained period that warrants national recognition.[63]

A spate of articles appeared on the Logan years. Hay, who went on to become Vice-Chancellor at Deakin University and then at the University of Queensland, had not always seen eye-to-eye with his former superior, but he described Logan's as 'the decisive vice-chancellorship' of the decade. If that were true, information and resources from a friendly Labor government helped him to make it so. The 10-year span of his vice-chancellorship, which provided a medium-term rather than short-term time horizon and increased the scope for risk, was another factor that made it possible. A third factor was those individuals who talked to Logan and shared a passion for engineering change: later Logan recalled the profound influence exercised by Alan Fels, mentioning also Leo West, Terry Hore, Louis Waller, Peter Spearritt of the National Centre for Australian Studies, and marketing manager Gary Neat. Downtown business contacts he consulted 'pretty regularly' included Geoff Allen, Russ Madigan, Hugh Rogers, Robert Gottliebsen, Peter Nixon and Ivan Deveson: 'Quite often I found business to have better ideas than academics'.[64]

A fourth factor was the people he shared the work with at Monash. It is stating the obvious to emphasise that Logan alone did not change the University's future. Wade was at the centre of the process of its remaking. Pritchard, Hay, the other DVCs and PVCs, Chancellors George Lush and Bill Rogers, most of the Clayton deans and, at times, many other individuals and groups, were also agents in the process. It was a difficult period for all; at times, especially during the mergers, the strains were immense. The willingness of Monash's partners at Caulfield, Peninsula, Gippsland and Parkville to concede to Clayton was even more essential than Clayton's willingness to accommodate them.

In the end it is the symbolic functions of leadership that are as important as any other. A single person's name comes to stand for a multitude of people and events, capturing the sense of the time. Monash underwent two different waves of modernisation, first during the making of the University in the 1960s, and then in its remaking in the late 1980s–90s. The early years are known as

Clifton Pugh with George Lush. The artist examines his own painting of Lush, Monash Chancellor (1983–92), who presided over the key decisions in the period of strategic change and merger.

the Matheson years, though they were the sum of many efforts. Then the governance structure of Monash was set, strong faculties joined to a forward-looking central leadership. Under Logan the Matheson structure was stretched to accommodate the mergers, an expanded leadership group and a plethora of business activities, Clayton became the hub of larger networks, and there was a great shift in the culture of the University. An engineer provided the hardware, a geographer with an eye on economics and politics provided the new operating system and changed the software. Monash became a combination of Matheson structure and Logan culture.

Monash merges

> The 'Idea of a University' was a village with its priests. The 'Idea of a Modern University' was a town, a one industry town, with its intellectual oligarchy. 'The Idea of a Multiversity' is a city of infinite variety.
>
> Clark Kerr, *The uses of the university*, Harvard University Press, Cambridge, MA, 1963, p. 41

Towards the multiversity

In 1963 the Victorian government's Ramsay Committee recommended that both Monash University and the University of Melbourne should develop as a multi-campus federation of institutions, like the University of California, with each federation growing to 18 000 students in size. The multi-campus model was supported by Matheson as a member of the Ramsay Committee, but was soon made irrelevant by the Commonwealth's Martin report in 1964, which preferred conventional universities of 4000–10 000 students.[1] The State's third university, La Trobe University in the northern suburb of Bundoora, soon followed. In 1988, 25 years after the Ramsay Committee had imagined 18 000 students in a multi-campus Monash, there were still only 14 768 students and all were at Clayton. The 1987–88 Dawkins policies brought the potential for a multi-campus institution back to the agenda, and reopened fundamental questions about Monash's geographical identity.

Under Ray Martin, Monash turned down the chance to spread itself, staying outside the 1981 round of mergers in Australian higher education in which the small teachers' colleges were closed, welded together or folded into larger institutions. It was at this time that the State College of Victoria (SCV) at Frankston joined the Caulfield Institute of Technology to form the new Chisholm Institute of Technology (1982). Monash might have taken in SCV Rusden, located in Blackburn Road. Instead, Rusden became part of the new Victoria College at Burwood, Toorak, Rusden and Prahran, and the opportunity was lost.

In 1988, with a bigger round of mergers in prospect, Monash adopted a different approach.

On 29 January 1988 the Victorian Post-Secondary Education Commission (VPSEC) circulated its 'Options for the development of higher education structures in Victoria'. It suggested merging Monash with Chisholm Institute of Technology and Swinburne Institute of Technology at Hawthorn, and transferring the Monash Faculty of Education to Victoria College (the last suggestion was to be ignored). Alternatively, Monash could merge with Victoria College or join with Chisholm and the Rusden campus of Victoria College. All three options constituted a minimal 50 per cent expansion in student numbers and the acquisition of at least three further sites. Grander ideas were in the wind. La Trobe University Vice-Chancellor John Scott floated with Logan the possibility of a two-campus Victorian State University, though nothing came of this.[2] Pritchard suggested an enlarged Monash 'on the University of California model', at Clayton, Rusden, Caulfield, Swinburne and the country sites of Ballarat, Bendigo and Churchill in Gippsland. Some might be university colleges, with others accorded full university status. As it turned out, the federal model was used in relation to Gippsland, not as a permanent solution but a transitional mechanism, a device for pacing the absorption of the campus into a unitary Monash.

As time passed, Monash's efforts became focused on two kinds of site: first, locations consistent with the notion of Monash as an institution for Eastern Victoria, particularly the area southeast of Melbourne, which prompted the University's interest in Chisholm, Gippsland, Swinburne and Victoria College, and later led to a new campus at Berwick; second, locations that brought Monash closer to the heart of the city—Caulfield and Swinburne, an office in the city, and the Pharmacy College, which was part of the Parkville medical precinct and located near the University of Melbourne. Realising the value of 'first-mover advantage', the University's leaders quickly consolidated the first group of options. On 26 February Logan issued a media release proposing federation with Chisholm, Swinburne and Victoria College, and reserving other possibilities. On 9 March 1988 the Professorial Board endorsed a resolution of the deans which supported discussion with Chisholm and other institutions. The road to merger was open.

Little did anyone know what lay ahead. In business and in educational institutions, mergers are rarely easy and are only slowly profitable. Expectations of reduced costs and increased diversity are rarely met, and can become contrary goals (chapter 3). Multi-site institutions carry additional costs in management, transport and communication between sites, and new overarching structures, and there is less scope for removal of duplication, such as with libraries and student services.[3] Something is usually lost, educationally and culturally. Old loyalties may be deliberately destroyed to enable a united institution.[4] The final outcome of a merger is shaped by the balance of power between the merger partners. Typically, large institutions taking over small ones use language such as 'a marriage of equal partners',[5] whereas, more often than not, in the post-merger period the distinctive features of the smaller 'partner' are eroded. Here mergers in higher education are the same as mergers in business. The vast majority of mergers are takeovers. Despite this, old institutional loyalties can be felt deeply, and live on in some people's minds for many years.

It is because mergers are such political processes that their resolution is sometimes bloody and always difficult, and usually more protracted than expected. Voluntary mergers are better because they lead to a more constructive climate in the new institution, but if the voluntary process is to succeed, people must participate actively and become convinced of the potential benefits. Every point of negotiation in a voluntary amalgamation is open to dispute. Particular groups may secure undue influence over negotiations through the threat to withdraw support from the merger.[6] After the deal is signed, the politics continue. Often the decisive decisions are during the implementation phase.

Centralisation to Clayton. Like a merger in business, a merger in higher education is more likely to be a takeover than a marriage of equal partners.

Monash and Chisholm

With 7110 students in 1987 Chisholm Institute of Technology was the third-largest CAE in Victoria after RMIT (11 175) and Victoria College (7692). In total, 4201 students were full-time. There were 1019 students at the postgraduate level, though only 37 in research higher degrees.[7] The campus at Caulfield was 10 kilometres southeast of the central business district of the City of Melbourne, halfway between the city and Clayton. It enjoyed good though declining standing in applied Engineering, its School of Social and Behavioural Sciences was in demand, and its Business Education and Computing courses were well regarded. The David Syme International Business Centre provided a government-subsidised program, assisting Australian companies to market their products internationally: 43 companies completed the program in its first three years.[8] Caulfield also offered full-fee places to international students. The Frankston campus, 40 kilometres south of the city, provided Education, Business and Nursing. In part Frankston operated as a feeder for Caulfield, with some students moving north at the beginning of their second year.

Each part of Chisholm had a longer history than Monash Clayton. Caulfield began with the enrolment of 200 students in the wheelwrights' and blacksmiths' courses at the new Caulfield Technical School in 1922. In 1925 the curriculum was expanded to carpentry, coach-building, sheetmetal working and the more modern pursuit of engineering drawing. Motor engineering was offered to diploma level. In 1944 diploma courses in art, mechanical and electrical engineering were added and the applied science laboratories in physics and chemistry opened in 1950. The School became Caulfield Technical College in 1958, with diploma, senior and junior schools, and was designated part of the newly formed State system of advanced education in 1964, being rechristened as Caulfield Institute of Technology in 1968. The data-processing department, later computing, began in 1964. Frankston Teachers' College opened with 109 students in 1959 and was redesignated as SCV Frankston in 1973. The merger between Caulfield and Frankston was formalised on 2 March 1982 as Chisholm Institute of Technology, with the TAFE division of Caulfield separating to form Holmesglen College.[9] This merger had its difficulties, especially at Frankston, but had settled by the late 1980s.

The idea of a merger between Monash and Chisholm was not new. There were rumours of it at Caulfield during 1986 and 1987, perhaps encouraged by collaborations between the institutions, such as the jointly managed Centre for Stream Ecology, a research and consultancy unit focused on freshwater resources; the Monash contribution to Chisholm Business Language programs in Chinese and Japanese, and bridging education in Mathematics; and some sharing of computing and library resources. On 4 December 1987 Logan attended a meeting at Chisholm that included Dawkins and VPSEC's Ron Cullen. With the Green Paper about to be released, merger talk was in the air.[10]

Chisholm's leadership may not have realised how keen were Logan and Deputy Vice-Chancellor John Hay to gain Chisholm. They saw it as the 'key merger' (Hay) for Monash. The reason was the Caulfield site: its proximity to the city, its role in part-time business education and attractiveness to international students, and its long-term potential. In the early stages Logan saw no great problem in simply adding the Caulfield courses to those of Clayton. In the US State universities a university could do almost anything provided there were structures in place for the validation of teaching and research.[11] Nevertheless, he knew this view was not necessarily shared at Clayton. A double diplomacy now commenced. Outside the University he opened its doors widely to Chisholm and other possible merger partners, emphasising the potential for mutually enriching change and the need to safeguard the qualities of small institutions. Inside the University he moved more cautiously, disarming opposition, advancing the cause as far as he could, presenting all mergers less as the meeting of equals and more as the strengthening of Clayton Monash, in which Clayton should feel little disturbed.[12]

From early on the leaders of Chisholm were favourably disposed towards a merger with Monash. The size limits specified in the Green Paper created, for all CAEs except RMIT, a strong pressure to merge with another institution. If Chisholm wanted to remain separate, to reach the government's benchmark of 8000 for full university status, it would need government support for the necessary operating grants and capital funds, but there was no certainty of such support. Neither Melbourne nor La Trobe were prospects. The options were limited to Monash, RMIT, Swinburne and Victoria College. RMIT was preoccupied by potential mergers with the Footscray and later Phillip Institutes of Technology. Victoria College offered little in the way of additional strengths, and promised the additional costs of a multi-campus institution. Geoff Vaughan, who had become Director of Chisholm only recently but was well liked and respected, became an influential advocate for the Monash option.[13] The personal relationship between Vaughan and Logan played a part.[14] Often in contact in those days (and both graduates from the University of Sydney as Logan was later to recall),[15] they established a level of affability and trust between them. Vaughan and Logan were good at resolving difficult issues by talking to each other, though some of those same issues were to return unresolved at a later time.

The Council was a significant factor at Chisholm, and the Deputy President of the Chisholm Council, soon to be President (1989) at the age of 36, was Paul Ramler. Committed to Chisholm's distinctive 'applied approach' to higher education, Ramler weighed the option of Chisholm remaining independent

Paul Ramler: the transition from Caulfield to Monash

Paul Ramler. (*top*) Ramler's role in tertiary governance began as a student representative on the Caufield Council. As President of the Chisholm Council he signed the merger agreement with Monash in 1989. L–R: Peter Wade, Mal Logan, Paul Ramler, Geoff Vaughan and Graham Trevaskis.

Ten years later. Ramler as Monash Deputy-Chancellor.

Paul Ramler arrived at the then Caulfield Institute of Technology in the first intake of marketing students in 1971. He led the development of a student union, wrote its constitution, spent two years as founding President and was the first student representative on the Council. He joined the Board of Studies 'and about 400 other committees'. Ramler topped his course and graduated at the end of 1974, becoming the first life member of the Caulfield Institute Student Union, and was invited back to Council as a full member.

The new graduate might have entered private industry, or worked as an educator or administrator in higher education. Instead he decided to enter the family furniture business, Ramler Furniture P/L, first as Marketing Director and later as Chief Executive Officer. On the Caulfield Council Ramler placed priority on the growth of community services. One of three members of the Caulfield Council to be appointed to the new Chisholm Council in 1982, he served two terms as Vice-President and became President in 1989. At the same time he was foundation President of the Holmesglen TAFE College Council (1982–89), and later a member of the Board of Governors of Mount Scopus College (1991) and the College Executive (1993). In 1997 he was appointed as Chair of the State Ministerial Committee on the future of the John Batman and Kangan Institutes of TAFE, and Chair of the State Ministerial Review Committee on the provision of TAFE in the Melbourne metropolitan area.

Convinced that the merger with Monash was the best option for Chisholm, at the same time Ramler was committed to Chisholm, proud of its Business School and determined to make a transition into Monash that would preserve Chisholm's strengths and enhance the opportunities for its people. From 1991 onwards Ramler was a Deputy Chancellor on the reconstituted Monash Council, Chairman of the Finance Committee, and Chairman and Director of the Monash University Foundation. He took leadership positions in Monash International, the Alumni Association, the Fundraising Advisory Committee, the Mt Eliza business school, the Berwick Development Committee, and a

> range of other areas. In 1997 he was appointed a Member in the General Division of the Order of Australia (AM).
>
> Looking back on the period of the merger, Ramler stated later that if he had the time over again he would do it 'slightly differently'. The main mistake was not to resolve the matter of Business Education prior to the merger. The outcome was the breakdown of the in-principle agreements on Syme, leading to bad faith and some loss of diversity in Business and Economics. Despite this, the merger was certainly the right decision for Chisholm students and staff. Monash's capacity to respond to new opportunities, and its international presence, had created the potential for richer educational experiences.[16]

within the Dawkins system, but judged it too difficult for the Council to sustain. From the standpoint of students, graduates and staff the Monash option made most sense. While parts of Chisholm such as Engineering might prefer to join Swinburne, there was little synergy between the heads of Chisholm and Swinburne, and little prospect of government support for the capital works that would be needed.[17] At Caulfield and Frankston, feelings about Monash were divided. There was a more pronounced industrial relations culture among Chisholm staff than Monash staff, and at Chisholm the academic and general staff associations were entrenched on Council and committees. The stance of the unions was important. While some academic union leaders would have liked to oppose the merger with Monash, a straw poll of their members found that about one-third supported the merger, many attracted by the lure of university status and culture, one-third opposed it, and one-third were indifferent. Many were reassured by the statement in the Heads of Agreement 'that there will be no forced redundancies as a result of the merger'. The unions concluded that the merger was inevitable and the only strategic option was to press for staff representation in the merger and post-merger structures, and to focus on protecting the industrial rights of staff.[18]

On 15 March 1988 there was a meeting on statistics and administration between Wade and Beilby for Monash, and Vaughan and John White for Chisholm. On 18 March Logan and Vaughan held a formal meeting, and on 7 April the Committee of Deans endorsed the pursuit of merger with Chisholm, the Rusden campus of Victoria College, and Gippsland. On 11 April Council authorised Logan to conduct negotiations with other institutions,

> particularly Chisholm Institute of Technology, the Rusden campus of Victoria College and the Gippsland Institute of Advanced Education, with the object of investigating amalgamations or arrangements designed to combine the academic and other activities of those institutions with

the activities of Monash University, In undertaking these activities the Vice-Chancellor will protect the academic standards of Monash and the value of Monash degrees and further so far as possible, opportunities for teaching and research by the staff of Monash and the staff of the other institutions concerned.[19]

Meanwhile Vaughan, having secured a positive response from his Council, reported to the Chisholm deans on 19 April that a document setting out Heads of Agreement was being drafted. Logan decided on a forward move at Clayton. On 28 April he told the deans that he believed that Monash should move to an in-principle merger with Chisholm. At a meeting with the Chisholm Planning Group on 9 May, Monash proposed a full merger, albeit one with a touch of federalism. The governing body would be an augmented Monash Council. Initially, the Professorial Board would coexist with the Chisholm Academic Board, with a coordinating body and management committee 'superimposed above both'. The proposal was well received by the Chisholm delegation, and the next day the Vice-Chancellor tested with his Committee of Deans the level of potential support in the faculties. However, there was a split among those faculties affected. Arts and Education were on the whole supportive, but there was opposition in Economics and Politics, and in Engineering. Science was noncommittal. Deputy Vice-Chancellor Ian Polmear was negative. In June a meeting of the Staff Association of Monash University (SAMU) revealed little enthusiasm for the merger. 'It got bumpy at Monash', said Logan later. There were 'feelings around the place'; 'Geoff and I decided to back off a bit'.[20] On 6 July a joint meeting of the two executive groups agreed that 'the institutions should not proceed with a formal association at this time'. It remained a possibility. 'In the meantime . . . every possible avenue for joint ventures and cooperative activities' should be explored. The Professorial Board endorsed this. Some of the deans urged Logan to keep the merger option open.

The merger had been halted, but it was being kept warm and 'somehow or other, we got it back on track' (Logan). Vaughan was crucial to this. More meetings were held, and in October Vaughan and Logan signed a formal Memorandum of Understanding providing for closer cooperation, 'in the spirit of moving towards a more formal association which could lead through a Heads of Agreement document to closer structural links'. This time Chisholm was seen to take the initiative. On 3 November Ramler proposed to the Chisholm Council that a more formal association be established. For example, Chisholm might

Geoff Vaughan. Director of Chisholm Institute and subsequently Monash DVC (1990–92), his support was crucial to the merger at every stage.

become a University College within the Monash system as Gippsland had done, with potential for closer integration.[21] On 13 December Chisholm Council agreed to the preparation of a Heads of Agreement. After the Christmas break, a joint Monash–Chisholm Working Party met informally on 31 January 1989, and on 8 February Logan told the Monash Professorial Board that 'Chisholm had written to Monash suggesting further discussions on links'. The Board agreed to negotiate a Heads of Agreement, and on 18 February endorsed formal association. This was agreed by Monash Council on 20 February.

At Council the Vice-Chancellor acknowledged there were some misgivings, and promised adequate consultation and representation of views. But events were now moving more rapidly. On 28 February Chisholm completed the first draft of the Heads of Agreement, and Dawkins and the Victorian Minister for Post-Secondary Education, Evan Walker, publicly supported a Monash–Chisholm merger. A flurry of drafting meetings in March led to a Heads of Agreement document, referring to the merger, which went to the Monash Professorial Board on 22 March. After a long debate a large majority of the Board agreed to support the document. Logan assured the Board that 'coercive mergers between like academic units of both institutions would not be considered', and that 'nothing should be done in furtherance of the merger that would affect the academic standards and status of the University', and these points became part of the Board's endorsement.[22] The draft Heads of Agreement went through Monash Council on 3 April 1989 and Chisholm Council on 11 April, and was signed at a formal ceremony on 10 May. It provided for a merger that would take effect on 1 July 1990.

Logan told his Council that the merger 'would create a new lease of life for the University'. The discussion was 'positive and constructive', according to Council minutes. Among the leadership and Council at Chisholm the level of goodwill was also high. There were outbreaks of symbolic warmth. Later in the year an old tree on the Frankston campus was blown down during a storm and had to be removed. 'In a spirit of cooperation during the lead-up to the merger between Monash and Chisholm' the Monash Chancellor, Sir George Lush, replanted a eucalypt outside Building A at Frankston to replace it. He also planted a tree at Caulfield. 'A commemorative spade is held in the Chisholm archives', recorded the final edition of the *Chisholm Gazette*, just before the archives, spade, *Gazette* and all of the trees were absorbed into the greater Monash.[23]

The timetable provided Chisholm with 14 months to negotiate the detail of the merger before it ceased as an independent entity and lost the larger part of its bargaining power. A joint Merger Implementation Committee of 20 people was created, including Logan, Hay, Vaughan and Ramler. At its first meeting on 14 June 1989 the Committee set up specialist working parties on academic programs and structures, governance and legislation, finance and administration, academic services, student services and organisations, and human resources management. A range of often sensitive items were open to debate, including the degree and the speed of the integration of the institutions, and the extent to which the new structures would be federal or unitary in character, the membership of the Council, the role of senior Chisholm personnel, the academic structures, the integration of management, budget systems, service departments and student organisations, and the character of the guarantees provided to academic and general staff concerning job security, their conditions of work and the nature of their jobs.

The process of implementation brought the role of John Hay to the fore. Hay was Logan's minister for mergers. He threw himself into the detail, using the verbal skills of a professor of English to the full and earning for himself at Chisholm and Gippsland the reputation of a formidable negotiator—politically sharp, aggressive and persuasive by turns. Hay's opponents did not always trust him, but they often found themselves being charmed by him. Those who dealt with Hay also knew that he was committed to making the process work. His departure from Monash in 1991 to become Vice-Chancellor of Deakin University probably made it harder for the University to deal with the problems of the post-merger stage.[24] At Chisholm Vaughan was central, but he was not always there at crucial meetings, and not as strong as some on the subtleties of position and vantage that an extended process of negotiation involves. It was Ramler that was seen by both sides as the person at Chisholm with the political acumen.[25] Nevertheless, Vaughan's role in creating the goodwill that sustained the merger should not be underestimated.

At Clayton the opposition Logan had encountered in the faculties in 1988, and the difficulty of steering the merger through the Professorial Board earlier in 1989, led him to change tactics. He made a conscious decision *not* to use the deans as the 'driving force' in the merger. The Merger Implementation Committee and its subcommittees reported to Council rather than Board. The Council and the Chancellor, George Lush, became mainstays of the mergers. 'I don't think he ever deviated once', recalled Logan when discussing the role of the Chancellor during this period.[26] Because the process was driven from Council, the deans and the Board found themselves reacting to initiatives that already had momentum. The Vice-Chancellor relied on individual deans to smooth the passage of the merger at the Board, including Williams in Law and Porter in Medicine, whose faculties were not directly affected.[27]

Though the Merger Implementation Committee began in a 'constructive and amicable' atmosphere (Logan), there was still disquiet at Clayton, especially in Engineering, Science, and Economics and Politics. In August 1989 SAMU conducted a plebiscite. The total number voting was small, representing less than 10 per cent of the academic staff; but, of the 250 who voted, two-thirds rejected a merger with Chisholm (Table 5.1).

TABLE 5.1 STAFF ASSOCIATION OF MONASH UNIVERSITY PLEBISCITE,
AUGUST 1989

Q. Would you support a merger [with Chisholm] which involved an integration of the staff, courses, degrees and students of the two institutions?

	Number	%
Yes	61	24.4
No	166	66.4
No answer	23	9.2
Total	250	100.0

Source: Academic Staff Association of the Chisholm Institute of Technology and Victorian Colleges and Universities Staff Association (Chisholm Branch), *Joint unions audit of the merger implementation arrangements between Chisholm Institute of Technology and Monash University*, March 1990, p. 5.

The proposition had been put in the terms most likely to disturb voters but it signified the climate at Clayton, in which the merger could still be lost. An unofficial SAMU gathering on 23 August 1989 adopted by substantial majority a resolution stating 'that this meeting declares itself to be totally opposed to Monash's amalgamation with Chisholm on the terms being discussed, in view of the lack of an intellectual justification for the current proposals'. There was bitterness at the prospect of being joined with former CAE staff, which was seen to signify the downgrading of academic standards and values in the post-Green Paper system.[28] On 6 September 1989 the Professorial Board again debated the merger at length, but the outcome was again strong support for Logan's position, with only one dissenting vote.[29] Though some of the professors were disturbed by both the substance of the proposed changes and the manner in which their old control over the agenda was slipping away, enough of their colleagues were convinced that in the framework of the Dawkins policies Monash had little choice but to expand, and that Chisholm was the best available option. For its part SAMU proved unable to build sufficient sub-professorial opposition or unify with the general staff, in contrast to the situation at Chisholm where the two unions worked well together. In any case, from a Clayton viewpoint the Board's endorsement of Logan's actions was not misplaced, in that Logan always handled the merger so as to maintain the primacy of the University. 'We did it all in such a way as to make it appear that the University was in the driving seat on everything', he said later. On the merger committees 'the University ran the show'.[30] The fears of Clayton academic staff that their academic identity would be lost were not realised.

Here the crucial element was the determination of Hay, backed by Logan, to secure a fully integrated academic structure, unitary rather than federal, in

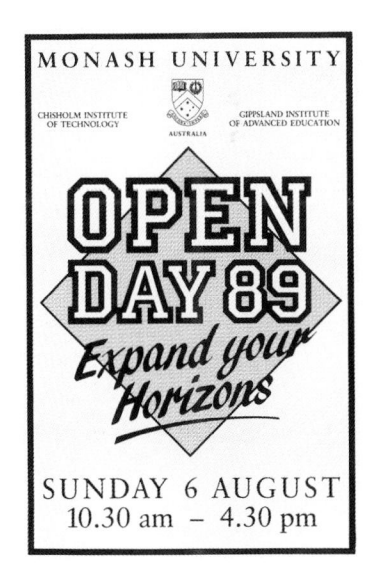

Anticipating the merger: the 1989 Open Day poster.

which faculties rather than campuses were the core units and the largely Clayton-based deans maintained their traditional Monash role. According to Hay in 1996, 'We had to integrate all of the departments in all of the campuses . . . If I railroaded anything, and I've been accused of railroading a lot of things, I didn't blink on that one'. The earlier notion of separate academic boards was abandoned, even as a transitional measure. At the time, there was some pressure to adopt a federal structure: to many people it seemed the logical form for a multi-campus institution, and one that enabled the full range of existing diversity to be preserved. It was also the easier option—the one that was more acceptable to critics and opponents of the merger, the one that enabled difficult issues to be postponed or avoided. On the other hand, the use of a federal structure in institutions premised on singular systems threatened to create incoherence, undue competitiveness and unevenness in standards. It would slow the spread of a university culture, and reduce the scope for central management and budgetary controls. While full integration meant a reduction in the range of academic options and approaches, a common framework for all programs promised to ease student movement and course combination. In the outcome, the federal model was never seriously debated.[31]

It was eventually decided that the 10 faculties in the enlarged University would be Arts, Law, Education, Science, Medicine, Engineering, which were all part of Clayton Monash; plus Economics, Commerce and Management (the greater part of the Clayton Faculty of Economics and Politics), Business (based on the David Syme School of Business at Chisholm) and two new faculties: Computing and Information Technology, and Professional Studies. The last included Librarianship, Social Work, Nursing, Police Studies, Art and Design, and some of the social and behavioural sciences at Chisholm. The decision to maintain the two separate faculties in the area of Business and Management was to be reviewed within three years of the merger.

By October 1989 the broad academic structure and undergraduate award programs were agreed, passing through the Monash and Chisholm Councils on 30 October and 14 November respectively. On 8 February 1990 the Merger Implementation Committee received the draft of what became the *Monash University (Chisholm and Gippsland) Act 1990*. Some outstanding matters remained, including the integration of staff structures and student unions.[32] As a consequence, there was a last-minute industrial dispute at Chisholm. The Chisholm union leaders had maintained their strategic assumption that the merger was inevitable, rightly judging that speculation about revolt on the Monash Professorial Board would come to little, and that SAMU would be ineffective. It was not until the formation of TRAG, the Teaching and Research Action Group in 1991, that there was a significant challenge by staff to the University's leadership at Clayton, and by then the merger had been an accomplished fact for almost a year (chapter 4).[33] However, as the negotiations unfolded, frustrations had developed at Chisholm. It was felt that the Monash negotiating team was not always able or willing to deliver on its assurances. Sticking points included Monash's failure to grant the David Syme School of Business the expected primacy, or make Vaughan the Senior Deputy Vice-Chancellor, or offer Chisholm more than one position in the senior management group, which would have signified something more like a merger of equals.[34] There was also concern about Clayton's attitude to the reclassification of Chisholm staff.

In March 1990 the Chisholm unions issued a *Joint unions audit of the merger implementation arrangements between Chisholm Institute of Technology and Monash University*:

> Despite Professor Logan's sincere intention to create 'a new and enlarged Monash' other members of the University are prepared, albeit grdugingly, to accept only an 'old and enlarged Monash' . . . many at Clayton still manifest a takeover mentality in which Chisholm will be a subservient adjunct to the University.

According to the Chisholm unions, Monash management was bypassing the Merger Implementation Working Parties, and 'signed and unsigned documents and statements emanating from Monash staff' had made 'inaccurate, ill-founded and derogatory remarks concerning Chisholm staff, courses, students and the Chisholm culture and tradition'. When compared to the Chisholm Council the proposed new Monash Council, with three academic and three general staff representatives out of 42 members, meant less staff representation, and the negotiation of the unions' industrial claims had not been advanced far enough by the university.[35]

The draft legislation had been approved by the Monash Council without dissent on 16 February, and on 13 March it was due for debate at the Chisholm Council. The joint unions decided to recommend to the Chisholm Council that the legislation not be endorsed 'at this stage' and the merger date be postponed until 1 January 1991. The legislation was passed by Council by a vote of 13 for, 3 absentions and 5 against. The five staff representatives recorded their dissent, and the two union bodies notified a dispute with Chisholm.[36]

The final negotiations over staffing now coincided with the passage of the Act through the Victorian Parliament, and were played out in the offices of the two Ministers of Education. On 1 May the bill received its second reading in the Victorian Legislative Assembly. In her speech the Minister of Education, Joan Kirner, stated that the merger of Monash with Chisholm and Gippsland would produce a 'greater' Monash, bringing together three institutions 'with complementary areas of expertise and strength'. Much was made of Chisholm's 'acclaimed David Syme Faculty of Business', the institution's reputation in business and government circles and the potential of the merger to strengthen Computing, Engineering, Business and Management education in the enlarged institution. Less accurately, the Minister predicted that the new Faculty of Professional Studies would 'create an academically and administratively sound framework for the location of professionally oriented disciplines'.[37] On 1 June an agreement was signed between Monash, Chisholm, SAMU and the Council of Academic Staff Associations (CASA) representing the Chisholm academic staff. The Chisholm unions achieved an increase of one on the number of academic staff representatives on the interim Council. There was also some loosening of the procedures for translating Chisholm staff onto Monash promotional scales.[38]

The final meeting of the Chisholm Council was held on 12 June. The Act provided for an interim joint Council for one year, to be followed by a newly reconstituted and integrated Monash Council of 43 members. The Professorial Board was replaced by an expanded and interim Academic Board, which, consistent with the collegial tradition in this respect at least, was charged with the task of preparing recommendations on its own future. In the 1990 Annual Report Logan declared that 'most of the turbulence associated with the merger is now dissipated'. Changes to the Council, Board and faculties had received 'near universal support', and 'some initial suspicions between staff of different cultures are now well behind us'.[39] It was an optimistic assessment. The process still had some way to go. There was plenty of mutual suspicion still.

Gippsland and Monash

The Gippsland Institute of Advanced Education (IAE), which had roots in Yallourn Technical School, formally came into existence in 1968, later moving to Churchill.[40] Like the power industry which dominated life in the La Trobe Valley region, Gippsland shared with Monash University an association with Sir John Monash, an association that meant a great deal in the Valley, bound closely to the State Electricity Commission of Victoria (SECV) that Monash had founded, and driven by Engineering, which was John Monash's profession. For a long time Gippsland IAE was the primary training institution for the technicians and managers who staffed the SECV. After Deakin University, which had 4334 external students, and the Warrnambool IAE (soon to merge with Deakin), Gippsland was the next largest provider of distance education in Victoria. In 1987 it enrolled 3410 students, including 1052 full-time students, 261 internal part-timers and 2097 externals. There were 345 postgraduate students, but only three people in research higher degrees.[41]

Given the Green Paper's size limits, a campus with a total student load of 2116 was scarcely in a position to stand alone unless it wanted to narrow the range of its courses. Association with a university had the potential to raise the educational horizons of people living in the region, and 'regional institutions which become part of larger institutions could use the resources obtained from these efficiencies for better regional delivery and the strengthening of their academic programs', as Dawkins had put it.[42] Gippsland's Director Tom Kennedy began talking to Pritchard and Logan. From early on, there was a 'powerful ease' between Logan and Kennedy, as Gippsland's Barry Dunstan later put it, similar to the rapport between Logan and Vaughan at Chisholm.[43] Interestingly, Kennedy had been Deputy Director at Caulfield before Chisholm was formed. On 24 February Logan wrote to Kennedy to state that Monash saw Gippsland as a potential part of a future multi-campus institution; two days later Kennedy replied in favourable terms. The Monash leader thought that Gippsland could undergo a period of University College status in which the potential for closer integration would be further explored. On 11 July Pritchard sent Kennedy a draft model of association along these lines, and on 23 August Logan told the Clayton deans that an association with Gippsland could head off a bid by Deakin to become the monopoly provider of distance education in the State. The consent of the deans was secured.

Gippsland. For Clayton the attraction of the merger was the Institute of Advanced Education's capacity in distance education. For the Institute at Churchill, the attraction was survival.

The University College model also suited Kennedy. If the merger had to happen, he wanted Gippsland to evolve slowly into Monash rather than undergo the fate of Chisholm; and in the meantime he wanted to use an association with Monash to broaden the horizons of an insular institution in an insular region. Monash had the potential to lift the image of the institution in the eyes of people in the La Trobe Valley. Monash was also attractive for its internationalisation. Gippsland had recently moved into Southeast Asia, creating offshore courses in Singapore (50 students) and Hong Kong (150 students). The campus at Churchill was divided about Monash: 'Half the staff were threatened and apoplectic about the whole idea. The other half couldn't get there quickly enough' (Dunstan). Gippsland's other option was to join with Deakin. The State government had floated the possibility of a federation-come-merger which would include Deakin and the CAEs at Gippsland, Warrnambool, Ballarat and Bendigo: the 'Country and Western University' as some called it.[44] For a number of reasons this was coming to grief: the question of Deakin's primacy was difficult to resolve, and Ballarat wanted to stand alone. Nevertheless, it was still possible for Gippsland to join with Deakin, uniting the two distance education providers.

For Monash, the main incentive for merger was the long-term potential suggested by Gippsland's role in distance education. This could provide the University with a head start in the future competition in distance education. The Commonwealth had specified that in future it would fund only a small number of Distance Education Centres (DECs). Deakin, a recognised leader in the field, expected to be nominated by the State government as sole DEC in Victoria. However, on 16 August 1988 representatives of Gippsland and Monash met at Clayton. They generated enough support for a combined Gippsland/Monash bid to ensure that Victoria would argue to the Commonwealth for *two* designated DECs in the State. Logan then worked his contacts in the Federal Minister's office. Rather to the surprise of Monash, and the chagrin of Deakin, the strategy succeeded. Victoria had two DECs, one of them Monash/Gippsland.

On 5 September 1988 the GIAE Council resolved to seek affiliation with the University on a University College basis. This was agreed in principle by the Monash Professorial Board on 7 September, and Council on 19 September, and finalised by each Council before the end of the year. On 24 February 1989 there was a ceremonial exchange of documents, with Dawkins present. As a University College, Gippsland was to retain a separate existence. There was no provision for eventual merger, but over the first three years of the agreement the parties were to 'work towards greater integration of research, teaching and administrative activities'. If after three years either party considered that there had been insufficient progress towards closer links, either could give one year's written notice of termination.[45] Gippsland's options remained open.

Over the next few months, without the sense of urgency that was powering the Merger Implementation Committee with Chisholm, the details of the University College were elaborated and the draft legislation agreed by both Councils and included in the *Monash University (Chisholm and Gippsland) Act 1990*. Monash was now committed and, with the Chisholm merger bedded down, the country campus received more attention. Logan became anxious about the progress of integration.[46] In December 1991 he circulated a paper which argued that 'it is now timely to ensure that the Gippsland campus occupies a position in the University which enables it to be seen as a full partner within the greater Monash'. Two months later Kennedy issued his 'Options for future development' paper, which inclined towards the extension of the affiliated college model. Dunstan stated later that:

> It was Kennedy's view that you had to control the process. He said that 'we want to take the best bits from Monash without being swamped by it, so therefore we need time'. He was a Chemist, and he always used

to talk about things in chemical terms: the slowest part of any transition was the rate controlling speed, and in this case that was the speed at which the slowest staff member came along [with the merger]. Kennedy's lectures used to be delivered in his office as a homily on Friday afternoons over a bottle of Scotch.[47]

Kennedy was maintaining the identity of Gippsland in case the merger process fell apart. To this point there had been practically no integration of academic functions or administrative systems. In 1992 DVC Robert Pargetter chaired a series of meetings of the relevant faculty groups, to plan closer integration. The pace of faculty integration varied, depending on the time and motivation of the deans and the extent to which Gippsland–Clayton and Gippsland–Caulfield synergies began to develop. Science moved first, taking a positive approach to Gippsland from the beginning. In 1993 the period of University College status expired. Kennedy was about to retire, and this enabled Monash to increase the 'rate controlling speed' of the merger. From 1 January 1993 Gippsland adopted the Clayton budget methodology, and from the start of 1995 its budget was fully integrated. Personnel, finance and planning systems slowly followed. There were problems, due to the heterogeneity of systems and the special costs of open learning; and with the integration of administration systems now moving ahead of the unification of some faculties, there was potential for conflict between the Gippsland administration's accountability to the campus manager, and its accountability to the General Manager and to his staff at Clayton. Hard work and hard talking sorted these problems through.[48]

Tom Kennedy. The Gippsland Director took integration slowly.

Logan did not want Gippsland to lose its regional character. He understood the local importance of the Churchill campus, the only higher education institution in a region characterised by low participation rates.[49] It had an even more crucial role in a region facing the partial collapse of the local economy. When the University first took on Gippsland in 1988, expectations for regional development were high, but soon after the SECV was privatised by the Victorian government. More than a quarter of its positions vanished: there were flow-on effects in other industries, and over five years more than 10 000 jobs were lost. Logan hoped that, in concert with employers, local authorities and community organisations, the campus would become a major player in regional socio-economic strategy. An important employer in its own right, it was a source of knowledge-based industrial development, and played a role in the arts and community services.[50] He also knew that, while there was scope for marketing

Gippsland as a quasi-vacation campus in the country, and as a safe haven for international students, it would never be a major money-maker. As Logan saw it, maintaining and developing Gippsland was part of Monash's public duty. He also knew that not everyone at Clayton agreed.[51]

Gippsland was the 'most difficult' merger for Monash (Logan), because it required a long-term commitment, and because it was hard to position the world university and regional university so as to make them work for each other. It was essential for Gippsland to transcend its old mindset grounded in isolation and regional disadvantage, a mindset that was becoming obsolete in an age of technology-based relationships but one that still sapped the confidence of people at Churchill.[52] Monash Gippsland's work in distance education, offshore courses and open learning was important here, because it allowed the campus to move beyond the framework of State and national higher education provision, where its historical role was not strong, and into the Southeast Asian region and beyond. Thus the global was implicated in the local. The difficulty was to bring the local to the global, so that Gippsland could take its part in the world university system without losing its local character, and contribute something distinctive to Monash's international work. At the same time, the teaching task at Gippsland was necessarily different from that at Clayton, with less concern with student entrance scores and more with providing access to families new to higher education. Gippsland was changing under the influence of Monash, but the faculties and departments at Clayton were beginning to realise that they also needed to change, to take in Gippsland's regional identity and to place its needs on higher priority.

Ones that got away

There were other potential mergers on the east side of the central business district, with Swinburne Institute at Hawthorn, and the multi-campus Victoria College including its Rusden campus. Both options were pursued by Monash, though with a certain inconsistency, and both eventually came to nothing.

Prior to the Chisholm–Monash merger, Vaughan and Logan held several meetings with Swinburne's Director Iain Wallace. Logan felt it would have been good to have Swinburne, with its strengths in Engineering, Computing and Business: 'they would have complemented us nicely'.[53] Some at Clayton saw Swinburne as a more desirable merger partner than Chisholm. But it became apparent that Swinburne would go its own way.

The University's leaders were more ambivalent about Victoria College. They did not favour a complete merger, which would add a large number of academics to the Faculty of Education, the one field where student numbers were likely to decline. Moreover, Victoria's Nursing promised more costs than benefits, and its sites were a mixed blessing. Although Rusden was a sensible acquisition, as the Monash Council indicated in its resolution of 11 April 1988, and the Victoria College mansion at 'Stonnington' in Toorak was an attractive piece of real estate, perhaps for a corporate headquarters, Burwood and Prahran had little to offer and would probably require substantial capital monies. For its part, Victoria College did not want to be broken up, or be a minor player in an existing university. Its council had resolved on 16 February 1988 that it would rather play a major role in a new university. In September 1988 Victoria announced plans to merge with Swinburne. When this fell through in the first half of 1989, hesitant negotiations between Monash and Victoria resumed. However SAMU was strongly opposed and Logan mindful of the need to protect the process of merger negotiations with Chisholm. He later remarked that by the time Rusden became a 'firm possibility' he sensed that 'Monash had had enough' of mergers and 'I could not push it any further'. Moreover, he had 'had enough' himself: 'There is a mental and physical limit to all of this and I think I had reached that limit'.[54]

On 27 September Logan wrote to Campbell rejecting a full merger 'at this stage', but suggesting an affiliation agreement that would encourage cooperation between parts of their respective institutions. Matters moved slowly, and by May 1990 there were reports that Victoria was discussing a merger with Deakin. Monash moved to keep its option alive, but was still unwilling to commit to a full merger, and on 30 August 1990 Victoria College chose Deakin. It affirmed that Rusden would be part of the enlarged Deakin University.

Monash still hoped to secure Rusden, possibly by influencing the subsequent legislation, though, as Logan told Council on 25 February 1991, the University was more interested in Rusden's land and buildings than in its staff and students. However, by the middle of 1991 it was apparent that Rusden was lost.

The Pharmacy College

If Rusden was a campus that Monash should have had and didn't, then Pharmacy was a steal, a totally unexpected outcome of the merger round. The School of the Pharmaceutical Society of Victoria dated from 1881, the Victoria College of Pharmacy from 1960. In 1988 the College enrolled 420 students. Following the publication of the Green and White Papers it was clear to its Council that it would not be in a position to survive as an independent entity. The obvious merger was with the University of Melbourne. Not only was that university located 1.2 kilometres down Royal Parade in Parkville but merger had been considered six times before, and the College already operated as

Melbourne's Department of Pharmaceutical Science for the purpose of supervising PhD candidates.[55] The research cultures of the two institutions were readily aligned.

However, the College's negotiations with Melbourne proved less than satisfactory. Melbourne would not consider a separate Pharmacy faculty: it had just folded its Dentistry faculty into Medicine, and expected Pharmacy to become a department within an enlarged Faculty of Medicine, Dentistry and Health Sciences. This implied that Pharmacy's professional status at Melbourne would be less than that of Medicine or Dentistry, and its academic autonomy and its control over resources and assets would be diminished twofold: first by the move to the University, second by location inside a Medicine-dominated faculty. The College was also concerned that it would be financially penalised by merging with Melbourne. Its premises in Parkville, owned by the Pharmaceutical Society, were leased at a peppercorn rental. The Society indicated that in the event of a merger with Melbourne it would expect a greater financial return. Melbourne stated that the additional cost would have to be borne by Pharmacy itself from within its departmental budget, and despite protracted discussions it refused to budge. Pharmacy's negotiators, including the Director Colin Chapman, wondered whether a merger with Melbourne was worth it.[56] Nevertheless, Melbourne's negotiating position seemed strong. Both the Commonwealth and State governments regarded a Pharmacy–Melbourne merger as the only possible outcome. The cooperation of the first was essential to future funding arrangements, and the cooperation of the second was essential to the legislation facilitating a merger.

The only other university in Victoria which had a Medical faculty, and thus the kind of full presence in the hospital system that complemented Pharmacy, was Monash. To Monash's surprise Pharmacy made approaches to it, and the Director and Deputy Director met Logan, Wade and Porter in May 1990. The Pharmacy College's minutes of the meeting record that the Monash team was 'extremely enthusiastic to forge links with the College. They are extremely keen to take in another respected health profession, to increase the University's strength in health sciences *vis á vis* the University of Melbourne, and to become part of the Parkville strip'. Equally importantly, 'the University would be happy to contemplate the College retaining its identity and autonomy in a similar fashion' to that proposed for Gippsland and would allow the College to report directly to Academic Board and Council, rather than through the Faculty of Medicine. Further, the University was 'willing to consider various options to resolve the question of the Society's property'.[57] The two institutions had something else in common: Geoff Vaughan, about to take office as Monash DVC, had spent many years as Director of Pharmacy before going to Chisholm.

Negotiations began in earnest. At first Pharmacy dealt with both universities simultaneously; then on 20 August it terminated discussions with Melbourne and signed a Heads of Agreement document with Monash on 23 October 1990. In February 1991 the University of Melbourne re-entered the picture, but its new offer did not resolve the substantial issues between it and the College. No doubt Melbourne still believed there was no prospect of a Pharmacy–Monash merger, and that Pharmacy's negotiations with Monash were a ploy designed to improve its bargaining position with Melbourne. Here Melbourne was outflanked by an audacious Monash strategy, kept secret until the crucial moment. As John Monash once remarked, 'surprise has been, from time immemorial, one of the most potent weapons in the armoury of the tactician'.[58] Wade recalled later:

> Melbourne correctly assumed that when it came to legislation it was very unlikely that the government would legislate to move the Pharmacy College to Monash when Melbourne was over the road. What Melbourne did not consider—and this was a lack of flexibility in their minds—was the option that legislation might not be needed. And what we discovered . . . was that [for a tertiary institution] the Pharmacy College was a very unusual place. It was a company not a statutory body. And when I went through the Monash Act I noticed we had company powers. What we did was a company merger with the Pharmacy College.[59]

Once done, it was politically difficult for the company merger to be undone. If a government legislated to undo a medium-sized company merger with no obvious question of company practice at stake, it would have sent shock-waves through the commercial world. 'At the end of the day' (Wade) both governments found themselves supporting the merger. This was announced on 25 June 1991. The College Council was replaced by a College Board. On 18 November 1992 the Victorian College of Pharmacy (Monash University) was formally wound up, and Monash University became its successor at law. Pharmacy became the smallest faculty of the University. Monash met the problem of the Pharmaceutical Society's request for a higher rental by making a one-off capital injection which provided the Society with meeting and workspace. This was held to offset the rental costs.

The Pharmacy College. Monash secured the merger with Pharmacy because it offered to provide greater autonomy and better support for rent and capital costs than did Melbourne.

Buildings and facilities

Mergers create more pressure on administrative staff and systems than academic systems, for administration has less room for local variations, and differences in phase-in time. There was a unitary approach to services, facilities and systems across the University, in which facilities were rationalised and modernised. Caulfield and Frankston were integrated first, followed by Gippsland and Parkville. One of the first services to be integrated was the library. In 1986 and 1987 decline in the value of the Australian dollar forced the Clayton library to cut a thousand of its 9000 periodicals and constrain book purchases. There was a small recovery in 1988, but no sooner was the crisis over than Clayton library staff were asked to provide a common set of services across the same faculties on each campus, even before fully integrating the systems. The library staff did exceptionally well to meet the challenge.[60]

The number of volumes held by all Monash libraries rose from 1.381 million in 1988 to 2.312 million in 1996, and periodicals rose by a third. The Chisholm campuses brought strengths in Business, Nursing and Computing to the network. Monash continued to lend more titles to external libraries than it received, though the margin was less than in earlier years,[61] and branch libraries such as Law and Pharmacy continued among the best in their field. The catalogue was on-line, and plans for a 24-hour electronic library were taking shape, though slower than expected. There was compensation for the pain of the merger in the new $5.8 million information services buildings at Clayton. This was connected by walkway to the main building to the north. It extended facilities significantly.

By the time the new library wing was taking shape the University was in the throes of the second great period of construction in its history. The new buildings, a direct outcome of the mergers, were facilitated by Monash's *guanxi* relationship with Canberra (chapters 3 and 4). In the first 15 years of the University's history there were 57 major Commonwealth-financed projects, before building slackened in the mid-1970s.[62] During the next 15 years of steady state, activity was largely confined to extension and refurbishing of the existing stock. The Gallery building completed in 1987 was financed by the University. In the next half decade the University won substantial capital grants. By 1991 a Civil Engineering building had been completed at Clayton, and other major building projects had begun or were in an advanced stage of planning on all campuses.[63] The backlog of work from the late 1970s and 80s was addressed and the new campuses were overhauled.

The building program was shaped by the Finance and Building Committees, and by the Campus Planning Committee which grew out of discussions between the Vice-Chancellor and administrative staff in 1989. The Campus Planning Committee set out to ensure that the physical development of the University took place in a balanced fashion across the six campuses, with some continuity in architecture and facilities. By late 1992 there were nine major building projects underway, costing over $70 million, including an estimated $18.8 million development at Caulfield,[64] a $7.4 million performing arts building at Clayton, information services at Clayton, and a $1.3 million new visual arts complex at Gippsland. The Caulfield project was for a three-storey building with lecture theatres, classrooms, computer laboratories and student union facilities, and a five-storey tower block for the Business School. The first part was part-funded by the Caulfield Student Union. Funding for the Gippsland arts building was split equally between government and University. Other projects in train or completed included Computing and general teaching sites at Clayton ($10.1 million), the fourth floor on top of the Clayton Law School, enabling expansion of the Law library ($3.1 million), the union community centre at Peninsula ($3.8 million), and student residences and recreational facilities at Gippsland. The ground floor of Gippsland's general teaching and distance education centre building ($7.7 million) was finished, as was the Gippsland clocktower, the practice golf range—a joint project with the City of Morwell—and the Peninsula technology building ($6.6 million).[65]

By 1994 the performing arts and information services buildings at Clayton, the general teaching building at Caulfield, the Union community centre at Peninsula and the Gippsland visual arts building were all completed, along with extensions to the university offices at Clayton and two Engineering buildings. Work on Clayton's first multi-level car park ($4.5 million) had begun. Within another year extensions to the sports and recreation centre ($7.9 million) and the Union building ($4.9 million), and the paving and refurbishment of the Library courtyard and Arts precinct, were all underway. Pharmacy was extended and an outstanding teaching space, the South Theatre Medical Faculty building, was added to Medicine. Nursing at Peninsula was rehoused. Of the 240 completed buildings on the six Monash campuses in 1995, 32 had been built since 1990.[66] All faculties had been expanded in physical terms, Business, Computing and Engineering had been improved dramatically, and there had been a major overhaul of union buildings and services.

The change at Peninsula was striking. Native planting and raw modern buildings combined to create a Claytonesque feel, but one newer and more coherent.[67] At Clayton the earlier buildings still outnumbered the new, some of the new buildings (like many of the old) were uninspired, and long-standing design problems were still unsolved.[68] Clayton lacked an architecturally strong centre corresponding to the sandstone hub of the older Australian universities.[69] The Menzies Building, too large for the eye to avoid or for the planner to remove, continued its slow decline. Fortunately, the outstanding new performing arts centre building escaped the constraints of the prevailing utilitarianism (chapter 8).

The other major initiative was the purchase of a building in the central business district. In 1988 Monash opened a rented office on the corner of Flinders Lane and Exhibition Streets and in April 1993 the Vice-Chancellor told Council that with the lease about to expire Monash was exploring other options. It was a good time to buy: city prices had fallen because of economic recession, and there was an oversupply of office space. On 12 May Wade reported to the Academic Board that the Monash Foundation had bought a 14-storey building at 30 Collins Street at the east end of the City, at a cost of $10 million. Located near corporate headquarters, the Supreme Court and the State government, the new building was used as an executive headquarters for negotiations with business and government, as a site for teaching, seminars and showpiece presentations, and for leasing purposes. Logan began to spend part of his week at his 11th floor city office, which overlooked the Melbourne Club, the Exhibition Buildings and the Princess Theatre.

Merging the faculties

The Merger Implementation Committee that managed the Monash–Chisholm negotiations had confined itself to the macro-structures. After 1 July 1990 the focus shifted to resource-sharing and course sorting in the faculties. Later the Gippsland courses came onto the agenda. The gradual integration which followed was easier in those faculties that were comfortable with the merger than in Engineering, and in Economics and Business.

For a time it was 'very hard' in Engineering (Hay).[70] The two Engineering cultures differed significantly. The Monash faculty saw itself at the forefront of global research and professional practice, and as a provider of education for high academic achievers. Applied Engineering at Caulfield saw itself as a solid introduction to Engineering methods and technologies, often directed to less academically able students. It ran smaller classes than Clayton and conducted much less research. Gippsland Engineering had a region-centred role (at one stage it provided virtually all the advanced engineering training for the SECV, though the relationship with the SECV was now less important than it had been) and modest research ambitions.[71] The only viable long-term strategy was the integration of the three groups into one, and at Clayton this triggered a deeply felt opposition to the merger, for resources were already stretched. It was feared that the merger would dilute the faculty's reputation, the quality of its students, and its research. The then Dean of Engineering, Peter Darvall, recalled later that 'there was fear and loathing in the air'.[72]

John Hay. DVC (1989–91) and Monash 'minister for mergers'. Hay's determination to secure integration on the basis of cross-campus faculties, rather than campuses, ensured that the post-merger University was a coherent institution.

TABLE 5.2 ENGINEERING AND SCIENCE ENROLMENTS* BY CAMPUS, 1995

	Clayton	Caulfield	Peninsula	Gippsland	Total
Engineering	1512	1120	36	613	3281
Engineering–Arts	108	0	0	0	108
Engineering–Law	30	0	0	0	30
Engineering–Business/Economics	97	0	0	9	106
Engineering–Science	424	0	0	0	424
Science–Arts	316	0	0	0	316
Science–Law	186	0	0	0	186
Science	2932	131	2	536	3601

* Excludes combined courses with Computing (Table 5.3) and Business (Table 5.5).
Source: Monash University statistics.

Darvall had argued against the merger at the Committee of Deans. But he was aware of the broader benefits of the merger to Monash, and the fact that it had majority support among the deans and on the Board and Council. He also knew that, like other officers of the University, the deans were customarily obliged to carry out the decisions of the majority once those decisions had been made. Darvall voted to facilitate the merger at the Board, and argued for it back at the faculty with as much conviction as possible, given his own position. An anonymous leaflet was circulated in the faculty, labelling the Dean a 'quisling'. It was a 'fairly brutal introduction in the necessity for Cabinet solidarity in the University context' (Darvall). Inevitably, the implementation phase was also difficult. The fact that Engineering was in three geographically separated locations reduced the scope for sharing, collaboration and course-mixing, and made it necessary to run the faculty as a confederation with distinct courses for four years after the official merger. But the different schools needed time to become similar before being pushed together. Under the Monash funding formula Caulfield gained more resources, enabling research, staff qualifications and goodwill to develop. Caulfield–Clayton communications remained weak, providing space in which the tensions could subside.[73] When he retired as Dean in 1994 the staff at Caulfield awarded Darvall the honorary degree of Doctor of Leadership Engineering (DOLE), in recognition of his even-handed handling of the merger.

The integration of Engineering at Gippsland proved slower. In his short tenure as Head of the Gippsland Engineering School Brendon Parker, originally from Clayton, 'turned the place around dramatically' (Dunstan). Unfortunately for Monash, Parker became Dean of Engineering at Wollongong University in 1995. For a while Faculty Dean Mike Brisk was the Head of School. The departmental integration of Gippsland began in 1997.

The Faculty of Science grew by almost one-third in size as a result of the merger (Table 5.2). It disestablished the Chisholm Applied Science degree in

TABLE 5.3   COMPUTING ENROLMENTS BY CAMPUS, 1995

	Clayton	Caulfield	Peninsula	Gippsland	Total
Computing and Information Technology	1592	1335	290	669	3886
Computing/IT–Engineering	166	0	0	0	166
Computing/IT–Business/Economics	0	302	94	0	396

Source: Monash University statistics.

1991 and gradually integrated activities at Caulfield, and later Gippsland. The Dean between 1990 and 1994, Ian Rae, 'wholeheartedly' supported the decision to merge. As in Engineering, the immediate impact of the merger was to bring to the faculty a large number of staff with low research profiles, and although not all Clayton staff were research-active[74] there was 'much enmity to overcome'. Rae was able to bring the Frankston staff on-side when he 'stood on' some of the Caulfield people, utilising resentments left over from the earlier Chisholm merger of 1982. Later, the melding of the faculty was assisted by Paul Rodan from Chisholm, who became Assistant Registrar in the faculty (succeeding Elizabeth Anderson, who transferred to Logan's office as Adviser to the Vice-Chancellor). Departments were rearranged piece by piece. Caulfield Physics and some Mathematics went to Clayton. Chemistry and Biology, combined at Chisholm, were split.[75] By the mid-1990s there was little Science left at Caulfield, though one exception was Barry Hart's successful group in Water Studies.[76] Rae believed that the regional role of Gippsland Science was worth preserving, and in the faculty reorganisation at Churchill he made some concessions to local interest.[77] Sometimes the details were tricky: for example, Psychology at Gippsland was linked to teacher education and had trouble fitting the 'rats and stats' mould in Science.

If the progress of the merger in Engineering and Science was measured by the extent to which the Chisholm school was subsumed into a pre-existing Clayton faculty whose nature remained unchanged, it was a different story in Computing and Information Technology. Chisholm's School of Digital Technology was brought together with Monash's Information Systems and Computer Science, and later Computer Education at Gippsland. 'The mergers created the Faculty', as the founding Dean, Cliff Bellamy, later put it.[78] The faculty was bigger and better than any of its pre-merger units. Clayton became seen by Caulfield staff as the best place to advance a career,[79] but there was something of a symbiosis in which Clayton, Caulfield, Peninsula and Gippsland all made distinctive contributions within a common academic framework managed by Bellamy from Clayton. Later, after the demise of Professional Studies (see below), Librarianship, Archives and Records were added. The development of the Computing Faculty was perhaps the outstanding long-term outcome of the merger round (Table 5.3).[80]

Bellamy knew that, to consolidate Computing in a university that saw itself as a research university, he would need to strengthen and generalise the research aspects of the faculty. The main constraint was the staff mix. At first there was some resistance at Caulfield and Peninsula to the idea that PhDs were relevant in employment and promotion. Bellamy found ways around this, for example by paying unqualified staff in positions of responsibility above their academic status. Gradually higher degree numbers rose.[81]

Professional Studies was the second new faculty out of the merger. Unlike Computing it was not centred on a single field but was a catch-all for a miscellany of disciplines, united by only two elements: their vocational orientation, and the University's inability to fit them easily elsewhere. Librarianship and Social Work from Clayton Arts were drawn together with Nursing at Frankston and Gippsland; Art and Design at Caulfield, Frankston and Gippsland; and Applied Psychology, Welfare Studies and Police Studies from Chisholm. The faculty covered much of the Chisholm School of Social and Behavioural Studies (the remaining components, Literature, Sociology and Politics, went to the Arts Faculty). As a largely Chisholm faculty with a Chisholm dean, Professional Studies lent some political balance to the rest of the structure. It also allowed the different groupings to be monitored, rationalised and developed as appropriate, leaving Monash with the longer-term option of retaining the faculty, augmenting it or dissolving it.[82]

The founding Dean, Richard Snedden, previously Chisholm's Deputy Director and Dean of Social and Behavioural Studies, had an almost impossible task. The faculty lacked intrinsic coherence and was disabled by congenital financial problems. Nursing, Librarianship and Art and Design were all creating sizable deficits. Nurse education had only recently entered higher education. It had no research culture to speak of, funding for clinical education in the hospitals had dropped out, nurse educators at Frankston were not talking to nurse educators at Gippsland, and some nurse educators at Frankston stopped talking to each other. The staff in Librarianship were good, but staffing was 50 per cent more than Snedden could afford. Art and Design supported a layer of full-time older staff without degrees. Despite its strengths in ceramics and graphic design, a more academically focused Visual Arts Department at Clayton, dominated by art historians, wanted nothing much to do with it. Snedden knew that he had to move slowly on industrial matters. He could not sack continuing staff.[83]

Over the next three years the faculty gradually entered the university environment. The Clayton Social Work Department, focused on the preparation of casework professionals, found itself at variance with Chisholm Welfare Studies, which was paraprofessional. The two groups learned to cooperate in professional placements and supervision arrangements. Police Studies lacked an academic vantage point on policing because it was too close to its main client organisation, Victoria Police, and found the transition more difficult.[84]

The faculty had received additional post-merger funds, but these were

The first four Deans of Education. L–R: Peter Fensham (1982–88), Peter Musgrave (1977–81), Syd Dunn (1971–75), Richard Selby-Smith (1964–71). Fensham's successor David Aspin (1989–93) was in the chair when student numbers grew by 141 per cent as a result of merger.

phased out, and on 16 June 1993 Wade told the Academic Board that it was in a parlous state. At the end of 1993 the faculty was running at a loss of $1 million a year in a budget of less than $12 million. By then, following a review chaired by Snedden, it was about to be dissolved. The Caroline Chisholm School of Nursing at Frankston and the School of Nursing at Gippsland became a subfaculty of Medicine. The School of Art and Design became a subfaculty of Arts at Caulfield. Applied Psychology joined the rest of Psychology in Science. Librarianship went to Computing, Social Work returned to Arts.[85]

Both Arts and Education grew considerably as the result of the mergers. During a time when most Education faculties were static or becoming smaller, student load in Education at Monash rose from 728 in 1989 to 1763 in 1991, the fastest growth of any faculty. The strong research orientation at Clayton was combined with Early Childhood and Primary Education at Frankston and regional specialties at Gippsland. Education moved faster than did most of the other faculties at Gippsland. Again, the drawing together of research and largely non-research groupings brought with it tension and skirmishing, and was followed by the gradual homogenisation of the non-Clayton units. Many Peninsula and Gippsland staff enrolled in higher degrees. From 1995, the faculty operated as a three-school confederation (Table 5.4).[86] The Clayton-based Deans of Education sometimes found themselves frustrated by opaque administrative processes outside Clayton.

TABLE 5.4 ARTS, EDUCATION, LAW, MEDICINE, NURSING AND PHARMACY
            ENROLMENTS* BY CAMPUS, 1995

	Clayton	Caulfield	Peninsula	Gippsland	Parkville	Total
Arts	4957	1462	449	1541	0	8524**
Arts–Education	0	0	78	0	0	78
Arts–Law	838	0	0	0	0	838
Education	1335	0	535	837	0	2707
Law	666	0	0	0	0	666
Law–Medicine	5	0	0	0	0	5
Medicine	1875	0	0	0	0	1875
Nursing	0	0	690	1119	0	1809
Pharmacy	0	0	0	0	463	463

* Excludes combined courses with Engineering and Science (Table 5.2) and Business/Economics (Table 5.5).
** Includes 115 at Berwick.
Source: Monash University statistics.

Student load in Arts grew from 3224 in 1989 to 6340 in 1991. Although there were differences in the *modus operandi* of the Clayton and Chisholm staff, there was significant research and publication at both Clayton and Chisholm. The Caulfield staff in Social and Behavioural Studies pressed for the creation of a separate Social Science Faculty and, when this failed, pressed for divisions of Social Sciences and Humanities within the one faculty. Instead the Arts Faculty opted for minimum structural change, so that in administrative terms the Sociology, Politics and Literature people were absorbed into the respective Clayton departments.[87] After the break-up of Professional Studies, the Caulfield-based subfaculty of Art and Design began to emerge as one of the strengths of the faculty and of the post-merger campus—the 'civilising influence' alongside Business and Computing, as John Redmond, the Director of Art and Design, was to put it. By then digital imaging was penetrating the visual arts, with new commercial possibilities.[88] Gippsland Arts Faculty activities remained distinct for a time, with very small teaching units in some disciplines. There were tensions when Gippsland wanted to develop courses in potentially popular areas such as communications and media that the Clayton faculty, wedded to the traditional humanities and social science disciplines, did not offer.

Business and economics

Merging was more difficult in Business and Economics than anywhere else. This was ironic, for Logan had seen the acquisition of the David Syme School at Caulfield as the chief potential gain from the merger process.[89] The value of a successful Business school with brand recognition in both the downtown business community and in the Southeast Asian markets was obvious. The problem was that Economics was a major faculty at Clayton, large and strong enough to make it central to any post-merger configuration in Economics, Business, Management and Administration. And the Syme and Clayton approaches not only were poles apart, they quickly became hostile competitors.

At Chisholm, Vaughan, Ramler and the other negotiators saw the Syme School as the jewel in the Chisholm crown. They believed that this was the one area where the merger should be a reverse takeover by Chisholm to balance the predominance of Clayton in other faculties. The Business school, with its applied orientation and its presence in Melbourne business circles, was at the core of Chisholm's identity. The first struggle over Economics and Business nearly scuttled the merger before it was launched. Chisholm's networks in business were mobilised, and eventually Ian Cathie, the State government's Minister for Post-secondary Education, warned Monash that Syme should be protected. The Chisholm negotiators secured guarantees of its survival, and it was understood that in the longer term Caulfield would be the main site for Business Education, broadly defined. Both sides accepted the temporary expedient of a separate Business faculty, and a three-year timetable for resolution, allowing Clayton for the moment to continue unchanged.[90]

The strengths of the Economics faculty at Clayton lay in research and its accumulated academic reputation. The core discipline was not Business, it was Economics, a discipline with a much longer history. Economics had been ascendant in commerce faculties in the 1960s, when Monash was established. The Clayton academics were scholarly in demeanour, mostly without a strong applied orientation or close links with the business world. The earlier collaboration between Economics and Law in commercial law (chapter 2) might have been the starting point of an enhanced role in advanced Business Education, but that collaboration had declined. In contrast the Syme School was overwhelmingly practical. It specialised in areas such as Marketing, Strategy and Finance, and differentiated its credential structure between the different branches of Business Education so as to maximise its share of the total student market. The Syme School brought a businesslike approach to business education. It fostered its relationships with the Melbourne business community and had built loyal alumni. Though it had little presence in global business circles, it was interested in the revenue-generating potential of international marketing.

As Clayton Dean of Economics and Politics Gus Sinclair saw it, the merger was creating an 'aggressive competitor within the institution'. That was also how the former Chisholm School saw itself.[91] The two parties were contending for the same role, and the balance of forces was relatively even. Each party was rendered increasingly insecure by the efforts of the other, and the potential for a stable division of labour gradually eroded, along with the goodwill. Relations deteriorated. At the time of the merger the Syme School, which under Peter Chandler had just been reorganised and re-equipped, was on the rise, 'a very highly motivated group that were making extraordinary progress', as Chandler (himself a marketing specialist) later put it. The acumen of the Syme staff in business spilled over into their capacity in self-marketing, a capacity that on the whole was lacking in the Clayton faculty. In the intra-Monash contest, the Syme School also had broader strategic options. Because it had always supported the merger it could claim to be an advocate of the common good. Clayton Economics had shifted from totally opposing the merger to demanding control of a post-merger entity that previously it had wanted nothing to do with. Syme often got the better of negotiating situations in front of third parties.[92]

Nevertheless, Syme did not hold all the advantages. Located in the junior merger partner, it was forced always to work from outside the centre of decision-making; and its lack of scholarly depth became an increasing handicap. It was a problem typical of Business Education in the CAE sector, never required to develop the academically codified knowledge, the layer of doctoral students and the peer-reviewed research projects and refereed conference papers typical of a university discipline. As Chisholm's Brian Costar saw it at the time of the merger, the business school at Chisholm was highly popular but 'academically shallow. And I wondered how long that could go on . . . You hit the wall somewhere'. There were only two research Masters students at Syme. A sociologist, Alan Simon, was brought in to run the PhD program because no-one inside could do it.[93] (The rapid growth of research and publication in the Syme School after the merger confirms Costar's point.) This was a weakness that the Clayton Economics faculty exploited and one that strengthened its determination to resist a Syme-led outcome.

Both groups genuinely believed that they were entitled to primacy. Clayton Economics, because only it was a *bona fide* university faculty with a strong scholarly record. The Syme Business faculty, because it had been granted primacy in the merger negotiations, and because this was Business Education: entrepreneurial functions were now important in all universities, and it had proved its capacity to attract students and business support. As Syme saw it, the academic discipline of Economics should feed into a Business-dominated faculty, rather than vice versa: 'Both parties assigned a role to the other that the other did not want' (Sinclair). To win their points, each used benchmarks that showed the other in an unfavourable light. This highlighted the differences, real and apparent, and further cut away the potential for goodwill. A ghetto mentality developed, especially at Clayton.

After the merger on 1 July 1990 the two faculties began to move into each other's territory, creating the contrary outcomes of short-term tension and long-term convergence (Table 5.5). In Malaysia, Monash marketed contending

TABLE 5.5 STUDENT LOAD IN BUSINESS AND ECONOMICS, 1990–96

	Total student load, Business and Economics	Total student load, Monash University	Proportion of total Monash student load in Business/Economics (%)
1990*	2321	14 062	16.5
1991	6324	26 358	24.0
1992	6824	27 366	24.9
1993	6918	28 311	24.4
1994	7239	28 681	25.2
1995	7672	29 938	25.6
1996	8173	30 699	26.6

* Prior to merger with Chisholm and Gippsland.
Source: Monash University Statistics.

courses in Business, Economics and Management. Though the difficulties this created were probably exaggerated for internal political purposes, no doubt there was some confusion in the market. Another outcome was that both faculties rapidly increased their international student numbers. Meanwhile, as Syme enhanced its research activities, and became the first to move into open learning mode, Clayton devised its own Bachelor of Commerce degree to run against Syme's Bachelor of Business. On 4 July 1990 the Syme Faculty of Business Advisory Board noted 'with some concern the confusion that this may create in the market place with the multiplicity of Monash awards', though the Advisory Board also expressed confidence that 'water would find its own level',[94] meaning that in a contest it expected that Syme would do well. Still, the Clayton BCom degree gathered strong student support, growing from 797 enrolments in 1992 to 2130 in 1995, though remaining smaller than the Caulfield-based BBus with 6084.[95] Because the BCom was Clayton-based, part of the traditional university, the cut-off scores for entry were generally higher than those at Caulfield.

Syme could scarcely insist on consultation, given that both faculties were pressing ahead with new courses, appointments and budgetary decisions with scant regard for each other's representatives on their decision-making bodies. The committee set up to iron out demarcation issues was ineffective, so that every specific initiative was fought out on the course approval committees and Academic Board. The rest of the University was an uneasily fascinated spectator to the resulting debate. There were 'bad days' (Logan), with the deans locked in head-to-head combat: 'It was a most awful period' (Chandler).[96]

The questions at stake were the orientation and location of the integrated faculty-to-be, its name and its leadership and the integration of its degrees, courses and departments. The name had become the symbol of the Syme orientation. Skirmishing continued. Students from Caulfield and Clayton were drawn in. Branches of Syme were created at Peninsula and in Gippsland, where the local staff were sympathetic to the Syme ethos, though ironically the similarity between Caulfield and Gippsland catalysed a new rivalry. Gippsland's Syme-influenced distance education course in business generated enough money to start several research centres.[97] Another branch of Syme began in Malaysia. Meanwhile, the Clayton departments declared their deeply felt opposition to any forced relocation to Caulfield.[98] Logan negotiated support from the Commonwealth for capital works that would enable an augmented Economics and Business Faculty to be developed at Caulfield, only to have the Economics Faculty Board withdraw support.

If there had been less conflict, and if the Clayton faculty had not been so adamant that Business and Economics was indivisible, then the University might have maintained two faculties. Chandler later argued that Syme should have become a separate private entity, segmenting the market rather than providing one standard product. Nevertheless, in the circumstances the University leadership thought it better to push them into one unit, localising the conflict and forcing its ultimate resolution. The immediate effect was to further intensify the conflict. The committee created to negotiate the detail of the merged faculty was acrimonious, 'probably the worst committee I've ever served on. They didn't want a bar of each other' (Bill Melbourne).[99] It was finally agreed that the David Syme title would be retained for the new faculty, and that the dean would be located at Caulfield. The faculty would consist of six schools: the David Syme School of Business, the School of Economics, the David Syme Graduate School of Business, the Graduate School of Economics, and the Syme Schools of Business at Frankston and Gippsland. At the same time, the two major schools in Business and Economics were to be integrated on the basis of cross-campus departments in Accounting, Banking and Finance, Economics, Econometrics, Management and Marketing. Although the strongly applied orientation of the old Syme school had been partly eroded, continuity of brand name was important and a powerful symbol. The outcome was seen as a victory for the former Chisholm elements.

At this point a 'third world war broke out' (Chandler). The Faculty of Economics stepped up its lobbying efforts, and there was much criticism of the proposed framework for the new faculty when Logan tabled it at the Academic Board on 9 September 1992. Monash did not allow personal names to be part of faculty nomenclature, declared one speaker, perhaps forgetting that the name of the whole institution came from just such a source. The proposal passed the

Peter Chandler. As Dean of the Syme School of Business (1990–93), Chandler found himself fighting 'world war three' with the Clayton Faculty of Economics. He was later Pro-Vice-Chancellor (1994–97) and campus Director at Caulfield.

TABLE 5.6 BUSINESS AND ECONOMICS ENROLMENTS* BY CAMPUS, 1995

	Clayton	Caulfield	Peninsula	Gippsland	Total
Business and Economics	2479	4126	826	2664	10 095
Business/Economics–Engineering	97	0	0	9	106
Business/Economics–Law	574	0	0	0	574
Business/Economics–Arts	303	239	161	0	703

* Excludes 396 combined enrolments with Computing (Table 5.4).
Source: Monash University statistics.

Board, but it was a near thing. Sinclair wrote to the Chancellor in protest. The matter reached Council on 21 September. Clayton students demonstrated outside the meeting. They claimed that the merger of the two faculties would lower the standing of their degrees. Clayton students required a higher entry score than did Caulfield students, yet graduation certificates would no longer specify which Monash campus the graduate had attended.[100] Council endorsed the merger but the name, departmental structure and the membership of the Implementation Task Force were referred back to the Vice-Chancellor for further consideration. On 2 November Council approved the Vice-Chancellor's revised merger plan, in which the Syme name was retained for individual units but was dropped from the faculty's title.[101] It seemed that the Clayton faculty had had the last word.

The new faculty began on 1 July 1993, with three generic degrees: the BBus with various specialisations, offered at Caulfield, Frankston and Gippsland and by distance education, and the BCom and BEc at Clayton (Table 5.6). It was still unclear how much diversification would be retained, and how it would be regulated. As Acting Dean from 1993, Deputy Vice-Chancellor Ian Chubb was committed to a diverse approach but unable to devise a lasting solution. John Rickard became Pro-Vice-Chancellor and Dean in late 1994. Again, diversity was endorsed in principle, but 'the Caulfield campus community',[102] including students, found itself fighting a rearguard action to preserve what remained of the Syme title. By then a further set of issues were on the agenda. Since 17 April 1989 Monash had been affiliated with the Australian Administrative Staff College at Mount Eliza, and on 29 July 1994 the Monash Mt Eliza Business School was established, offering high-fee graduate courses in Management.[103] In the later 1990s the respective roles of Clayton, Caulfield and Mt Eliza in Management education were still being sorted out.

Business and Economics was increasingly important to the University: with 12 597 students in 1996, it was probably the largest university faculty in Australia. In 1995 it earned $17 million in fees and other non-government income.[104] The post-merger faculty was moving forward: Economics was stimulated in a more practice-driven environment, while Business and Accounting were developing a stronger research agenda. Gippsland was pioneering electronic commerce.[105] In the first half of the 1990s, too much energy had been expended on internal conflict that might have been better utilised in teaching and research. Nevertheless, the vocational power of Business was still growing, and the fund-raising potential of the faculty was clear. Over time it could only become stronger.

Outcomes of the merger round

At the end of his vice-chancellorship in 1996 Logan stated in *Montage* that 'without question' the mergers were the toughest job of his time in office.[106] In a study of university mergers Harman and Meek note that 'the post-merger and integration phase generally is long and painful'. The process is always more complex and far slower than expected. The short-term costs, 'financial and emotional', are high.[107] It can take up to a decade for the wounds to heal and the new realities to become generally accepted, longer still for the full benefits to appear.[108] Monash was fortunate in that all four of its mergers were consent-based, and for the most part the negotiated arrangements proved durable. Still, the scale of change was vast, and the process was still being completed in the late 1990s.[109]

Mergers are an institutional investment. Whether the short-term burdens are worthwhile depends on the size of the medium-term and long-term pay-offs. At Monash the medium-term benefit was that the mergers helped the University to transform itself. They were also associated with a growth in operating resources and the transformation of capital facilities on all campuses. Unlike mergers in some other universities, the Monash mergers did not lead to weak federal structures and educational incoherence. The decision to use the faculties rather than the campuses as the basic units was vital. In the mergers that failed in other universities in the early 1990s, the fault lines of the new institution were locational and historical boundaries rather than the boundaries of the mind, the divisions created by teaching and research.[110]

Whereas at the beginning of 1990 all Monash students were enrolled on the one site, by 1996 just under half of all students (49.2 per cent) were attending classes at Clayton (Table 5.7). A total of 21.5 per cent were enrolled at Caulfield and 8.2 per cent at the Peninsula campus at Frankston, with 19.6 per cent enrolled at Gippsland, many of them external students. Size and diversity brought with them a capacity to 'sustain enrolments in the face of rapid fluctuations in the areas of undergraduate student demand', as Logan put it in the 1990 Annual Report, and helped to prepare the University for a more customer-driven age to come. At the same time Monash became very big indeed, and there was a danger it would begin to creak under its own weight. Here the

TABLE 5.7   ENROLMENTS AT MONASH BY CAMPUS, 1990–96*

	Clayton	Caulfield	Peninsula	Gippsland	Pharmacy	Berwick	Total
1990	15 894	0	0	0	0	0	15 894
1991	16 864	7773	2792	5367	0	0	32 796
1992	17 624	8136	2885	6275	0	0	34 920
1993	18 657	7857	2982	6493	478	0	36 467
1994	19 853	8488	2893	7258	470	0	38 962
1995	20 395	8715	3161	7988	463	115	40 837
1996	20 427	8935	3418	7874	462	427	41 543

* Enrolment census in first half of each year; refers only to enrolments in Monash University, not predecessor institutions.

Source: Monash University statistics.

reform of the University's financial and administrative systems (chapter 7) was vital. The period of restructuring that was opened up by the mergers facilitated this process of administrative reform.

At the end of Logan's term of office there was still unfinished merger business for his successor David Robinson to deal with. It remained for the University to develop a long-term plan for the fuller utilisation of the non-Clayton sites, for example by locating major specialties at Caulfield and Frankston.[111] The integration of Economics and Business had a way to go. Course quality at Mt Eliza needed improvement. In the longer term, maintaining administratively separate Nursing schools at Gippsland and Peninsula was probably undesirable. Equally important was the need to restrengthen the core disciplines in Arts, Science and Engineering that had been placed under such pressure during the merger period. Hay remarked later that one unintended consequences of mergers is that, because of the need to deal with structural change, academics might 'take their eye off the ball' and fail to keep up with change in their disciplines.[112] At Monash the mergers were focused on faculty rather than departmental reorganisation and, though the process of change led to disciplinary modernisation, the effect was not automatic. At the same time, some faculties were outside the process altogether. The burdens and the benefits were unevenly spread.

What about the outcome for students? Student Union facilities in the new sites were greatly improved. It proved too difficult to create a single cross-campus union, and the traditional variations in student culture survived: Clayton focused on political representation, Caulfield and Peninsula focused more on services and business activities. At Caulfield, Peninsula and Gippsland, course cut-off scores rose after the merger.[113] Graduates gained, because their degrees were now Monash degrees. (At Pharmacy there was probably little change in the standing of the professional qualification.) While courses such as the Bachelor of Applied Science were discontinued, overall, students found they had the choice of a larger number of courses, course combinations, locations and modes of study. Within the larger Monash they could move midstream between many options. Whether there was a loss in course *range* is more difficult to assess. While Chisholm's distinctive offerings in Business, Engineering and Science were modified under pressure from Clayton, with the disappearance of the CAE sector it is unlikely those courses could have survived in their old form. At the same time, a more applied orientation and a stronger focus on links to industry and on graduate outcomes was taking root throughout the post-Dawkins university system, including Monash.

Did Chisholm, Gippsland and Pharmacy gain or lose overall? Gippsland and Pharmacy had no choice but to find a partner. Arguably, Monash provided Pharmacy with more independence and perhaps more respect than Melbourne would have done. Gippsland gained significant facilities, and became stronger at a time when matters in the La Trobe Valley were difficult. Much of the regional flavour of the campus remained. Of all the institutions that joined with Monash, it was Chisholm that brought the most with it, and Chisholm that held the highest expectations about its own future. Chisholm saw the negotiations with Monash as a process between equals, and for a time the forms were preserved. Yet it was never a merger between equals: it was always closer to a takeover,[114] not just because of Monash's size but because of its university status, coupled with the decision to pursue an integrated model. Chisholm carried the main burden of adjustment. Senior Chisholm figures had mixed fortunes in the new university. Ramler achieved a lasting role, becoming Deputy Chancellor and Chair of the Finance Committee. As Deputy Vice-Chancellor at Clayton, Vaughan received unappetising portfolios. He became disillusioned, and left Monash in late 1991.[115] Snedden retired early with ill-health. The talented Chandler, who under better circumstances might have been Dean of the combined Faculty of Business and Economics, was moved sideways to Pro-Vice-Chancellor and campus manager at Caulfield and Peninsula. He also retired early. Generally, Clayton people remained in charge of administration, with exceptions such as Paul Rodan in Science; Ken Hobbs, who became Registrar in Computing; and the significant role of the Chisholm finance branch in the post-merger University. John White became Deputy General Manager under Wade, and later Director of the Caulfield and Peninsula campuses.

Old hands felt the loss of the particular Chisholm culture, the intimacy of a medium-sized tertiary institution, the sense of family. Some hankered after the influence exercised by the lively staff unions at Chisholm. Richard Whyte found the Monash Council 'one step up from the morgue'.[116] On the positive side, many staff appreciated the enhanced standing that Monash brought. 'Now I can put Monash on my business card' stated one during a staff association survey at Caulfield in 1993. The merger benefited younger staff, for whom it provided research opportunities.[117] Funds for building and facilities were obtained that were beyond the reach of the old CAEs. 'The merger has been the making of this campus', remarked Whyte of Peninsula.[118] Landscaping, trees, glass, steel, carpets, air-conditioning: they were not the sum of higher education, but they helped. New buildings and Monash letterheads elevated the dignity of students and staff; and in their sudden, continuous and very visible transformation, the newly acquired campuses recreated something of that boisterous modernity that had been the hallmark of Clayton in its first phase of growth.

Gone global 6

> Globalisation . . . has been broadened not only to encompass movements of goods and services but of investment, people and ideas across national and regional frontiers . . . The resources of education, training and self-directed learning are essential in addressing the challenge of valuing diversity.
>
> Organisation for Economic Cooperation and Development, *Lifelong learning for all*, OECD, Paris, 1996, pp 29–30

The bigger picture

Monash had always been open to international influences, to a greater extent than most Australian universities. Melbourne, Sydney and the other 19th and early 20th century university foundations were linked closely to Britain, though they also maintained connections in America and Europe. Australian academics often travelled abroad, many for their postgraduate training, a tradition that continued even after local doctorates became more common. Monash, the Australian National University and the University of New South Wales—the next wave of universities, founded in the post-Second World War period—shared these orientations, but from their early days each developed an interest in East and Southeast Asia. In the 1960s Monash created a Southeast Asian Study Centre and began an extensive program in Asian languages; the University flourished as a teacher of Bahasa Indonesian well before the subject was taught in Victorian schools.[1] From the early days, internationalisation took yet another form. As well as Monash studying Asia as the 'other', in the Eurocentric manner of the times, Monash found that the 'other' was becoming part of it, through the onshore education of international students from countries in the Southeast Asian region.

Under the terms of the Colombo Plan, a cooperative pact started in 1950 by Australia, Britain, Malaya, India, Pakistan and Ceylon, New Zealand and

Canada, later joined by the USA, Indonesia, Burma and the associated States of Indo-China, Australia provided university places for students from South and Southeast Asia.[2] With student quotas at Melbourne and Sydney, Monash and the other newer universities provided more than their share of Colombo Plan places. Many Colombo Plan students were destined to become leaders in government and business in their own countries, and to look back on their Monash days with affection. These students added much to Clayton, but the real impact of internationalisation on the Anglo-Australian majority was limited. Few local students enrolled in Asia-specific subjects. International students found themselves required to assimilate in a cultural setting that was largely unchanged by their presence. Though international 'exchange' was talked about, the relationship was largely one-way.

Aid not trade: Economics and Politics Faculty Dean Donald Cochrane (L) with the Malaysian High Commissioner and three Malaysian students, 1971. At this time international education was defined by the Colombo Plan as foreign aid not economic export, although there were also many private students.

About halfway through Logan's term of office as Vice-Chancellor, a decisive change occurred. The international dimension moved from the margins to the centre of the University. For a time, until the idea became thoroughly established, Monash styled itself 'Australia's International University'. A university does not internationalise overnight: the change was built on the three previous decades of experience. Nonetheless, a deep change in orientation did occur. Internationalisation was more than a marketing pitch, more than the marketing of fee-based courses in the region. Internationalisation developed unevenly between the faculties, and among University personnel, but it profoundly affected those parts of the University that were externally engaged.

The reorientation of Monash foreshadowed in *Strategy for the future* had its first fruits in the mergers, in the enlarged role within Victoria that the mergers created, and in the modernisation of structures and facilities that followed. The second fruits were in the creation of a global role, the building of economic, educational and technological networks enabling Monash to operate on a completely new scale. In both developments the common themes were openness, engagement, encounters with diversity: all consistent with the idea of Monash as a State university of the American kind, now operating on the global plane.

The internationalisation of the University was driven by two intersecting forces. The first element was 'globalisation', the growing impact of *world systems* in economic, political, technological and cultural life, systems that extended beyond the framework of the nation–state. The growth of these world systems was facilitated by the deregulation of finance and, later, the development of world-wide telecommunications-based networks. The second element was

Monash's own strategic response to the new opportunities and pressures emerging in the global realm. Globalisation was often unpredictable, and the responses to it were often little more than improvisations; to a certain extent it carried the University (like all universities) along with it. Nevertheless, Monash was not merely responding to the new global environment, but was one of the shapers of that environment. Itself an agent in the globalisation of higher education, Monash created new and different forms of international education, became the only front-rank university in Australia to be a significant player in delivery at a distance; and was large enough to be a collaborator with governments in Asia-Pacific regional development.[3]

The opening of the University to global influences also made other changes possible, as Logan was well aware. It helped to legitimise entrepreneurial management. It began to make flesh the notion in *Strategy for the future* of an engaged university, in which educational activities were synchronised with the polity and the economy. Though such a synchronisation could (and should) never be perfect, in international education, especially its marketing, the synchronisation was closer than elsewhere. At times it seemed that educational changes at Monash were being driven directly by the global economy.

Globalisation

By the early 1990s globalisation had become a front-rank influence in the evolution of education. The economic, technological and cultural effects of globalisation fed each other. Growing people movement and better communications brought about more cultural contact, and facilitated market development in education and other sectors; in turn this led to more people movement than before. A volatile worldwide capital market emerged, associated with a rapid growth in short-term transactions such as currency dealing and facilitated by the instantaneous data transfer via telecommunications networks and computer. By reducing communications costs, new technologies helped to globalise production and financial markets, assisting the marketing of education and other tradable services. Communications networks and financial markets intensified economic competition in all sectors. Research and development, always international, became more so. No longer were knowledge and information primarily ordered by national boundaries.

'Today's world involves interactions of a new order and intensity', as one theorist of globalisation put it.[4] In addition to communication via phone and computer screen, there was migration, tourism, business and education. Table 6.1 shows the fall in the costs of global networking between 1970 and 1990. Costs fell further during the 1990s.

Globalisation did not lead to the formation of one world, or even one world

TABLE 6.1 DECLINING COSTS OF GLOBAL TRANSPORT AND COMMUNICATIONS, 1970–90

	Average air transport revenue per passenger mile	Cost of a 3-minute phone call between New York and London	Cost of computer power (US Department of Commerce index)
1970	100	100	100
1990	69	11	5

Source: International Monetary Fund, *World economic outlook*, IMF, Washington, DC, May 1997, p. 46.

economy. Though some networks were now ordered on a global basis, national identity and national governments still mattered. Nevertheless, it changed the setting in which national entities worked. It meant that economic and cultural isolation was no longer possible (whether for nations or for individual universities) and all governments faced the question of how to orient to the global level. Further, national identity was more unstable than before, and national governments and universities found themselves having to rework their roles in a more global environment. In this, Australian universities had an immediate advantage. The new global technologies, the products and symbols and icons (Hollywood, McDonald's, Nike), the modes of marketing and management, the content of business education—all were Anglo-American in character. Globalisation drove a sudden spread of English-language forms in software, education and research. Australian universities could readily develop global educational prototypes and compete with US and British institutions. Increasingly, a Western education was a vocational advantage—even a business necessity—in many Asian countries.[5]

Yet global influences were not always one-dimensional, or one-way. In nations such as Malaysia and China there was a trend to Americanisation, and also resistances to it. Ultimately there was potential for more than one kind of globalisation. The continuing salience of national identity meant that in the longer term, to engage effectively on the global plane, it was essential to develop a capacity in cultural understanding and diversity.

As early as 1980 there were more than a million international students worldwide. As well as facilitating cultural transmission and exchange, globalisation was a great boost to the growth of the economic market in international education. By the late 1980s the form of that market was established. Two-thirds of all international students journeyed from developing countries to the schools, industry training and higher education institutions of the OECD countries. Half of these attended institutions in the USA; 2 per cent came to Australia, mostly from Singapore, Malaysia and Hong Kong, and smaller groups from Indonesia and Thailand. An international education provided access to the growing global labour force of technicians and professionals, able to take their skills to many parts of the world and, often, to use this global mobility as a means of migration into the OECD countries. In the 1980s the international student experience changed. With both transport and communications made cheaper and more accessible, the cultural costs were also reduced. People who left home could talk more easily to the families they left behind, and they returned home more often. They more readily retained their original cultural identities, even while coming into contact with new ones. In short, in a more mobile and interactive world, multiple cultural identity was more readily sustained and this, too, modified the trend to a universal Anglo-Americanism. For non-Anglo families it reduced the risks inherent in international education.[6] It also meant that in the longer term cultural diversity was bound to become a larger educational issue on campus, though for the most part the traditional single model of good education held sway in Australia.

Culture becomes more complex: When global transport and communications costs became cheaper, international students could live in more than one cultural world at the same time.

'Asianisation' and education

The Australian government was increasingly preoccupied with the place of Australia in the future world economic division of labour, with Australia's future economic relationships to its fast-growing Asian neighbours, and with the cultural changes needed to secure a more global approach in Australia. Between 1960 and the late 80s the share of world manufacturing exports held by Japan, South Korea, Taiwan, China, Hong Kong and Singapore rose from 8 to 20 per cent. Taiwan accumulated the world's largest pool of foreign reserves. South Korea demonstrated its competitive capability in almost every area of manufacturing, from steel to shipbuilding to automobiles to electronics, and Singapore and Hong Kong were leading manufacturers and financial centres. Between 1980 and 1991, South Korea experienced an average growth rate of 8.7 per cent, China 7.8 per cent.

Even without China, the population of East and Southeast Asia was almost twice that of Western Europe. The World Bank estimated that by 2020 the 10 largest economies would include Japan, China, Korea, Taiwan, Thailand and Indonesia. Already by 1988 almost half of Australia's total trade was with its four largest Asian trading partners.[7]

The Commonwealth Minister for Foreign Affairs, Gareth Evans, and Industry Minister John Button worked to improve Australia's profile in East and Southeast Asia. As the government saw it the task was not to turn Australia into an Asian country. Australia's heritage was Anglo-American and European. Australia did not look, or feel, or even smell like an Asian country, as Logan remarked to the Council in 1992.[8] Rather, the objective was for Australia to become fully integrated into the economic life of the region, not only in its traditional role as a mineral and agricultural producer but as an exporter of technologically advanced manufacturing and services. More sophisticated economic links required in turn a greater level of linguistic, cultural and social familiarity with the region.[9] In Canberra the policy was dubbed, rather dramatically, 'Asianisation'. The Vice-Chancellor's connections to the government and his own interests in globalisation and Southeast Asia made him instinctively sympathetic. 'While some of us may look backwards at a disinterested type university system', he argued at the Pacific Rim University Presidents Conference at Tamkang University in December 1990, 'it is important for us in this part of the world to realise that, increasingly, education is becoming integrated in regional economic and international relations'.[10]

'Asianisation' also had its critics. Populist conservative politicians played on Anglo-Australian fears of a generic Asian 'takeover'. Some academics had their doubts. In 1993 the American political scientist Samuel Huntington published an influential article titled 'The clash of civilisations', which described the emerging global order as a bipolar battleground between 'the West' and 'the Rest'. In a footnote to his article Huntington attacked Australia for proposing to 'defect' from the West and redefine itself as an Asian country. He argued that Australia lacked a common cultural base with East and Southeast Asia and lacked a national consensus on the desirability of the move, so that it was doomed to fail. Huntington's polemic did draw attention to some of the difficulties inherent in the official 'Asianisation' project. But he had misconceived that project, and his argument appealed more to the isolationist conservative tradition in America than to Australians. The Huntington thesis received stinging criticism at Monash.[11]

Monash itself became a player in the governmental aspects of Asianisation, mainly through the Vice-Chancellor's links in Canberra. In 1989 Minister Evans invited Logan to become involved in the Pacific Economic Cooperation Council (PECC). PECC had 20 member Asia-Pacific nations. A little-known but significant body, PECC's role was to advance public and private sector cooperation in regional development. It provided formal input into the Asia-Pacific Economic Cooperation (APEC) forum, a regular meeting of Asian and Pacific nations that for a time was perhaps the principal arena of Australian foreign policy. The Vice-Chancellor served on the Australian Pacific Economic Cooperation Committee (AUSPECC) which shaped Australia's role in PECC, and chaired the PECC Human Resources Development Committee. In 1995 the Committee's secretariat was transferred from Singapore to Monash, and located next to Logan's office. It prepared and distributed reports, organised regional meetings and coordinated human resource projects. Philip Adams from the Monash Centre for Policy Studies also assisted PECC, through economic forecasting.[12]

In 1994 Monash bid jointly with the University of New South Wales for the provision of the APEC Study Centre, housed in twin premises at UNSW and the Melbourne central business district. The primary focus of the Centre's work was related to trade and economic development. It undertook research in cooperation with business and other universities. Monash also won a tender to provide postgraduate courses for the Department of Foreign Affairs and Trade. The courses were delivered by Monash personnel but were located at the ANU in Canberra, closer to the students.[13]

Nevertheless, Monash's main contribution to 'Asianisation' was to be through higher education itself. The government saw education as a service sector in which Australia enjoyed a competitive advantage within the region, a potential source of significant export income (chapter 3).[14] Education also had a larger role. In the second half of the 1980s education was the main basis for entry into Australia by Thai nationals (60.5 per cent of visas) and Chinese nationals (44.9 per cent) and important to entry from Indonesia and Korea.[15] More generally, the government believed that universities had a broad strategic role in opening their nation to a more global world, especially in fostering a more export-conscious business sector. International education was deliberately fostered by the Commonwealth as an instrument of globalisation: 'Education is a business in its own right but it also underpins everything else. That's why it's so important' (Logan).[16]

From the late 1980s the international dimension became more significant in every Australian university, in some more than others. Internationalisation included face-to-face courses for international students on-site in Australia, franchising and twinning arrangements whereby offshore institutions provided all or part of Australian degrees, international distance education, staff and student exchange, research collaboration, and changes in domestic curricula. Mission statements were overhauled to incorporate a global dimension. Airport lounges were clogged with university officers on their way to China, Malaysia or Indonesia to sign collaborative agreements with partner universities; by 1995 there were 997 such agreements for staff exchange alone, although many of them were not activated.[17] After years of serving academics, general staff in international programs found themselves with a licence to travel, manage an expense account and make strategic educational decisions. Above all, the number of fee-paying students steadily grew and, after a pause, support services mushroomed in their wake. Monash was in the forefront of these developments.

The market in international education

After the first guidelines for full-fee international marketing of education were specified in 1985, the following year overseas student entry procedures were streamlined to encourage education institutions to market their courses overseas on a full-cost basis. From the start the government determined that fee-based places would be additional to, rather than a substitute for, publicly funded domestic student places, also that there would be no subsidisation of market activities from public funds. This 'quarantining' of fee-based places meant that there would be no direct conflict between access for domestic students and international marketing.[18] Previous critics of the growth of international enrolments, such as Monash Engineering Dean Lance Endersbee (chapter 2), were happy to support the new policy.[19] Institutions now had a strong incentive to raise fee-paying student numbers as much as possible, winding down their involvement in the existing 'subsidised scheme' for international education. At first fees were regulated from Canberra and set at full-cost levels, including profit. Universities retained all the income generated.

By 1990 the economic market was the dominant form of international education, though some places were still subsidised for foreign aid reasons.[20] The fledgling export industry was underpinned by the government-supported International Development Program (IDP), education centres attached to the Australian embassies in Asian capitals, part-funded by the universities and coordinated by IDP, and grants under the Export Market Development Program.[21] The times favoured the international marketing of Australian education. The nations of East and Southeast Asia had fast-growing middle classes and domestic educational systems unable to provide for local demand. Malaysia had a slightly larger population than Australia, yet in 1991 there were only 62 113 students enrolled in its public universities, less than one-eighth the Australian total.[22] Demand for engineers in construction and related fields was at 10 times the domestically generated supply of places.[23] Chinese-Malaysian families experienced more restricted access to public universities than did Malays, and they had strong private motives to invest in education abroad. By 1991 there were 7294 Malaysian students in Australian universities, and a similar number in each of Britain, Canada and the USA. The Malaysian government supported international education because it augmented total public and private Malaysian investment in higher education, despite the loss of foreign exchange and the drain of part of the graduate labour force.

Though specific factors affected each home country market, Australia had a positive educational image through the region and was seen as a safe and healthy place to live. University education was if anything cheaper than in rival English-language countries. Australia's main drawback was that there was no particular field of study where its higher education was seen as superior to other countries. Nor were its individual universities as well known as Oxford or the American Ivy League. The USA was seen as stronger in business education, which constituted almost half the international market. But in Hong Kong, Singapore and Malaysia Australian universities were both close at hand and a valid substitute for British institutions. For Koreans Australian education was a second or third choice for students unable to access the highly competitive Korean universities or afford to study in America. On the other hand, in Indonesia the Australian universities had a strong reputation for quality and were often the first choice.[24]

In the early years total fee-paying enrolments in Australian higher education grew quickly, from 1019 in 1987, to 16 805 in 1990, to 35 182 in 1993. By 1996 there were 52 899 full-fee international students, and the Australian share of the world market had risen from 2 to 4 per cent. The main demand was for Business Education, followed by Science, Engineering and Computing. In 1994/95 fees and living costs of international students generated $1710 million for the Australian economy.[25]

Universities focused largely on onshore provision (i.e. education in Australia) rather than offshore provision. Much as in the Colombo Plan era, the main source countries were Malaysia, Singapore and Hong Kong, followed by Thailand and Indonesia. Newer markets were emerging in Taiwan and mainland China. The dominant role of Malaysia, Singapore and Hong Kong produced a relatively homogeneous group of international students who shared both Chinese culture and English-language schooling. Bicultural and cosmopolitan in background, they found it easier to handle the Anglo-Australian education system and social setting than did many others. Their capacity to bridge the gap between Southeast Asia and Australia masked the more difficult educational problems faced by students from other countries, such as Indonesia, and perhaps enabled universities to postpone a more fundamental internationalisation of curriculum, teaching methods and student services.

But the curriculum often remained unchanged: It was relatively easy to recruit international students in the context of growing demand and capacity to pay; it was harder to internationalise the curriculum.

TABLE 6.2 INTERNATIONAL STUDENTS AT MONASH, 1987–97

	Total international students	Full-fee-paying international students	Change in number of international students from previous year (%)
1987	1593	35	–
1988	1518	223	–4.7
1989	1450	424	–4.5
1990	NA	NA	–
1991	2912	2365	–
1992	4064	3770	+39.6
1993	4225	4120	+4.0
1994	4620	4508	+9.3
1995	5168	5126	+11.9
1996	5795	NA	+12.1
1997	6491	NA	+12.0

Source: Monash University statistics. NA means data not available.

Monash and the market

International marketing had the potential to both augment the University's income and drive its integration into the region. At the Professorial Board and Council, initial doubts were expressed, and marketing did not get into full swing until 1989. After that the growth of full-fee-based enrolments at Monash was faster than in the nation as a whole. The mergers boosted the number of fee-paying students: the Caulfield courses in Business and Computing had an international reputation in their own right, and Chisholm's post-arrival services were better than the norm. Gippsland brought with it international enrolments in distance education. Already by 1992 Monash had 4102 international students, according to Commonwealth statistics, the largest enrolment in Australia. UNSW with 3223 had the second largest. Monash also enjoyed a relatively high take-up rate on its offers of places to international students.[26]

If not all faculties were heavily involved in international marketing in the early years, it was a high priority in Business and Computing. Logan later remarked that international marketing released an unexpected commercial genie from the academic bottle:

> It's a funny thing about academics. When you lift the lid off them and deregulate them as Dawkins did with the international stuff, some of them just go crazy. They're really into it in a big way, very money-making oriented people. And that's something I never expected.[27]

At Monash there was less internal opposition than might have been expected. Perhaps the mergers were drawing the main fire of critics unhappy with the more entrepreneurial direction that the University was taking, while the income earned from the growing number of international students (Table 6.2) carried a force of argument of its own. The deans retained 70 per cent of the income generated by fee-paying international students, with 30 per cent flowing back to the University centre and used for marketing and support services.[28] In 1992 Monash's total export revenues were $41.2 million, of which $2.6 million came from offshore provision. In 1993 and after the University featured in *Australian Business Monthly*'s top 500 Australian exporters.[29]

From 1991 international students and their families in the main source countries were provided with offshore Monash graduation ceremonies. In August 1992 Logan reported to Council that in Kuala Lumpur there were 157 graduands from nine faculties, and another 61 graduands from six faculties in Singapore. November saw 210 graduands in Hong Kong. By 1995 there were almost 800 students at ceremonies in Kuala Lumpur, Hong Kong and Singapore; Singapore graduands were addressed by Professor Ang How Chee of the National University of Singapore. The University did the ceremonies 'in style' (Logan) and ensured that its leading officers were there.[30] At the same time it stepped up its networking efforts among Southeast Asian alumni. By 1993 there were 7000 Monash graduates in Malaysia alone, and all were seen as potential advocates for Monash's business interests and its contacts with government. In 1993 Logan announced that the University was setting up 'Monash societies' in Singapore, Indonesia, Hong Kong and Malaysia.[31]

The year before, the University had drawn up plans for future international marketing. Source countries were placed in three broad groups for strategic purposes. First, there were 'defensive strategies' to sustain enrolments in main source countries such as Malaysia. Second, there were developmental strategies in nations where there was substantial potential demand but the Monash intake was as yet relatively low, such as India, Thailand, Sri Lanka and the Middle East. (Indonesia fell between the first and second groups.) Developmental strategies included the creation of academic links designed to raise the University's profile, education exhibitions and school visits, and contact with government departments, as well as direct recruiting in course areas likely to

Offshore graduation ceremony. From 1991 onwards students in Singapore, Hong Kong and Kuala Lumpur could graduate at home with their families in attendance.

prove popular. Third, in Vietnam, Laos and Cambodia, potential demand for full-fee courses was low but there was scope to increase the number of subsidised students and establish long-term links with governments and educational institutions. There was strong interest in Vietnam, which was expected to become a 'tiger economy' in future. Through an initiative of Le Nguyen Binh in the Faculty of Engineering, the government of Vietnam asked Monash to provide advice on the possible development of a National University of Vietnam in Hanoi. In November 1993 Logan, Darvall and the Vice-Chancellor's adviser Elizabeth Anderson toured Vietnamese higher education, accompanied by Truong Truong of the University of NSW and BHP's Peter Laver, who was the Chair of the National Board of Employment, Education and Training. The delegation completed a report for the Vietnamese Ministry of Education and Training at the end of the trip.[32] It was hoped that this might lead to an ongoing role for the University in Vietnam, but there was no immediate follow-up.

Monash International

At first the University's efforts were not well coordinated, and sometimes not coordinated at all. Different campuses, courses and individuals pursued their own interests, using the Monash brand name. They were not always loyal to each other. In Business, Caulfield–Clayton rivalry was compounded by Gippsland independence. Gippsland sent its own people to Malaysia, who acted unilaterally: 'I never knew what they were doing' (Logan).[33]

Clearly a more disciplined approach was needed, without losing all the freedom of initiative facilitated by deregulation. In 1991, Leo West became Australia's first Pro-Vice-Chancellor for International Programs and Development,[34] and in July 1994 the administration of international programs was restructured as a corporation, Monash International P/L, 100 per cent owned by the University. The first Directors were Logan, Ramler, Wade, West, Chandler, Will Bailey of the ANZ Bank and former Minister for Industry, Visiting Professor at Monash and friend of the Vice-Chancellor, John Button.[35] The formation of Monash International did not abolish all the tensions between the sections of Monash engaged in international marketing, but it kept those tensions within bounds.

By 1996 there were almost 50 people employed in the Monash Caulfield office of Monash International, and a varying group worldwide. The company commissioned others on a consultancy basis at need, including John Dawkins, who had recently retired from politics when he worked for Monash International between November 1994 and January 1995. Monash International was now the University's main face outside Australia, particularly in East and Southeast Asia, and in this context its role was more than a commercial one. For example on 5 May 1995 Leo West received a letter from Angela Leach, an American student full of praise for the efforts of Monash International after she was injured on an excursion and needed special help. The company's role also extended to educational initiatives. The lead time for developing courses for international students could be shorter than the norm. The Vice-Chancellor explained in the *1994 Annual Report* that Monash International enabled 'greater flexibility in off-shore arrangements including the ability to move more quickly in finalising teaching programs and in negotiating memoranda of understanding with off-shore bodies',[36] though all courses were subject to the same ultimate faculty standards. Crucial to the success of Monash International was the calibre of its manager, Tony Pollock, recruited from the University of Melbourne in 1992.

Logan chaired both Monash International and the Academic Board, so he controlled relations between the commercial and educational drivers of decision-making. The structuring of Monash International as a separate company allowed it to be detached from the University at his convenience. Thus, when members of the Academic Board became concerned about the cost of offshore graduation ceremonies, Logan was determined to maintain the ceremonies so as to connect Monash to home country families. The cost was transferred to Monash International: no longer visible in the University budget, it was no longer a target for attacks.[37] Logan told *The Age* towards the end of his term in office that he had 'driven the Asian agenda pretty strongly in the personal sense . . . If we had argued it through all of the processes of the university, we might never have got it through'.[38]

Sometimes faculties found the strategies of Monash International to be restricting. Pharmacy wanted to tackle East Asia in a consortium with other Australian universities that had Pharmacy courses, not on its own, but this was not the Monash way.[39] Still, the payoffs were clear: in 1995 Business and Economics received $10 million from international students. The faculty was $12 million in surplus, which it was allowed to retain. Computing and Information Technology received $5 million from international students and had a surplus of $4 million. Even Arts took in $2 million.[40] In 1995 there were 5126 full-fee-paying international students at Monash, with 1926 at Clayton, 1515 at Caulfield, 1389 at Gippsland (mostly distance education students in Business and Nursing), 261 at Peninsula, and 35 in Pharmacy at Parkville. There were 2452 students in Business and Economics, 47.8 per cent of the total, some of whom were enrolled in combined courses. A total of 1012 were involved in Computing. More than half of all international students at Monash were women.[41] Hong Kong had taken over from Malaysia as the main source country. Singapore was second and Malaysia was third (Table 6.3).

The student body at Monash became more diverse in cultural terms. This was due not only to internationalisation but to the changing cultural composition of Australian citizen families as a result of immigration. In 1991, 29 per cent of all Monash students were born outside Australia. By 1996 this proportion had reached 36 per cent. There was little change in the number of students

TABLE 6.3 MONASH INTERNATIONAL STUDENTS, 1996, COUNTRY OF ORIGIN

Country of origin	Number of international students	Proportion of international students (%)*
Hong Kong	1622	28.0
Singapore	1428	24.6
Malaysia	1262	21.8
Indonesia	480	8.3
Sri Lanka	119	2.1
Thailand	96	1.7
Taiwan	86	1.5
Japan	78	1.3
China	67	1.2
India	59	1.0
South Korea	46	0.8
All other countries	452	7.8
Total	5795	100.0

* Rounded to one decimal place
Source: Monash University statistics.

born in Malaysia (1998 in 1996) but significant rises in the Hong Kong-born (2083), and those from Singapore (1535), Vietnam (915), Indonesia (566), China (536) and Sri Lanka (526). Those born in the UK fell from the third-largest to fifth-largest grouping. More 'Asianised' than Australian higher education as a whole, Monash was much more 'Asianised' than Australian society. In 1996, 24 per cent of all Monash students had been born in Asia and the Middle East. No fewer than 12 808 (30.8 per cent) of all Monash students came from homes where English was not the main language spoken, including 5646 (13.6 per cent) who spoke Cantonese, Mandarin, Hokkien or one of the other Chinese languages. Aside from English-speaking homes (28 735) the largest European language group was Greek (928).

From Monash to the world

Despite the growth in the number of onshore enrolments, the Vice-Chancellor regarded offshore activities as more significant to the global role of Monash in the longer term. He believed that in future Southeast Asian governments would expand national domestic capacity in higher education. Malaysia had already indicated this. Monash would need to mesh with these domestic systems in the region, becoming a partner in their evolution.[42]

Monash's offshore activities took several forms. The Monash University Foundation Year (MUFY) provided preparatory tuition for international students in English and in preparatory subjects for Monash courses. Though most of the

MUFY places were provided onshore in Australia, from 1992 a parallel program operated in Indonesia jointly with the University of NSW. The program in Indonesia led to 116 new Monash students in 1993, 139 in 1994, and another 160 in 1995. By the following year a Thailand-based MUFY was under discussion.[43] At the same time, the University was extending its 'twinning' arrangements with regional institutions. Early twinning partnerships had been created by Gippsland in distance education, and Chisholm, with business courses in Kuala Lumpur. Later, Monash established a stable partnership with Sunway College in Malaysia. Students enrolled for the first year of their Monash course in Malaysia, and then transferred to Australia for the remainder. Sunway had a similar association with four universities in Australia, and others in New Zealand, the United Kingdom and the USA. The Monash–Sunway partnership proved fruitful. In April 1995 Dato Dr Jeffrey Cheah Fook Ling, head of the SungeiWay Group of companies in Malaysia and founder of Sunway College, was awarded an honorary Monash doctorate.[44] The University was increasingly

Sunway College. Monash's 'twinning' partner in Kuala Lumpur in Malaysia and the foundation stone for later offshore developments.

active in China. Monash Mt Eliza provided short non-degree courses for metal industry executives. Monash worked with the Australian government-funded agencies Ausaid and Austrade to bring business education to Beijing and Shanghai. It was planned to offer parallel streams in Mandarin and English, leading to Chinese and Australian qualifications respectively.

The ultimate objective was to develop branch campuses of the University outside Australia. The creation of a Monash campus in Malaysia became a high priority.[45] First floated by Bob Baxt as Dean of Law in 1985, under Ray Martin ('I just got absolutely nowhere'), the prospect engaged Logan from the beginning of his term in office.[46] For the Malaysian government, the issues were complex. It wanted to stem the drain of foreign exchange in education and develop higher education in Malaysia itself, both to facilitate national economic development and cultural maintenance in a globalising world and to enable Malaysia itself to become a significant exporter of education. From Malaysia's viewpoint, a Monash campus could assist local economic and educational development. At the same time, its cultural character was a sensitive issue. On visits to Malaysia, Logan talked about the potential for Monash–Malaysian cooperation to help meet Malaysian objectives. In a speech before a distinguished audience in Kuala Lumpur in January 1994, he talked up education as a factor in regional economies. Here, he suggested, there was a vacuum to be filled. 'Just why Singapore . . . has not become the educational hub of ASEAN is something of a mystery to me', he stated. Then a page or so later:

> It is not impossible for Malaysia to seize the opportunity to establish itself as the educational hub of the ASEAN region; nor is it impossible to see the twinning arrangements already established with Australian universities as providing the launching-pad for such a pre-eminent position.[47]

After a preliminary announcement in 1991, the Malaysian government announced in 1993 that it would entertain applications from international universities to establish branch campuses. Monash's proposal for a Malaysian campus was developed in conjunction with the SungeiWay Group. Progression of the application was slow, but in January 1996 the Clayton newsheet *Etcetera* reported that a memorandum of understanding had been signed in Malaysia, witnessed by the Australian Prime Minister.[48]

In Laos, the University purchased 30 per cent equity in an English-language college. The college was used also for vocational education, in Laos a more pressing need than higher education.[49] There was talk about a degree-providing university in Laos, a Monash campus in South Africa, and a private university in Thailand. Much energy went into plans for a private university in Indonesia in conjunction with local business.[50]

From the world to Monash

Logan hoped that the links with Southeast Asian countries formed through twinning and international distance education would encourage curriculum change in Australia, leading to a more thoroughgoing form of internationalisation affecting all Monash students. Rather optimistically, he told the Pacific Rim University Presidents Conference in 1990:

> With these developments will come a change in the nature and content of courses. Courses in Australian universities, for example, have traditionally given greater attention to Western culture and development of ideas. This is beginning to change and will continue to do so. I do not just mean that we will have more Asian studies and Asian languages. I mean that history, literature, music, medicine, science, engineeering, law, indeed all disciplines will as a matter of course give appropriate attention to Asian perspectives and culture. The reverse will be true in Asian universities with respect to Australia.[51]

In this deeper practice of internationalisation, teaching would be adjusted to embrace a diversity of learning styles.[52] The manner in which international education (especially offshore education) evolved as a corporate operation at Monash, partly separated from the normal academic life of the rest of the University, probably inhibited spontaneous cross-cultural fertilisation. The University's managers partly compensated for this by driving a selective Asianisation of curricula at Monash direct from the University centre. In 1988 an Institute of Contemporary Asian Studies was opened to capitalise on the University's strengths in Asian studies, largely centred on the Arts Faculty. It was hoped the Institute would encourage Asian-related courses and research in Economics and elsewhere, and become a resource for government and business.[53] In 1991 the Monash Asia Institute was established. Under Director John Mackay its role was to coordinate interdisciplinary teaching and research activities in Asian studies, encourage the inclusion of Asia as 'a normal reference' in all disciplines, manage exchanges with universities in Asia, assist Monash students and staff wishing to study and research in Asian countries, and develop specialist Asian-focused centres at the University. These included the Development Studies Centre, the Centre of East Asian Studies, the Japanese Studies Centre, the Centre of Malaysian Studies, the Centre of South Asian Studies, and the Centre for Southeast Asian Studies. Monash was part of a consortium in the National Key Centre for Korean Studies.

Monash maintained one of the world's best Southeast Asia-focused library collections, and study tours, research projects, guest lectures and seminars in relation to the study of Asian countries grew.[54] The University offered courses in Japanese, Korean, Mandarin, Cantonese, Hindi, Thai, Vietnamese, Lao, Khmer, Bahasa Indonesian and Bahasa Malay. Language students spent a semester in the home country of the language of study: $650 000 was allocated to this program in 1994. A growing number enrolled in Engineering–Arts and Business–Arts courses in order to gain access to language study.

Nevertheless, the University's leaders were concerned that, despite the great growth of international student enrolments, few Australian students had corresponding experiences. Student exchange programs were on a small scale. Compared with French or American students, Australian students lacked the capacity 'to shoot over to another culture for a semester or a long vacation' (Wade). Yet a period of international study was often an advantage to young graduates applying for jobs. The University's leaders began to think that there might be an emerging market in study abroad: if so, Monash should attempt to obtain first-mover advantage. It was hoped the creation of offshore campuses in Malaysia and elsewhere would provide one medium in which domestic students could experience international education. The focus would not necessarily be regional, as domestic students might prefer Europe or North America: 'We have to think globally rather than regionally' (Wade).[55] But the area remained underdeveloped.

Links to international universities expanded and diversified. In the late 1980s, as earlier in the decade (chapter 2), the schedule of student and staff exchange agreements was modest, and largely focused on American institutions. In 1989 it included only the University of California, the most active arrangement, the University of Illinois, the University of Waterloo, the University of British Columbia, Rikkyo University and the Free University of Berlin. A new agreement with the Indonesian Universitas Gadjah Mada was signed during the course of the year, but the agreements with the universities of Nanjing and Chengdu were inactive due to the cost of servicing them.[56] However, in May 1990 Council endorsed Logan's view that the University needed to identify a small group of universities with which it wanted to develop links, with an emphasis on leading universities in Hong Kong, Korea and Indonesia. Events began to move more rapidly. In December 1992 Logan reported to Council that in January 1993 he would visit 15 Chinese universities in five days to conclude exchange agreements. By 1994 there were formal cooperative agreements with 50 overseas institutions, including very active staff exchange with Gadjah Mada University in Indonesia, the University of Indonesia, and Prince Songkla University of Thailand.[57]

Relations with Europe and North America were also moving. At the Australian end there was the Centre for European Studies at Clayton. At the global end, the University supported Australian Studies centres at the University of London, Potsdam University in Germany, and Georgetown University in the USA. The Potsdam centre was backed by the Brandenburg government and by

Boral and Siemens, major German companies with Australian connections. 'The hierarchical conservative structure of the German universities' created some difficulties, Logan told Council in December 1993.[58]

Results and prospects

The annual *Good Universities Guide* ran a 'University of the Year' contest 'to recognise and publicise outstanding efforts to improve the quality of undergraduate education'. The focus for the award changed year by year. In 1994 it was internationalisation, with emphasis on the Asia-Pacific Region. The criteria were the number of international students, and the quality of educational and other services provided to them; offshore programs; programs enabling domestic students to study and work abroad; and, 'above all, the extent and quality of opportunities for undergraduates to develop a genuinely international and cosmopolitan perspective'. West and Logan (by now President of the Board of IDP) documented Monash's activities with care. The University won.

The *Good Universities Guide* found 'Monash is exceptional in being at or near the cutting edge in all four areas'. The extent of 'Asianisation' of the curriculum stood out, as did the University's $43 million in export income in 1993. The *Guide* also emphasised the cosmopolitan character of the Monash campuses:

> The Japan Times classifieds, offering vacation employment in Tokyo, are pinned to the careers office notice-board. In the union buildings a board outside the sizeable travel agency offers bargain flights to every Asian capital, and the Asian food bar has the longest queues. With more than 2500 local NESB (non-English speaking background) students as well as the 4500 internationals. Asian, African, Mediterranean and Melanesian faces are everywhere. Over the lunch break students browse the South China Morning Post, the Singapore Straits Times and the Bangkok Post. Cross-cultural couples cuddle in the lounges. German exchange student Berndt Meyer, at Monash for less than a semester, wonders at the extraordinary mix of a student body speaking more than 80 languages ranging from Brunei and Burma to Taiwan and Vietnam (and even one from Mongolia). He and 1300 others live in on-campus halls of residence where proportions of internationals and locals are carefully regulated, right down to decisions about who gets rooms next to whom.[59]

'University of the Year' status was very helpful. Marketing director Gary Neat and his colleagues spread the news energetically through the Southeast

Asian media. A 12-minute video 'targeting prospective international students' was also prepared.[60]

The core objective of the Monash internationalisation strategy was to establish the University as a significant educational-corporate presence in the countries of Australia's geographical region. By the mid-1990s this objective had been achieved. As a provider of places for international students, Monash was the national leader, though the RMIT sometimes exceeded Monash's numbers, and the University of NSW was stronger in postgraduate education, which was likely to become an increasingly important aspect of Australia's educational role in the global market. Monash was the best-known Australian university in Malaysia, and probably in the region as a whole. In terms of long-term potential, Monash's offshore presence and the beginnings of the internationalisation of the curriculum in Australia were important. Monash had avoided the mistake made by some Australian universities of placing too much emphasis on the immediate commercial returns. As Logan put it, universities had to 'genuinely engage in the region':[61]

> The relationship we have with the region is a fragile one. It cannot be built on trade alone, and on the cult of 'short-termism' that characterises so much of our thinking. Trust is all important and it is based on long term relationships.[62]

In the next decade and beyond, internationalisation would be more challenging. Greater cultural diversity of approach would be required. Given their population size, China, India and Indonesia were home to the most important emerging markets: in those countries the bulk of the hard work was still to be done, and Australian universities would need to become more competent in languages other than English. Towards the end of his term Logan expressed frustration at the slow rate of developments in Indonesia, and also in Korea; though because of MUFY in Indonesia, the University's capacity in Asian languages and the success of its business courses, it was better prepared than most.

Future developments in international education would be determined not only by the efforts of Monash, but also by the larger political, economic and cultural setting. In 1996, following a change of government in Australia, spending on programs to promote international education links was cut by more than a third and Canberra withdrew support from the Australian International Education Foundation, an industry–government partnership for the generic promotion of educational exports.[63] More seriously, the campaigns of maverick politician Pauline Hanson and others against Asian immigration and other manifestations of globalisation threatened to undermine the work of Monash and other universities. On the eve of retirement, Logan warned that the only thing which could destroy the momentum for the internationalisation of education was 'a developing perception in Asia, which has resurfaced in recent times, about Australia being ethnically an uncomfortable place to live'. This was 'an enormous threat'.[64]

Ethnic tension was not a problem at Monash itself. The level of tolerance was so high that it became taken for granted. The early 1980s Clayton debate about the 'balance' between the numbers of Asian and Australian students had faded. Not only was international marketing structured so as to avoid direct conflict over places, there were now many Australian citizen students from families with Asian origins. The old distinctions that had sustained that debate in the early 1980s were disappearing and were not going to return.[65] There were still cultural barriers between international students and many local students, but they were lower than they had been, and there was more mixing than before.

The full potential of internationalisation was yet to become manifest. The distribution of international students was skewed towards Business and Economics and Computing (in Engineering the international student presence was significant, but less than in the early 1980s), and Clayton and Caulfield. In research, collaboration with colleagues in North America, the UK and Europe was much stronger than in Asian countries, despite the progress of basic research in Singapore and Taiwan.[66] These factors did not diminish the achievement. In the decade after 1986 Monash had gone global. It was probably the most important aspect of the remaking of the University. It was also an unequivocal 'win–win' outcome for everyone, in contrast with the more two-sided experience of the mergers.

The new educational technologies

By the early 1990s the global potential of new information and communications technologies in education was becoming apparent. The personal computer and the modem enabled departments at Monash to link directly via e-mail with students, to collaborate instantaneously with universities around the world, and to maintain more effective contact with alumni. Technically it was now possible for the University to issue electronic bulletins to all staff and students with e-mail access, to conduct interactive teaching and electronic meetings, to provide course materials via the Internet, and to maintain an electronic library. Computer-based simulation enabled a range of new research and learning tools. The new potentials for management included direct marketing of courses to potential students, business networking on a global basis, the tracking of financial transactions and speedy up-to-the-minute balance sheets, better cost control and risk management, and the accumulation of performance data on staff and departments. Technologies such as broad-band multimedia, satellite transmission, videoconferencing and CD-ROM also had a range of educational and administrative applications.

The promise of the new technologies was flexibility of time and location. They made possible a variety of alternatives to traditional face-to-face teaching, for both the University as 'producer' of education and the student as 'consumer'. There was distance learning via broadcast media (radio and television) and by e-mail, and the prospect of 'virtual university' courses, whereby all course materials could become available on-line and assessment conducted electronically on an interactive basis. A 1995 Commonwealth report, *Converging technologies*, noted that interactivity is central to learning. It 'enables the learner to self-direct research, respond, question, interrogate and collaborate instantly over long distances'.[67] For example, using the Internet enabled students to more freely explore learning sources and to directly interrogate staff at need by e-mail, even to design their own educational programs from the electronic services on offer. Students might come to see university not so much as an induction into the mysteries of didactic knowledge but as a set of tools for that student's own vocational and academic projects. Potentially, the teacher–student relationship itself could change, especially in postgraduate and work-based learning. Universities could use electronically based distance education techniques even with their face-to-face students. At the same time, in distance education, universities faced potential competition from other electronic providers.

The implications for international education were immense. When students could be reached directly on-line, it was no longer so essential to bring them to Australia or to rely on twinning or franchising with home country institutions, providing telecommunications and computing were in place. While learning on-site would still be valued because of its effects in developing the person and in forming personal and professional networks, electronic learning opened the potential for vast new international markets in postgraduate and continuing education. For example, universities could provide their professional alumni with regular upgrading courses.

At Monash there was much discussion of the potential of the new technologies. *Directions for the future* (1995) positioned the University as a technological leader: Monash 'was now embracing electronic learning as the most effective means of teaching nationally through a network of campuses', and 'a fundamental part of the University's policy agenda into the next century'. *Directions* foresaw a big role for the virtual university, and saw electronic learning as the means whereby students could mix and match course options from the different Monash campuses.[68] Actual practice fell far short of these grand visions. Virtual universities were some way off. The remaking of courses in electronic form was a matter for faculties and departments, but as yet students had taken to the new technologies more quickly than staff. In practice,

The digital revolution. Communications and information technologies created a new potential in off-campus learning.

the achievement of Monash's technological potential depended on the development of distance education modes and open learning, and distance education at Gippsland was still largely print-based. And in common with other universities Monash found it difficult to negotiate agreements with major publishers and broadcasters, not least because of the tradition that individual academics owned their own intellectual property rights in articles and textbooks. The only curriculum materials the University could confidently claim as its own were study guides and coursenotes.[69]

Distance education

Distance had always been profoundly important in shaping Australian life, yet the distance education mode never became as strong as in some other parts of the world. This was a function of the high level of urbanisation of 20th century Australia, and the decision to provide all students in the cities with face-to-face education. In 1991 there were 56 922 external students in Australian higher education, 10.6 per cent of all students, spread between many institutions. On a world scale Australian distance education was small. In 1995 worldwide there were 10 publicly supported distance education institutions with 100 000-plus enrolments, including China's TV University, with 530 000 students in degree programs alone. The Korean National University also used videoconferencing, cable TV and some computer-mediated communication in reaching its 196 000 students. The UK Open University with 150 000 students, an important provider of access, was more sophisticated and cost-efficient than the distance education centres at any Australian university.[70] It also offered more face-to-face options than these Australian operators could muster.

Technically, distance education had evolved through three phases. The first phase was correspondence courses conducted through the post. In the second phase radio and TV broadcasts, and multimedia such as audiotapes and videotapes, were used to supplement printed materials. In the third phase (in the early 1990s it was more a potential phase than an actual phase) satellite delivery, e-mail and on-line courses came into the picture, and the potential for interactivity and student-directed learning emerged. The advent of the third phase meant that all existing distance education providers had to reinvent themselves, technologically, pedagogically and also economically, for it was possible to be cost-efficient at a much lower number of students than before, opening up the field to greater competition.[71] The third phase also brought with it an enhanced potential for combining distance techniques with on-campus learning techniques. In Australia a growing number of courses were provided in both modes, with on-campus students drawing on the resources provided in distance mode.

On-campus students found printed course materials useful, and there was potential to make general use of e-mail and Internet-based document delivery, with the choice of either printing out the document or reading it on screen.

The *1958 Monash University Act* sanctioned the University's involvement in distance education, but it was not until the 1988 Monash–Gippsland bid for distance education status that this became a reality.[72] After the merger, distance enrolments at Gippsland doubled in less than three years—the Monash name made a difference—and by 1994 there were 6171 students: 1017 international, 3396 from Victoria and 1758 from elsewhere in Australia. Most of the Victorian students were from the east of the State. On the western side Deakin was dominant, except in Science and Engineering, which it did not provide.[73] Under John Harris, who succeeded John Evans as director of the Distance Education Centre in 1992,[74] $350 000 was spent on desktop publishing and graphic design. Funds for new technologies were slower in coming. There was high unmet demand: people at Gippsland estimated they could have enrolled up to 10 times as many students if the funded places were made available within Monash's overall student load.[75]

From 1994 the Commonwealth abandoned its policy of supporting a small number of distance education centres, instead favouring the development of mixed-mode delivery in all institutions.[76] Two years later, 60 Monash award course were in distance education mode, largely concentrated at Churchill, where most courses were provided in dual mode, on-campus students received distance learning materials free of charge, and there were 540 'mixed-mode' students.[77] Logan talked about distance education, but the faculties at Clayton were mostly unmoved, and both the faculties and the University's leaders were more focused on open learning.[78] Unlike distance education, open learning was organised in a company structure controlled by the leadership group at Clayton. They believed that open learning offered the best potential for creating prototypes for the virtual university, enabling Monash to secure a first-mover advantage in future electronic developments.[79]

Some Caulfield Business courses were offered by distance, and there was Nursing by distance mode at Peninsula and Gippsland. The only distance courses at Clayton were in Social Work and the Centre for Bioethics. Distance courses in Science, Computing, Engineering, Arts and Education were confined to Gippsland.[80] It seemed that while the concentration of distance education at Gippsland had provided that campus with a distinctive role, it had also marginalised the development of the distance mode itself, especially in the form of international delivery where there was huge potential. At Clayton there was concern that international distance education would choke off the growth of onshore international education. It should have been possible to develop distance education alongside onshore and offshore face-to-face education, exploiting the potential for greater flexibility, with students moving between the modes during course life. Instead the growth of distance education was restricted, and the mode was little promoted by Monash International. These restrictions began to lift only in the mid-1990s.[81]

Open learning

Open learning evolved in Australia as a particular form of distance education that was characterised by the use of broadcast media and designed to provide open access to tertiary education. Courses were much cheaper than conventional distance education ($305 per subject in 1996) and there were no prerequisites or quotas. Anyone, no matter what their educational background, could enrol in the open learning course of their choice. Students who passed two open learning units became automatically eligible for entry to conventional degree programs. In Australia open learning was conceived in 1991 by the Labor Minister for Higher Education, Peter Baldwin, as a pilot TV-based open learning project with courses in Australian Studies, the Environment, Anthropology, French, Marketing, Religious Studies and Statistics. Monash and four other universities were involved. The programs were provided on free-to-air TV, while students paid for study materials and formal assessment. Monash staff played a crucial role in a number of these television productions, including units on marketing (Peter Chandler and Sally Joy) and the 13-part 'Out of empire' series in which Peter Spearritt and colleagues tackled the decline of the British monarchy and the rise of republicanism.

In the pilot year 5453 students bought open learning study materials, and the Commonwealth government committed itself to a larger initiative in the 1992/93 budget, allocating $52 million for the next three years to subsidise student enrolments and finance an open learning agency to act as broker between students and the universities providing courses.[82] A number of university consortia formed to bid for these funds, and the Monash-led group won the tender.

On 18 January 1993 the government appointed the Open Learning Agency of Australia (OLAA) as broker to implement the open learning strategy. The company was established and owned by Monash, but included representatives of Deakin, the University of New England, Griffith University Queensland, the University of South Australia, Curtin, the University of Southern Queensland and Charles Sturt University on its board.[83] Tony Pritchard was seconded from the post of Registrar at Clayton to become managing director of OLAA. Enrolments began in March 1993, in 31 undergraduate-level courses, which took the form of 13-week units. In 1994, 9057 students enrolled in a total of 22 508 of these open learning units between them. The absence of prerequisites and quotas was particularly helpful to older people. Almost two-thirds of OLAA students were aged over 25 years, compared with one-quarter of other students.[84] There was less staff contact than with conventional distance education, but students could buy one-to-one assistance on a telephone basis.

The number of undergraduate units grew quickly, and graduate programs also developed. All provided printed materials, the majority were in broadcast mode, and some had an interactive electronic component. In some the print materials were as extensive as for orthodox distance education courses; in others there were no readings, just a unit study guide. By 1997 eight universities provided degree courses, and shareholding in the company had been broadened from Monash to include ANU, RMIT, the Universities of Queensland and South Australia, Curtin, Griffith and Macquarie. Monash itself provided about half the units altogether, in 90 subjects in 1996 in Business and Economics, Computing, Engineering, Science and Arts. Often departments took to open learning more readily than to orthodox distance programs; a number with no previous distance education experience developed good open learning units, such as Spanish and Philosophy. The first OLAA graduate finished his business degree at Monash in December 1996, completing it in the same time as an on-campus student while working full-time as a bank officer in Queensland. Many students moved from open learning to distance education, highlighting the new flexibilities while slowing enrolments in open learning.[85]

Student servicing was shared by the academic departments and Gippsland, with Gippsland handling copyright services, the storage and dispatch of study materials, initial student liaison, and assignment tracking services. It was hoped Gippsland's expertise in distance education could be swung into open learning. But negotiations failed to reach an understanding on costs.[86] Clearly the solution was to integrate the management of the two areas, but by the end of Logan's term in office in February 1997 it still had not happened.[87] Ironically, the distance between Clayton and Churchill was still difficult to bridge. The technological preconditions had been created for an integrated university, in instantaneous contact with itself, but it seemed that the organisational and cultural preconditions had not. The velocity of technological change had exceeded that of the merger process.

Plate 1 **All smiles, but . . .** Staff and students from the Monash Orientation Scheme for Aborigines (MOSA). It was often hard for MOSA and the Koorie Research Centre working at the edge of the mega-university, which sympathised but did not always understand.

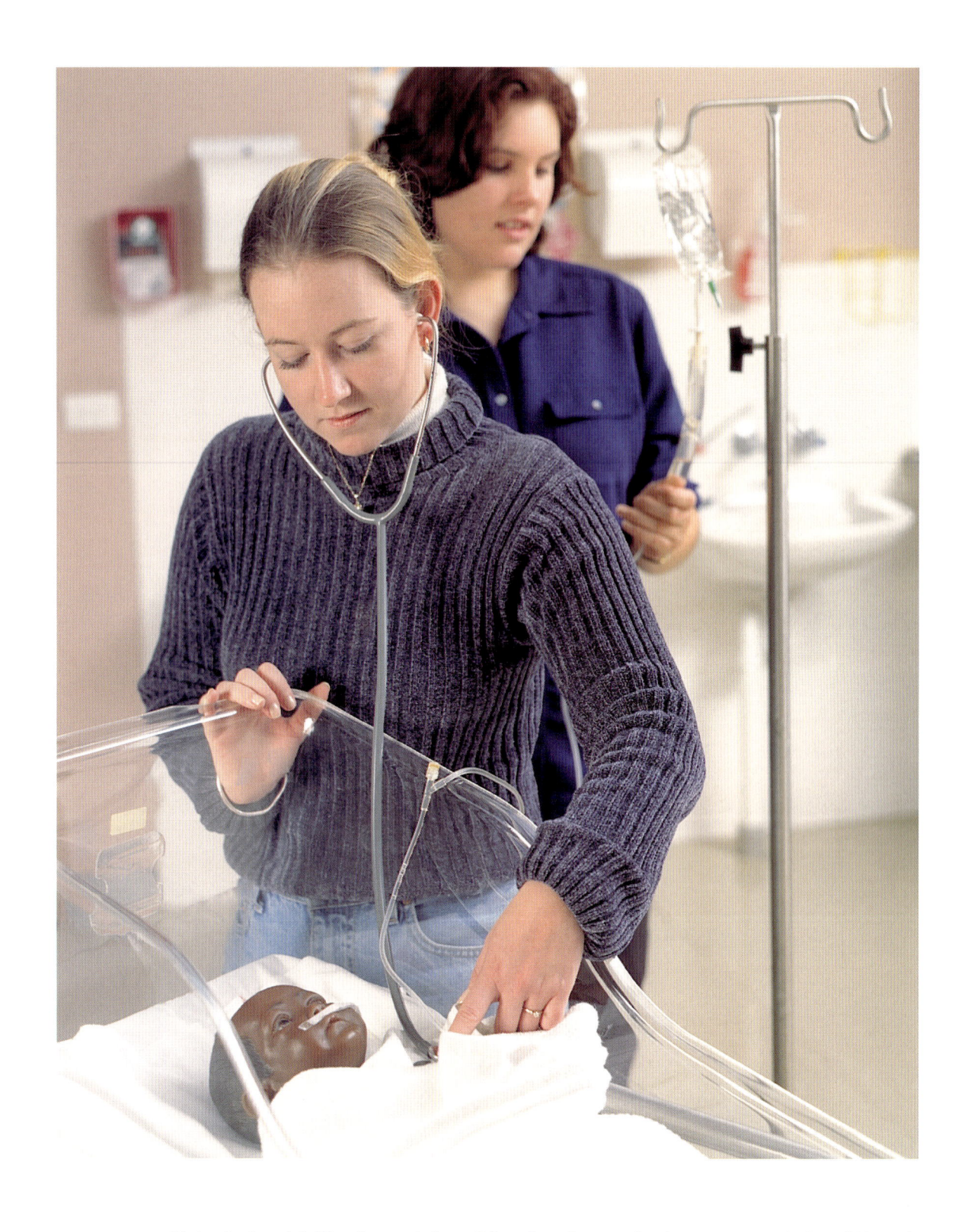

Plates 2, 3 and 4 **The rise and rise of female science.** By the 1990s a majority of Monash medical students were women, and female numbers had increased significantly even in the traditionally male-only Engineering faculty

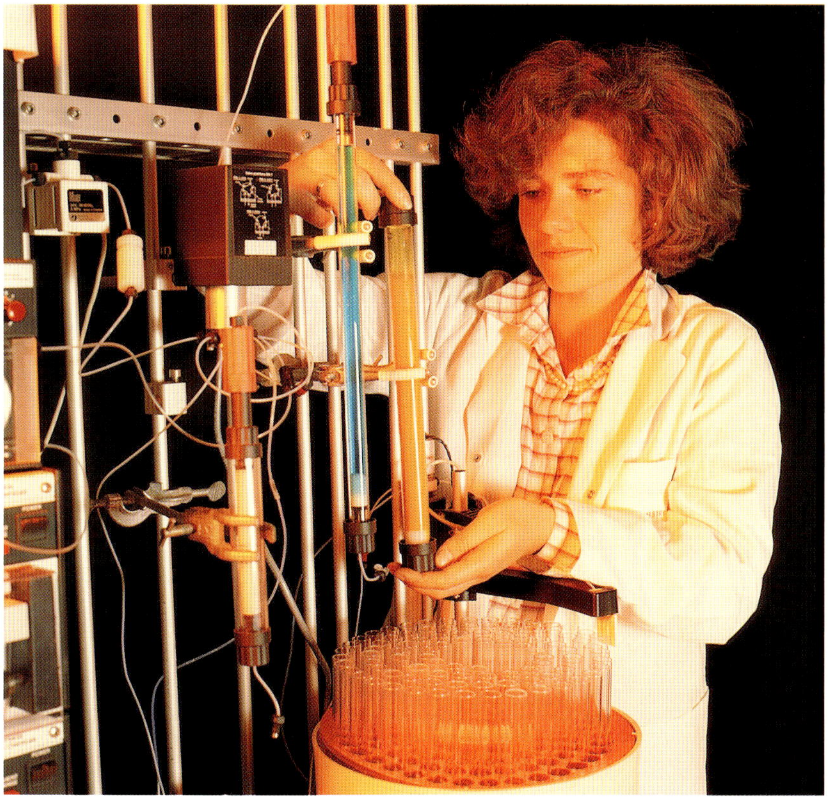

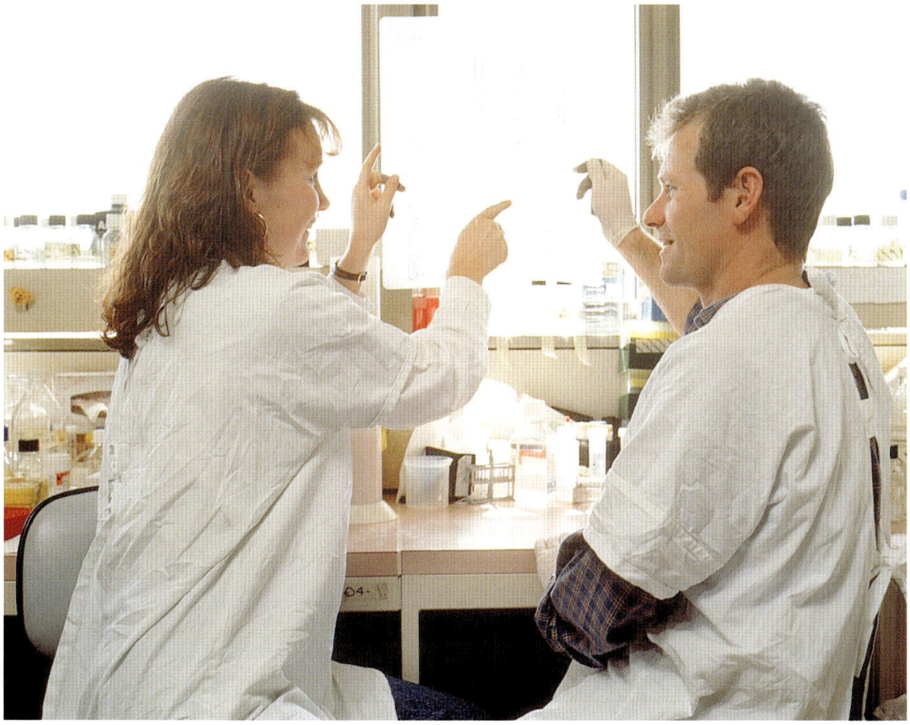

Plates 5 and 6 **Many cultures, one university, global reach.** By 1996 there were 5795 international students and 31 per cent of all students were from homes where English was not the main language spoken, creating new educational potentials and challenges.

Plates 7 and 8 **Time to talk:** as the graduate labour market deteriorated in the early 1990s the mood on campus became more vocational, but there was always time for friendship.

Plates 9 and 10 **Not by bread alone.** When art, music and literature are absent, said John Monash, 'to that extent is our vision and outlook limited and cramped'.

Plates 11 and 12 **A sound priority:** the opening of the Performing Arts Building at Clayton in 1996 was a great boost to Music, which had suffered in the Menzies Building from lack of space. Monash was unusual among Australian universities in the priority placed on the arts.

Plate 13 **Not bad for a practice venue:** the Music auditorium in Performing Arts seated 250 people. There was a lunchtime concert on most days of the week. The Australian Broadcasting Corporation and many other community groups used the Monash facilities.

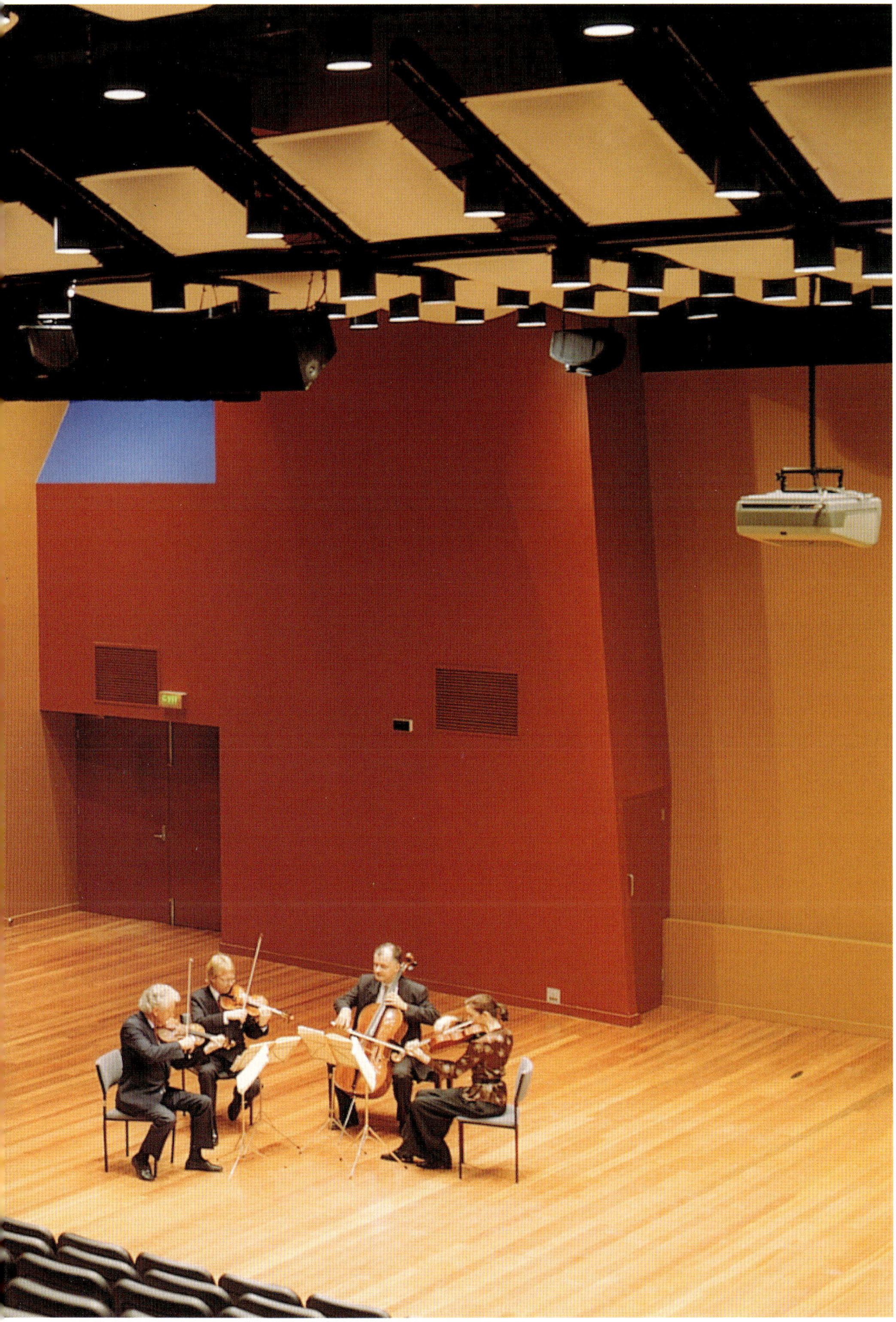

Plates 14 and 15 **Good buildings are possible after all.** The exterior of Performing Arts, painted in the colours of the Australian landscape, blended with the native plantings at Clayton. It was much the best of the 1990s constructions at Clayton.

Plates 16 and 17 **Pushing out the boundaries:** the Berwick campus, in the far east of suburban Melbourne, opened to students in 1995. Located on the site of the old Casey airport, the striking main building evoked an airport terminal.

Plates 18 and 19 **Renovator's delight:** the Caroline Chisholm School of Nursing and the student union at Peninsula. At the renovated Frankston campus native plantings and raw modern buildings created a 'Claytonesque' feel, but more coherent and attractive.

Plates 20 and 21 **Closer to the action.** In 1959 contenders for the Monash site were Clayton and the Caulfield racecourse. The merger with Chisholm Institute of Technology in 1990 finally brought the University to Caulfield, halfway to the Melbourne city centre.

Plate 22 **Regional leader.** After the privatisation of the State Electricity Commission and the loss of 10 000 jobs, the Monash Gippsland campus at Churchill became the chief employer and *de facto* civic leader of the La Trobe Valley region in eastern Victoria.

Plates 23, 24 and 25 **Diversity of purposes, variety of styles**: (*top*) the entrance lobby at 30 Collins Street in the central business district of Melbourne. (*lower*) The French window at the west end of the Robert Blackwood Hall and the Gallery Building, both at Clayton.

Plate 26 **Regional presence**. The Japanese garden at Clayton. Like the University of NSW and the Australian National University in Canberra, the other 'second wave' universities founded between 1945 and 1960, Monash emphasised East and Southeast Asian Studies from the early years.

Greater Monash

7

Hobbs that afternoon, backed by his brigadiers, anxiously drew attention to the strain on his troops. 'I was compelled to harden my heart', Monash later wrote, 'and to insist that it was imperative to recognise a great opportunity and to seize it unflinchingly'.

The capture of Mont St Quentin, Western Front 30 August 1918, Geoffrey Serle,
John Monash: a biography, Melbourne University Press, Melbourne, 1982, p. 355

Monash everywhere

In the first semester 1990 there were 15 894 students. Five years later there were 40 837, and Monash was educating 6.5 per cent of all higher education students in Australia and almost one in four (23.3 per cent) in Victoria. The next-largest universities were Melbourne with 17.9 per cent and RMIT with 15.3 per cent. Monash Clayton had become Greater Monash.

Perceptions of the University were reshaped by its new and aggressive magnitude. 'New universities are opening all over the country', ran one joke in the wake of the Dawkins-induced changes to higher education, 'and most of them are called Monash'. The State government might have heard the same joke, because when the municipal boundaries in the Melbourne metropolitan area were redrawn in 1994 part of the Glen Waverley and Oakleigh districts were combined into a new City of Monash.

In truth, Greater Monash *was* several universities. It was an international university and a Victorian State university; and within the State it had more than one role. In the inner eastern region, with a school-leaver participation index of 42.2 at the beginning of the 1990s, it competed with Melbourne as a university for the privileged and the middle classes. It also provided access in the Mornington Peninsula (17.5), the outer east (20.0) and Gippsland, regions where participation rates were among the lowest levels in the State.[1] Monash–Gippsland was attended by nearly 50 per cent of higher education students

TABLE 7.1   MONASH STUDENTS BY SEX, 1988–97*

	Women	Men	Total persons	Growth in total from previous year (%)	Women as a proportion of all students (%)
1988	7 305	7 463	14 768	–	49.5
1989	7 427	7 420	14 847	+0.2	50.0
1990	7 948	7 946	15 894	–	50.0
1991	16 395	16 401	32 796	+106.3	50.0
1992	17 496	17 424	34 920	+6.5	50.1
1993	18 551	17 916	36 467	+4.4	50.9
1994	19 816	19 146	38 962	+6.8	50.9
1995	21 373	19 464	40 837	+4.8	52.3
1996	22 246	19 297	41 543	+1.7	53.5
1997	22 651	19 393	42 044	+1.2	53.9

* Number of enrolments as at the annual census date in the first semester. In 1990 there was a change in the compilation method. The data for 1989 and 1990 are not strictly comparable.

Source: Monash University statistics.

from Gippsland, and also provided distance education for students throughout Victoria and Australia.

The mergers changed the character of the student body as well as its size. With the old CAE sector providing half the post-1990 Monash students, the weight of part-time and external students increased and that of research higher-degree students declined. In 1987, 73.1 per cent of the students at Clayton were full-time, but in 1995 only 55.0 per cent of all Monash students were full-time, with 17.2 per cent external. At Gippsland, where external studies was centred, almost half of the student body was aged 30 years or over, compared to less than a quarter of students at Clayton, Caulfield and Peninsula. In 1987 the proportion of Clayton students enrolled in Masters or PhD programs was 17.1 per cent, but in 1995 it was only 13.3 per cent, despite the system-wide growth of postgraduate study. The number of students in research degrees doubled, but the number of undergraduates rose three times. The proportion of students who were women rose slowly to 52.3 per cent in 1995 (Table 7.1). The long-term trend to female enrolment in higher education had been partly cancelled out by the more masculinist composition of the CAEs that merged with Clayton.

The balance between fields of study also altered. In the two years before the 1990 Act there were substantial increases in student load in Economics, Arts and Engineering, slower changes in Law, Education and Medicine, and not much change in Science at all. After 1990 the mergers brought sizable growth to faculties directly affected, especially Business, Engineering and Education (Table 7.2). Business and Economics continued to expand in the 1990s,

TABLE 7.2 STUDENT LOAD BY FACULTY, 1986–97

	Eco/B	Arts	Science	Health	IT	Engin.	Educ.	Law	Pharm.	T&R	Total
1986	2207	2739	2378	1533	–	945	775	947	–	–	11 523
1987	2278	2869	2582	1592	–	932	746	1002	–	–	12 001
1988	2537	3109	2634	1658	–	990	787	1059	–	–	12 774
1989	2853	3224	2620	1680	–	1059	728	1012	–	–	13 176
1990	3054	3502	2663	1701	–	1168	823	1149	–	–	14 060
1991	6324	6340	3705	2599	2055	2260	1763	1287	–	26	26 359
1992	6824	6220	3632	2959	2029	2593	1743	1354	–	13	27 366
1993	6918	6114	3510	2993	2515	2676	1713	1423	428	21	28 311
1994	7239	6426	3467	2831	2688	2599	1584	1388	429	30	28 681
1995	7672	6537	3803	3002	2840	2520	1716	1387	427	34	29 938
1996	8173	5889	3554	3117	3109	2437	1644	1428	422	61	30 699
1997	8358	6003	3435	3104	3319	2463	1636	1396	459	40	31 072
Increase 90–97 (%)	173.7	171.4	30.0	182.5	–	110.9	198.8	21.5	–	–	122.1

Note: While Gippsland enrolments were formally separate from those of the faculties in 1991, here they have been distributed according to their faculties-to-be, unlike Table 6.2. The 1986–97 series is not consistent in all faculties. For example, Economics and Politics (1986–90) split into Economics, which went with Chisholm Business Studies to eventually form Business and Economics, and Politics which went to the post-merger Arts Faculty. Computing took place before the formation of the Computing and IT faculty, but was located in other faculties such as Science. For more discussion of these and other changes, see text.
Eco/B = Economics, Commerce, Management and Business courses. IT = Computing.
T&R = teaching and research centres. Health includes Medicine and Nursing.

Source: Monash University statistics, various years. These data have been collated on a different basis from those in Table 2.3, which includes some double-counting.

and student load in Computing also rose sharply. There was slower growth in Arts and Engineering, while the student load in each of Science and Education fell every year from 1991 to 1994. Law dropped from fifth-largest faculty to eighth. After 1993 the Law faculty decided not to expand further (see chapter 9).

Staff numbers expanded along with the growth in the student body. By 1995 there were 3163 effective full-time academic staff and 1618 staff in other capacities.[2] The proportion of academic staff who were women at 31 per cent in 1991 was similar to the female ratio for higher education as a whole. The upper and lower levels of the academic hierarchy were divided on gender lines. The proportion of Monash tutors who were women (59 per cent in 1991) was higher than the national average, while the proportion of women among senior lecturers (14 per cent) and in higher academic positions (8 per cent) was lower. In full-time equivalent terms, 8 per cent of all Monash staff were casuals.[3] Of the staff in full-time positions in 1995, 57.5 per cent were men, while the majority of part-time staff were women.[4] A high proportion of casual staff was young and female.

TAFE and the Berwick development

The 1990 mergers had not exhausted the potential for regional expansion. Negotiations on a new outer eastern campus began in 1991. Supported by the State and Commonwealth governments, the project was also welcomed with enthusiasm by municipal authorities. In 1992 the State approved the location of a new campus at Berwick and agreed to purchase a site for the campus on 52 hectares of land at the old Casey Airport in Clyde Road, opposite the Berwick campus of Casey College of TAFE and not far from the Berwick railway station. The Commonwealth allocated $9.1 million for new buildings and another $2 million for the telenetworking of Monash campuses and learning centres, enabling the Berwick campus to trial innovations in interactive electronic teaching and learning.[5]

From the first enrolment in 1995, Monash Berwick provided cross-sectoral courses in cooperation with Casey TAFE. All courses were combined courses that led to two qualifications—a degree in higher education and a diploma or associate diploma in TAFE—after four years of full-time study. Students enrolled in the Monash program of Bachelor of Communications and combined this with TAFE courses in either Marketing, Professional Writing and Editing, or Information Technology (Technical and User Support). In the first year, students did three-quarters of their program in TAFE and one-quarter in higher education, in the second and third year half of the program in each sector, and the whole of the fourth year in higher education; the fourth year also could be completed at Clayton or Gippsland, or by distance education mode. After three years students qualified for the TAFE Diploma or Associate Diploma; after one more year they had the degree as well. It was a flexible structure, and the double qualification was attractive to employers.

In 1996, expecting a student load of 260, the University offered two additional courses, the Gippsland-based Bachelor of Business and a Bachelor of Tourism. Casey commenced a Diploma in Hospitality (Management), and this opened up combinations such as Tourism–Hospitality and Business–Hospitality. In addition, Berwick students could now combine a Berwick degree with another Monash degree, opening up combinations such as Business and Communications, Business and Tourism, and Communications and Tourism. Berwick's first academic school was formed, the School of Communication, Tourism and Business, as part of the Faculty of Business and Economics.[6] Courses were delivered by face-to-face teaching, teleteaching and computer-based tutorials.

A 50-metre telecommunications tower linked the Berwick campus to microwave dishes on the top of the Gippsland Administration Building and the Menzies Building at Clayton. Students in a new 250-place lecture theatre at Berwick joined counterparts on other campuses, via large-screen videotransfer. The lecturer could respond to questions from anyone in the augmented audience, a spectacular display that often impressed international visitors.[7] Berwick also began to trial tutorial delivery at a distance using personal computers.[8]

Capably managed by Jill McLachlan, Berwick was nevertheless a high-risk venture. Student support was not guaranteed. Though Berwick was located in a growth corridor, the history of Clayton had shown that patterns of educational use are not driven by demographers' models per se. Other factors, such as the proximity of shops, services and facilities, are often more important. On the positive side, unlike Clayton, Berwick had the advantage of a nearby railway station, as well as providing students with ample parking spaces. Further, the relationship with TAFE opened a new mode of entry to the University. There was better understanding of this at Frankston and Gippsland than at Clayton. Though TAFE graduates enrolled in Monash courses did better than school-leavers, those faculties receiving good-quality students, as measured by school leaver cut-off scores, did not see the need for another pathway.[9]

The entrepreneurial centre

The ultimate success of the potential opened up by the coupling of Berwick and Casey depended on the University's capacity to implement a common policy across all faculties and sites. This pointed to the larger problems facing Greater Monash. In a University grown to three times its previous size and spread across six sites instead of one, how would coherence be achieved? And how could a strategy-setting central management secure the consistent cooperation of the Monash faculties, with their tradition of independence?

The solution chosen was consistent with the history of Monash, and with Logan's personal preference for organisational systems which left a good deal of discretion to the academic units. The approach of the leadership group was not so much corporate as entrepreneurial (chapter 4). It did not rely on top-down direction or detailed performance requirements. The faculties were held in a common financial framework by budgetary formulae and accountability and data requirements, but educationally they were expected to devise their own targets and make these transparent, rather than follow targets regulated at the centre. Meanwhile the entrepreneurial centre gave itself the maximum room to move. It developed initiatives in the form of 'add-ons' to the existing structures, such as Monash International and the other commercial companies, the Monash Foundation, and publicity and promotion activities. This provided the centre

The Executive Group under Logan. L–R: Robert Pargetter, Leo West, Ian Chubb, Elizabeth Anderson, Mal Logan, Gary Neat, Peter Wade, Peter Darvall. Expanded executive groups became central to most Australian universities in the wake of Dawkins.

with more than one option: it could either work through the faculties or bypass them. The faculties, too, had a choice. They were encouraged to be externally engaged and entrepreneurial, to look for opportunities for non-government incomes and a larger role, but entrepreneurship was not made compulsory. One result was that the operational grip of the leadership, and engagement with the new culture of Greater Monash itself, were uneven between the faculties, across the campuses, and over time.

The pivotal elements of the Matheson structure were retained: the strong deans and the strategic vice-chancellorship, under the authority of Council. What changed was the systems of decision-making and resourcing that lay between the vice-chancellor and the faculties. In the 1960s the intermediate bodies were the collegial structures of Professorial Board and Committee of Deans, while the faculties had faculty boards, assemblies of the academic staff. The Committee of Deans discussed most matters of university-wide import,[10] and the Board was the educational personality of the University and the main channel to Council. When Matheson retired in the mid-1970s the collegial assemblies were already less potent, and the deans' role in University-wide matters was in decline (see chapters 2 and 4). The trend continued under Martin, and culminated under Logan. Full-time managers at centre and faculty levels became more important than before. The elements that now joined the vice-chancellor to the faculties were the executive group and the reformed mechanisms of formula funding and financial management. The quasi-democratic collegial structures were maintained in form, but in practice largely superseded by management and executive power. The Committee of Deans and Professorial Board, later Academic Board, became consultative instead of decision-making forums. The exception was times of conflict, when they regained some significance, for Monash continued to be held together by discussion and consent, by words and politics as well as managerial *fiat*.

The deans continued to be powerful on their own turf, more so as the deanship became more explicitly managerial and the faculty boards declined. Some of the roles of Committee of Deans and Academic Board had been shifted to the executive group, some back to the faculties.[11] It was all consistent with the Dawkins recipe. Similar changes were occurring in most other Australian universities.[12] Perhaps the distinctive feature of the Monash model was the degree of independence in educational matters retained by the deans.

The executive group consisted of the Vice-Chancellor, the Deputy Vice-Chancellors (DVCs), the Pro-Vice-Chancellors (PVCs), and the Registrar, Comptroller (later General Manager) and, from time to time, others. Its weekly meetings were semi-formal in statutory terms, being unrecognised in the Act, but matters of importance were normally discussed in the executive group before they went before the deans, Board and Council. The number of people in the executive group expanded dramatically. In 1986 there were two DVCs (Westfold and Logan), and in Logan's second year in 1988 one DVC (Polmear) and one PVC (Endersbee). By 1996 there were three DVCs and two PVCs, and they were joined in the executive group by the General Manager, the Communications Director and the Vice-Chancellor's Adviser. Through the Council, Logan created new positions to fulfil emerging needs, or simply to rearrange the configuration of duties. One after another, senior executives shuffled their portfolios and strutted their stuff on the Monash stage. There was a high turnover rate. Only the Vice-Chancellor and General Manager were constant.

The DVCs and to a lesser extent the PVCs were at the heart of the changes at Monash. The executive group shared a common culture, and a common interest in maintaining its standing within the University. Logan and most of the members of the group were located within a few metres of each other in the University offices at Clayton.[13] Yet in some respects DVC and PVC were not happy parts to play, and this was one reason for the high turnover. 'The emphasis is not on who reports to who, but on a pooling of brainpower to solve problems and to take initiatives', Logan told Council in 1992.[14] Nevertheless, members of the executive group were not equal to each other, and all were vying for role and effect in an unstable setting. The Vice-Chancellor sustained a certain ambiguity and tension. At times relationships were under strain. All of the executive group exercised real authority; on some issues the faculty deans reported to the DVCs rather than Logan.[15] At the same time the DVCs were extensions of the Vice-Chancellor, with less independent authority than a dean and far fewer resources at their command. As one dean, Ian Rae, remarked of the transition from dean to DVC that was followed by four of the group:

> You'd had a thirty or forty million dollar budget and suddenly you had an office, you were given a secretary and a bit of a travel fund. It struck me that during the time I was there [as Dean of Science] that the senior officers below the level of Vice-Chancellor, except for the General Manager, are relatively powerless at Monash compared to Deans.[16]

The DVCs were a buffer between the Vice-Chancellor and deans. Some deans resented reporting to the DVCs because it diminished their access to the top.[17] At worst the DVCs did the 'hatchet work' for Logan. From time to time the Vice-Chancellor encouraged them to confront the established centres of power in the faculties. If the deans hit back hard, where necessary Logan intervened as the diplomat. When the credibility of the DVCs was exhausted in relation to the matter of conflict, they were moved on to other jobs.[18]

The first DVC to assert his role in this manner was John Hay. Logan 'deliberately gave Hay quite a long lead', and Hay used it (Darvall).[19] After Hay's resignation in 1991, to become Vice-Chancellor of Deakin University, Logan reviewed the executive structure. He secured the support of Council for the creation of a senior Deputy Vice-Chancellor position—though it was another year before this was filled—and the appointment of two faculty deans, Porter (Medicine) and Pargetter (Arts), as part-time DVCs, providing the executive group with a line back to the Committee of Deans. Later, Darvall as Dean of Engineering also became a part-time DVC. The Vice-Chancellor's Executive Assistant Leo West was promoted to Pro-Vice-Chancellor for a three-year term and took responsibility for the international office. In effect, the executive group had been remade as a hybrid body combining the Vice-Chancellor's office with part of the Committee of Deans. The outcome was not

All in a day's work: DVCs were generalists who did whatever was required, including sausages. L–R: Robert Pargetter (1992–96), Lauchlan Chipman (1995–96), Peter Darvall (from 1993).

satisfactory. Some faculty deans had been privileged relative to others; the part-time DVC positions were difficult to work, partly because of the time demands; and there was now a direct role conflict between faculty and University inside the executive group.

On 1 March 1993 Ian Chubb, the former head of the Commonwealth Higher Education Council, took up office as DVC. In welcoming Chubb to the Academic Board on 10 March, Logan described the new position in terms of the role of provost in North American universities. Chubb was to take primary responsibility for educational matters, build 'links and bridges' with the academic community and deputise for the Vice-Chancellor at need, freeing Logan to concentrate on strategic development and the representation of Monash in external forums.[20] Chubb rapidly developed a working overview of the University. His administrative ability and drive, his disdain for the niceties and his dominating style of work created anxieties among his peers, exposing the structural flaw in the part-time positions.[21] On 16 June 1993 the Vice-Chancellor told the Academic Board that Porter had decided to relinquish the position of DVC (Research) to return to Medicine as full-time dean. Darvall was appointed part-time DVC (Research) in his place; he later became full-time (see chapter 9). Pargetter left the Arts deanship to be a full-time DVC. The hybrid DVC/dean positions were not revived.

Porter's return to Medicine did not end the conflict around Chubb, though it translated some of it downwards. Logan's approach to the deans was to integrate them into the corporate culture without disturbing their sense of ownership of their own affairs, to persuade the deans it was natural to move with the centre. If the deans decided not to move, there was little he could do. Chubb used more direct methods. He was concerned at what he saw as a lack of clarity about educational objectives and was keen to achieve a coherent approach across the University. He wanted identifiable improvements in teaching and learning, and saw students, not the deans, as his primary reference point. As the deans saw it, by creating an Education Committee with a network of associate deans (Teaching), and setting up his own policy unit with a mandate to monitor faculty performance, Chubb DVC was threatening to bypass the deans and 'much of the process of the place' (Pargetter). It was 'a turbulent era' (Darvall). The sheer size and inertia of the University, the independence of the faculties and the absence of uniform goodwill made it difficult for Chubb to succeed. In addition to his DVC role he was Acting Dean of the troublesome Economics and Business Faculty (chapter 5) and responsible for management education at the newly merged Mt Eliza campus. It was a heavy workload that was very broadly spread.

Despite some support in Science, Arts and Education, and from Staff Association and Student Union activists who admired his commitment to educational goals and saw him as a potential ally, the 'can-do' Chubb began to feel frustrated. His prospects of becoming vice-chancellor after Logan receded: 'There were a variety of people who thought that Ian should not succeed Mal and took steps to make that happen' (Williams). He resigned from Monash, effective 24 February 1995, to become a successful Vice-Chancellor at Flinders University in South Australia. The attempt at a provost-style position was not repeated.[22]

Most of Chubb's role in educational policy was assumed by Pargetter, who used a more Loganesque approach to the deans. Involved in teaching quality, school-leaver entry, course structures, open learning and relations with TAFE, in his last two years (1995 and 1996) Pargetter also handled academic planning, and framed academic business for the University decision-making bodies. For a while the sharp-minded Pargetter—who was said to sleep only a few hours a night, which left him more time to think and plan—loomed large in the University, if not as large as Chubb.[23] Lauchlan Chipman, who managed Gippsland and Berwick and led equal opportunity policy, was promoted from PVC to DVC in 1995. He later became Vice-Chancellor at Central Queensland University. Darvall and Wade were the only member of Logan's inner circle who continued into the Robinson era.

Although female students were in a majority, the number of women in professorial chairs—the starting point for an internal run at dean, PVC or DVC—was small. Logan supported the Senior Women's Advancement Scheme, a training in career-building and executive functions. Participants reported that 'they felt more self confident, more empowered, more positive about themselves' and they understood the University better,[24] but opportunities for women remained limited.

Corporate images

If the entrepreneurial centre was sometimes frustrated by its lack of direct steering power in the faculties, it was potent in external relations, enabling it to shift the conditions in which the faculties operated. Logan understood public relations not in the traditional sense of making public the University's teaching and research (especially the latter) but as corporate image-making. Here the product to be sold was Monash itself, and the Vice-Chancellor knew that the character of that product would be partly determined by the processes used to sell it. Precisely because an aggressive approach to promotion was subversive of the academic tradition, it could be used to magnify the distance between the old Monash and the new, and to steal the march on competitor institutions. In late 1987 a department of external relations and alumni affairs was established, including fund-raising (which at this stage was confined to the annual library appeal).[25] Subsequently Gary Neat became Director of Communications. Neat had a certain swagger about him and for a while exercised quite an influence. He had little time for the professoriate, but his direct manner and corporate experience ensured that the senior manager-leaders would take him seriously. Neat radically changed advertising, publications, media liaison and image-making. Sitting on the executive group, he was 'a major player' at Monash (Logan).[26]

A Neat trick. From the original Monash crest to the chevron and stars.

Neat managed relations with the press on behalf of Logan so as to strengthen the carefully crafted image of an open, dynamic, modern and global university. He was adept at deflecting attention from problems of the mergers and dissent from the leadership: only one substantial story about the TRAG revolt was ever printed.[27] He also secured positive coverage in Southeast Asia, at a time when international marketing was stepping up. However, the decisive change implemented by Neat, with Logan's involvement, was the creation of a singular corporate image for the University, permeating every aspect of external relations.

That image was spare, modern, global and emphatic—MONASH in capitals. It incorporated a new symbol, a chevron with five stars representing the Southern Cross. There was little that was academic about the symbol: except for the proclamation that Monash was 'Australia's International University', it was an image that might have been designed for any large corporation. Council did not actually decide to substitute the new symbol for the old Monash crest, or to replace the scholarly motto *Ancora imparo* with 'MONASH: Australia's International University'. These changes simply happened, carried off by the sheer weight of advertising and publications. The old symbol and motto stayed on the books but had little role in the new order. Even a new University tie was developed, in heavy silk with multiple bold stripes, replacing the old and sombre navy blue and two stripes. The crest was still there but it was downplayed, positioned at the bottom of the tie. The ties and other souvenir items were sold by yet another new company, Monash Merchandising.

There was a great expansion of advertisements for Monash courses and activities in the national, metropolitan and local press, growing from 547 in 1991 to 850 by 1994. Regular publications were targeted at specific audiences, such as *Business Victoria* and *Schools Update*. There was a marked growth in generic promotional publications. Design formats were standardised so that each new publication contributed to the accumulation of the common image. Few academics were comfortable with the flood of glossy booklets with their carefully crafted sameness, verging on the banal, the recycled pictures of smiling young people with mixed cultural backgrounds and reassuring messages. But the intended audiences were not academic; they were external to the University and often external to Australia, and there was no doubt that the material was professionally produced.

Inevitably, there was resentment at Clayton. In an Occasional Paper issued by the Arts Faculty office, Gay Baldwin charged that in contemporary Australian universities truth-telling and internal democracy were being displaced by a new set of values in which 'corporate loyalty' and commitment to the 'platitudinous "boosterism" of the "we are the greatest, another first for X University"' kind took primacy: 'The millions of words churned out by public relations departments can only be described as propaganda, a form of communication which should be anathema in universities'.[28] When the new Professional Development Centre building was erected at 700 Blackburn Road, long-standing Centre Director Terry Hore made sure the old crest was prominent on the front of the building. Next door was Personnel, sporting the corporate chevron and stars. Someone from the Communications Department rang Hore to complain about the clash of images. 'Well, that's unfortunate', stated Hore, 'but the crest says "I am still learning" and that is a perfect motto for a staff development centre'. The crest stayed.[29] There was no doubt that Neat's image-building had strengthened Monash's position in what had become a more competitive environment. Corporate times required corporate methods. Perhaps what was in question was the degree to which overt product branding and other corporate techniques should determine the character of Monash.

While the corporate image was being developed, the executive group was becoming more integrated with the external business world, in which the Neat style of operation was commonplace. Relations with business were carried mainly by Wade, who had retained good links with business throughout his career, and Logan. The Vice-Chancellor put much energy into developing a rapport with the chief executive officers (CEOs) of major companies. It was a favourable time to do this. Business was becoming more interested in education and more open to partnership arrangements.[30] Logan believed that business would inevitably be more crucial to universities in future. In Australia there was little tradition of business investment, but perhaps this could be enhanced. Closer relations with business also promised to provide insight into labour market trends affecting graduates.[31]

Logan decided not to wait for busy corporate leaders to come to the University but to take the initiative. He started inviting corporate CEOs to the Monash city office to explore matters of mutual interest. Rather to his surprise, almost every one of these invitations was accepted. The CEO to CEO aspect of the invitation was well received. Monash's recognised strengths in Business and Engineering education helped. Similarly, business leaders were willing to attend seminars provided by the Monash–ANZ Bank Centre for International Briefing. The

University began to build a strong portfolio of contacts. Monash was the only Australian university to become a member of the Pacific Basin Economic Council, an association of business leaders designed to promote free trade.[32] Sometimes business links flowed into resources—if never as much as was hoped. For example, the head of Visyboard, Richard Pratt, provided funding for the Australian Centre for Jewish Civilisation.[33] The growing links to business leaders became expressed in the pattern of honorary degrees: miner Arvi Parbo in 1989, Richard Pratt in 1990, banker Will Bailey in 1991, BHP managers Brian Loton in 1993 and John Prescott in 1994, and banker Don Argus in 1995.

In 1992 Logan told Council that 'business people now talk about Monash in a different way', and that Monash received more media coverage than any other Victorian university. No doubt the rise of Greater Monash was a matter of public interest. Nevertheless, public and business perceptions of Monash were largely constructed by the University itself.[34]

Manufacturing a DVC (Hay) . . . and a VC (Logan). Early examples of image making by Clayton photo-designers. In the first half of the 1990s the University's communications switched from journalism mode to marketing mode.

Entrepreneurial financing

Within the University, the most flexible organisational form for securing an entrepreneurial mission steered by the executive group was that of the commercial company. Companies were readily focused on outcomes rather than process, and made quicker decisions than collegial bodies.

Rather than being inherently conservative they were innovation-prone, albeit innovation of a commercial kind. Monash International facilitated the international marketing of courses (chapter 6). Monash IVF provided medical services in the market for infertility treatment and in-vitro fertilisation. Montech and Montech Medical Development developed intellectual property and brokered staff consultancy services.[35] The training facilities in the central business district were run by the Sir John Monash Business Centre. In 1995 all companies received $30 million in fees and charges, double the previous year. The work of the Monash solicitor grew in tandem with commercial activity. Staff were not always comfortable with all this. Some were disquieted by 'the spinning off of corporate bodies' outside the control of the governing bodies, as one staff representative on Council saw it, Jenny Strauss from Arts.[36] Others experienced the University companies as a regulatory constraint on their own commercial activities.

The budget statements issued annually by Wade's office recorded the financial growth of Greater Monash, and its entrepreneurial activities. Between 1986 and 1995 operating revenue rose from $138 to $553 million, and expenses rose from $134 to $501 million. The University's assets grew from $341 to $893 million. Logan was fond of stating that the Monash budget was larger than the entire State government budget for Tasmania.[37] Monash had the third-largest university budget in Australia, after Sydney and Melbourne. It was a good year in 1995 (see Table 7.3). Operating surplus was up 21 per cent, consolidated operating surplus had doubled, and income from fees and charges to companies controlled by the University had almost doubled. Revenue from fee-paying international students was up 13.4 per cent, and revenue from postgraduate fees was up 23.7 per cent. The bond and share markets had been favourable, so that investment income was up from $7 to $18 million.[38] The balance sheet was reported in the business press. Though public funding per student was falling, the University seemed to be flourishing financially.

At the same time entrepreneurial funding differed from public funding, in that it was not distributed on a formula basis between faculties. It was ploughed back into the commercial activity itself, and into the subsidisation of selected teaching and research. At a time when public funding per student was in decline, alternative revenues were becoming crucial even to the maintenance of core operations. Faculties that generated their own commercial revenues were therefore much more strongly placed than those that did not.

Logan and Wade talked up the importance of raising private incomes. In aggregate terms, private funding was certainly on the rise. Between 1988 and 1995 it jumped from $3 million to $43 million, reaching 17 per cent of the University's recurrent funds.[39] Monash enrolled 4929 fee-paying international students, 10.6 per cent of all such students in Australia, and 2360 fee-paying postgraduates (10.2 per cent).[40] In both categories it was the largest enrolment

TABLE 7.3   SOURCES OF INCOME, MONASH UNIVERSITY, 1995

		$million	Proportion of total (%)
Commonwealth government	Base recurrent grant*	250.1	64.0
	Research infrastructure	3.4	0.9
State government	Making Places Initiative	5.5	1.4
Both governments	DEET/State special purpose	2.6	0.7
Research not elsewhere included	Australian Research Council	8.2	2.1
	National Health & Medical RC	8.5	2.2
	Cooperative Research Centres	6.4	1.6
	Other research grants	21.1	5.4
	Contract research	2.7	0.7
Student fees	International	37.0	9.5
	Postgraduate fee-paying**	5.3	1.4
	Non-award courses	0.9	0.2
	Open learning	2.0	0.5
Other non-government	Monash University Foundation	4.7	1.2
	Prior year funds	3.4	0.9
	General donations	7.1	1.8
	External earnings	21.4	5.5
Total***		391.0	100.0

   *   Includes HECS-related income payable to Monash.
  **   Does not include international fee-paying postgraduates.
 ***   Figures have been rounded to one decimal place.
Source: Monash University, *1996 Budget*, p. 31.

in the country. Annual postgraduate fees ranged up to $14 000 for the Graduate Diploma in Business Administration and $45 000 for a Mt Eliza MBA. (Of the fee-paying postgraduates 58.9 per cent were men, who were more likely to receive help from employers with the cost of fees.)[41] Australian universities derived less than 7 per cent of their income from international and postgraduate fees, but the equivalent figure at Monash was 10 per cent.[42] Nevertheless, financing varied greatly by faculty. 'Some Faculties had shown a capacity to supplement their incomes by exploiting their high standing', the Vice-Chancellor told Council in 1992, though 'others have not been willing or capable of pursuing this course'.[43] Of course some faculties were better placed to attract fee-paying students, notably Business and Computing. In 1995, 38 per cent of operating income in Business was from student fees, and 36 per cent in Computing, compared with 7 per cent in Arts (Table 7.4). This was a function of supply as well as demand. Arts, Science, Law and Education did not share the entrepreneurial drive of the Business faculty, where consulting activity was often more important to individual academics than was research.

As a university founded in the postwar period, Monash lacked the large

TABLE 7.4   SOURCES OF THE INCOME OF EACH FACULTY, 1995

Faculty	Government ($m)	Student fees ($m)	All sources ($m)	Government (%)	Student fees (%)
Business and Economics	21.1	13.0	34.1	62.0	38.0
Computing & IT	11.1	6.2	17.4	64.1	35.9
Engineering	19.9	4.0	23.9	83.2	17.8
Law	6.2	0.5	6.7	92.2	7.8
Medicine	29.1	2.2	31.3	93.0	7.0
Science	27.2	2.0	29.2	93.1	6.9
Pharmacy	5.4	0.4	5.8	93.2	6.8
Arts	31.7	2.2	34.0	93.4	6.6
Education	9.7	0.4	10.1	96.4	3.6
All faculties*	161.4	30.9	192.5	83.9	16.1

* Figures have been rounded to one decimal place.
Source: Monash University, *Budget 1996*, p. 36.

alumni lists of universities like Melbourne and Sydney. One of the long-term imperatives was to build an asset base additional to the land and buildings. As chair of the Finance Committee of Council, James McNeill was a strong advocate of building a separate fund. The Monash Foundation was established in 1984 and its development soon entrusted to Wade. He carefully crafted a set of decisions that would enable him to manage cash flow in a consistent manner across the University. Income from the Commonwealth, international students (who paid a semester in advance) and other sources was parked in a mix of short-term money market, share market and bond market investments, and a fixed 50 per cent of interest earned was channelled into the Foundation. A fixed 50 per cent of other interest earnings was also earmarked for it.[44] The deans complained at losing the interest earnings on their budgets, but there were compensations: for a while the other 50 per cent of interest earned was channelled into works and maintenance. The Foundation started to grow. At times there was pressure to shift part of it into operating budgets, 'buying our way out of problems instead of solving them', but 'we held the line' (Wade).

Using these techniques, $30 million in interest earnings was channelled into the Foundation. Once there, the money was reinvested in a bundle of shares, property, bonds and short-term funds. The resulting earnings were used partly to sustain the value of the Foundation against inflation, and partly returned as income to the university. 'What started off as University interest earnings was soft money', but once part of the Foundation, so that the interest generated further interest, 'it hardened up enormously' (Wade). The Foundation began to live on its own earnings, and no longer needed half the interest earned, freeing that money for other purposes. At the close of 1995 the gross value of the Foundation stood at $109 million and its net value was $101 million, compared with $15 million in 1985.[45] It was a tremendous achievement. By 1995 it was generating nearly $7 million per annum in hard money income to the University, 2 per cent of operating income—similar to the annual funding from Australian Research Council Large Grants projects. Money from the Foundation was more flexible than the income from most bequests. It could be deployed at will to areas of high priority, such as research initiatives. The Monash Development Fund distributed funds to the faculties on a dollar-for-dollar basis. In those faculties where budgets were under high strain the additional funding was particularly welcome, while from the point of view of the University's leaders it allowed them to exercise influence over academic development: 'But in running these seeding funds you've got to be very rigorous in your thinking to make sure that they truly are seeding operations' (Wade). Seed funding was for a couple of years, after which the faculties had to decide whether to raise income from another source, allow the initiative to wither, or support it by internal reallocation.[46]

With Monash now almost 40 years old, alumni funding had a growing potential and the University expanded its fund-raising infrastructure. It began to send a glossy magazine to alumni, *Mosaic*, which often emphasised alumni from Malaysia.

The funding formula

The more entrepreneurial spirit in some of the faculties, as well as the new problem of administering diverse activities in several campuses, made it all the more essential to establish a modernised financial regimen across the whole University, a regimen less variable and politicised and more transparent and rigorous than before. The introduction of a new formula for distributing government operating funds between faculties, and new systems of recording and reporting financial transactions, was managed by Wade. There was an effective division of labour between Vice-Chancellor and the Comptroller (later appointed as General Manager following the secondment of Registrar Pritchard to Open Learning). Logan and Wade were contrasting personalities with different skills, but both were realists, and they each respected the other's capacities. Unlike the DVCs, Logan and Wade were not competing on the same terrain. Logan was not enamoured of administrative detail, and left to Wade some matters that Matheson and Martin might have handled themselves.[47]

The allocation of funding was governed by the Central Budgets Committee, which included most members of the executive group but excluded the deans, and where Wade and Logan were the key players.[48] Over 1990 and 1991, after

Peter Brian Wade, Comptroller and General Manager

As a Council member (1969–87), Deputy Chancellor and Chair of the Finance Committee, Sir James McNeill left a mark on the University. The 1985 McNeill report paved the way for a new management structure and a more strategic vice-chancellorship (chapter 4). It was McNeill's idea to set up the Monash Foundation. Not the least of his contributions was to persuade Peter Wade to take up the position of Comptroller in 1985.[49]

Wade was then one of the stars of the Victorian public service. A Masters graduate in Economics and former President of the Victorian branch of the Economic Society of Australia and New Zealand, he reached Deputy Head of the State Treasury in 1977 at 34 years of age. One of his portfolios was university funding, and he became well acquainted with the three-way relationship between institutions, State and Commonwealth.

After five years as Deputy Head of Treasury and three at the Ministry of Transport, the mid-career shift to Monash was a gamble. It turned out to be good timing for both parties.[50] Wade threw himself into the new job. Within two years the University was in the process of its greatest changes since the mid-1960s. In 1993 Registrar Tony Pritchard left Monash on secondment to manage open learning, and Wade's position was renamed General Manager, an amalgam of Comptroller and part-Registrar with responsibility for most of the operational side of the University. Five divisional heads reported to him.

Outside university governance and management circles the fact that Wade was a non-academic manager tended to diminish awareness of his role. Yet the General Manager's importance was probably second only to the Vice-Chancellor's, as deans were aware.[51] Wade's reforms to budgeting and financial reporting modernised faculty devolution; his cash flow management built the Monash Foundation. In between he promoted Monash in the business sector, was an active Director of Monash IVF and Monash International, chaired the Playbox Theatre for Monash, and took a great interest in the Monash galleries. He also found time to lecture occasionally on university management to students in the Monash MBA courses and the Faculty of Education's professional doctoral program.

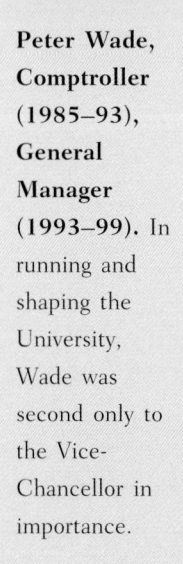

Peter Wade, Comptroller (1985–93), General Manager (1993–99). In running and shaping the University, Wade was second only to the Vice-Chancellor in importance.

extensive discussion, it was decided to reform faculty financial management.[52] As a result of the reforms, the faculties gained greater control over their resources. They could retain surpluses and they were no longer penalised for raising private funding by losing some of their government funding. The formula used to distribute operating funds, partly the creation of former Chisholm staff John Harris and John Levine, was a version of the Commonwealth's relative funding model. Research and equipment funding were joined to funds for teaching, further increasing faculty discretion.[53] Monash became one of the first Australian universities to prepare a public budget. Thus the open and manageable politics of the funding formula was substituted for the old under-the-table politics of funding distribution. As Dean of Law Bob Williams put it later, 'we still squabble, but we squabble over the small change'.[54]

Under the formula, funds were distributed on the basis of weighted student units, varying upwards from 1.00 in undergraduate Business and Economics to 2.90 in undergraduate Medicine, and from 2.20 for most research higher degrees to 4.90 in Medicine, Engineering, Science and the behavioural sciences. The original Commonwealth formula from which the model was derived was based on national average costs in each discipline. However, teaching practices varied between universities, and costs in particular faculties at Monash did not always correspond to the formula, despite its modification for local use. The main losers were Law and Education. Monash Law provided smaller classes and more intensive teaching than did universities such as Melbourne and Queensland, which had influenced the national model. At the 27 November 1991 meeting of the Academic Board, Williams moved a resolution deploring the model, stating that it had been formulated without prior debate, and recommending that it not be used. The motion was lost, and on 16 December Council adopted the budget, including the funding formula. A year later it was Education's turn. When the 1993 budget was presented at the 18 November 1992 meeting of the Board, the Dean of Education (David Aspin) proposed an independent body to advise on funding distribution. The Vice-Chancellor replied that the Committee of Deans was such a body. The funding formula had survived, and it became entrenched.[55]

The deans and devolution

The authority and responsibility of deans varied from faculty to faculty, and was never precisely codified,[56] a function of the strength of their disciplines, their individual knowledge of the University, and their capacity to hold a negotiating position. (Medicine, Engineering and Computing under Bellamy were good at this.) Nevertheless, all deans found that, with the mounting Commonwealth requirements for data, the work arising from the mergers and other changes, and financial devolution, the role of full-time dean had become more demanding. Longer-standing deans such as Gus Sinclair in Economics found it impossible to continue research and journal editing alongside administration.

Faculty budgets were flexible instruments. The main constraints were the funding formula, the requirement to meet certain University policy objectives, the proportion of total resources that was tied up in fixed staff numbers, and the two-way flow of data on expenditure and student numbers, between the offices of General Manager and Dean. After the installation of computer-based systems it became impossible for deans to resort to time-honoured ploys such as running up debts, or over-enrolling in one year and securing extra funding the next. There was little that they could do about this. It was easy to defend the new system as both fairer and more efficient.[57]

As noted, the deans had plenty of scope on other fronts. In effect they were told: 'here is your bucket of money, get off and do your job' (Williams). Hay stated that: 'in my first year of Dean of Arts the thing that made it most interesting was the certain knowledge that the Vice-Chancellor wouldn't interfere'.[58] This habit of independence meant that while the Deans' Committee was largely reduced to a consultative forum, it was still a place where consent was needed. The deans saw most items on the way to the Board and Council. At some meetings, the deans would spend their time taking notes for reporting back to their faculties; at other meetings they engaged in animated discussion, or freewheeling debate. A number of deans working together could still kill a proposal, and they also used the meetings to draw support from each other for their own faculties.[59] There were no permanent alliances on the Deans' Committee: it was every faculty for itself. From time to time particular executive group decisions might hurt individual faculties, but 'temporary breakouts' by 'disaffected Deans' were 'very rare' (Darvall). The Vice-Chancellor could normally persuade the deans that it wasn't worth the fight, and anyway, what happened to one today might happen to another tomorrow.[60] And after the deans had discussed a matter, as Logan told the Council in his 1992 paper *Monash: toward 2000*, regardless of any disagreement at the committee, 'each Vice-Chancellor in Monash's history has come to rely on a high level of Decanal solidarity'.[61]

An early draft added the words 'with one exception I have enjoyed such support'. This was removed from the version finally tabled at Council.[62] As this suggests, the relationship between deans and centre fluctuated. At one stage the Deans' Committee meetings began to take on the form of an augmented executive group. The DVCs and PVCs came with Logan and, after Chubb's appointment, Chubb's staff as well. Logan no longer managed all business himself. The deans began to feel both outnumbered and bypassed. A number of deans chafed at this, organising deans-only meetings—without the Vice-

Chancellor—to discuss what was happening in the University. At the next properly constituted meeting of the Deans' Committee Logan sharply criticised this practice, but he took the point. There was a return to smaller Deans' Committee meetings chaired by the Vice-Chancellor.[63] This incident and Chubb's departure were hailed by some deans as a renaissance of decanal power, but it was not so. At best the deans had defended their faculty prerogatives. In University-wide matters, the trend to the executive group was unabated. Logan continued to consult, but towards the end of his term he did less of this himself and became more dependent on the DVCs for the grassroots intelligence and the fostering of consensus.

The evolution of the Deans' Committee paralleled that of the Academic Board. The first reconstituted Academic Board meeting on 17 July 1991 consisted of 50 professors, 27 non-professorial academic staff, 10 senior officers and members of the executive group, the Librarian, the Director of the Computer Centre, and five students. As on the old Board, decisions were framed by the executive group. Some Board members, frustrated by their declining importance, attempted to establish monthly rather than six-weekly meetings;[64] and for a time in the post-merger period more frequent meetings did occur. Nevertheless, in reality the Board was merely a 'safety valve' (Bellamy) for handling policy conflicts, becoming important only in moments when key initiatives were not bedded down and consent was needed (chapters 4 and 5). Logan normally sounded out key figures, sometimes the whole Board, before pushing sensitive matters to a resolution. He made good use of the Monash tradition whereby the Vice-Chancellor chaired the Board. 'This gives you the right to control the agenda and the minutes, and drive your policies from the chair', he noted later. If the Board had elected its chair as in some universities, 'I don't know how I would have handled that. To be frank, we might have lost everything' (Logan).[65] Consent was secured by personal authority. The Vice-Chancellor was a masterful chair of the Board, knowing just how long to allow debate to flow before moving for closure.

As the larger role of the deans and the Board fell away, the entrepreneurial centre was freer to evolve independently of the faculties. For their part the faculties were tethered to the centre via the Logan personality and the culture of Greater Monash, and bound by Wade's financial systems and drivers. After the merger the main organisational priority was cross-institutional integration. As noted, along with administration and finance, faculty structures were primary instruments for integrating the campuses into Monash, so that the fault lines fell between faculties rather than campuses (see chapter 5). One outcome was that the campuses became tied more closely to the institution than were the faculties, for after the mergers were in place the old faculty independence reasssserted itself.

Within the faculties, collegial tradition survived better than in most Australian universities, though it had lost its overall hold. Greater Monash was more than the sum of its faculties: the entrepreneurial centre was important. At the same time, the faculties were not subordinated to the centre. Indeed, faculties and centre enjoyed an independence of each other that was unusual in Australian universities. A corporate centre might have centralised Monash; an entrepreneurial centre would not, and could not. With its reliance on the self-regulation of teaching and research, and its leaders' dependence on culture and consent rather than coercion, Greater Monash was not a closely integrated institution.

The quality assessment

A loosely integrated structure was an advantage, in that it enabled different fields of study to develop their own traditions and provided scope for grassroots entrepreneurial activity. It could be a definite disadvantage when whole-institution responses were needed, especially when the matters concerned were in areas that the faculties regarded as their prerogative. This problem was compounded in the first few years after the merger, when systems were in flux and the faculties yet to create their own coherent systems across the campuses. Thus the first assessment of institutional 'quality' by the Commonwealth Committee for Quality Assurance in Higher Education in 1993 did not come at a good time for Monash.

The issue of quality came on the Australian higher education agenda in 1990–92 following similar developments in Britain. 'Quality' had more than one meaning in higher education. It could refer to a single standard of excellence or exceptional performance. It could refer to a variable standard, whereby an institution was judged according to its success in meeting its own mission ('fitness for purpose'). It could also refer to the *mechanisms* used to monitor performance and secure improvements, such as strategic planning and evaluation of outcomes, measures of research performance, student evaluation of teaching, and 'benchmarking' of performance against that of other universities.[66] In its reviews of the quality of individual Australian universities in 1993, 1994 and 1995, the Commonwealth Committee took all three meanings into account. It also published rankings of the universities based on their performance in relation to research and teaching, and quality assurance mechanisms.[67] In a more competitive climate, these rankings were bound to be the focus of attention. The first quality assessment in 1993 took on a particular importance, as the first official sorting of the hierarchy since the Dawkins reforms.

Pargetter chaired the working party of Academic Board that began the shaping of an approach to the Commonwealth. The working paper tabled its first document on 9 September 1992, 11 months before the Commonwealth evaluation team was due to appear. While some faculties were looking at ways of monitoring quality, and Logan had introduced awards for teaching excellence, there were few processes in place of the kind likely to find favour with the Commonwealth. Logan, who had little intrinsic interest in the kind of detailed regulation favoured by quality assurance systems, hoped that the arrival of Chubb as DVC in early 1993 would enable a plausible Monash response to be put together. Chubb had presided over the Commonwealth policy papers on quality and was passionately committed to quality assurance as a means of securing better learning outcomes. However, he did not have enough to work with. There was no great concern in some faculties, which regarded the quality assessment as another in a series of corporate window-dressing exercises.[68] In Chubb's office there were emergency meetings and a growing sense of panic. When the Commonwealth Committee visited Monash, its interrogation was testy and sometimes hostile.[69]

In the outcome, the University was placed with the University of Sydney in the second of six groups, behind Melbourne, NSW, Queensland, Adelaide, WA and ANU. The Committee found that Monash lacked overarching principles on teaching and learning, diminishing its capacity 'to apply good practice systematically across the university'. There was also 'a lack of clear formal pathways of reporting back'.[70] It was a reverse that pleased Melbourne, irked by all the attention that Greater Monash was getting, and baffled some in media and government circles. It shocked many at Clayton. Logan was devastated. For him, it raised questions about Chubb's capacity to deliver. He also vented some of his ire on the Commonwealth Committee, in whose processes he had no great faith. How could Monash have first-class outcomes and second-class procedures as the Committee had suggested? Did all of the universities in the top band have strong procedures? Nevertheless, the damage had been done, and shooting the umpire was not the way to win.

In retrospect the Committee's decision appears less surprising. It used uniform criteria in preparing the rankings, so that particular circumstances affecting each university affected its rating, but these circumstances were not sufficiently acknowledged in the outcomes. Of the eight leading universities, two were placed in the 'B' category, and these were the two that had undergone substantial mergers. At both Monash and Sydney the mergers brought in a large group of academics with weak research records. (On research outcomes Clayton alone would probably have secured a top rating.) The mergers also retarded the emergence of quality assurance measures. Subsequently at Monash the unexpected B rating in 1993 freed Chubb's hand and accelerated the speed at which quality assurance was tackled. Clearly, Monash had to recover the lost ground. The University's new education policy specified there would be defined objectives for every course, common policies on assessment and postgraduate supervision, a more explicit emphasis on teaching quality and evaluation, and clear reporting lines. The University was able to tell the Commonwealth

Committee in its second year of operation in 1994 that all the new strategies were being implemented, though compliance was slower in Arts, Education and Science than in other faculties.[71]

The Committee was impressed by the achievements of the associate deans (Teaching) on the Education Committee, and Monash received a top rating in the 1994 assessment of teaching practice, though Chubb received insufficient credit for this: the University was still trying to digest the outcome of the first round. In the 1995 assessment of research and community service—by which time Darvall (research) and Pargetter (community service) had taken over the quality portfolio from Chubb—Monash was placed in the top group for research outcomes, research management, and all facets of community service.[72] The Committee found that research planning was 'effective and consistently deployed across the institution'. Monash used 'a devolved management system which places research management as a primary responsibility of the faculties'. Faculty research management plans were reviewed according to central guidelines and compliance was centrally monitored. There was good progress in enhancing research at the former CAE campuses and 'the cross-campus faculty structure is proving effective in promoting this'. The Committee found that, overall, in 'the strength and breadth of its research activities' Monash was 'in the leading group of institutions in the country'.[73]

There was a sigh of relief at Clayton. The process of quality assessment was 'grossly imperfect' remarked Logan afterwards, but 'coming first beats the hell out of coming last'.[74]

The arts

8

One of the ways you measure the character—indeed, the greatness—of a country is by its public commitment to the arts. Not as a luxury . . . but as a commitment arising from the belief that the desire to make and experience art is an organic part of human nature, without which our natures are coarsened, impoverished and denied, and our sense of community with other citizens is weakened. The arts are the fields on which we place our own dreams, thoughts, and desires alongside those of others, so that solitudes can meet, to their joy sometimes, or to their surprise, and sometimes to their disgust. When you boil it all down, that is the social purpose of art: the creation of mutuality, the passage from feeling into shared meaning.

Time's art critic Australian Robert Hughes in a speech at a fundraiser for a fine arts school in New York, reported in *The Age*, 10 June 1996

Vision and outlook

All should know art, music and literature, stated John Monash, for, to the extent these things are lacking, 'to that extent is our vision and outlook limited and cramped'.[1] From the beginning, the arts were important at Monash University, but over the 40-year history of the University the cutting edge shifted between the different branches of the arts.

In the late 1960s days of street politics, Monash excelled in innovative student theatre. Graduates such as John Romeril, David Williamson, Richard Murphet, Lindy Davies, John Hawkes and Lindzee Smith later formed the nucleus of the Australian Performing Group at the Pram Factory in Carlton, perhaps the most influential *avant-garde* in the history of Australian theatre. By the second half of the 1980s Monash theatre had been mainstreamed. It excelled in performances for local children. Student theatre had not disappeared and still had memorable moments, but was less active and less significant than before. Music, lacking space and less exciting than theatre in Matheson's time, became more varied in its offerings in the 1990s. Meanwhile the cutting edge had shifted to the University's collection of paintings and sculpture, and its role as an exhibitor.

In part this was a function of the program of capital works. If the absence of the arts led to the cramping of vision and outlook, then the cramping of the arts left them confined to their devotees, with little scope for the larger formative role that John Monash imagined. For much of Monash's history, both music and the visual arts were retarded by lack of room. Too much space could also be a problem. The large Alexander Theatre and Robert Blackwood Hall created a bias towards performances likely to attract large audiences. Correspondingly, the right kind of new buildings made many things possible. The Gallery that opened in 1987 enabled the University art collection and exhibitions to flower. Later, the brilliant facilities in the Performing Arts Building (1996)—much the best construction in the wave of capital projects under Logan—opened the potential for a new era in music, dance and drama.

The art collection and Gallery

The Monash art collection had its origins in Matheson's March 1961 proposal to the Professorial Board, on the urging of Jock Marshall, that 'a modest sum' be provided each year for the purchase of works of art.[2] Like the grounds and buildings, the bias of the art collection was national and modern. The decision to concentrate on work by contemporary Australian artists was ahead of its time, though it was grounded in economic as well as aesthetic sensibilities: the Art Purchasing Committee (later the Art Advisory Committee) began with only 500 pounds a year, and it was thought better to spend the 'modest sum' on a larger number of promising works by younger artists. The acquisition policy also allowed senior members of the Committee to play the role of patron, pursuing their own artistic tastes and their skills in talent spotting. The first painting bought under these guidelines was *Two foxes* by Clifton Pugh, a friend of Marshall's with whom he shared a fascination with the Australian bush. Later the Committee branched out to sculpture, ceramics and other work. The University also supported local artists by setting aside a small proportion of the funding for each new building for works of art to embellish the building, such as murals or sculpture, though this policy was later allowed to lapse.

In the outcome Monash created a collection of contemporary local art before it was fashionable.[3] The acquisition mandate was formalised in 1976 with the help of Professor Patrick McCaughey from the Department of Visual Arts, from 1981 the Director of the National Gallery of Victoria. The aims of the collection included 'to build up a broadly representative collection of Australian art in the years since the foundation of Monash', though holdings were not confined to this ambit.[4] The limited budget was used well, with some remarkable purchases made for relatively modest sums, such as John Brack's *Crossing* (1978). The Gallery, established to display works from the collection and house a growing number of exhibitions, provided a public service, especially in the southeastern suburbs. Until the creation of State-supported galleries such as Heide and the Australian Centre for Contemporary Art, and the development of University of Melbourne galleries, the Monash Gallery was the main public exhibition space in the zone between the large State collection at the National Gallery of Victoria and the commercial galleries.[5]

Grazia Gunn was the first full-time curator (1975), succeeded by Jenepher Duncan in 1980. The Gallery was located on the seventh floor of the Menzies Building in the Department of Visual Arts. The curator played only a minor role in the Department's teaching program while the physical limitations were obvious, and in 1983 a group calling itself the 'Friends of Russell Drysdale', including former Dean of Medicine Rod Andrew, organised an auction of paintings that raised $100 000 towards the cost of a new building to house the Gallery. This sum was augmented by the University, and the multidiscipline centre was designed by Daryl Jackson Architects and opened in early 1987.[6] The first exhibition was a Russell Drysdale retrospective that drew 4200 visitors.

The Department of Visual Arts was to follow the Gallery into the new building, but space allocation became a problem and it elected to stay in Menzies. As incoming Vice-Chancellor, Logan also became Chair of the Art Advisory Committee and strongly supported the separation of Gallery and Department. This decision was to have an enormous long-term impact. It meant the Gallery gained its own budget and ceased to be financially dependent on the Faculty of Arts, just at the time when that faculty's economic position was about to worsen. The Monash Art Foundation was established, with half of the money placed in interest-building deposits and the other half used for the purchase of works of art. In 1990 the building embellishment fund was revived, and 0.5–1.0 per cent of the funding allocated to each new building was used to buy works of art. The new works were designated as part of the Collection rather than being allocated permanently to their buildings.[7]

The Curator was renamed Gallery Director, and the Art Advisory Committee was renamed the Gallery Committee. The Committee was chaired by Logan throughout his term of office, and Wade also played a significant role both as Committee member and as the University officer in charge of the Gallery. The senior managers were located on the first floor of the new building while their

Patrick McCaughey. Professor of Visual Arts (1974–81) and a principal influence in the development of the University collection, along with curators Grazia Gunn (1975–80) and Jenepher Duncan (from 1980).

quarters in the University offices were renovated, so that works in the collection slipped into their consciousness, encouraging mental leaps between the management of art and the art of management.[8]

The acquisitions policy was revisited in 1988, and one of the goals became 'to develop a major public art collection for the purpose of demonstrating the University's continued commitment to the study, patronage and advancement of the visual arts in Australia'. The emphasis on contemporary Australian art was retained, and 'fair representation of Australian women artists' was made explicit.[9] Nothing as big as the Drysdale retrospective was on show, and total Gallery attendance was down, but there were seven exhibitions in 1988 compared with the five in 1987. The most popular exhibition was the review of the Australian work of Walter Burley Griffin, the designer of Canberra. Les Kossatz, designer of the stained glass prepared for the Religious Centre, became the first practising artist to be a member of the Committee. Attendances were up again the following year, acquisitions continued, and the Gallery found that in its new premises it was already running out of storage space.[10]

In 1989 and again in 1990 there was an exhibition of work by postgraduate students from Chisholm and Gippsland, a goodwill gesture on the brink of the mergers and a departure from the Gallery's normal conception of itself as a public exhibition space rather than a gallery for student work. The mergers extended the scope of the Committee to the management of the art holdings of Chisholm and Gippsland and the display of works from the collection on all campuses, including 30 Collins Street from 1992. Acquisitions were also centralised. In a field as naturally heterogeneous as the arts, the normal merger difficulties were compounded, and the enlarged responsibility of Committee and Director were not easy to implement. On 29 December 1990 those responsibilities were further extended when the affiliation agreement with the Australian Centre for Contemporary Art (ACCA) was signed.

The ACCA was situated next to the Botanic Gardens in South Yarra, not far from the National Gallery of Victoria. Created in 1984 as a State government initiative to supplement the National Gallery in the field of contemporary art, the ACCA held exhibitions in painting, photography, sculpture, performance and sound. In the annual number of exhibitions and size of attendances it was similar to the Clayton Gallery, while its central location made it a stronger site in the evenings, and a useful space for seminars and public events. The government was keen to involve Monash in the ACCA's operation because the main source of non-government funding had collapsed, and there were insufficient monies to support both the staff and the exhibition program. In effect the ACCA became part of the Monash network

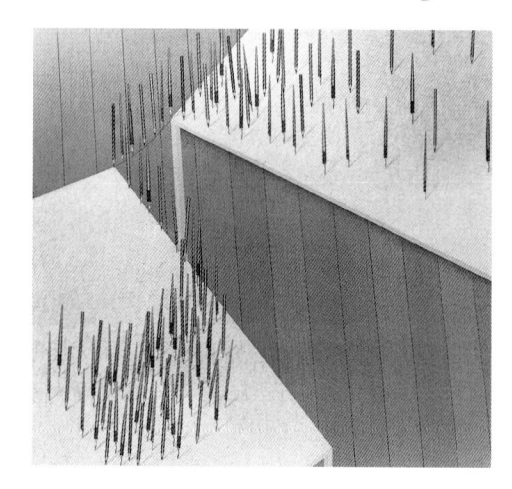

John Brack's *Crossing* **(1978).** Oil on canvas, purchased in 1979.

while retaining its autonomy and public funding. Logan took over the ACCA chair in April 1990 and Wade became Treasurer in January 1991. Monash funded one full-time staff position and was represented on the ACCA Board of Management. By 1993 the annual deficit had been eliminated. In 1994 there were 21 exhibitions and 18 lectures, performances and other public events, including international photographic exhibitions by Jean Baudrillard and Pierre Molinier.[11]

Meanwhile the University collection continued to build. In 1992 the Committee bought 13 works totalling $50 800 and received 15 gifts valued at $64 850: the collection now contained 700 works. The Gallery at Clayton held seven exhibitions including 'The Angelic Space', which commemorated the work of Piero della Francesca 500 years after his death, and the Art Gallery of Western Australia's 'Ian Burn Minimal-Conceptual Work 1965–1970'. There were also two displays drawn from the Monash collection, including 'The body in question'. 'Contemporary Gippsland artists', which consisted largely of the work of art teaching staff from the Gippsland campus and focused on positive images of regionalism, concluded a two-year national tour at Clayton.[12] Together with the Department of Ecology and Evolutionary Biology, the Gallery negotiated details of a seven-month British tour of the Banksia watercolours painted by Celia Rosser.[13] As a stalwart of the Gallery Committee and Chair of the Friends of the Monash University Gallery, Rod Andrew argued that the collection should be on permanent display. He believed that this had been the understanding reached when the monies raised by the 'Friends of Russell Drysdale' was donated to the University a decade before. However, permanent display of the collection would have reduced the capacity to mount other exhibitions, and Andrew's foray into Gallery policy was unsuccessful.[14]

Clayton Gallery attendances were down in 1993 and it was decided to issue personal invitations to staff to build greater interest. The collection bought 22 works totalling $124 070, including balance payments from the previous year. A total of 97 works from the collection were on display throughout the Clayton, Caulfield and Peninsula campuses. The first inventory of artworks from the Caulfield campus was undertaken. The rented studio at Collingwood, a venue used mainly by Caulfield postgraduate students, was losing money, and closure was imminent. In October 1993 in a memo to the Vice-Chancellor's adviser, Elizabeth Anderson, Duncan suggested the creation of a Monash Art Prize for the acquisition of works by emerging artists. Logan found the funds and 21 artists were invited to contribute for the inaugural competition in 1995. The first prize of $8000 was awarded by the panel of three judges to a large painting by the Sydney-based artist Mathew Jones, with the second prize of $6000 for work by Callum Morton. The idea of an Artist in Residence was discussed—the Vice-Chancellor was 'most interested' according to Anderson—but space was now at a premium, and the proposal was reluctantly discarded.[15]

In 1995 there was a strong focus on women artists and a rise in attendances due to the targeting of secondary schools by Gallery staff, which now included a Director, Assistant Director, Administrator, part-time Assistant Curator, Secretary and Security Officer. Public events held in conjunction with the ACCA included forums, lectures and performances. Curator Natalie King helped to organise a joint exhibition of the work of young Australian artists alongside their Singapore counterparts, to be held in Singapore. This generated representations from Monash International, and the Committee agreed that the company had an important role in the coordination and financing of Monash's cultural activities in Singapore. In 1996, in a long discussion about Gallery development, it was noted there was a need for more exhibition space so as to display elements of the collection alongside the rotating exhibition program.[16] By then the collection included more than 1000 works in diverse media, including pieces by Sidney Nolan, Ian Burn, Fred Williams, John Brack, Peter Booth, Dale Hickey, Susan Norrie, Julie Rap and Mike Parr.

The Gallery retained its orientation to the contemporary, experimental and emergent. On Tuesday 19 March 1996 it sponsored an appearance by performance artist Stelarc as part of the week-long celebrations attendant on the opening of the new Performing Arts Centre complex. In the show, *Split Body, Voltage In/Voltage Out*, Stelarc attached a robotic limb and electrodes to his body. 'The cyborg-like transformation means that his body can be controlled by a computer program generating electric shocks', reported *Etcetera*.[17]

The Robert Blackwood Hall

If the Galleries were the *avant-garde* face of the arts at Monash, the main performance spaces at Clayton, the Robert Blackwood Hall and the Alexander Theatre, were the mainstream. The economics of *avant-garde* performance arts are tougher than the economics of exhibitions in *avant-garde* painting and sculpture. The Hall and the Theatre shaped their programs to fit the needs of public service and cultural commerce, with the service function sustained by subsidies from the University. This public service function was part of the Hall from its opening in 1971, for half of the cost of building had been raised by public subscription. In addition to University functions and ceremonies—the Hall with its powerful West window designed by Leonard French was the site of examinations and degree conferrings—the Robert Blackwood Hall and the Alexander Theatre became the main providers of music, theatre, dance and other performances for the eastern suburbs of Melbourne. The Alexander Theatre was sustained by its successful children's theatre program, and both Hall and Theatre were used extensively by schools, drama groups, dancing schools, callisthenics clubs, ethnic and service clubs and music groups.

In 1987, Harold Karpin's first year as Manager, the Robert Blackwood Hall was used for 140 University functions, including graduations, orientation ceremonies, examinations, re-enrolments, career contact for graduates, concerts and public lectures. The Australian Broadcasting Corporation (ABC) provided its usual six major concerts by the Melbourne Symphony Orchestra, and conducted 51 rehearsals and recording sessions. Two commercial film scores were also recorded, and 68 other concerts, competitions, religious meetings and conferences took place during the course of the year. The University had financed Monday lunchtime concerts for almost 15 years, though the 1300-seat Hall was too large for them.[18] The Army and Police Bands provided eight performances attended by almost 10 000 school children. Thirty schools and colleges used the Hall for graduations, speech nights and concerts. Something was happening in the Hall for 78.1 per cent of the year, including the weekend days and holiday periods, underlining its role as a community facility.[19]

The following year, the Hall's Management Committee became increasingly concerned with relations with the ABC. Bookings were cancelled sometimes on a day's notice. Then, after many years, the ABC withdrew its concert series, though it continued to use the Hall for rehearsals. As Chair of the Committee, Engineering Professor Noel Murray complained to the redoubtable David Hill, Managing Director of the ABC, that the Orchestra's administration seemed to look on the Hall only as 'as a place to be exploited' for rehearsals for concerts held at the Concert Hall or the Melbourne Town Hall. Hill told Murray that the ABC had become concerned at declining audiences. The venue was too far from the city centre, and lacked catering and refreshment facilities. Logan became involved, inviting Hill to Clayton for lunch to talk things over. The matter of catering was 'not insurmountable', he stated. But the Canberra network did not work this time. Hill suggested that the invitation was more appropriately directed to the General Manager of the Melbourne Symphony Orchestra. Though the University was disappointed, there was nothing it could do.[20] The size of the music program in the Hall was not much reduced by the ABC's decision, and total use of the facilities continued to grow. By 1992 there were 50 per cent more activities than in 1987, just over half being University activities, and 40 schools staged graduations, speech nights and concerts. At the end of 1993 Noel Murray stood down as Chair of the Management Committee after 14 years, leaving Roy Jackson the Director of the Hall as the longest-standing Professor on the Management Committee, as well as the occasional referee in the sometimes acrimonious disputes between the Hall's manager and different users of the Hall over scheduling and access.[21]

In 1994, after all the drama, the ABC's Melbourne Symphony Orchestra concert series quietly returned. Ticket sales went well. In February 1994 the builder of the Louis Matheson pipe organ, Jurgen Ahrend, revisited the University, restoring the organ to its original condition; in 1995 the long-awaited harpsichord for the Hall was delivered. The project, first mooted 10 years before and supported by a public appeal, was delayed by the illness of its maker, Australian Bill Bright, placing the University under pressure from donors. It seemed that Noel Murray had done much to encourage Bright to finish it.[22] The number of subscribers to the ABC concerts doubled from 1994–95, and over the two years the Melbourne String Quartet, Victoria de los Angeles, the Aboriginal Islander Dance Theatre, and the Quang Dong Acrobats of China, among others, all performed there. 'What a wonderful acoustics your Hall has', declared Victoria de los Angeles after she sang there in 1995, 'and what a relief it is for a singer'.[23]

Servicing the organ. In 1994 the builder of the Louis Matheson pipe organ, Jurgen Ahrend, revisited the University and restored the organ to its original condition.

The theatres

Despite the financial support of the University, the Alexander Theatre never became associated with a self-sustaining Monash student theatre tradition. It was not that the Alex was a poor venue in itself. With distinctive (and expensive) sloping walls, it was opened by Senator John Gorton in 1967 as the best-equipped theatre in Melbourne outside the central business district. Rather, potential student players were drawn off to suburban theatre companies; audiences for student theatre varied alarmingly and the Alex was expensive to maintain. And it was simply wrong for many student plays: its fixed proscenium arch stage, broad shallow playing area and large audience capacity were incompatible with the experimental, minimalist, confronting productions that many student companies wanted. Student theatre often found itself in the Union—where it had to compete with the Film Society—the Manton Rooms on the ground floor of Menzies, and the Chemistry Gardens, sometimes used by the Shakespeare Society.[24] The Union Board employed a line of fine directors of student theatre, such as Nigel Triffit, Stephen Dee, Bob Burton and Jim Lawson. Peter Fitzpatrick from English directed many student plays.

After Philip A'Vard was appointed Manager of the Alex in 1969, the theatre began to establish a coherent and businesslike role, if less *avant-garde* than some had hoped. A'Vard knew that income from outside hiring was crucial to the

Theatre's operations, and that it was necessary to maintain a high technical standard in the 500-seat theatre so as to attract those outside bookings. By the mid-1970s the Alex was largely maintained by children's theatre, especially the Saturday Club which began in 1972, and by hirings to suburban theatre companies and others.[25] The long-term pattern had been established. Children's theatre underwrote adult and student theatre, these remained the lesser parts of the total operation, and in most years the subsidy from the University was kept down to mutually tolerable levels. For example in 1986, 58 per cent of the audience was for children's theatre. Adult theatre comprised 25 per cent of all performances, and local gymnastic, callisthenics and dancing schools 15 per cent.[26]

The perennial problem of parking seemed the only factor inhibiting children's theatre at Monash. It appeared impossible to devise satisfactory parking for outside theatre-goers, even on Saturdays. The problem peaked when the school holidays overlapped with normal semester time. A'Vard called it 'angry letter season'. Nevertheless, despite the children's theatre phenomenon the nagging feeling remained that the Theatre needed to start a new direction if it was to find a place within Melbourne theatre. In 1988 negotiations were conducted with the Playbox Theatre Company to extend some of its 1989 seasons to Monash, with assistance from the University.[27]

The first Playbox productions at Clayton were *Nice girls* by Linden Wilkenson, and *Coralie Lansdowne says no* by Alexander Buzo. Staff buying a ticket for the whole season, which included Willy Russell's *Educating Rita*, received a good discount.[28] Average evening audiences were 77 per cent.[29] Over dinner in a Hawthorn restaurant, Logan discussed with Playbox Artistic Director Carrillo Gantner the potential for a longer-term association. From the start, the idea was that Playbox would become a part of Monash but it would enjoy a greater artistic and financial independence than the Melbourne Theatre Company (MTC), which was linked to the University of Melbourne, a relationship that exhibited periodic strain. Wade managed negotiations from the Monash end. There were a number of benefits. Student productions were staged at the renovated Playbox headquarters at the Malthouse in South Melbourne. The Playbox contributed to the theatre and drama studies program at Monash, and offered discounts to Monash students.

A community service. The children's program, especially the Saturday Club, became the mainstay of the Alexander Theatre and a significant contribution to eastern suburbs life in Melbourne.

The Playbox at Monash. Theatre Manager Philip A'Vard is on the right. The posters advertise the first two Playbox productions at Clayton.

Meanwhile A'Vard ducked and weaved successfully enough to evade proposals for the relocation of 9 am Faculty of Economics and Politics lectures to the Alex. He had an argument, for in terms of audiences the Theatre was going from strength to strength. In 1990 all previous figures for total attendance (141 400 people) and usage (518 occasions) were broken. The Monash Play Season was again successful, in terms of both numbers attending (13 901) and its contribution to promoting the University, though it required a significant subsidy ($35 000). In the second half of 1990 Theatre operations were reviewed by the Sydney-based arts consultant and administrator Justin Macdonnell. He praised the Theatre, its staff and its manager.[30] With the merger agreement now signed, the review included the 350-seat George Jenkins Theatre at Frankston, which was the community theatre for the Peninsula area. The review led to an overarching University Theatres Board, and A'Vard's role was extended to managing the George Jenkins Theatre. Programs at the Alex were brought to Frankston. Macdonnell also supported the inclusion of the Robert Blackwood Hall in a common administrative structure with the theatres, but this was strongly opposed by Murray and the Hall's Committee of Management.[31]

University funding was becoming tighter. Both theatres came under pressure to reduce their subsidised deficits. The problem was compounded by a loss of $204 708 on the Monash Play Season for 1991, the first year of operation at the George Jenkins Theatre. Too many performances had been attempted. A'Vard began a more systematic attempt to attract sponsoring companies, and in August 1991 the Victorian Health Promotion Foundation provided the children's season at the Alex with $88 278. The financial position improved in 1992, mostly because of better-than-expected box office receipts at the George Jenkins Theatre, where attendances were double those of 1991. Surprisingly, the long success in children's theatre now began to falter. For a time the Alex was less adventurous in its choice of productions. Next year, attendances at the Alex picked up again, and the number of community groups involved in productions increased, to 46 at the Alex and 43 at Peninsula.[32] In 1994 total attendances at both theatres reached 30 171. The deficit was $83 016. The University seemed to have settled into the role of subsidising a mainstream theatre operation that ran at a loss, though from time to time it tried to turn the grant into a loan.[33] The theatres were an important public service, yet there was little that took them to the cutting edge. That was left to other branches of the arts at Monash.

The Performing Arts Centre

The creation of the $10.5 million Performing Arts Centre building[34] confirmed Clayton's role as the largest concentration of arts activity in Victoria outside St Kilda Road. By providing boutique performance facilities for drama, dance and music, it rendered more flexible the total facilities for the arts and broadened the potential range of performances. It enabled the mass venues of the modern era, the Alex and the Robert Blackwood Hall, to be partly replaced by smaller, technologically sophisticated post-modern venues. The new Centre included soundproof practice rooms, a music archive, the Asian Orchestras Room, the Early Music Room, recording studios and dressing rooms, plus seminar space and academic offices. The new building was associated with an administrative revamp which revived Macdonnell's idea of a more integrated approach. The new Performing and Creative Arts Committee covered the theatres, the Robert Blackwood Hall and the new Music Auditorium and Drama Theatre. Pargetter was Chair of the Committee and A'Vard was the first Director of Performing and Creative Arts, though given the size of his responsibility in relation to the theatres it was difficult for him to become closely involved in all aspects of performance at Monash.[35]

The University celebrated the launch of the Centre with a week-long arts festival on all campuses. The indigenous rock band Yothu Yindi began the week's activities with a lunchtime concert in the Arts Centre courtyard on 18 March 1996, followed by indigenous opera singer Maroochy Barmbah. Other offerings included *Temple dreaming* by Indian dancer and resident Monash fellow Tara Rajkumar, performance artist Stelarc, the Melbourne String Quartet and the Melbourne Symphony, Team of Pianists and 'the tap dancing sensation', Tap Dogs.[36]

The new building brought a qualitative change to all of the performing arts. In their old premises in the Manton Rooms drama students and staff had stood on rickety eight-foot ladders to hang a maximum of 15 lights; the new theatre had 80 lights, and with 250 seats it was better than the Alex for University-based productions. Within four years, the Centre for Drama and Theatre studies alone had staged more than 40 productions.[37] There were also half a dozen shows a year in the Union. Monash now had four active theatre venues.[38] The other major winner was music. The Department of Music dated from 1965, though it had taught musical performance only since 1990. Under Margaret Kartomi it specialised in Southeast Asia (especially Indonesia), Japan, Africa and indigenous Australia. The move to Performing Arts enabled the Department to run specific classrooms in each specialty area, while the music auditorium seated 250, which was a better size than the Blackwood Hall for lunchtime concerts.

In addition to the University lunchtime series the Department provided its own concert series, and in some weeks there was a concert in the Performing Arts Centre every day, with Tuesday reserved for student performances. E-mail was an effective means of advertising. Lunchtime attendances grew and Logan funded a part-time concert manager. There were also concerts in the Religious Centre for part of the year, so that when the Robert Blackwood Hall was included the University had three music performance venues.[39] Composition was an emerging area of strength, now becoming digitalised. Students made up the New Monash Orchestra, the Monash Wind Symphony, the string orchestra Simphonia, and the Departmental choir Viva Voce.[40]

Specialising in East and Southeast Asian music: Margaret Kartomi with Jose Maceda from the University of the Philippines' Department of Asian Music. The instrument is a kacapi bambu from Sumatra.

Caulfield Art and Design

Outside Clayton there were three main areas of activity. The Switchback Gallery at Gippsland began as a student gallery and became an important regional exhibition space, working in conjunction with the La Trobe Regional Gallery. Peninsula specialised in crafts, including ceramics, which were also strong at Gippsland. Caulfield had the School of Art and Design, which despite its post-merger problems (see chapter 5) was an educational leader in graphic design and industrial design, fine arts, ceramic design and craft.

The appointment of John Redmond as Head of the subfaculty (later the Faculty) of Art and Design brought a restless, aggressive innovator onto the Monash arts scene. Redmond felt that Monash Gallery policy tended to serve the Clayton campus to the exclusion of others. He argued that there should be one visual arts entity at Monash, and Gallery activities should be integrated with teaching and research. He wanted to pursue his own exhibition program in association with the subfaculty at Caulfield, and was frustrated by what he saw as the Gallery's privileged access to central University funds. He argued that the Caulfield campus was a more important teaching site in the visual arts than was Clayton. He also proposed that exhibitions at Clayton should tour Caulfield and Gippsland. In response, Jenepher Duncan defended central funding of the Gallery, its 'supra-faculty' orientation and its independence of teaching, the association between the Gallery and collection, and the potential created by administrative and spatial proximity to the University leadership. There was no doubt that the Gallery and collection had benefited from the post-1987 relationship with the University, and Duncan's handling of the matter was supported by the University's leaders, who had invested heavily in a Gallery and collection centred at Clayton and saw them as important to Monash's public face.[41]

Nevertheless, this check did not exhaust Redmond's energy for reform. He began to push for a closer relationship between the arts and teaching across all Monash courses. 'Sensory and creative capabilities, marginalised by the scientific rationalism of the industrial age', were becoming 'increasingly important', he stated. He pointed to examples of medical students who took drawing classes to improve their capacities to perceive and communicate: 'drawing forces people to see'. An understanding of the dynamics of creativity was useful to graduates in any field, from Engineering to Business, he argued.[42] It was a good sign that even in the midst of the harder-driven vocational culture of the later 1990s, courses in the arts felt able to bid for a central place in the curriculum.

9 Learning, teaching, research

> Research . . . is the point on which the academic community turns, and it is by their research performance that academics take on their professional identity and are judged by their peers. Teaching accomplishments take a back seat. . . But if we are seriously interested in promoting the quality of higher education, of improving the effectiveness by which teachers teach and students learn, it is to the teaching process that we must look.
>
> Ronald Barnett, *The idea of higher education*, Society for Research into Higher Education and Open University Press, Buckingham, 1990, p. 135

Student life in the late 1980s and 90s

In 1987 at Clayton, on the brink of the great change in the University, conservative student politicians—their preferred code words were 'moderate' and 'non-aligned'—were on top in the Student Union. Jenny Munz and fellow *Lots Wife* editor Steve O'Mara[1] campaigned to stop 'anti-Zionist extremists' from winning the student newspaper. The Monash Association of Students was largely inactive due to the election of an executive whose sympathies did not lie with student unionism, though it joined the new National Union of Students (NUS), replacing the now-defunct Australian Union of Students, in December.[1] The Union was preoccupied with the question of the future of the Community Research Action Centre (CRAC), attacked by the Monash Jewish Students' Society (MONJSS) for supporting a Palestine Human Rights project; CRAC's long tradition of radical campaigns and innovations on policy issues came to an end when it was disbanded in mid-year. However, a new wave of activism was foreshadowed in the government's introduction of the $250 Higher Education Administration Charge, which spelled the end of free higher education.[2]

In 1988 the big issue in the Union was whether a bar should be opened on campus. This had been the subject of recurring debate. When the Union was drawing up the final plans for completion of a licensed facility, one member of the Union Board contested the otherwise unanimous decision, and it was agreed to put the matter to a referendum of students and staff. Some of the religious clubs campaigned against the bar, but it was strongly supported by *Lots Wife* and the Union hierarchy, which took it for granted that the referendum would be carried. To widespread surprise the proposition was defeated by a good margin. The silent majority had spoken.[3] Nevertheless, the apostles for alcohol had other venues for their rites. Farm Week (see chapter 2) was revived, including the famous scavenger hunt. It was thinly disguised, with a change of name to 'Green Week': the name was said to be derived from the colour of the can used by the brand of beer sponsoring the event, Victoria Bitter! (Perhaps it should have been titled 'Beer Week'.) The same year, Student Radio 3MU began transmitting on the FM band,[4] and with the announcement of the Higher Education Contribution Scheme (HECS) the student fees issue hotted up. David Strover and others organised a campaign against the introduction of HECS, occupying the university offices for two days. Later, Strover, Erica Pearson and Luna Ruiz were elected *Lots Wife* editors for 1989 on the strength of their involvement.

The Unions at Chisholm and Gippsland remained separate from the Union and Students' Association at Clayton, and Caulfield and Peninsula stayed in a common organisation, preserving a residual Chisholm consciousness. Pharmacy also kept its student association. Focusing on student services more than student politics, and with new premises on both campuses, Caulfield-Peninsula was one of the largest student unions in Australia, with a turnover of $11.5 million in 1996. Its bookshop opened a branch at the Australian Catholic University. Representative functions were handled by a student association within the Union structure; the issues included parking (especially at Caulfield), student accommodation, and the retention of the name David Syme at the School of Business. The Union at Caulfield and Peninsula was 'very business oriented'.[5] At Clayton, student government, activism and cultural activity were often more important.

In the 1990s the Clayton student politics ebbed and flowed. It was perhaps less imaginative and distinctive than it had been in the first decade of the University in the 1960s, and even the early 1980s.[6] After two decades the bold impression left by Albert Langer was finally fading. The number of people active in the Union, Monash Association of Students (MAS) executive and committees, *Lots Wife* and the whole gamut of clubs, societies and cooperatives was in the hundreds rather than thousands. Some academics decried what they saw as

Monash trained him. Liberal club activists with a banner advertising the electoral claims of Federal Treasurer Peter Costello, who cut his political teeth in the Monash Union in the late 1970s.

the conservatism of students, recalling the earlier years (when those same academics had often been on the other side of the barricades) with nostalgia.[7] Perhaps these sentiments merely signified their isolation from contemporary student life, for if mood was more vocational than before, Monash students were neither socially scared, culturally timid nor politically backward. By external standards, rather than those of Monash past, the label 'conservative' was scarcely accurate. There was still plenty going on. If the faces on election posters were now those of 'nice kids' more often than 'bomb throwing revolutionaries', as one student leader put it, and not every cultural activist was drawn to the addictive excitement of the politics of social change, Edwina Hanlon, who edited *Lots Wife* with Mark Jeanes and Selena Papps in 1993, found Monash to be 'a thriving metropolis' with 'a great variety of activities and a great variety of students'.[8]

The main change in student politics was that it was more closely aligned to mainstream Labor–Liberal politics. Militant student activism was still a factor, particularly in relation to ecology and education policy, but it did not set the whole mood. While at the Universities of Melbourne and Sydney student activism retained some of the classic features of the young bourgeois in revolt, it seemed that a more sober and realistic tone had come to Monash. The balance of power tended to lean towards Labor and the non-aligned left.[9] From time to time explicitly conservative groups played a role. There was another effort to establish a bar in the Union, and again the attempt was unsuccessful. A funded women's officer position was created in 1993, raising awareness of the issue of rape on campus; as a result the University improved the lighting and provided a bus to ferry students at night from the library to the car parks. Parking was a continuing issue. The same year there was a Koori Awareness Week, and *Lots Wife*, facing a hostile MAS executive, picked up the traditional political role of MAS by organising Tom Keneally to speak at Clayton on republicanism, accompanied by an article in *Lots*. The theatre was packed out.[10]

The Clayton Union building was the central mixing point on campus because most students had their lunches there. It was largely empty at night and there continued to be little student life in the neighbourhood of Clayton, aside from the Halls of Residence and the Nott, which was less important than it had been in the University's first two decades. Monash's suburban location remained both a strength and a weakness. It created a sharp distinction between university life and home life. The University lacked the inner-city 'street cred' enjoyed by Melbourne and RMIT, with their proximity to the fashionable districts for student living and entertainment. On the other hand, Clayton, like Caulfield, was geographically accessible to the families living in suburbs with the highest rates of participation in higher education; and the wide open spaces at Clayton enabled a more relaxing atmosphere, particularly compared with RMIT.[11] The quadrangle between the Union and Menzies was often full to overflowing, especially on sunny days.

One part of the Union building which stayed open at night was the *Lots Wife* office. *Lots* provided fast-track learning in writing and editing, desktop publishing, layout nights, fast foods, stress management, people management, and the finality of printers' deadlines. It gave editors the opportunity to have a vision and put it into practice. Editors changed annually and their efforts were highly variable, though *Lots* usually improved during the year as the format, editing style and intraoffice politics sorted themselves out.

> The most amazing thing about a *Lots Wife* layout night is driving home on a Friday morning and thinking about it all. In about 48 hours you have just been through this complete range of emotions whereby you have absolutely lost it with people, you've been rapt with an idea, something's working, something's not working, you've got typesetters and volunteers cracking the shits, you've had relationships formed and broken, it's absolute undergrad excess. It's the best. And it is the only thing aside from getting an edition back that makes the job worthwhile . . . at the end of that two week period you have this thing to look at for two weeks. It changes every two weeks. It is a constant process of renewal.[12]

In 1988 there was a combined issue of all the Victorian student newspapers, with a 40 000 print run. The project was a raging success (especially in the minds of the editors) and was repeated more than once in the next few years. *Lots* editors faced the recurring dilemmas of whether to entertain or to argue a case; and whether to pitch for maximum readership by being deliberately provocative, or by being professional and inclusive. In Hanlon's year the editors opted for the latter strategy, publishing 20 issues with plenty of advertising. They were attacked for bias only once, in sharp contrast with some of their predecessors, and by the end of the year found that they were having to print more copies. In 1994 Cody, Forrest and Paton prepared a CD issue of *Lots*, assisted by a grant from the University. They distributed 6000 free CDs, including a segment on the Commonwealth quality assurance agenda, snippets of humour and live recordings of bands that had played at Monash. It was one of the years that *Lots* was not very political.[13] Stated Cody later:

'If it's not on it's not on. The first Aidswatch in 1988.

> My one regret as editor of *Lots Wife* was that we produced a newspaper that was thoroughly vacuous and we made no attempt towards furthering any aims of any kind whatsoever barring the entertainment of its readers.[14]

But even if its aim was only to entertain, the future of *Lots Wife* was now uncertain. Through its Voluntary Student Union (VSU) legislation the Victorian government wanted to cut off support for all student activities with political potential. The intention was to allow student unions to collect fees but to limit the activities they could finance. Student newspapers were on the excluded list. For a time the Commonwealth Labor government provided funds earmarked for student union activity, allowing universities to circumvent the intent of the State legislation. The Students' Association and *Lots Wife* campaigned vigorously against VSU.[15] The legislation achieved the opposite of its intention. Such is the contrary logic of political repression. According to Symon Rubens, an editor of *Lots* in 1996: 'It wasn't often as editors that we had a definite agenda in the paper. When it came to VSU we had an agenda. That was because of our own survival'.[16]

Like the anti-HECS campaign, the anti-VSU campaign created another generation of activists. Once again, new students began to learn the old techniques of radical politics—leaflets, meetings, megaphones, rallies and confrontations—and the heady excitement that came with it. As another *Lots* editor put it: 'I think that is why people become involved in things like *Lots Wife* and student politics. Because it is a real adrenalin rush. They love it'.[17] The VSU debate generated some of the largest student general meetings in Monash's recent history. At one meeting only nine students supported the VSU legislation and over 1400 students voted against it. The election of a Federal Coalition government in 1996 meant that student unions were no longer protected from the VSU. The funding from DEET dried up overnight and *Lots Wife* was closed. To the surprise of the editors, there was a rally of 2000 people in the Union building. The mainstream media were sympathetic and strong public support was expressed, especially in the arts and music communities. Eventually the Students' Association refloated the newspaper, but its temporary closure had galvanised opposition to the VSU perhaps more than any other measure could have done.[18]

Not all the activities that moved and motivated students were happening in the Union building. One form of association was the Halls of Residence. In the union people stuck together with others from home, whether from the country or overseas, but in collegiate corridors and eating areas they rubbed shoulders with everyone else. The Halls taught their inmates tolerance. Many came into contact with indigenous students for the first time. Relationships formed in the Halls could become profoundly important to personal development.[19]

Some very serious friendships were built up. Although there was a mainstream culture of drinking, beer swilling, footy-playing—and that includes the women because we had a women's footy team—there was room and space for everyone.[20]

For many students the most important connections were with sporting clubs, religious organisations and other affinity groups. One was the Monash University Regiment, which proudly celebrated its 25th anniversary in 1995 with a record number of officer cadets and the establishment of a solid presence in the Gippsland region. Officer cadets were trained concurrently by the Regiment and the Royal Military College at Duntroon, and those who passed became graduates of the Military College. Members of the Regiment conducted a successful march in the Netherlands.[21] No doubt John Monash would have been pleased.

The first half of the 1990s saw a strengthening of faculty student societies, to an extent not seen since the 1960s. Law, Engineering and Medicine had always sustained their own pre-professional identities, and Science and Arts students also had recognisable styles. There was an informal dress code, never quite universal: law students with Country Road clothes and leather briefcases, engineers with tracksuit pants and Dunlop runners, arts students with old school bags and backpacks, and often dressed in black. The newly created Economics and Commerce Students Society grew very quickly. New clubs also began in Science and Arts. The clubs in Law and Engineering were particularly strong.

Some argued that faculty organisations were unduly segregating the University. The tutorials and counselling services duplicated similar services also offered by MSA. The growth of commencement and recovery balls organised by Law, Economics and Science led to the disappearance of the corresponding MSA functions. The rise of faculty societies was a sign of a student body that was more course- and career-focused than before and a university grown to three times its earlier size. The faculty groups also helped to bridge the gap between the different metropolitan Monash campuses, and the segregation effect was partly offset by combined degree enrolments and cross-faculty participation in social affairs.[22]

Vocationalism

Students were more sensitive to the graduate labour market than their predecessors had been. With total unemployment hovering around 10 per cent, not all graduates were certain of a job, and of those that were employed many faced difficulties in securing the kind of job they wanted. Graduate employment fluctuated along with the economy. In the boom conditions of the mid- to late 1980s, a growing number of graduates was absorbed

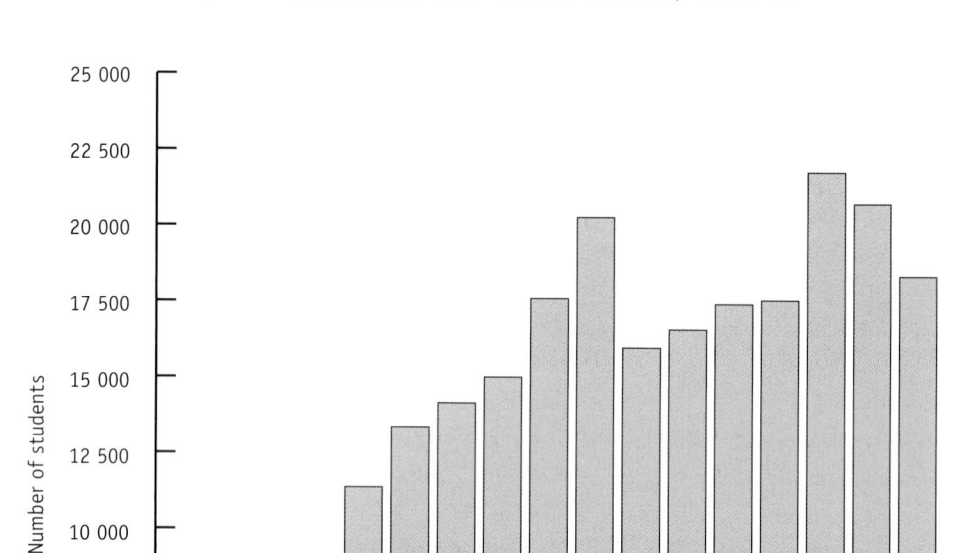

FIGURE 9.1 JOB VACANCIES REGISTERED AT THE MONASH UNIVERSITY STUDENT EMPLOYMENT AND CAREER SERVICE, 1980–96

successfully and graduate salaries were rising, compared with overall workforce earnings. There was slower demand in the public sector, once the dominant employer of graduates, but expanding demand in management, marketing, finance and information technology, and solid opportunities in engineering. The beginning of the 1990s saw a severe economic recession in Australia. In 1990 the number of job vacancies registered with the Clayton Student Employment Service fell by 21 per cent (Figure 9.1). The supply of new graduates was still growing everywhere, and the outcome was a more competitive graduate labour market, greater individual insecurity, and intensified competition between universities.

In Victoria the recession was particularly severe. Nevertheless, new graduates from Monash, especially from Clayton, felt it less harshly than graduates from most universities. At the peak of the recession in 1992, 22 per cent of Victorian Bachelor-level graduates were unemployed or underemployed[23] in the

April after graduation, compared with 17.5 per cent of Monash graduates. The 1993 Monash rate of unemployment and underemployment fell to 15.8 per cent while the Victorian rate was still at 20.9 per cent.[24] One reason that Monash graduates were relatively employable was the strong labour market performance of the professional faculties—not only Law and Medicine, but Engineering, Business and Economics, and Computing. In Law, with the expansion of the number of law schools in the 1990s many graduates from other universities could not enter the profession,[25] but most Monash Law graduates obtained articled clerkships in the year after graduation. Social work graduates also enjoyed good employment prospects.[26]

Arts and Science graduates faced greater difficulties. Pass graduates not going on to further study might find themselves working in supermarkets, sales or clerical jobs. However, 4 in 10 Bachelor-level Monash graduates in these disciplines immediately entered further study, and others returned later; with a second qualification, often a vocational one in either higher education or TAFE, their prospects of entering professional work improved greatly. Education and Nursing graduates had a difficult time in the early 1990s but then graduate outcomes improved, especially in Nursing. In 1996 virtually all Nursing graduates from Peninsula and Gippsland went straight into positions in the profession, though some were part-time or casually employed.[27] Like Medicine, Pharmacy was recession-proof, providing certain employment for its graduates.

The collapse of the labour market in the early 1990s accelerated the longer-term trend to a more vocational student culture at Monash and elsewhere. Vocationalism was shaped also by University marketing and course development, which fed into the hard-headed, career-minded approach now fashionable. The spread of user charges encouraged this. Failing a course meant not only a lost opportunity but financial penalties as well. Even Arts and Science were becoming justified in terms of their utility at work, rather than their formative effects on students or contributions to science and intellectual/cultural life. The growth of Business Studies, and vocationally tagged Arts degrees, brought work and learning closer together. So did 'cooperative education', whereby students spent part of their course working in industry: already in 1992, 1662 Monash students were involved in such programs.[28] There was a growing focus on learning work-related skills such as teamwork, oral communication and problem-solving, though the impact of this agenda varied by course.[29] Another sign was the emergence of the successful Deakin Australia, the commercial arm of Deakin University which provided full-fee professional upgrading, including in-house training negotiated with their professional associations for occupational groups such as accountants and engineers. In late 1994 and early 1995 Logan tried to create a similar company at Monash. However, there was 'no great enthusiasm'

Just the beginning. Graduation no longer led automatically to a full-time career job, and many students found themselves enrolling in second qualifications to strengthen their position in the labour market.

(Logan), either on Council or in the academic community, and it was discarded.[30]

Long-standing Monash academics were struck by the change in student outlook. Gus Sinclair, Dean of Economics at Clayton from 1983 to 1992, found students becoming more focused on the completion of their degrees and less active outside the classroom than their predecessors. Jim Warren, who taught in Science from 1962 and was Dean in 1994–96, found the students of the 1990s less engaged with and excited by the scientific disciplines. As a staff member from 1972 and Dean of Law from 1988, Bob Williams found the students of the 1990s 'more professional, more hard-working, more vocationally oriented'. They had less time to enjoy themselves, but somehow they still managed to do it.[31] Student leaders also noticed the change. Already when Munz was editor of *Lots Wife* in 1987 there were concerns about too much emphasis on hard work and achievement and not missing lectures, fears that the student body was becoming 'yuppified' and the Chocolate Appreciation Society was rising above the Labor and Liberal clubs: 'I mean how vacuous' (Munz).[32] Nick Economou, active in *Lots Wife* and the Union from 1981 to 1986, noted in 1996 as a lecturer in Politics that students were 'scared about the future. They want their degrees to be about getting into a profession and they try really hard, almost too hard'.[33]

There was also resistance to the tide of careerism, especially in Arts where the commitment to pure disciplinary traditions and learning for its own sake was strong. 'Students are not customers', argued Gay Baldwin in a paper distributed within the faculty: 'Customers are people from whom sellers wish to make money. Students are people whom teachers wish to see grow and develop intellectually'. The two roles were 'completely different and incompatible'. If they were confused, 'the activity of teaching will become compromised and subverted'. Certainly, plenty of students were still touched by the love of learning. The 1996 *Counter Faculty Handbook* was full of compliments for some of the Arts subjects at Clayton. 'I cannot praise this subject enough, everything about it is brilliant', one student commented on 'Literary women of the eighteenth century'. The more practical subjects in Business and Engineering failed to elicit such fervour, though they drew better student numbers.[34] But even Arts students whose primary interest lay in the content of their courses also had half an eye on the post-graduation employment prospects.

Surveys by business organisations found that employers from global companies often wanted graduates equipped with a broad liberal education, fostering flexible thinking and higher order intellectual skills. Other employers wanted specialists. Some employers wanted a preparation that was both broad and specialised.[35] The growth of enrolments in combined degrees such as Arts and Business, Law and Arts, Engineering and Arts, and Engineering and Science suggested that employers, and students, valued a combination of vocational preparation and generalist education. The number of Monash students in combined courses rose from 1546 in 1988, and 2780 in 1991 after the mergers, to 4338 in 1996.[36]

Transition and access

As the 1990s proceeded and the more competitive and market-oriented approach took root in higher education, accompanied by rhetoric about the needs of the student customer, Monash's leaders cast around for ways that they could strengthen the University-to-student relationship. They were constrained by the decline in public funding, and faculty autonomy in matters of course development. This left two main avenues for intervention: programs designed to improve the quality of teaching (see below); and actions designed to attract more and higher-scoring students to Monash and to ease the educational difficulties in the transition from schooling to first-year university. Logan told the Council in 1992 that:

> There is evidence that students are becoming more discriminating in selecting both courses and institutions. If there is a change of government, student choice will to a very large extent determine the future of the University. It therefore becomes particularly important to focus on teaching effectiveness, especially at first year level, and to differentiate what we offer from what others offer . . . an aspect of equal importance is the communication between the University and schools/parents/students. We do not know clearly enough just what it is we are trying to communicate to schools and the way we do communicate is not yet based on a functionally integrated approach.[37]

There were several ways of entering the University. The main school-leaver route into undergraduate education was highly competitive; other routes were not. Like the American State universities, Greater Monash was so large and diverse that it could be exclusive and accessible at the same time. Entry to Medicine and Law and the top echelons of most other faculties was similar to entry to the University of Melbourne. It was determined by competitive year 12 scores and often dominated by students from eastern suburbs private schools. Mature-age entry, distance education and entry from TAFE produced students older than the school-leaver norm, and less exclusive in terms of parental incomes and social status. Once they had entered the University, students from both groups worked to the same academic standards and performed at much the same level as each other.

In 1993, 35 per cent of school-leavers entering Monash were in the top one-fifth of Victorian secondary school-leavers by score, compared with 47 per cent at the University of Melbourne, 6 per cent at both La Trobe University and RMIT, and 2 per cent at Deakin.[38] At Clayton 51 per cent of school-leaver applicants had scores in the top one-fifth, and at Pharmacy in Parkville the figure was 91 per cent.[39] Elsewhere the proportion was 31 per cent at Caulfield, 8 per cent at Peninsula, 4 per cent at Gippsland, and 24 per cent in the first Berwick intake, illustrating the mix of selectivity and access at Monash.[40]

Before the mergers the largest group of students came from Glen Waverley, Mount Waverley, Mulgrave, Vermont and Wantirna, suburbs to the west and north of Clayton. Significant numbers also came from affluent suburbs closer to the central business district such as Balwyn, Brighton, Caulfield and Toorak.[41] By 1996, there were also demographic bunchings around the Caulfield and Peninsula and Gippsland campuses.

In 1991, 30 per cent of the school-leaver entrants to Monash were from independent private schools and 22 per cent from Catholic schools, with 46 per cent from government schools. The independent school share rose slightly to 31 per cent by 1995. Yet only 18 per cent of final-year secondary students in Victoria were from these schools.[42] The role of the independent schools was much greater in relation to entrance to Monash, than in education as a whole. It was greatest at Clayton (35 per cent), Caulfield (37 per cent) and Parkville (40 per cent).[43] Most of the schools providing a large number of first-year Monash students were independent or Catholic (Table 9.1).[44] Nevertheless, government institutions located near the Monash campuses played a significant role, as did Melbourne Boys and MacRobertson Girls high schools.

Monash aimed to improve its relationship with feeder schools by strengthening its standing with principals, careers teachers and curriculum coordinators.[45] The educational objective was to reduce failure rates in first year. The installation of a more collaborative and interactive approach to education in years 11 and 12 had sharpened the contrast between school and first-year university, with its individualised learning, large lecture groups and paucity of direct teacher support. It was felt that secondary students would gain from prior contact with the University.[46] In 1990 the Careers and Appointments service was restructured as the Course and Careers Centre, and a Schools Liaison Service was added. By 1995 the Service had six full-time staff and was visiting over 100 schools in metropolitan and regional Victoria, Tasmania, Canberra and on the NSW border. Pargetter estimated that he was working personally with over 200 principals a year; the Vice-Chancellor hosted a series of dinners with principals, and there was an annual conference between senior Monash officers and 30 principals. Faculty staff visited schools and lectured to secondary students.[47] Inevitably, in response to Monash, Melbourne upgraded its own program of schools liaison.[48]

One fruit of this growing relationship with feeder schools was the Enhance-

TABLE 9.1 THE 20 SCHOOLS PROVIDING THE LARGEST NUMBER OF SCHOOL-LEAVERS TO MONASH UNIVERSITY, 1991 AND 1995

Schools providing the largest number of school-leavers to Monash in 1991	New students, 1991	Schools providing the largest number of school-leavers to Monash in 1995*	New students, 1995
Melbourne High School *G*	94	Taylors College* *I*	88
Wesley College *I*	93	Melbourne High School *G*	84
Mount Scopus Memorial Coll. *I*	84	Glen Waverley Sec College *G*	66
Haileybury College *I*	74	Wesley College *I*	65
Kurnai College *G*	72	Kurnai College *G*	64
Xavier College *C*	52	Haileybury College *I*	59
Karingal Secondary College *G*	47	Frankston High School *G*	57
De La Salle College *C*	47	Presbyterian Ladies College *I*	57
Catholic Reg Coll Sydenham *C*	46	Wesley Coll Glen Waverley *I*	56
The Peninsula School *I*	44	Methodist Ladies College *I*	54
MacRobertson Girls High School *G*	44	Mount Scopus Memorial Coll. *I*	54
Presbyterian Ladies College *I*	43	Scotch College *I*	49
Methodist Ladies College *I*	41	Xavier College *C*	49
Mount Eliza Secondary Coll. *G*	38	Mount Waverley Sec College *G*	45
Mazenod College *C*	38	Caulfield GS Wheelers Hill *I*	43
St Michaels Grammar School *I*	38	Catholic Reg Coll. Sydenham *C*	42
St Leonards College *I*	37	Melbourne Grammar School *I*	42
Toorak College *I*	36	McKinnon Secondary College *G*	40
St Kevins College *C*	35	St Johns Regional College *C*	40
Caulfield GS Caulfield *I*	35	MacRobertson Girls High School *G*	39

C = Catholic school, *G* = government school, *I* = independent private school.

* In 1995 international students were included in the data for the first time, boosting Taylors College (which provided 76 international students to Monash in 1995) to first place on the table.

Source: Monash University, *Enrolled VTAC applicants by school,* 1995.

ment Studies Program, provided at both Monash and Melbourne, which became fully established in 1995. The Program was targeted at the top 5 per cent of secondary students. Students applied for inclusion in the program with the support of their school. They studied a first-year university subject, credited to their year 12 record, at a cost of $770 (1996). Subjects were provided in Science, the Arts, Computing, Engineering, Music and Business, and both university academics and school-based personnel took part in teaching, with students spending some time in the university setting. The program was provided in face-to-face delivery and distance mode. Some schools participated on a cluster basis in Enhancement Centres. By 1996 over 600 students were involved. In 1995 Monash Teaching Fellowships were offered for the first time, bringing six VCE teachers into the University setting to teach first-year students. Another initiative was the Monash Prize for academic excellence, awarded at 125 of Monash feeder schools to students at the end of year 11. Recipients received a trophy and $500, and were promised another $500 if they enrolled at Monash.[49]

Despite the Enhancement Studies Program and the demand for Medicine and Law, the University of Melbourne continued to enrol most of the students with scores in the State's top 1 per cent. This owed itself more to tradition and location than to the quality of schools liaison or undergraduate teaching, and there was not much that Monash could do to change the situation quickly. Sometimes Monash academics felt shut out of the inner circle of educational power and social influence. In September 1996 *The Australian* published an internal memo by Law Dean Bob Williams, in which he stated that the award of Rhodes Scholarships was slanted in favour of students from Melbourne. Since 1986 Melbourne students had won nine of the last 10 State-based scholarships and nine of the Australia-at-large awards, while Monash students won only one in each category. In his memo Williams pointed out that the interviews for the Rhodes were held at Melbourne and the scheme was administered from that university, originating as it had in the days when Melbourne was the only university in the State. The selection panel contained a high proportion of people with current or former Melbourne connections. In the previous year all five of the candidates selected for final interview had been students or graduates of Melbourne. In response, the honorary secretary of the Victorian Rhodes Committee stated that Melbourne students' dominance simply reflected their greater academic prowess. The honorary secretary was Jim Potter, the Registrar of the University of Melbourne.[50]

It was easier to make progress in opening up Monash to underrepresented groups. The Disability Support Program was established in 1992 to improve access for people with disabilities or long-term medical conditions. It included procedures to assist the processing of enrolment and employment, better mobility and safety on campus, access to courses, curriculum, information systems and university services. A full-time Disability Liaison Officer was employed. With 1300 students with disabilities (1994) the Program implied a major commitment in infrastructure and equipment alone. It was going to take time to put this in place, and services were uneven across the University. A 1993 survey of disabled students ranked the Disability Liaison Office highest for quality, Student Administration the lowest, and identified continuing problems

Bridging the gap. The second group of Year 11–12 teachers awarded one-year fellowships to teach at Monash and improve the transition from school to university (L–R): Tanya Kantanis, Roger Brown, John Raven, Catherine Lang, Tom Fisher, Carol Bullimore, Angela Vaughan.

in Monash's student unions. Once needs were recognised, the work of the Disability Liaison Office grew. In 1995 direct services were provided to more than 250 individual students, a rise of 47 per cent on 1994.[51]

The work of the Monash Orientation Scheme for Aborigines (MOSA)[52] continued. To the one-year preparatory course for Arts and Law, a two-year preparation for science-based disciplines was added in 1986 and a preparatory Business course in 1996. The University set itself the modest goal of expanding indigenous participation from 0.4 to 0.5 per cent of enrolments, but the 1994 enrolment of 111 effective full-time students fell short of the target level of 147.[53] Completion rates were also low. Between 1984 and 1994, 181 students enrolled in MOSA; 82 passed their course, with the same number progressing to an undergraduate program, mostly in Arts–Law or Arts. But by 1994 only 15 former MOSA students had completed an undergraduate degree. A further 17 were still studying.[54]

Managing teaching

The mergers broadened the expectations placed on academics. Applicants for promotion were expected to base their case 'on varying mixes of teaching, administration, research, scholarship, professional activity and community service. There have been recent examples of promotion to Associate Professor based primarily on community service', the University told the Committee for Quality Assurance in 1995. Thus former Chisholm and Gippsland staff were accommodated. Still, despite all the talk about 'equal but different', research and scholarship remained the wellsprings of academic status. It was performance in these areas that signified that former advanced education staff had 'made it' in orthodox terms. It was important to sustain Monash's status as a research university, and research-generated income from both government and commercial sources, especially after Commonwealth operating funds became linked to research performance. There were strong imperatives driving the extension of the Clayton research culture, inside and outside Clayton.

It was not a favourable time to step up research performance. Student–staff ratios were rising, as were average workloads.[55] Yet not only was there more attention to research, there was more emphasis on the quality of teaching, in policy, public discussion and university management, for example in the appointment and promotion of staff. In public discussion, this new emphasis on teaching was often touted as an alternative to the traditional emphasis on research. In fact there was greater pressure to perform in both areas, driven ultimately by accountability requirements, competitiveness, and the scarcity of funds and opportunities. Of the two areas, research was the more visible. The number of grants and publications was readily computed. The quality of teaching was less easy to measure.

Nevertheless, in 1988 *Strategy for the future* had defined 'excellence in teaching' as Monash's first objective. Underpinning this declaration was the Higher Education Advisory and Research Unit (HEARU), successor to the Higher Education Research Unit founded under Matheson in 1969.[56] The voluntary programs provided by HEARU included induction courses for new university teachers and advice on learning technologies. Despite this, most Monash academics did not regard teaching quality as the proper object of central managerial intervention. Teaching was seen as specific to and exclusive to each of the academic disciplines themselves, and its improvement dependent on peer attitude and individual academic effort. In some quarters the view lingered that only staff whose teaching was deficient would go outside the discipline to a generic advisory unit such as HEARU. In these faculties, staff who used HEARU did not mention it to their deans.[57]

The culture of teaching varied across the University. In Medicine and Engineering there was a faculty-wide approach to teaching;[58] a similar practice was emerging in Law, and was natural to the Education Faculty. An organised focus on teaching was slower to catch on in Business and Economics, while in Arts and Science teaching quality was considered a departmental rather than faculty matter. In Science, Rae's attempt as Dean to create a faculty-wide education committee faltered when he was strongly resisted by some departments. Still, the departmental approach paid educational dividends when Chemistry—followed by Physics and later Mathematics—set up successful student help centres.[59]

The formation of the Vice-Chancellor's Task Force on Teaching provided management with a way into the delicate issue of teaching quality. The arrival of Ian Chubb as DVC at the beginning of 1993 provided the potential for strong leadership on the issue. For a while Logan backed the crusade. In April 1993 he stated that 'the simple fact is that the quality of teaching and the learning environment for many first year students is just plain not good'.[60] This suggested the need for fundamental reforms, with the potential to challenge the prerogatives of the faculties in educational matters. Of the Task Force's five subgroups, one was concerned with rewards for excellence in teaching and another with student evaluation of teaching. The former led to the Vice-Chancellor's Distinguished Teaching Award, which began in 1992 with three awards per annum. Winners received a plaque, $5000 in cash and a permanent citation in the University calendar. In addition, some faculties presented their own teaching awards. The second of the subgroups led to the creation of a single system of student evaluation of teaching, Monquest, administered by a Teaching Evaluation Unit supervised by HEARU.[61] There were grumblings in Engineering, where faculty-specific surveys had long been used and were reckoned more appropriate than a generic University-wide questionnaire. In corners of Science there was resistance to questionnaire-based evaluation of teaching, of any kind.[62] Most Arts academics refused to use the official instrument, and the faculty cooperated with HEARU in developing a questionnaire of its own.[63] But formal evaluation of teaching became a fact of life, and though departments were encouraged to continue their own specific surveys 'for developmental purposes', the common Monquest data were used in conjunction with applications for tenure and promotion, and carried weight. A powerful set of data on teaching performance began to accumulate.

Other initiatives included the strengthening of references to teaching in the regulations governing promotion and staff selection; and a restructuring of programs at HEARU, whose work was merged with staff development for general staff to form an expanded Professional Development Centre.[64] HEARU's scope was extended to all campuses other than Gippsland, whose Educational Development and Research Unit still held sway.[65] It was a mild dose of regulation, but significant in a University unused to central intervention in teaching. Chubb's key initiative was the creation of Associate Deans (Teaching) in each faculty, responsible for enhancing teaching and learning, parallel to a similar network in research (see below). The associate deans formed the new Education Committee, chaired by Chubb. He saw the Committee as assuming a leadership role in educational matters that the Academic Board did not exercise. The position of the associate deans was ambiguous. Representing the faculties at the centre, they were also the instrument of centrally driven reform in the faculties. The ambiguity helped the Education Committee in preparing new education and research policies and bedding down student evaluation, but ultimately it fuelled decanal resistance to the DVC[66] and probably retarded achievement of his policy objectives. There was concern, in both faculties like Medicine where a faculty-wide approach to teaching was working well, and Science where it was absent.

After Chubb left in 1995 the Education Committee concentrated on reconciling faculty initiatives with central guidelines.[67] The conflicts of the Chubb era evaporated, along with the potential for more radical educational change that Chubb's forceful style had offered.

Managing research

For the first time in 1989 all higher education institutions were required to submit research management plans as a condition of Commonwealth funding, and Monash listed its policies and priorities along with the rest. More a tour of existing activity and a statement of intent than a guide to action, this was the harbinger of a more managed research era to come. But as with teaching, so in research: independent faculties resisted full 'managerialisation'. It was a time when many universities introduced more centralised research management, driving an increase in research grant income by using formula-based systems for improving performance without much regard for disciplinary niceties.[68] Monash academics who complained about the rise of corporatism in their own institution did not realise that in relation to research and scholarship the University was less corporate than most. Yet traditionalism in research was now a weakness as well as a strength. Research funding, especially from the Commonwealth, was governed by quantitative performance indicators. Under a devolved system of management, in which academic development took a natural discipline-directed course rather than being force-driven by manager-leaders, the good research faculties and departments remained strong, the weaker faculties did not necessarily improve, and activities were determined more by the evolution of the discipline than strategies designed to maximise performance indicators. All else being equal this meant less research performance in official terms, less research funding, and less research status.

In April 1992 the Board's Research Review Committee, chaired by Louis Waller, proposed a full-time Deputy Vice-Chancellor with responsibility for research, a Research Committee consisting of Associate Deans (Research) in each faculty, and a centrally administered Research Fund. Nevertheless, it declared firmly against the notion of research run from above by professional managers:

Louis Waller. Law Professor since 1965, Dean (1969–70) and chair of the 1992 committee which reviewed research organisation in the University.

Research administration should *not* be designed to manage, to control or to direct the research efforts of the staff who are employed, wholly or partly, to do research in the university. On the contrary, the role of research administration should be to provide the environment in which those research efforts can flourish . . . We specifically reject any model of research administration that places a research 'manager' in a position of authority over those charged with the responsibility of carrying out research. Such management models are not seen as appropriate to the climate of free intellectual inquiry that characterises a great university. The business of research management is best and most appropriately conducted locally, that is, through the deans of faculties, then heads of departments or schools and the directors of research and other centres.[69]

The Committee also argued that resources for research support should be sensitive to differences between disciplines. It criticised funding formulae that gave the main weight to income for research rather than time spent on research; and favoured disciplines in which success was measured in terms of grant income rather than scholarship and publications. The Committee's report was adopted. It led to an internal funding formula which gave more weight to publications than did the Commonwealth—an approach which helped Arts and Law[70]—while its policy of devolution became the cornerstone of research management. Engineering Dean Peter Darvall became acting Deputy Vice-Chancellor (Research and Development) in mid-1993, and in April 1994 was chosen by Council to fill the position on an ongoing basis. Like his predecessor Bob Porter, Darvall was committed to research systems in which individuals and faculties controlled their own agendas. In the words of one of his successors as dean of Engineering, Darvall 'let everyone fly themselves' rather than imposing his own priorities,[71] and he carried this into the DVC's office.

It was a tricky time to take over as research manager-leader. The ground was shifting. In the post-Dawkins environment there were a larger number of sources of project funding, and 'grantpersonship' (skill in working the competitive grant system) was more important. At the same time it was becoming harder to reconcile financial objectives and intellectual values. Two months after the Waller Committee report was tabled, the Vice-Chancellor told Council that all was not well with research at Monash. The University was slipping behind its comparators. There had been little change in its share of ARC Large Grant projects despite the increase in size: Monash trailed Melbourne, NSW, Sydney, Queensland and Adelaide, though it did win one in five ARC Senior Research Fellowships in 1992.[72] Monash researchers did better in National Health and Medical Research Council (NHMRC) grants, vying with Queensland for third place behind Melbourne and Sydney. Still, 'if our research grants were expressed on a per effective full-time staff basis we would appear in an even less favourable light', stated Logan. In 1992 Monash was fifth in aggregate terms in nationally competitive research grants, but tenth in grants per academic staff member. Monash academic staff received $13 252 per head compared with $20 857 at Melbourne and $27 543 at the University of Western Australia (UWA).[73] The University had a problem.

In a more competitive era, this placed in doubt the University's reputation as a research institution. Three factors were working against it. One was the mergers, which led to an automatic decline in grants per head, and tied up resources in extending the research role to the former CAEs rather than building on existing strengths. Second, the Monash reliance on faculty-driven performance made it difficult to secure the kind of quick improvement in measured outcomes across the whole university simultaneously that some other institutions were achieving. Third, the official measures of research performance emphasised income for research rather than publications and other measures of output. The Commonwealth allocated a proportion of operating funds in the form of the

Peter Darvall: change and continuity

The core business of the University is teaching and research

Peter Darvall's career path shadowed the University's changing preoccupations, and he was part of many of its dramatic moments—staff representative and long-standing member of Council in the more collegial era of the 1970s, a mover in the transition to a modernised leadership in the mid-1980s,[74] Dean of Engineering when the mergers hit at the beginning of the 1990s, and DVC (Research and Development) at a time when measured research performance was coming on to the policy and funding agenda. In the second half of the Logan years, moving into the Robinson years, Darvall, along with General Manager Peter Wade, provided the continuity in a leadership structure prone to short-term appointments and a high turnover. Energetic, acerbic and good-humoured by turns, a stickler for numerical accuracy, structural thinker and people person, and always an engineer at heart, in 1994 he told Monash staff gathered to receive their 25-year service medals:

> It must always be remembered that, whatever the seductions of corporatisation, the core business of the university is teaching and research, and that core business is conducted and supported by individuals, like yourselves. The work of administration, or management, or leadership, is to facilitate the work of those individuals. The purpose is to allow people to fly intellectually, and as high as possible.[75]

Darvall completed a Doctorate in Structural Engineering at Princeton in 1969. After a variety of work roles in the second half of the 1960s, including surveying on the Casement Glacier in Alaska and engineering on an Egyptian archaeological dig, he took a lectureship in Engineering in 1970, succeeding Lance Endersbee as Dean 18 years later. His research specialty was the use of reinforced and prestressed concrete, a passion of John Monash 60 years before. Darvall's deanship saw substantial improvement in research grants, publications and links with the profession. He raised over $1 500 000 in industry funding for student scholarships, and began a Women in Engineering program. A strong supporter of combined degrees, his own interests had taken him to the Arts Faculty, where he completed three years of Spanish in 1975–78 and Latin American literature in 1977.

Darvall's interest in Engineering education led him to a Diploma of Education (Tertiary) in 1972, extensive publications, and early examples of instructional videos: in 1976 he made a 20-minute film on *Elementary Engineering Communication* with K.J. Atkins. Commitments to university governance and the academic profession led to the Presidency of the Staff Association of the University (1977–80) and of the Federation

Peter Darvall, DVC (Research and Development) from 1993. The smaller photo shows three Deans of Engineering (L–R): Lance Endersbee (1976–88), Ken Hunt (1961–75) and Peter Darvall (1988–94). In the larger photo Darvall (R) and fourth-year Civil Engineering students enter the *Sir John Monash* in a 1985 concrete canoe race.

of Australian University Staff Associations (1979–81). Later he chaired the Academic Board Committee, which established Monquest as the system of student evaluation, and the committee handling the Vice-Chancellor's awards for teaching and supervision.

As DVC (Research and Development) from 1993 Darvall presided over the first University-wide research policies and strategies, restructured Research Services, and led the response to the 1995 quality assessment which restored some of the status lost in 1993. Coming from a faculty with a strong research tradition and professional identity, his notion of good management in research was to facilitate the faculties in monitoring and managing their own performance. It was a formula that worked well in areas where Monash research was near the top of the field; though as the 1990s proceeded researchers faced more pressure and distractions. Darvall regretted the absorption of academic energy in the mergers with Chisholm and Gippsland, but saw little alternative to the strategy of the time. Always an institutional loyalist, he was proud of the Greater Monash that resulted.[76]

'research quantum', largely calculated on the basis of success in obtaining nationally competitive research grants. The quantum had become the principal measure of strength in research. This did not favour Monash, because of the University's discipline mix. The universities that did best under a grant-based measure were those with a high proportion of their staff in the science-based disciplines attracting large grants. Monash had strong research in Medicine, Engineering and parts of Science, but the total proportion of staff in Law, Arts, Education and Business was higher than in the top research universities. These disciplines did not require heavy equipment or large research teams. Their main research tool was the library and their main resource was the time of individual scholars. Average grant size was relatively small. For them, the main indicator of research activity was not grants but publications.

If the main measure of research performance had been publications rather than grants, Monash would have done much better. Despite the mergers, in 1993 it was number one in Australia in publications per staff member, well ahead of Queensland and Melbourne (see Table 9.2).[77]

The first research management plan consisted of faculty research management plans, centrally monitored to meet planning requirements, plus selected central initiatives. A total of 12.25 per cent of the recurrent budget was allocated to the faculties on the basis of research income and publications, providing a performance driver. From there the strategic decisions about research programs were made at faculty or departmental level.[78] Each faculty defined its own targets and means of achieving them.[79] The 1995 report of the Committee for Quality Assurance was comfortable with Monash's decentralised research management. Research planning was 'effective and consistently deployed across the institution', it stated, placing Monash in the leading group of nine institutions for research outcomes, in the leading group of 14 for research management, and in the second of four groups for the improvement of research outcomes.[80]

In the same year the University changed its formula for distributing research support to the faculties to more closely approximate the Commonwealth quantum. Instead of 55 per cent allocated on the basis of research grants and 45 per cent on the basis of publications and other measures of output, the new ratios were 70 per cent on the basis of research grants, 22.5 per cent on the basis of publications, and 7.5 per cent on the basis of higher-degree completions.[81] There was a redistribution of research resources away from Arts, Law and Education, and in favour of Medicine, Engineering, Pharmacy and Science.

In addition to the funding allocated to faculties as their share of the research quantum ($18.3 million in 1996), specific projects were supported from the Monash Development Fund and the Monash Research Fund: the University channelled $2.4 million through the Fund in 1996, plus $1.7 million allocated to Cooperative Research Centres (CRCs) in which Monash was a participant, and $0.7 million to seven other research centres. Almost $5 million was spent on Monash postgraduate scholarships, and $150 000 on postdoctoral fellowships, titled the Logan Fellowships. Five new awards were made each year.[82] The Research Services Division administered research grants, fellowships, schol-

TABLE 9.2 RESEARCH PUBLICATIONS AND RESEARCH GRANTS PER HEAD,
            1993: SIX UNIVERSITIES COMPARED

	Research publications per FTE academic staff member	National competitive research grants per FTE academic staff member ($)
Monash University	3.30	12 580
University of Queensland	2.87	24 005
University of Melbourne	2.86	22 143
University of WA	2.50	28 875
University of NSW	2.41	20 838
University of Sydney	2.37	19 594

Source: Australian Vice-Chancellors' Committee finance and publications research data collection. Publications data are a weighted average across the different kinds of publication.

arships, ethical clearance for projects, and PhD candidacy. Monash's success in bidding for funding under the Cooperative Research Centres (CRCs) program, particularly in Engineering, underlined the University's capacity in applied research and in linking to industry. The CRCs were jointly funded by government, industry, the CSIRO and the universities themselves. By 1996 Monash was involved in 11 CRCs. It was also very successful in competition for industry-based Commonwealth research scholarships. Monash raised a larger share of the nation's private funding for university research (almost 10 per cent) than public funding (7 per cent). Engineering and Pharmacy were the main magnets for industry funding.[83]

Among the areas of research strength, the Institute of Reproduction and Development's work on in-vitro fertilisation (IVF) was probably the best known: outstandingly important in scientific terms, it was also a public service and a source of income. The work of the Accident Research Centre had a high public profile. The Monash disciplines with greatest citations impact in the United States were Mathematics—which, judging by citation between 1981 and 1992, would have ranked in the top third of the leading 100 US institutions if based in the USA—and Engineering. The two individuals with the greatest citation impact, David de Kretser and Alan Trounson, led the IVF program.[84] In the mid-1990s there was a slight improvement in research performance as measured by official indicators. In new NHMRC grants Monash moved from third to second behind Melbourne; and, though its ARC ranking stayed at fifth, the share of ARC funding rose. There was celebration at Gippsland, where staff won two large ARC grants. Publication rates rose at Caulfield, Frankston and Gippsland.[85] There was still a nagging feeling that the University should be doing better, and the mergers had been accommodated at the cost of research at Clayton. Towards the end of his term Logan stated that Monash still had not 'got it right' in research. If so, the problem was left for his successor.[86]

Medicine and Nursing

Robert Porter returned to Monash to be Dean of Medicine in 1989, following a stint as Director of the John Curtin School of Medical Research in Canberra. The Monash faculty was more collaborative and more open to modernisation and reform than the Curtin School had been. Porter threw himself into the job with enthusiasm; under him Medicine's position in the University became even stronger. Porter was a key player on the Committee of Deans and the Academic Board, and a national leader in Medicine.[87] It was a reforming time in medical education. The 1988 Doherty report called for better communication skills among doctors, more attention to ethical matters, and the integration of medical education with community health care outside hospitals. The new dean was sympathetic to these perspectives. He also found that the faculty's research work needed reinvigoration. The curriculum was overhauled. Traditional disciplines like Biochemistry or Physiology were replaced by programs designed to expand knowledge in a medical context, such as subjects on cancer and tissue injury; clinical experience was brought forward to the first year; and courses in 'Clinical and Communication Skills' and ethical considerations were set up.[88]

From 1990 the faculty interviewed prospective students. With year 12 scores no longer the only determinant of entry, about 10 per cent of the enrolment were non-school-leavers. A growing proportion of entrants were from rural areas, and from southern European and East Asian-origin families. In contrast with Melbourne Medicine, women now constituted well over half of the student body. The Monash and Melbourne Medical faculties competed vigorously for high-scoring school-leavers. Neither followed the graduate entry system introduced at Queensland, Sydney and Flinders or the problem-based curriculum used at Newcastle and at McMaster University in Canada. Porter watched developments elsewhere closely. By the mid-1990s he was expressing concern that the faculty was spending too much time force-feeding students with information, and not enough time on reflective approaches and self-directed learning. The Monash approach was too traditional, he felt.[89]

In 1994 chairs in surgery, cardiology, infectious diseases and venereology were created, also a Centre for the Study of Nervous Diseases. In conjunction with the College of General Practitioners the Department of Community Medicine provided continuing education for GPs, pioneering the use of flexible learning and CD-ROMs.[90]

A faculty generating more than 40 per cent of the University's income for research, receiving a third of the research funding from industry, and publishing at a rate similar to the Arts Faculty and twice that of Science, was financially well placed even in lean times. In 1995 Medicine received $17.1 million for research and $7.5 million in external earnings and donations, together totalling

44 per cent of its budget.[91] A history of this length cannot do justice to all areas of research strength. Geoffrey Thorburn's work in fetal physiology was highly regarded. Mollie Holman led the worldwide study of electrical activity in smooth muscle cells, the neural control of smooth muscle, and other branches of autonomic neurophysiology for 30 years. Appointed to a personal chair in Physiology in 1970, one of the first women professors in Australia, she had officially retired but continued to research and teach. In 1994, in conjunction with colleagues from Pharmacology and Chemistry, Bevyn Jarrott won a $1 million Australian Medical Research and Development (AMRAD) Corporation grant to develop drugs to protect the brain in ischaemia, which occurs during strokes, head injuries and possibly Alzheimer's and Parkinson's diseases.

Jim Goding was the first graduate to return as a full professor when he accepted the chair in Pathology and Immunology at 37 years of age in 1984. With an international reputation in the genetics of the immune system, including the isolation of the mechanisms used to identify foreign substances, he revitalised the department. Research income rose from $20 000 in 1984 to $1.3 million in 1995. Goding's research programs generated a long series of spin-offs for the study of AIDS, diabetes and iron deficiencies, among other areas.

The first IVF baby was born in London in 1978 and the first Australian baby arrived in 1980, the outcome of collaborative work by teams at Melbourne and Monash. IVF had enabled many childless couples to have children and was associated with a growing array of research projects devoted to refining the techniques and creating new methods for fertility control and new adaptations. It was also a source of continuing controversy. The capacity to engineer life brought an immense power with it, and there were continuing questions about the potential and limits of that power; about the rights and obligations of scientists, parents, pre-embryos and embryos; and about the effects of the commercialisation of health care in this most sensitive of medical domains.

In all of this Monash was at the forefront. Monash IVF was a medical business which, alongside Melbourne IVF, provided the main fertility enhancement service in Victoria, with city premises at Richmond and Clayton and clinics in five country centres. Monash IVF began with a handful of people in the Infertility Medical Centre at St Andrews Hospital in 1980; the key figure in the early days was Carl Wood (chapter 2). The Centre changed its name to Monash IVF in 1992. It was a private company 100 per cent owned by the University, a structure developed by Peter Wade which enabled it to work around the committee structure of the Medical faculty while retaining collaborative relations.[93] Net revenue from Monash

Mollie Holman. Appointed to a personal chair in physiology (1970–95), one of the first women professors in Australia.

In-vitro fertilisation

In-vitro fertilisation (IVF) was the scientific name given to the process used to conceive a child by bringing egg and sperm cells together outside the body (*in vitro* being Latin for 'in glass', though in fact plastic containers had replaced glass). The technique was used in cases where natural conception could not readily take place—in men whose sperm were dead or deficient, women who had problems with ovulation (egg formation) or whose fallopian tubes were blocked, and so on. In the IVF procedure women were given hormones to stimulate egg production, and multiple eggs were formed. When these reached a sufficient stage of maturity they were picked up with a very fine needle, washed chemically and maintained at body temperature. The partner sperm were added to each egg and, if fertilisation occured, a zygote (pre-embryo) started to develop. This remained in an incubator for one or two days until it had divided into 2–4 cells, when it was transferred to the woman's uterus using a fine tube. Two weeks later blood tests were taken to find out whether the embryo had successfully transplanted and pregnancy begun. There were many variations on this basic procedure, such as different methods of stimulating egg production, or not using stimuli and relying on the one egg naturally produced each month; the use of donor sperm in cases where the male partner was wholly infertile; micro-drop insemination to improve the chances of sperm–egg collision, or microinjection in which a single sperm was inserted directly into the centre of the egg.[92]

IVF's Alan Trounson. In the early 1990s the two most cited Monash researchers were Trounson and David de Kretser of the IVF research program.

IVF flowed back to the University and to support the research of the Institute of Reproduction and Development (e.g. $448 823 in 1994). In 1987 IVF Australia was set up to take the service to the United States. Changing its name to IVF America, it generated an immediate $20 million when floated on the New York stock exchange. In 1994 it sent back $300 000 to the Institute's research program.[94]

The Institute of Reproduction and Development was possibly the largest scientific research establishment in the field in the world. It had its origins in the Centre of Early Human Development in the Faculty of Medicine under John Maloney in 1978. Alan Trounson became director in 1985. He began his research career in animal reproduction and worked at Cambridge, Utrecht and Calgary, before returning to Melbourne as a Ford Foundation Senior Research Fellow to work with Wood on the early stages of IVF. The Institute was formed in 1991, incorporating the Centre for Human Development and linked to the

Departments of Obstetrics and Gynaecology, and Paediatrics, and the neonatal and perinatal units of the Monash Medical Centre in its new site at Clayton. The director was David de Kretser from Anatomy, with Trounson as deputy director. De Kretser's major research achievements were in relation to male reproductive systems. The Institute was part of the Faculty of Medicine and contributed to its teaching programs. The objective was to combine people from different departments in order to create critical mass sufficient to take the work further. By 1996 the Institute was taking in more than $7 million in grant income per year, there were over 130 people, including 30 postgraduates, working in overcrowded conditions—mostly on one-to three-year grants—and it was talking about obtaining its own building.[95]

The key to this growth was the potential opened up by the technologies themselves, and the quality of the research that kept Monash scientists and their technologies at the cutting edge. Trounson and de Kretser found their jobs expanding exponentially. They spent much of their time simply raising grants. Long-term projects with broad implications were funded by NHMRC: more applied projects were funded from Monash IVF revenues on a one-year basis. Other sources included the ARC, other government agencies and one-off public projects, foundations and private donors. Trounson estimated that about four submissions in 10 were funded. From the beginning there was close contact with other scientists in the field. By the mid-1990s there were collaborative programs with—among others—the University of California in Los Angeles, the University of Calgary, and universities in Germany and Italy. An important link had been negotiated with the University of Singapore, managed by Trounson and Christine Hi at the Monash end.[96]

The IVF-related technologies were capable of other applications. Multiple embryos from genetically valuable livestock could be implanted in host mothers. Embryo freezing promised an easy, cost-effective alternative to transporting livestock over long distances. The Institute also studied the reproductive habits of indigenous Australian fauna and developed techniques for genetic identification, semen collection, sperm and embryo preservation, and embryo transfer, to enable artificial breeding of animal species. This offered a viable route for long-term conservation on the basis of genetic diversity. Sperm, eggs and embryos were stored and catalogued in the Animal Gene Storage Centre of Australia, jointly operated by the Institute and the Zoological Parks Board of NSW.[97]

Having only just entered higher education, through the CAE sector, Nursing was at a different stage of development. As a research field it was still defining itself. There was tension between Nursing knowledge in the clinical setting, and philosophical, sociological, anthropological and educational constructions of Nursing. Clinical specialisation offered the potential for science-based research, but touched on the unequal relationship between nurses and doctors. After the demise of professional studies, Nursing became a subfaculty in Medicine, which provided more support for research.[98] A Centre for Graduate Studies in Clinical Nursing was created in 1994. That year Sue Elsom from Peninsula was one of three recipients of the Vice-Chancellor's Awards for Distinguished Teaching.[99]

Pharmacy

The merger with Monash enabled the Victorian College of Pharmacy to modify its courses and research: honours were introduced and in 1995 the college/faculty began to redesign its three-year Bachelor-level course as a four-year course, integrating what was previously a clinically based pre-registration year into the course proper. There were new opportunities for research collaboration, for example with Chemistry and in Medicine. There were also new burdens in the internal paperwork and the committee meetings that came with being a part of the University structure. Essentially, however, the work of the College went on as before. Student numbers were steady. The research program continued. Relations with the Pharmaceutical Society of Australia (Victorian Branch), which occupied premises at Parkville, remained close.[100] Perhaps the most obvious gain from the merger was the building and refurbishment of Parkville, including a new foyer and reception area, classrooms and administrative offices, research space, and additional space for the use of the Pharmaceutical Society of Australia and the Pharmacy Board of Victoria.[101]

Pharmacy had 2 per cent of the University's students but in the period 1992–93 earned 22 per cent of total research funds from industry. Its higher-degree research load was also well above the Monash average. The best-known research achievement was the development of a drug to prevent or treat influenza. Clinical trials in the USA in 1994 were encouraging. The research team under Mark von Itzstein worked with the CSIRO Division of Biomolecular Engineering and Glaxo Research and Development.[102]

Science

If Monash Science had fallen somewhat from its great days, it still included a brilliant research department of Chemistry, and carried out important work in many other areas. The malaise lay not so much in a decline of Monash Science as in the changing role of the natural sciences as a whole. Science faculties were affected by a fall in the proportion of high-scoring school-leavers aspiring to Science: some were enrolling in the professional faculties, others in Business and Computing. There was also a decline in government funding, compared to the 1960s and 70s, when the natural sciences were at the centre of public research programs. Science at Monash did not enrol many fee-paying students and only Earth Sciences was well placed to raise industry funding. Many faculty members were out of sympathy with the entrepreneurial new Monash.

The popularity of the Biomedical Sciences was increasing. Mathematics attracted some of the best secondary students, though continuation into second year declined.[103] Physics, the discipline of space exploration and nuclear power, once the aspiration of more bright school students than any other, faced difficulties. Research in Monash Physics was not as strong as it had been, and there were few physics jobs for graduates, though it was a powerful generic intellectual training for business or government. As Dean, Ian Rae felt Physics was underperforming and held too many resources relative to other departments, but he ran into a wall of resistance when he tried to make one staff member redundant.[104] The department had not exhausted its potential for educational innovation. In 1996 a new Astrophysics major grounded in Mathematics and Physics was introduced.[105]

The success of Chemistry overshadowed the rest. In 1988 it earned $0.982 million in research grants, more than twice as much as the next department, Mathematics. It continued to lead the faculty in the 1990s. Apart from Mathematics and Chemistry, other departments with high citation rates included Materials Sciences, Geosciences, and Plant and Animal Sciences. In 1992 and 1993 the faculty received 18.7 per cent of all the University's income for research, and 20.9 per cent of competitive grants from schemes such as ARC, second to Medicine in both categories; it produced 13.4 per cent of Monash publications and 21 per cent of research graduates.[106] In 1995, $10.1 million (24.6 per cent) of faculty income was for research: ARC grants raised $3.0 million and CRC program grants $2.5 million.[107]

Some of the best-known faculty research was sustained by small groups, even a single individual. The work of physical vulcanologist Ray Cas had implications for mineral exploration and for governments concerned to minimise property damage and loss of life in the wake of volcanic explosions. In the department of Ecology and Evolutionary Biology, Sam Lake's research on the regulation and maintenance of natural communities was at the centre of contemporary ecology. His interests included heavy metal contamination and other aspects of the ecology of freshwater communities, the ecology of Lake Pedder in Tasmania, Australian wetlands, rainforest ecology and, more generally, the regulation of species diversity.[108] Lake's research was continuously funded by bodies such as the ARC, the Australian Water Resources Advisory Council, the Land and Water Resources Research and Development Corporation, and the Australian Nature Conservation Agency. In 1993 Monash, the University of Canberra and other partners obtained funding for a Cooperative Research

The Prentice predictions

Two hundred years ago the French astronomer and mathematician Pierre Simon de Laplace proposed that the solar system had begun as a vast gas cloud that was furiously hot inside and spun fairly slowly around a central axis. As the cloud cooled, it contracted under its own gravity and began to spin faster and faster on its central axis, shedding rings of gaseous material at its equatorial edge which condensed later to form the planets and their satellites. Laplace's theory achieved wide acceptance until the mid-19th century, when scientists began to argue that the sun seemed too large relative to the planets, and rotated too slowly, to have been formed according to Laplace's theory. Monash mathematician Andrew Prentice came across Laplace's theory while at Oxford in the late 1960s. He developed an adjunct to the theory, 'supersonic turbulence', to explain the gap. Supersonic turbulence was caused by strong downwinds within the original gaseous cloud, which forced the condensation of the core of the sun, together with weaker 'upwinds' (thermals) that expanded the outer layers of the cloud. In 1972 Prentice returned to Australia to Monash, and began a computer program based on his theory.

The program grew enormously, containing nearly all known data on the thermodynamic properties of the gases and major minerals of which the sun and the planets were made, and how those minerals behaved under extremes of temperature and pressure. By 1996 the program had 20 000 lines, each of 80 characters, and absorbed 400 megabytes of a mainframe computer. The program computed the mass and temperature of the gas rings that, Prentice theorised, were cast off by the primitive sun, and the properties of the gas rings later shed by Jupiter, Saturn, Uranus and Neptune. The mathematical model took into account the heat released by rocks and kept track of temperatures inside each satellite since its formation. Prentice used this computer program to foretell the successive discoveries of NASA's deep space probes to the outer planets Jupiter, Saturn, Uranus and Neptune.

In 1977 he predicted a rocky moon belt at four planetary radii from Jupiter's centre. Two years later a rocky ring was discovered, though closer to Jupiter at only

Andrew Prentice.
An applied mathematician with a long record of unorthodox theorisation and accurate predictions in solar system astronomy.

two planetary radii. He predicted two new moons or moonlet streams placed 2.5 and 3.5 planetary radii from the centre of Uranus. Nine years later a new moon (Puck) was found at 3 radii and a family of nine moonlets at 2.5 radii. In 1981 he predicted that the mass of Saturn's moon Tethys was 20–25 per cent larger than the generally accepted level. Three months later that moon was found to be 21 per cent larger. In 1989 he predicted a new family of four large dark moons at 5, 3.5, 2.5 and 1.8 radii in Neptune's equatorial plane. Later that year four dark moons were discovered at 7, 3, 2.5 and 2.1 radii and all in the equatorial plane. He predicted that dry ice would be the major carbon-bearing chemical on Triton. Infrared measurements confirmed this three years later. In 1995 he predicted the sulphur content of Jupiter's atmosphere to be twice that of the sun; this was confirmed the following year. The list goes on.[109]

European journals published his work, even if the American journals did not. Prentice did not help his case by accusing his opponents of a 'herd mentality', and by focusing the research program on its applications rather than on more conclusive proofs of the theory.[110]

> Some people would like me to have spent the last, and the next, 25 years consolidating my model of supersonic turbulence. But I don't want to find when I'm 80 years old that it's a good theory but I have missed all the opportunities to make predictions. I'm lucky to have been born when I was, because these NASA missions have cost well over $1 billion each and I'm able to use the missions to test my mathematical theories. At the moment I'm trying to keep just ahead of them by making predictions of what they'll find. It is a very exciting time for me.[111]

By then Prentice was already turning his mind to Saturn, due to be visited by the spacecraft Cassini/Huygens whose launch was scheduled for later 1997.

Centre for Freshwater Ecology, and in 1994/95 the CRC received more than $2 million from the Commonwealth and $5 million from the Centre's partners.

Mathematician Andrew Prentice had a worldwide reputation for his extraordinarily accurate astronomical predictions and the controversy these generated. Prentice supported a neo-Laplacian theory of planetary formation out of favour in the US scientific establishment—prestigious journals such as the *American Journal of Geophysical Research* refused to publish him—but the Jet Propulsion Laboratory of the National Aeronautics and Space Administration (NASA) program in California was very interested in his work.[112]

Palaeontology is the study of ancient life forms, their biodiversity and ecology, and changes in life forms over time. Life in Australia stretched back almost 4 billion years but had been less studied than that of North America

Pat Vickers-Rich. Pioneering vertebrate palaeontology in Australia and popularising science and the indigenous dinosaur to a generation of school students, she was appointed to a personal chair in 1995.

and Europe. When Pat Vickers-Rich emigrated from the United States in 1971 she found hardly anyone working on vertebrate (backboned animal) fossils. She began teaching the history of vertebrates in Australia, New Zealand and the Southwest Pacific, and coordinated the preparation of *Vertebrate Palaeontology in Australasia*. Her fieldwork began with studies of Australian mammals and birds, but she and her husband (Thomas Rich, a palaeontologist at the Museum of Victoria) came across so many dinosaur fossils that they changed focus, discovering many new species of dinosaurs. The work began to attract media attention and public interest.[113]

Vickers-Rich began at Monash in 1976 and in 1979 travelled to China, where she found that palaeontology was very short of funds. She organised an exhibition of dinosaurs from China which travelled through Australia and around the world, being seen by half a million visitors in Australia alone. Funds went to the Institute of Vertebrate Palaeontology and Palaeoanthropology in Beijing. She also collaborated on the production of a Chinese–English and English–Chinese Dictionary of Vertebrate Palaeontology. In 1992 she helped organise another fund-raising exhibition, this time of Russian dinosaurs; in 1993–94 more than a million Australians saw the exhibition, which generated over $4 million in revenue.

In 1993 Vickers-Rich published *The Wildlife of Gondwana*; this explored the flora and fauna of the supercontinent Gondwana which was integral until 100 million years ago and once included Australia, New Zealand, South America, Antarctica, Africa, India and part of Southeast Asia. The book won two major awards: the Eureka award from the ABC and the Australian Museum, and the Whitely Medal for the best natural history book published in Australia. Vickers-Rich also wrote a number of children's books. Keen to attract children to science at an early age, she found dinosaurs to be the perfect ambassadors for the scientific kingdom. Children were fascinated by them. The interest in children's education led Vickers-Rich to begin to develop the idea of a Monash Science Centre, with encouragement from Logan and from the faculties of Science and Engineering. Funding was secured from the Monash Development Fund and from private sources, and the Centre was opened in 1993. With a staff of 20 enthusiasts, mostly part-time, it provided a variety of short lectures and courses for primary and secondary schools, and developed new teaching modules. Meanwhile Vickers-Rich own research continued, taking her to Argentina to examine the fauna of another part of Gondwana, and Alaska to compare the polar dinosaurs of Australia–Gondwana with those of Alaska. She was awarded a personal chair in Palaeontology in early 1996.[114]

Engineering

'Engineering provides the basis of our civilisation', trumpeted a mid-1990s pamphlet on the Faculty of Engineering, pitched at year 12 students. No-one could accuse the faculty of undue modesty. Though Endersbee retired in 1988 the brash, engaged style that had always typified Monash Engineering was maintained in the years that followed. In truth there was much to boast about. The three-volume Williams report (1988)—the Commonwealth discipline review of Engineering education—was positive indeed:

> The faculty aims and objectives and its Five Year Program are to some extent visionary, but their credibility is supported by achievements to date . . . The aims are being achieved to date primarily because of staff activity in generating strong industrial support for research which reflects in teaching to an international level.[115]

Under Darvall a turnover of departmental heads strengthened the Dean's hand and diminished internal conflict. The faculty's finances became more transparent, and the onus was placed on people to earn the money they needed rather than rely on supplicancy to dean or head of department.[116] It was a period of growth in student numbers, though from 1994 onwards demand for undergraduate places slowed, a trend affecting other Engineering schools. In 1995 the faculty was third in the University in industry funding as a proportion of income, and in income from competitive research grants. It earned 25.6 per cent of its total income from research funding.[117] Growth created space problems. At Clayton these were solved by the opening of Building 69 in early 1995, providing for laboratories, research centres, seminar rooms, offices and the electron microscopy site; and shared access to Building 70 the next year. Space at Caulfield remained constrained.[118]

Student evaluation of teaching became general after the first of the quality reviews in 1993. There were seminars on teaching students from diverse cultural backgrounds. Staff involvement in the Australasian Association of Engineering Education was encouraged. In 1988 Engineering began hosting an annual 'Tournament of the Minds', a competition in creative problem-solving involving thousands of senior primary and junior secondary students every year. It also introduced an elective for fourth-year students which consisted of assisting a school with a technology studies project, a scheme later copied by other Engineering schools. In January 1994 the Centre for Engineering Education began under Zenon Pudlowski. Its purpose was to assist developing countries to build courseware and software. Monash had won the UNESCO-sponsored tender.[119]

Darvall's deanship saw the spread of cooperative education programs, in which students spent part of a semester working in industry. Industry also financed prizes and scholarships. The faculty's good standing in the Williams report and regular professional accreditations made it easier to sustain good external relations without losing autonomy.[120]

In the first half of the 1990s expenditure on research activity almost tripled (see Table 9.3). Nearly all activity was at Clayton. Caulfield's main research contribution was through the Research Centre in Timber Engineering. Gippsland was a minor player, though in 1995 it received $220 000 for collaborative research with the South China University of Technology at Guangzhou, aimed at developing a solar-powered refrigerator.[121]

The faculty had many ongoing research strengths. Ray Jarvis and his colleagues in the Intelligent Robotics Research Centre produced world-class work. Jarvis' particular interest was in the development of computer vision systems for robotic applications—'hand/eye' systems in the language of artificial intelligence. Jarvis became interested in robots as a means of testing ideas about vision, 'the same way that humans can test their ideas about vision by hand–eye coordination'. He realised that the capacity of the computer to correctly analyse data could be verified by the computer's ability to trigger an appropriate robotic response. For example, its capacity to detect a cup on a table would be confirmed if the computer could direct a robotic arm to pick up the cup. The metaphor developed a life of its own, becoming the research program. Jarvis

TABLE 9.3   EXPENDITURE ON RESEARCH, ENGINEERING, 1991–97 ($MILLION)

1991	*1992*	*1993*	*1994*	*1995*	*1996*	*1997*
3.349	3.856	4.620	7.411	9.039	10.282	11.135

Source: Budget 1996, p. 61; Budget 1997, p. 65, Budget 1998, p. 44.

explored the potential of computer vision systems to aid robotic navigation in various work environments.

Robots were already part of the factory assembly line. The Robotics Research Centre started thinking about roboticised tractors in agriculture, and robotic vehicles in hospitals, able to carry meals to a patient and freeing the nurses for the human side of medical care. The problems of robotic navigation differed in indoor and outdoor environments. Inside, the robot's computer received signals from a sensor capable of detecting barcodes placed at intervals along the wall. Outside, 'global positioning' was used, whereby the robot oriented to at least four of a group of the 23 American satellites put in place for this purpose. This enabled 10 centimetre accuracy in outdoor settings, so that the roboticised tractor could go up and down the rows and avoid trees and other obstacles.

Jarvis became interested in virtual reality as a tool for robotic control. Sites of robot activity could be modelled and pretested using simulation. He also developed 'robotic swarms', many small devices each about the size of a matchbox; the objective was a system where the robots cooperated to carry out a task that no one robot could achieve. Between 1987 and 1996 the ARC awarded more than $1.5 million to the Centre. In 1989 it received over $1 million for a project on robotic vision with BHP as the industry partner; by 1994 collaboration with Electrodrive P/L had led to the Centre's first commercial product, an automated industrial trolley. The Centre developed links with robotics groups at Oxford, Tokyo University, the Electrotechnical Laboratory at Tsukuba in Japan, INRIA at Nice in France, and the Helsinki University of Technology in Finland.

There was much research activity in transport, and in electronics and communications. In the Department of Mechanical Engineering, Bill Melbourne led research on the response of tall buildings and structures to wind action and turbulence, and the dispersion of atmospheric pollutants. By 1996 the University

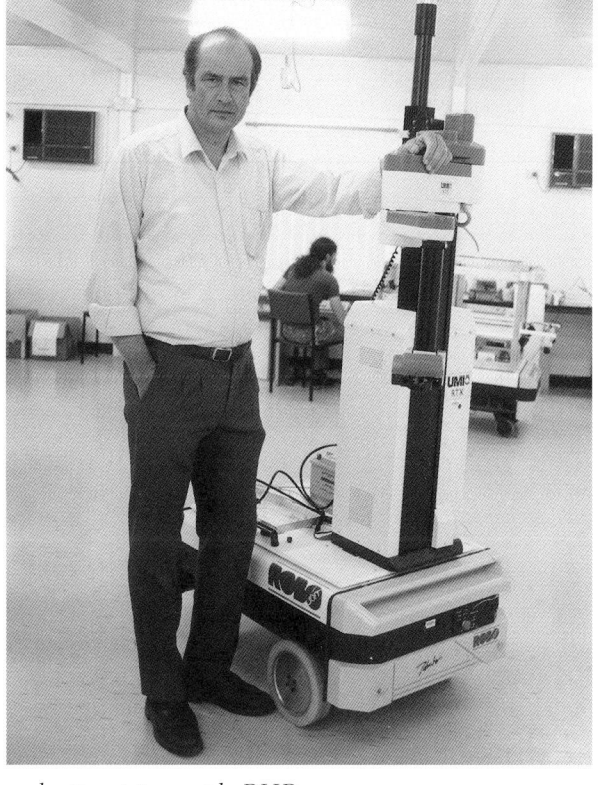

Ray Jarvis. His interest in computer vision systems for robotic applications ('hand-eye systems') led to a series of grants, awards and applications.

had two major wind-tunnel facilities, a 450 kilowatt boundary layer wind tunnel and a 1 megawatt wind tunnel, designed to replicate natural wind activities, into which models of buildings and bridges, aircraft parts and vehicles were inserted. The larger tunnel was a closed circuit, with working sections varying to up to 40 metres long, 12 metres wide and 5 metres high. Wind engineering data were provided for many different commercial clients and to many countries.[122]

Engineering also contributed to the Monash University Accident Research Centre, founded in June 1987 with four staff to do road safety research for the State government. A decade later there were 60 staff undertaking research in various fields of injury prevention, and the Centre was working with the Commonwealth and various State government agencies, the Victorian Health Promotion Foundation, the Transport Accident Commission, VicRoads, and the Royal Automobile Club of Victoria. Its work had contributed to a halving of the annual road toll in Victoria, from 776 deaths in 1989 to under 400. The Centre drew on expertise in Engineering, Medicine and Science. It was conceived as a centre of the University rather than attached to any one faculty.

The Centre conducted injury surveillance and exposure studies, analysed trends, identified countermeasures, and evaluated interventions meant to reduce injury. One role was to study the effects of advertising campaigns designed to discourage drunkenness and careless driving. It conducted projects on women's and children's injuries in the home, product safety, farm injuries, sporting injuries and the like; it encouraged child-resistant cigarette lighters, and the prevention of finger jam injuries in doors. It studied injuries to pedestrians. It rated cars on the basis of the capacity to provide protection in a crash, pressuring manufacturers to upgrade standards. The research had an international impact: for example, the American Automobile Manufacturers Association used the Centre's airbag evaluation study to petition for a change in airbag regulations in the USA.

The University regarded the Accident Research Centre as a major priority, a showpiece of community service. A foundation member of the Centre Board, Wade chaired it from 1994 to 1996, followed by Darvall. In 1996 the Centre received $2.756 million in research grants and $0.406 million in research quantum and infrastructure funding.

Much of the faculty's research activity became concentrated in the Co-operative Research Centres (CRCs), which were funded on a shared basis between government, CSIRO, industry and the universities themselves and designed to stimulate commercially realisable research and development. After securing support for one CRC in the first round, Engineering was a partner in five successful bids in the second round. One collapsed, after ICI Australia withdrew from research in ceramics, leaving five CRCs in operation. Later the faculty was involved in successful bids for two more CRCs, making seven altogether: Low Rank Coal Technologies, Hardwood Pulp and Paper Science, Aerospace Structures, the telecommunications-based Research Data Network, Polymer Blends, Maritime Engineering, and Catchment Hydrology. In 1995 the CRCs between them generated $3.1 million out of a total $9.6 million in faculty research income, 32 per cent; and provided additional postgraduate places: between 1989 and 1994 the number of higher-degree students expanded by 50 per cent.

The Low Rank Coal Technologies CRC in Chemical Engineering set out to tackle the technical problem that had engaged John Monash at the State Electricity Commission more than 70 years before—how to build a viable power industry on the basis of low-quality water-filled brown coal. Monash staff patented a drying process that was bought by a company from Germany, the country from which Sir John had obtained most of his technology. Technological leadership had reversed.

At the same time other Engineering schools were improving, especially in research and dealings with industry. Not as wealthy as the Sydney and Melbourne faculties, with less money in bequests, Monash Engineering was correspondingly more dependent on the efforts of its current staff. Taking office as Dean, Darvall stated that the greatest difficulties the faculty faced were 'fatigue and complacency'. There was too much happening for complacency to gain a hold, but with an ageing staff fatigue was more of a problem. There were as many cars in the Engineering carpark on Saturdays and Sundays as from Monday to Friday. As busy academics moved from one completed project to the next, many of the potential research papers remained unwritten. There simply was never enough time.[123] The faculty had proven its competitive credentials. Morale was high. Nevertheless, a greater dependence on 'soft' money in the post-Dawkins era meant that research activities were less secure and stable than in the days of Matheson and Martin. In the tougher environment of the mid-1990s the faculty found itself running harder just to hold its ground.

Computing and Information Technology

Computing empathised not so much with Mathematics and Science as with Medicine and Engineering. It was an applied science focused not on ideal cases but on solving real-life problems, and on preparing students for work in computing and information technology fields. In the mid-1990s it produced a quarter of all Victorian graduates.[124]

At Peninsula total expenditure more than doubled between 1991 and 1995, cut-off scores rose and international recruitment also grew. There were initiatives in Medical Informatics and a summer semester. Medical Informatics was the use of information technology to process the massive amounts of information generated in health care. It began in the early 1970s. Monash became the first Australian university to develop a curriculum in Medical Informatics, and in 1996 established a Centre for Medical Informatics under Branko Cesnik as the founding director. It offered courses both inside and outside Medicine and drew on other faculties located at the Peninsula campus, including Nursing, Computing and Business. A handful of doctoral students were enrolled and a graduate diploma was planned, aimed at health and business management professionals. The Centre was also involved in industry developments.[125] The largest activity in the early stages was the HIV/AIDS hypermedia project, funded by the AIDS Council and consisting of 1200 screens of information, patient interaction, reference materials and animations. It was adopted for use in seven countries and over a dozen medical schools. Another commitment was the improvement of communication in rural health. Cesnik's own research was focused on the extraction of concepts from text and the construction of category and referencing systems in Health. 'Branko Cesnik is like a space shuttle taking off', observed Bellamy: 'He's at full power and he's into everything'.[126]

Gippsland proved stronger than expected. The former Division of Computing in the Gippsland School of Applied Sciences became a school in the Computing Faculty in 1995. Like some other parts of the campus it had good community links. In 1996 *Montage* reported that a group of farmers from the Maffra region had approached the Gippsland School for advice on how to make better use of information technologies. Students surveyed the area to determine existing technology use and assess needs. The School designed a cost-effective regional computer network linking more than 800 farms to the Internet. Local wool, milk and beef cooperatives established their own web pages and there was a data service with prices, suppliers and weather.[127] Thus the faculty's technological capacity was used to remake local identity in a global context, while at the same time strengthening that local community's viability, in its own terms, within a globalising world.

Entering the faculty after the demise of Professional Studies and bringing 18 research students, the Department of Librarianship, Archives and Records made a successful transition to the technology-based approach. 1995 was the first year of the Bachelor of Information Management. Subjects from the degree were offered at Berwick in 1996.[128]

International students were crucial to Computing and Information Technology's early development. In 1995 their fees brought in $5.3 million, 26.9 per cent of total faculty funding for that year. Taking into account fee-paying postgraduate students as well, fee revenue was 55 per cent of the level of income from the Commonwealth and State governments for teaching purposes. Another $1.2 million was obtained in external earnings. Short courses netted half a million dollars a year.[129] This did not preclude research and publications. In 1995 the faculty generated 1.3 per cent of the University's research funds but 4.8 per cent of its research higher-degree completions and 4.1 per cent of all publications.

Business and Economics

In 1987 the Public Sector Management Institute began within the Graduate School of Management, with the help of Commonwealth funding; Henry Ergas from the OECD, an expert in the emerging area of telecommunications policy, was persuaded to take a professorial chair.[130] The Centre of Policy Studies survived at Clayton but lost the public funding it previously enjoyed, and lost director Michael Porter to private ventures.

In the three-year period after the merger with Chisholm in 1990, the period of separate Business and Economic Faculties, the pace of development quickened (see chapter 5). In 1992 the David Syme School of Business began a fully articulated graduate studies program with honours studies, graduate diplomas in both Accounting and Finance, a Master of Business (Accounting) by coursework, and a PhD program. The mostly fee-paying courses were popular, and 200 students were enrolled by 1993.[131] Despite this, Dean Chandler was never convinced that the Syme School should change fundamentally. He believed that, from the business viewpoint, a research mentality and a business mentality were mutually exclusive. Syme's emphasis should be on how to achieve comparative advantage, he thought.[132] Nevertheless, the appointment of John Rickard, the former Pro-Vice-Chancellor of Deakin University, as Pro-Vice-Chancellor and new Dean of the combined faculty from August 1994 brought in a leader who believed that in principle, the teaching of strategic management should be joined to a research culture, rather than posed against it.

Despite the continued tensions between Syme and Clayton, what held Business and Economics together was its tremendous popularity with local and international students, and its capacity to earn non-government income. In 1995 international students brought in $9.7 million, 23.3 per cent of all funding. Total revenue from fees was $11.9 million, and the faculty took in another $4.7 million in external earnings, 10.1 per cent of income.

In many areas relations with business were strong, while the faculty's international reputation was developing. Graham Peirson in the Centre of Research in Accounting and Finance was involved in setting national and international financial accounting standards. Increasingly, Asia-Pacific countries used international rather than local standards. Peirson's work on the harmonisation of standards assisted financial globalisation. Robert Chenhall took management accounting to the edge of industry innovation, producing books and reports on industry innovation and comparative advantage, leadership, devolution and employee participation, and the role of small business in

Australia. Economics at Clayton remained strong, and Monash continued to lead in econometrics, especially in relation to statistical theory. The University scored a coup when Peter Dixon was persuaded to move his economic model, research team and outside clients from Melbourne to Monash.

The work of Yew Kwang Ng in welfare economics, imperfect competition and other areas was widely cited. Joining Monash at Clayton in 1974, Ng established a reputation as an unusually broad-ranging economic thinker, publishing seminal theoretical papers in several branches of economics. His *Welfare economics* examined how efficiency in resource allocation contributed to increases in social welfare. In 1980 an article on 'Macroeconomics with imperfect competition' began a process of creating a new set of foundations for macroeconomics, based on imperfect competition. Orthodox economics assumed that the foundations of economic behaviour were the laws of perfect competition, whereby the sole objective of economic actors was to maximise individual utility and price was determined at the meeting point of supply and demand. These assumptions were unrealistic, and the predictions of economic models were often contradicted by the actual course of events in the real world. In moving beyond the limitations of the conventional approach, Ng synthesised macro-level insights with microanalysis, terming this 'mesoeconomics'. He assumed that the firm operating at a microeconomic level took into account aggregate variables such as output and price. The model was extended by other scholars. Mesoeconomics entered teaching programs, though largely outside Australia.

John Rickard. Dean of Business and Economics and Pro-Vice-Chancellor from 1994.

In addition, together with his colleague Xiaokai Yang, Ng co-authored *Specialisation and economic organisation: a new classical economic framework* (1993), which restored Adam Smith's themes of the division of labour, specialisation and the structure of economic organisation to a central place, and opened new issues to quantitative analysis. He extended welfare economic methods to the new field of welfare biology to study animal consciousness and suffering, complementing the work of Peter Singer (with whom he co-authored articles) in philosophy. Ng published not only in economic journals but in *Biology and Philosophy, Behavioural and Brain Sciences, Journal of Mathematical Psychology, Journal of Theoretical Biology,* and *Quarterly Journal of Applied Mathematics*. He also wrote popular commentaries on Chinese economic reform, poems, and a Chinese-language novel covering economics, kung fu, mystery, love and poetry—as well as teaching, writing, and research and model-building as part of simultaneous ARC Large Grant projects.

Despite the work of outstanding individuals, the evolution of research in the faculty had some distance to run, especially outside Clayton. Many staff preferred consultancy to research, and it was often difficult to persuade good students to stay on for research degrees because of the forgone earnings. The faculty enrolled a quarter of all Monash students in 1994, provided only 5.9 per cent of all higher-degree completions in the two years 1993–94, and published 9.9 per cent of the publications.

Law

The Law Faculty was not directly affected by the mergers, and the transformation of Monash after 1988 provided fewer opportunities for the Dean of Law, Robert Williams, than for some of his counterparts. The faculty's reputation was strong: in the legal profession its undergraduate program was widely regarded as better than Melbourne's. It seemed that the strategic imperative was to sidestep the turmoil of the times and consolidate its position. Despite this, Williams was induced by Hay to expand enrolments in the 1989–91 period. Then the University's adoption of formula funding wiped the special funding deal Williams had negotiated with Hay (chapter 7), and the faculty was in trouble. In 1992 first-year intake was culled drastically and staff numbers were reduced. New Arts–Law and Law students fell from 304 in 1990 to 178 in 1991. There was a reduction of similar magnitude in Masters intakes.[133] Staff appointments were frozen for two years.

By 1993 the faculty was back in the black, but the expansion was not resumed. As Williams and his colleagues saw it, there was a danger Monash Law would become 'quantity' to Melbourne's 'quality'. It decided that its best interests lay in maintaining elite status, while competing with Melbourne for the best school-leavers as hard as possible.

> While we are a large Law faculty by Australian and international standards, we remain a small part of the University and have deliberately sought to contain growth. We have chosen to focus our efforts on quality; to the achievement of high standards in comparison with what we have achieved in the past and in relation to other parts of the tertiary sector. We do not apologise for this, but consider high standards to be one of the routes to continued professional and academic leadership.[134]

This was consistent with the history of the Law school, though somewhat at variance with the spirit of Greater Monash, in which size was often the engine for development, and supply expanded to meet demand. The faculty might have harmonised with Logan's strategy if it had developed entrepreneurially in postgraduate studies. However, as Williams saw it, the quality of a Law school was measured by its undergraduate rather than its postgraduate program.[135] The outcome was that with growing emphases on specialisation and continuing education within the legal profession, the rival Melbourne Law school stole a march on Monash, sustained partly by its close location to the city and funding from the leading law firms. Monash moved its postgraduate coursework to various premises in the CBD, including law firms, but it seemed unable to overcome continuing perceptions that the courses were still located at Clayton. Melbourne had also moved belatedly to reform its undergraduate program, and by the mid-1990s was threatening to outdo Monash in that area as well.

The Monash faculty's strengths continued to be the quality of its staff and its intensive teaching program, and its legal scholarship. The curriculum emphasised the formation of legal skills, the clinical programs provided in conjunction with Monash-Oakleigh and Springvale Legal Services, and a critical understanding of legal theory and social context.[136] Law was the first Monash faculty to introduce mandatory student evaluation of staff, and good teaching was mandatory for appointment and promotion. The teaching program was reviewed regularly. Under Williams, faculty administration lifted markedly. At the end of the 1980s there was a cultural change in the Law Students' Society, so that it became more vocational in temper. As well as a large-scale mooting competition, culminating in the final moot before a group of Supreme Court judges, it managed a tutorial program using later-year students as tutors, financing the program with donations from law firms; monitored the law firms for graduate employment; and organised career fairs.[137] The faculty's relations with the legal profession were underpinned by the lecture series it ran in conjunction with leading law firms and banks. Between 1991 and 1994 speakers included the Japanese Ambassador to Australia, the managing directors of three major banks, the deputy governor of the Reserve Bank, the Solicitor-General, the Chairman of the Australian Securities Commission, the Commissioner of Taxation, the heads of the Seven Network and the Herald and Weekly Times, and Justices of the High Court and Supreme Court.[138]

The Law library was extended to a fourth floor and continued to be a tremendous asset. CD-ROM technology and electronic databases enhanced its offerings, which was fortunate because it was used by staff and students from Melbourne, La Trobe and Deakin, and law firms and members of the public. Inevitably, a user charge was introduced for outsiders. The mood among staff was collaborative and purposeful. In the five years after 1990, 36 major legal texts were solely authored or shared by members of staff. Seniors made decisions as a group. The heart of the faculty was still in criminal law. Commercial law was perhaps not as strong as under Bob Baxt but there were new specialisations, such as Sam Ricketson's work in intellectual property. Ricketson was at the top of the field in Australia, and known around the world for his work on the Berne Copyright Convention. His *Law of intellectual property* was often cited in the courts.

In a University with so few female leaders, Law was an exception. In 1995, seven out of 19 academics at Professor or Associate Professor/Reader level were women, and 30 out of 63 academics at all levels.[139] Enid Campbell had served as Australia's first female Law school Dean. Marcia Neave was one of the University's best-known Professors. She was appointed to a chair at the University of Adelaide in 1986 and transferred to Monash in 1991. Managing an eclectic portfolio of research and policy interests in property law, family law and law reform, she left a considerable mark on each. Neave co-authored *Property law: cases and materials* (1972), which ran through a number of editions and was still in widespread use almost three decades later. Much of her subsequent work focused on women's issues, where she interwove feminist theory with traditional 'black letter' law. She was particularly interested in issues related to the division of property after the breakdown of relationships. In such disputes the law often produced inequitable results for women. Much of her work involved thinking about ways to ameliorate the position of women who had lost earning capacity because of their commitment to child-rearing and domestic work. She published *Australian family property law* in 1984, with Ian Hardingham.

In 1983 and 1984 Neave was research director of the New South Wales Law Reform Commission and involved in preparing papers and reports on de-facto relationships and accident compensation and advising Parliamentary Counsel on the drafting of legislation. The Chair of the Commission, Ron Sackville, later paid tribute to her work on accident compensation, which helped to shape the Commission's deliberations. In 1985 she headed the Victorian government inquiry into prostitution and prepared the reform of prostitution law. Most of the proposed reforms were adopted, but she was unsuccessful in securing the abolition of criminal penalties for women involved in prostitution and the designation of safe areas for street prostitution, and continued to press for these changes.

While at Monash, Neave worked on a book with Susanne Liden on the legal response to the sexual division of labour, covering labour law, family law, social security and other fields, including an assessment of the effectiveness of initiatives to remove discrimination from the law. She also became involved in orientation programs designed to educate family court and other judges in gender inequality in judicial process; for example the biases in particular legal rules, and preconceptions about the relative credibility of women and men as witnesses. She was a part-time member of the Victorian Law Reform Commission from 1986 until its abolition in 1992, and was President of the Administrative Review Council.

Arts

When John Hay arrived from Western Australia to become Dean of Arts in 1987 the faculty was ready for change. A number of new centres were founded, which proved to be effective mechanisms for

Centre for Human Bioethics. Helga Kuhse and Peter Singer: their critical reflections on the IVF program became part of the development of the program itself.

shaping innovative teaching and research programs, and cross-field collaboration, without unduly disrupting the workings of departments.[140] The Centres for Australian Studies, for European Studies and for Development Studies, and the Women's Studies Centre, all opened that year. The Centre for Human Bioethics, founded half a decade earlier, was also in Arts—its leading light was Peter Singer—though it established its role in monitoring the IVF program. The IVF scientists talked regularly with the Centre. IVF technology was often pointing at the unknown: 'once you unlock a door, you don't know where it will take you' (de Kretser).[141] Helga Kuhse, Centre Director, stated in 1996:

> There are no firm boundaries in science any more and there's no ultimate truth. Some of us would say that we are trying to get a bit closer to the truth. One way that you can achieve this is not by going out and doing empirical measurements, but by putting arguments that people can agree or disagree with on reasonable grounds.[142]

Consulted by governments and community groups, the Centre was also a vigorous academic publisher. Kuhse was general editor of a series of books on bioethics published by Oxford University Press, and Kuhse and Singer were invited to co-edit an international journal. In 1988 the Australian Studies group, carefully orchestrated by Hay, was successful in winning national funding as a Key Centre for Teaching and Research, against competition from many other institutions. Under director Peter Spearritt the National Centre for Australian Studies, as it became known, was a powerhouse of activity, one of the generators of the reviving interest in national identity. It secured more funding, from the Victorian Education Foundation, and was soon receiving student load funding and student fees. It started applied postgraduate courses in Tourism, Communications, Museum Studies and Cultural Policy, and Australian Studies itself; and a fee-paying graduate diploma in Publishing and Editing. It early realised the significance of the World Wide Web. It prepared open learning units. Staff conducted research in bibliography and biography, cultural policy, indigenous studies, heritage studies, urban and transport history, trade union history, and published the *Guide to New Australian Books* and a biographical dictionary of 20th century Australia.[143]

Robert Pargetter became Dean of Arts in 1989, and one of his most important decisions was to support the creation of the Centre for Critical Theory and Cultural Studies, where Philosophy and cultural theory met English. The Centre was the right move for the times. Drawing together the distinctive talents of Elizabeth Grosz and Kevin Hart, it proved very popular with students. Its PhD numbers grew rapidly. Hart came from English at the University of Melbourne in July 1991. Originally a philosopher, he was interested in Catholic theology. Grosz was a feminist from General Philosophy at the University of Sydney. To many at the time it seemed a strange pairing. Pargetter recalled later:

> The issue was, could they ever work together? So I talked to each of them. Liz was in America at the time: I happened to be going to America, so I chatted to Liz at the LA airport. I decided, having talked to each, that they could get on. Each was aware of each other's work and admired each other's work and that seemed to me crucial.[144]

While Liz Grosz was still an undergraduate at Sydney in the early 1970s there was a strike in the Philosophy Department in support of the introduction of a course in feminist philosophy. Eventually the Department was split into General Philosophy (which included feminist philosophy), where Grosz later worked, and Traditional and Modern Philosophy. Her doctoral thesis focused on Jacques Lacan's reading of the work of Freud. Working at Sydney throughout the 1980s, she published a broad array of work including *Sexual subversions*, on the work of three influential French feminists—Julia Kristeva, Luce Irigaray and Michele Le Doeuff. The prospects opened up by the Monash Centre and critical theory program excited her. It was 'a golden opportunity to begin a program on contemporary theory', she stated later. No other Australian university was doing this at the time.

Grosz became founding director of the Centre, moving beyond psychoanalytic theory to the theorisation of the body. For feminists who understood gender oppression in terms of consciousness and experience, and saw relations between the sexes in terms of equality rather than difference, the focus on the body was a radical change. Here Grosz drew on Foucault, for whom the body was 'something positive, rather than an obstacle to be overcome'. For her the body was 'the fundamental site of sexual difference'. *Volatile bodies: toward a corporeal feminism* (1994) and a companion volume of essays (1995) won awards and critical acclaim. Awarded a personal professorial chair in 1995, Grosz held visiting professorships at the University of California (Santa Cruz and Davis), Johns Hopkins University, George Washington University and the University of Richmond.[145]

Kevin Hart was one of Australia's foremost literary critics and poets. Interested in French and German philosophy but finding himself locked into an Anglo-American tradition, Hart shifted across to English in 1986 at a time when the discipline was drawing on outside influences. He began to weave together English, Philosophy and Theology. Teaching in both the new Centre and the English Department at Monash, he encouraged students to read poetry in association with history and cultural theory. His personal interest was in 'the poetics of the negative'—that which is 'other' or unsayable. Hart's major books included *The trespass of the sign* (1989), *A.D. Hope* (1992) and *Economic Acts: Samuel Johnson and the culture of property* (1997). He also edited the *Oxford book of Australian religious verse*. His poetry, published in seven volumes, had won many awards.[146]

Back in the departments it was not always easy to reconcile the excitements of feminism, post-modernism, post-structuralism and post-colonialism with the reproduction of the disciplines. In the new environment knowledge itself was seen as constructed, and socially determined, creating an ultra-modernist sense of perpetual movement in which nothing was certain. For some staff this was stimulating, and the success of English showed that many students agreed. Other staff found it threatening, but soldiered on. Ageing tenured academics and feisty young academics without tenure (and few opportunities to obtain it) were not always comfortable with each other. The collapse of disciplinary certainty made everything harder: supervising students, marking theses, designing courses, making appointments, explaining the discipline in public:[147]

> In English it is the crisis about 'what are English studies?' The general public are abusing us for not teaching the students grammar. We start kicking the school teachers for not having taught them grammar. At the same time we have people wandering round the place and asking 'what is grammar anyway?' And not waiting for an answer.[148]

Numbers in Arts plateaued after the merger, which was fortunate because facilities in the Menzies Building were inadequate. The opening of the Performing Arts building led to the relocation of Music, Drama and Theatre Studies but this added little to total space. The building needed a major renovation—'it's a slum' was how one Dean described it[149]—but the funds were not there. The inhabitants had to be content with minor renovation and refurbishment. Fortunately the educational offerings were more exciting than the architecture. English, History and parts of Philosophy and Linguistics continued to be strong. Bob Birrell was a busy and productive sociologist with a gift for media comment. The University maintained the largest group of languages of any Victorian university, offering culture and history as well as communication. Honours and postgraduate programs grew; the faculty provided 27.3 per cent of higher-degree completions at Monash in 1995, and 22.9 per cent of the publications, though receiving only 7.5 per cent of the research grants.[150] As Dean, Pargetter fought for a Monash funding formula based on a 50/50 split between research income and publications, but was unsuccessful.[151]

Following Pargetter's appointment as DVC the deanship went to historian and women's studies academic Marian Quartly in 1994. Her job was more difficult than that of her predecessors. By the mid-1990s government funding was very tight, foreshadowing a longer-term crisis in Arts. The faculty had few options if the position worsened, for more than 90 per cent of its income was tied up in salaries, and the level of non-government earnings was low.[152] The National Centre for Australian Studies showed that it was possible to support both traditional scholarship and entrepreneurial activity under the same roof. Nevertheless, it was hard to persuade most academics working in the Arts departments to chase commercial opportunities, the more so given the growing difficulties they faced in sustaining the workload of ordinary teaching programs. Divided along disciplinary lines even more than was Science, the faculty lacked coherence in policy and resource management. The action needed to change its funding base seemed beyond it. Departments focused on their own immediate position to the exclusion of all else.

Education

The Education Faculty was a national leader in its field, strong since its beginnings at Monash,[153] especially in research and higher-degree work. The faculty built its main reputation in Science and Maths education, and from time to time its personnel provided assistance to the Faculties of Science, Engineering and Medicine. The work of Peter Fensham, Dick White, Jeff Northfield, Dick Gunstone and others was well known in Britain and North America. The Monash faculty was established in the American Educational Research Association. Many visiting scholars spent time at Clayton, and from time to time the faculty sustained large-scale policy research projects in Southeast Asia.

In 1987 the *Times Higher Education Supplement* asked the heads of British university departments of education to nominate the international faculties of education at which they would most like to work. The answer was Stanford, Harvard and Monash.[154] It was an accolade that at the time had been well earned; yet it was a sign of the insecurity of the discipline of Education within the University that faculty leaders cited this passing incident many times in the course of the next decade. Education was prone to retreat behind its walls, and sometimes to dwell on past glories; though the faculty had built a solid internal culture, its relations within the University were prone to tension and misunderstanding. The underlying problem was that Education was a poorly paid mass profession with none of the prestige of Medicine or Law or even Engineering.

Other academics did not always take the study of Education seriously, despite the salience of issues related to teaching, in every discipline.

Relations with the University centre worsened during the Logan years. Peter Fensham, Dean from 1980 to 1988, remarked later that one problem was that 'Education had a very democratic culture' and was uneasy with the Vice-Chancellor's entrepreneurial approach.[155] Under David Aspin the Dean was more cooperative, but the troops continued to be restless. After the mergers, beneath the strong deanship typical of Monash, there was no departmental structure as such and political rather than managerial distribution of resources. Funds were often shared out on a pro-rata basis. Education was productive of publications, competitive in ARC grants, and attracted some funding for research and consultancy projects, but it was a weak income-earner in other respects: in 1995 only 3.4 per cent of total funding was from fees. External earnings constituted 9.0 per cent ($1.2 million), much of them from the Centre for Continuing Education at Frankston. The faculty provided 6.2 per cent of the University's publications, 6.2 per cent of higher-degree completions, and 1.2 per cent of research grants,[156] a similar profile to that of Arts. This heavy dependence on government-funded student load threatened to create future problems.

Though the integration of Education at Peninsula and Gippsland was slow, the teaching and research profile of Peninsula was ultimately transformed and it was hoped that it would be a faculty strength in future years.[157] In course structures, the main initiatives were the introduction of a professional doctorate, the EdD (Monash was the first in Australia) and the introduction of combined courses. The combined course with Arts proved popular. Ironically, the first Monash Dean of Education, Richard Selby-Smith, had attempted a combined degree with Arts but had failed. His goal was achieved 25 years later.[158] Apart from science education, there were research programs in the Economics of Education and Training under Gerald Burke, in Educational Psychology, Administration and Policy, and later in Adult and Vocational Education. With Dick Selleck, Andrew Spaull and others Monash was a leader in Educational History. Despite this, the faculty in the 1990s was perhaps not as dominant in the discipline as it had been. Like several other Monash faculties, it had become somewhat set in its ways and it faced a problem of renewal. The departure of Fensham and Selleck left a gap, though they continued to be research-active. Other leading scholars were close to retirement.

The agenda was broadened by International Education, a new subdiscipline created by Fazal Rizvi, appointed from the University of Queensland in 1996. Rizvi had broad-ranging interests, including internationalisation, questions of racism and identity, the arts and cultural politics and their implications for education. In forming the Monash Centre for Research in International Education in 1997 he situated this emerging field in the context of studies of globalisation, international marketing and the growth of cultural exchange. A member of the Australian Foundation for Culture and the Humanities, a former member of the Australia Council for the Arts and contributor to *Creative nation*, the Commonwealth statement on cultural policy, Rizvi focused on the identities of people moving between cultures, such as migrants and international students, and 'the creativity which comes about because of cultural exchange and cultural borrowing and appropriation'. He was also interested in 'how new technologies allow some of these things to happen'.

Rizvi's agenda had a practical relevance to the University. The new postgraduate courses in international education grew quickly: students included members of the staff of Monash International. The Centre for Research in International Education also took up issues of curriculum change and cultural encounter. In an ARC-financed project on the experience of Malaysian students studying in Australia, all the students that he interviewed told Rizvi that they hoped to make friends with local students. It was apparent that most of these hopes had failed. There was an unrealised potential for 'hybridity'—what happened when different cultures come together. Rizvi's approach was emblematic of globalisation itself. He wanted to connect studies in and about education to other fields with something to say about culture and policy, including International Relations, Politics, Sociology and Youth Studies. He saw Education as a primary facilitator of this intellectual mixing. It was a novel addition to the faculty's traditional role of preparing teachers for Victorian schools.

The faculties in 1996

The continuing independence of the Monash faculties created the question of how University-wide organisational coherence was to be achieved. At a time when competitive pressures were growing and the need was for strategic change, the question was thrown into sharp relief. In a university there were good reasons not to rely primarily on top-down corporate control as the means of securing coherence, and this was doubly so at Monash, where Logan's strategy depended on cultural factors and voluntary compliance (see chapter 4). Nevertheless, at the end of his term of office the integration of the new entrepreneurial culture into day-to-day operations remained uneven.

In the faculties the outcome was patchy. If Business and Economics, Computing and Engineering were comfortable with the mix of government-funded and market activity that had come to characterise the times, and Medicine and Pharmacy had become accustomed to working both public and private sources of research grants, Law and Education were less enterprising. Arts and Science were yet to develop strategies to compensate for a declining government funding share. In disciplines which (however crucial they were to the larger map of knowledge and to the foundations of research and the

David Antony Robinson, Vice-Chancellor, February 1997–

'Universities have to continually make and remake themselves'

David Robinson, Vice-Chancellor from 1997. A reputation for decisiveness and the capacity to make effective use of resources in a new context.

David Robinson was born in 1941 and began his university career at University College, Swansea, with an honours arts degree in Politics and Sociology. Within three years he had gained a doctorate from the University of Wales in Sociology (1967) and begun the specialisation in medical sociology which dominated his work for the next 20 years.

Robinson spent nine years at the Addiction Research Unit in the University of London Institute of Psychiatry (1971–80) before being appointed Acting Director of the Institute for Health Studies at the University of Hull, becoming promoted to Professor in 1984. He worked on a series of World Health Organization (WHO) projects and consultancies, chaired several WHO committees, managed over 1.3 million pounds in funded projects at the University of Hull alone, and served on research committees of the Medical Research Council, the Medical Council of Alcoholism and the Economic and Social Research Council. At the same time Robinson generated a large scholarly output: between 1968 and 1989 he wrote, co-wrote or edited 12 books on medical sociology, alcohol dependence, self-help and related issues; plus 18 chapters, 51 journal articles, and other materials.

For him health issues were 'endlessly fascinating', with their span from the micro to macro, from doctor–patient relations to 'global markets in legally addictive substances like tobacco', and to issues of health policy in between. Inevitably, he was forced to curtail his research interests as he took on a greater weight of administrative responsibilities at Hull, though he was still publishing in the 1990s. Dean of the School of Social and Political Sciences in 1986, Robinson became Pro-Vice-Chancellor in 1989 under Bill Taylor. The Hull years were a severe lesson in institutional economics. As he stated later: 'when you get a 17 per cent cut in government funding overnight, it really concentrates the mind'.[159]

In 1992 came the change of country, when Robinson applied successfully for the position of Vice-Chancellor and President at the University of South Australia (USA) in Adelaide. (Later he became a dual British and Australian citizen.) USA was formed out of the merger of the South Australian Institute of Technology with the three campuses of the South Australian CAE. The institution was one of the success stories of the

> Dawkins reforms, developing quickly under the new Vice-Chancellor. Robinson built a reputation in higher education for decisiveness and the capacity to make effective use of existing resources in a new policy context. He became active in Open Learning Australia, and strengthened his interest in internationalisation. They were good attributes to bring to Monash.

professions) lacked a role in postgraduate vocational training or immediate applications in business it was genuinely difficult to generate market incomes. The problems of the non-entrepreneurial faculties had been made more difficult, and their solution more urgent, by the decline in public funding per student. Faculties were forced to raise teaching loads, and it was hard to employ new young staff. With a large number of staff aged over 50 years, there would be dramatic change in Arts and Science early in the 21st century; in the meantime it sometimes seemed that innovation was impossible.

Everywhere people were working harder than earlier in the University's history.[160] In the later 1990s the capacity of academics had to be greater than that of their predecessors, not just at Monash but at all Australian universities. It was no longer possible to 'coast'. To survive and prosper needed stamina as well as intellect,[161] and skill in improvisation, in stretching the same resources further. There were limits to this. Better quality was not solely reducible to management, and could not be achieved by marketing. More resources were needed. There was no sign of these in sight, except perhaps through student fees.

A new era begins

Logan's successor David Robinson was chosen 10 months before taking office, soon after the election of a Liberal–National Party government in March 1996. Once again Monash had timed a change of leaders in synchronisation with a change in policy. The change of government cut the special ties between Monash and Canberra, and spelled a tougher fiscal regimen for all universities. In the August 1996 budget it was announced that operating funds would be reduced—Monash was to lose 3.9 per cent in real terms between 1996 and 1998—and that universities would not receive cost supplementation for future rises in salaries, resulting in a further reduction of 10 per cent or more in the coming years. This meant that the corporate sector and private funding sources would become still more important.[162]

The new Vice-Chancellor was a Yorkshire-born sociologist who had come to Australia as Vice-Chancellor of the University of South Australia (USA) in 1992. He accumulated a strong reputation in an institution making a success out of a difficult merger. USA had built quickly in size to become the largest university in South Australia, and like Monash had used its opportunities well, diversifying teaching, building research, creating a new city campus, and strengthening international education, distance education and open learning. The recent history of the two institutions had much in common, and Robinson had a prior connection to Monash and to Logan, having worked on the Board of Open Learning Australia since 1992.

Robinson shared with Logan a commitment to higher participation and improved access to social groups underrepresented in universities, and to distance education and open learning. They had another quality in common: Robinson, too, was a moderniser. Nothing was sacrosanct, including the legacy of his predecessor. He told *Montage* soon after his Monash appointment was announced that universities had to be 'street wise organisations'; and had to 'demonstrate their quality, not just claim it'. 'Universities have to continually make and remake themselves if they are to survive and prosper', he stated.[163]

Afterword

A large university is a beast with many faces. Its activities are various and complex. The continuing vitality of curiosity-driven research, of extra-curricular student life and of the arts at Monash is a reminder that the essence of a university is more than political economy. Yet projects of economy and government are too important to dismiss. In truth there is no single essence of the university as an institution. Neither its academic practices nor its social purposes are valid for every time and place, but are continually renegotiated.

In the transformation of Monash into Greater Monash, its leaders realised that after Dawkins had opened the doors to the outside world and globalisation had brought that world larger and closer than before, external pressure for change had become more or less continuous. In the globalised environment a university, like a nation, retains its distinctive personality, its inner life. Change touches every aspect of the university's affairs, but is neither even in tempo nor programmed according to a single formula. There is space for the university to strategise, and while organisational innovation carries risks—the risks are greater in a more competitive setting, with less backup from government funding—if the institution is strong enough there is scope for remaking the nature of the university itself.

All Australian universities grew in the 1990s and many expanded their functions, but they followed established patterns. Imitating behaviour was dominant.[1] Monash not only remade itself—to a significant degree it remade the Australian university as an institution. It created a new prototype, not so much in size as in the diversity and responsiveness of its activities. The range and intensity of its external engagements brought Monash to the cutting edge. In 1988 Australia was yet to develop an institution like the American State university (suburban, regional, national). Monash achieved that model and added an international and global dimension to it. In doing so, the University created the longer-term possibility for itself of becoming a great international university.

No Australian university fell into this category—the category of Oxford or Harvard, UCLA or the Sorbonne. Until recently it had been quite beyond reach.

To achieve it, Monash would need more than a keen eye for the main chance: it would also need absolutely front-rank research and teaching. There was also a larger problem to figure out: that of the future role of Australian institutions in a globalising environment. Worldwide communications networks had reduced the old constraints of distance. With an established presence in East and Southeast Asia, Australian universities were playing an intermediary role between North America and Asia, and Europe and Asia. It remained to be seen whether this could turn itself into a new kind of global presence. The road to world university was still long. To complete it would again require the ingenuity of the 1980s and 90s, sustained over a greater time. Nevertheless, a real beginning had been made.

Monash always suffered from being the second university in a city whose leading citizens had mostly attended the first. By the 1990s that had changed somewhat, and its international role allowed the University to reach beyond its local limits. Nevertheless, the weight of history meant that Monash's leaders always had to be better at what they did, just to achieve an equal place. Monash selected only three full-term vice-chancellors in its first 38 years of life, and whether by chance or design each was unusually appropriate to the times. Louis Matheson (1960–76) was an engineer with an eye for a structure that would last. Ray Martin (1977–87) protected the research mission of the University in the steady state. Mal Logan (1987–97) moved remarkably quickly to take advantage of the changes in government policy. In a period when the new form of creativity in universities was organisational creativity, he worked emerging opportunities where none had been before.

At the end of the Logan years the remaking of the University was still a project in progress. The merger process was unfinished. The engagement of faculties in their external environment was uneven. The culture of a responsive university was yet to be fully generalised inside the institution: Monash could not yet take full advantage of the new opportunities it had opened for itself. The old unhelpful abrasion between administrative and academic functions lingered. It was vital to achieve a better synergy between the administrative and the academic. Too often, the distinct character of faculties was expressed in their organisational autarky, rather than disciplinary innovations; while administration sometimes showed in the weight of procedure rather than the facilitation of outcomes. And teaching and research had been stretched too thin by resource constraints.

If the remade Monash were to flower in the next period, the most important priority was to strengthen the academic heartland. Academic quality was integral to whatever lay ahead. A new blossoming of research and teaching would also provide more favourable conditions for integrating the University's academic activities with its institutional goals and systems.

Endnotes

Data in numerical date form (for example 7.11.95) refer to research interviews. These were conducted by the author, except for interviews with personnel in the arts and the IVF program (Isabelle Normand), with former *Lots Wife* editors (Daryl Dellora) and with leading researchers (Bridget Nettelbeck).

Preface

1 Graeme Davison (1991), 'Paradigms of public history', in *Packaging the past? Public histories,* edited by John Rickard and Peter Spearritt, Australian Historical Studies, Melbourne University Press, Melbourne, pp 4–15.
2 McCalman, Janet, *The Australian*, 3 January 1996.
3 For example, the works by John Poynter and Carolyn Rasmussen, *A place apart—the University of Melbourne: decades of challenge*, Melbourne University Press, Melbourne, 1996; and Stephen Foster and Margaret Varghese, *The making of the Australian National University, 1946–1996*, Allen & Unwin, Sydney, 1996.
4 Interview with Cliff Bellamy, 19 June 1996 (hereafter Bellamy 19.6.96).

1 Beginnings

1 Robert Blackwood, *Monash University: the first ten years*, Hampden Hall, Melbourne, 1968, pp 10–11; Louis Matheson, *Still learning*, Macmillan, Melbourne, 1980, p. 66.
2 Geoffrey Serle, *John Monash: a biography*, Melbourne University Press, Melbourne, 1982, p. 510. This is an outstanding work.
3 Serle records that Anderson and Monash were responsible for the graceful Morrell Bridge over the Yarra River at Anderson Street near the Botanical Gardens, using the Monier technique, which combined cement mortar with a grid of iron rods (1899). However, although Monash was an early advocate of this technique, the firm responsible for the construction of the bridge was Carter, Gummow and Co. of Sydney (designer W.J. Baltzer, construction manager G. Forrest). Monash's partner Anderson assisted the Sydney firm in negotiations for the contract, and Monash kept in touch with proceedings during the construction phase. The Morrell Bridge introduced Anderson and Monash to the Monier system—Lesley Alves, Alan Holgate and Geoff Taplin, *Monash bridges: typology*

study, reinforced concrete bridges in Victoria 1897–1917, 2nd edn, Monash University Faculties of Engineering and Arts, Monash University, Clayton, 1998, pp 47–9.

4 *ibid*, p. 435.

5 *ibid*, p. 462.

6 'Until the last shot was fired, every day was filled with loathing, horror, and distress. I deplored all the time the loss of precious life and the waste of human effort. Nothing could have been more repugnant to me than the realisation of the dreadful inefficiency and the misspent energy of war', John Monash, *The Australian victories in France in 1918*, Hutchinson, London, 1920, p. 297.

7 The opposing commander Ludendorff called 8 August 'the black day of the German army', in which the ultimate outcome was made clear to both sides—*ibid*, p. 131.

8 Serle, *op cit*, specially pp 375–403.

9 Monash, *op cit*, p. 96.

10 Serle, *op cit*, p. 396.

11 *ibid*, p. 481.

12 *ibid*, p. 148.

13 *ibid*, p. 479.

14 *ibid*, p. 253.

15 Serle, *op cit*, p. 507.

16 *ibid*, pp 192, 460, 507.

17 Matheson, *op cit*; see also Blackwood, *ibid*; and John Rickard, 'The "university in a hurry"', in F.W. Kent and D.D. Cuthbert, *Making Monash: a twenty-five year history*, Monash University, Clayton, 1986, pp 6–24.

18 Simon Marginson, *Educating Australia: government, economy and citizen since 1960*, Cambridge University Press, Melbourne, 1997.

19 Nicolas Brown, *Governing prosperity*, Cambridge University Press, Melbourne, 1995.

20 Poynter and Rasmussen, *op cit*.

21 Keith Murray (chair), *Report of the Committee on Australian Universities*, Commonwealth Government Printer, Canberra, 1957, pp 7, 23, 86–7.

22 *ibid*, p. 91.

23 The account that follows is influenced by Rickard *op cit*, pp 6–8 and Matheson *op cit*.

24 Blackwood, *op cit*, pp 1–2; Poynter and Rasmussen, *op cit*, p. 102.

25 Blackwood, *op cit*, pp 4–9. 'The Melbourne Technical College did not give up without a fight, launching on October a twelve-point plan to achieve university status and claiming a capacity to ease the pressure on Melbourne University until the new "general" university was open. When all of these manoeuvres were ignored, it made a final, unsuccessful attempt to be incorporated into the new Monash; failure condemned the College to spend another three decades on the wrong side of the binary tracks'—Poynter and Rasmussen, *op cit*, pp 195–6.

26 Blackwood, *op cit*, pp 17–21.

27 John Legge, 'Monash—then and now', in *Monash University: 1961–1986—the first 25 years*, Monash University, Clayton, pp 19–20; Peter Darvall 4.2.1997.

28 Matheson, *op cit*, pp 92, 173. 'Ancora imparo' is attributed to Michelangelo.

29 *ibid*, pp 14–15.

30 *ibid*, pp 22–7.

31 The 1958 *Monash University Act* made provision for agriculture and veterinary science, but the attention of rural lobbyists switched to the reopening of a separate veterinary school at Melbourne, and the Monash option was not debated—Poynter and Rasmussen, *op cit*, pp 229–32.

32 Terry Hore 23.7.1996; Louis Waller 29.7.1996.

33 Matheson, *op cit*, p. 4.

34 Poynter and Rasmussen, *op cit*, p. 266. For the crisis at Melbourne see pp 264–92.

35 Matheson, *op cit*, p. 34.

36 Matheson, *op cit*, pp 166, 172–3.
37 Graeme Schofield, 16.7.1996.
38 Matheson, *op cit*, p. 58.
39 Rickard, *op cit*, pp 10–11.
40 *ibid*, pp 40, 44; Blackwood, *op cit*, p. 198. 'Ming' was one of Prime Minister Robert Menzies' nicknames.
41 Rickard, *op cit*, p. 9. By the 1980s the Menzies Building was experiencing a different kind of press. 'It has all the grace of a gargantuan pigeon loft . . . so fat, so square and so brutally stark . . . this mistake of the university's youth', wrote Bill Hitchings in *The Herald*, 2 August 1984. He praised the grounds, however: 'an air of peacefulness that it would be difficult to find outside the Botanic Gardens'.
42 Blackwood, *op cit*, p. 198.
43 Matheson, *op cit*, p. 43.
44 Marian Quartly, 'Looking backwards, looking forwards', in *Ming Wing: winds of change*, brochure prepared for a photographic exhibition commemorating the Menzies Building in the 1960s, Monash University.
45 Waller, *op cit*; Lance Endersbee 26.6.1996; Matheson, *op cit*, p. 65.
46 Bob Williams 9.7.1996.

2 Clayton in steady state

1 Marginson, *op cit*, chapter 4.
2 *ibid*, chapter 9; Milton Friedman, 'The role of government in education', in *Capitalism and freedom*, University of Chicago Press, Chicago, 1962, pp 85–107.
3 Margaret Thatcher, Prime Minister of the United Kingdom, *1981 Sir Robert Menzies Lecture* at Monash University, Melbourne, 6 October 1981.
4 Michael Porter, 'Our costly and cosseted universities', *Australian Financial Review*, 21 August 1984.
5 Bruce Williams (Chair of Committee), *Education, training and employment*, Report of the National Inquiry into Education and Training, AGPS, Canberra, 1979.
6 Between 1975/76 and 1982/83 annual spending on building works fell from $360 to $140 million (constant 1984/85 prices)—Australian Bureau of Statistics, *Expenditure on education*, ABS Catalogue no. 5510.0
7 Department of Employment, Education and Training (DEET), *The Tertiary Education Assistance Scheme*, Australian Government Publishing Service (AGPS), Canberra, 1988, p. 63.
8 ABS, *op cit*; Department of Employment, Education and Training (DEET), *Participation in education* statistics, DEET, Canberra.
9 *ibid*, CTEC data.
10 Commonwealth Tertiary Education Commission (CTEC), *Review of efficiency and effectiveness in higher education*, AGPS, Canberra, 1986.
11 Don Anderson and Aart Vervoorn, *Access to privilege*, Australian National University Press, Canberra, 1983.
12 Terry Hore, '"Reflection" has at least two meanings; post-secondary education for what?', in Terry Hore, Peter Chippendale and Leo West (eds), *A new era for tertiary education*, Darling Downs Institute of Advanced Education, Toowoomba, 1980, pp 25–6.
13 Commonwealth Tertiary Education Commission (CTEC), *Learning and earning, Vols 1 & 2*, AGPS, Canberra, 1982. Male retention to year 12 in schooling fell from 34.6 per cent in 1975 to 31.9 per cent in 1980. Female retention rose from 33.6 to 37.3 per cent to outstrip male retention for the first time—ABS, *Schools Australia*, Catalogue no. 4221.0.

14 Excluding student assistance, total public funding rose from $2039 million in 1975/76 to $2185 million in 1976/77 before falling away to $2007 million in 1982/83. ABS 5510.0, *op cit*.
15 Ray Martin. 'Report of the Vice-Chancellor', *Annual Report 1983*, Monash University, p. 6.
16 'Staffing need is paramount', *Monash Reporter*, 2 March 1983; '"Hold steady" year with hopes high for future', *Monash Reporter,* 7 March 1984, p. 1.
17 *ibid*, p. 2. The multidisciplinary building was completed in 1986.
18 'The big questions in higher education', *The Australian*, 28 November 1984. In 1984 an estimated 45 000 qualified applicants for university places were unsuccessful: Helen Trinca, 'The tertiary "boom" brings optimism to the campuses', *The Australian*, 28 February 1984.
19 'Ceiling stays on Monash funds: UC', *Monash Reporter,* 1 June 1983, p. 2.
20 *Monash Reporter*, *op cit*, p. 1.
21 ABS 5510.0, *op cit*; DEET, *National report on Australia's higher education sector*, AGPS, Canberra, 1993, p. 74.
22 Matheson, *op cit*, p. 170.
23 '"Hold steady" year', *op cit*, p. 1.
24 Monash Council meeting 5/84, 9 July 1984.
25 Joe Bornstein, *A new university—the search for excellence*, graduation address Monash University, 29 March 1985.
26 Martin, 'Report of the Vice-Chancellor' 1977, *op cit*, pp 2, 5.
27 Ray Martin, 'The way ahead', in *Monash University: 1961–1986—the first 25 years*, Monash University, Clayton, 1986, p. 2.
28 *Monash University Statistics 1984*, Monash University, Clayton.
29 John Hallows and Helen Trinca, 'How to choose your university', *The Australian*, 14 July 1984.
30 *Monash Reporter*, 7 March 1984.
31 Endersbee 26.6.1996; Mal Logan 7.11.1995; Bill Melbourne 9.11.1995; Robert Porter 7.11.1995.
32 Jim Maher, 'The chiefs are learning—the hard way', *Herald*, 20 July 1984.
33 Nick Economou 23.8.1996.
34 Matheson, *op cit*, p. 171; Legge, *op cit*, p. 14; Peter Wade 19.10.1995.
35 Logan 12.12.1995.
36 'Sir Richard retires', *Monash Reporter*, 8 April 1983, p. 2.
37 *Monash Reporter*, 2 November 1997, p. 8.
38 *Annual Report 1983*, Monash University.
39 Schofield, 16.7.1996.
40 Martin, 'The way ahead', *op cit*, p. 2.
41 Bellamy, 19.6.1996.
42 'Singer to write for *Britannica*', *Monash Reporter*, 8 November 1984.
43 See various articles in *Monash Reporter*, 8 November 1984.
44 *Monash Reporter*, 5 November 1982, p. 10.
45 'VC proposes office to boost outside links', *Monash Reporter*, 8 November 1984, pp 1, 15, 19.
46 Endersbee 26.6.196.
47 'University–community gap narrowing, says historian', *Monash Reporter*, 6 June 1984.
48 'Legal services meet growing demand', *Monash Reporter*, 8 November 1984.
49 'Student changes', *Monash Reporter*, 2 March 1983, p. 1.
50 There is an extensive literature in relation to this correlation. See for example Trevor Williams, Michael Long, Peter Carpenter and Martin Hayden, *Entering higher education in the 1980s*, Australian Council for Educational Research, Melbourne, 1993.

51 *Monash Reporter*, 5 October 1983, p. 9; 'Ryan urges changes in tertiary approach', *The Australian*, 20 September 1984.
52 Terry Hore and Leo West, *Access and equity,* paper issued by HEARU, Monash University, January 1984; Leo West, *Social composition of Monash 1986; an update*, HEARU, February 1987.
53 Council minutes and the archival records of the 1983–84 meetings of the Council Childcare Review Committee.
54 Council minutes 10/82.
55 'Goal is Aborigines in the professions', *Monash Reporter,* March 1984, pp 1, 3.
56 *Sun*, 23 May 1984.
57 'Universities and the new government', *Monash Reporter*, 1 June 1983, p. 2.
58 *Lots Wife*, 6 September 1983; Council 8/83, 10 October 1983.
59 '"Hooligans" bring Farm Week ban', *Monash Reporter*, November 1984.
60 Kevin Brianton 23.8.1996.
61 *Annual Report 1983*, Monash University.
62 Anonymous interview with 1980–83 Monash student, 19 March 1996.
63 Legge, *op cit*, p. 17.
64 Peter Nugent 16.8.1996.
65 Wade 6.3.1996.
66 *The Sun*, 22 June 1984.
67 Anonymous interview with 1981–87 Monash student, 15 April 1996.
68 Economou, *op cit*. While active in Monash student politics, Economou was enrolled at the University of Melbourne.
69 Deborah Blashki 19.8.1996.
70 *ibid*.
71 'Sports and Recreation should separate from Union: Tadgell', *Monash Reporter*, November 1984.
72 Commonwealth Minister for Schools and Vocational Education (1996–1997), Commonwealth Minister for Employment, Education, Training and Youth Affairs (from 1997).
73 Council meeting 5/84, 9 July 1984.
74 Press Release, Monash University, 18 January 1984.
75 1980–83 student, *op cit*.
76 'Five held in uni drug raid', *The Sun*, 27 July 1984; Tom Noble, 'Nine held in drug raid at Monash', *The Age*, 27 July 1984; *Lots Wife*, 30 July 1984.
77 'Wholefoods cooks share their secrets', *Monash Reporter*, November 1984.
78 *Box Hill Eastern Standard*, 5 April 1984.
79 'Vivian takes Caltex prize', *Monash Reporter*, November 1984.
80 Martin, 'The way ahead', *op cit*, p. 2; Legge, 'Monash—then and now', in *ibid*, p. 4.

3 The 'Unified National System'

1 J.H. Newman, *The idea of a university*, Oxford University Press, Oxford, 1892 (originally published in 1853).
2 Michael Porter, *Competitive advantage: creating and sustaining superior performance*, Free Press, New York, 1985; Robert Reich, *The work of nations*, Alfred Knopf, New York, 1991.
3 Organisation for Economic Cooperation and Development (OECD), *Structural adjustment and economic performance*, OECD, Paris, 1987.
4 *OECD contribution: background report*, paper for the OECD conference on the transition from elite to mass higher education in Sydney, July 1993, OECD, Paris.

5 Sheila Slaughter and Larry Leslie, *Academic capitalism: policies, politics and the entrepreneurial university*, Johns Hopkins Press, Baltimore, 1997.
6 Included in Business Higher Education Round Table (BHERT), *Learning from others*, BHERT, Melbourne, 1993, pp 53–6. See also OECD, *Structural adjustment, op cit*, pp 36–7, 93–113.
7 BHERT, *Promoting partnerships*, BHERT, Melbourne, 1992, p. 6.
8 John Dawkins, *Higher education: a policy discussion paper*, AGPS, Canberra, 1987, pp 2, 8.
9 Ken McKinnon, 'Higher education and industry', *Higher Education Quarterly*, 42 (2), 1988, pp 179–92.
10 Dawkins, 1987, *op cit*, p. 3; DEET, 1993, *op cit*, p. 26.
11 BHERT, *Educating for excellence*, BHERT, Melbourne, 1992, p. 4.
12 CTEC, *Review of efficiency and effectiveness in higher education*, AGPS, Canberra, 1986, pp 244–5.
13 Logan 7.11.1995.
14 'No, Prime Minister', Paola Totaro, *Good Weekend*, pp 26, 31–2.
15 Logan, 7.11.1995; Steve Lewis, 'Questions being raised by Dawkins' "purple circle"', *Financial Review*, 7 August 1990.
16 Dawkins, 1987, *op cit*, pp 1–2, 9–13; DEET, 1993, pp 332, 338.
17 ABS, *Schools, Australia, op cit*.
18 DEET, *Selected higher education statistics*, various years; DEET, *Education participation rates, Australia*, DEET, Canberra, 1994; NCVER, annual collection of Vocational Education and Training (VET) data; annual surveys of unmet demand by the AVCC.
19 DEET, *Selected higher education statistics, op cit*.
20 *ibid*.
21 DEET and the Higher Education Council (HEC), *Resource allocation in higher education*, DDET/HEC, Canberra, 1994, p. 1.
22 DEET, 1993, *op cit*, pp 12–18; Logan 7.11.1995.
23 DEET, *Report of the Task Force on Amalgamations in Higher Education*, DEET, Canberra, 1989, pp 7–17, 26.
24 CTEC, 1986, *op cit*, pp 59–60; Dawkins, 1987, *op cit*, pp 30–4.
25 Roy Lourens, University of WA, 'University management: tensions in a changing environment', paper to an AVCC Administrative Staff conference, Hobart 1990.
26 The exception was the big institutes of technology such as RMIT that were considered ready to become universities in their own right, and hence ready to be senior partners in a merger.
27 Logan 7.11.1995.
28 CTEC, 1986, *op cit*, p. 60; Dawkins, 1987, *op cit*, p. 31.
29 'The whole process was time-consuming, irritating and, in my view, unnecessary', stated Matheson of the capital program: *op cit*, p. 73.
30 Dawkins, 1987, *op cit*, pp 75–80.
31 There is more discussion of these issues in Simon Marginson, *Markets in education*, Allen & Unwin, Sydney, 1997, pp 220–77.
32 ABS, 4224.0, *op cit*, p. 54.
33 Simon Marginson, 'Steering from a distance: the reform of higher education in Australia', *Higher Education*, 34, 1997, pp 63–80. This argument was confirmed by the government itself in DEET, 1993, *op cit*, pp 118–19.
34 Helen Trinca, 'So let the hard men win . . .', *The Australian*, 23 September 1992.
35 Dawkins, 1987, *op cit*, pp 47–51; Dawkins, 1988, *op cit*, pp 101–4.
36 CTEC, *op cit*, pp 144–7; Dawkins, 1987, *op cit*, p. 65; DEET, 1993, *op cit*, p. 26.
37 Don Aitkin, 'How research came to dominate higher education and what ought to be done about it', *Australian Universities Review*, 33 (172), p. 12; Gregor Ramsey, 'The new challenge to higher education: growth, increased outputs and new directions', in Grant

Harman and Lyn Meek, *Australian higher education reconstructed?*, University of New England, Armidale, 1988, pp 26–7.
38 Geoff Maslen and Fiona Whitlock, 'University challenge', *The Age*, 8 October 1988.
39 Ian Rae 15.7.1996.
40 Mal Logan, *Monash: towards 2000*, report to University Council, p. 11.
41 John Button 27.11.1996.
42 Slaughter and Leslie, *op cit*.
43 'The closing of the Australian mind', *Background Briefing*, ABC Radio National, 16 April 1989.
44 Ronald Barnett, *The idea of higher education*, Open University Press, Buckingham, 1990, pp 3–15.

4 Strategic management and cultural change

1 John Micklethwait and Adrian Wooldridge, *The witch doctors*, Heinemann, London, 1996, p. 17.
2 Universities Commission, *Sixth report May 1995*, AGPS, Canberra, p. 140; ABS, *Social Indicators*, Catalogue no. 4101.0, ABS, Canberra; DEET, *Higher education statistics 1994*, DEET, Canberra.
3 Micklethwait and Wooldridge, *op cit*, pp 96–8.
4 *ibid*, p. 81.
5 Robin Middlehurst, *Leading academics*, SRHE/Open University Press, Buckingham, 1993.
6 Micklethwait and Wooldridge, *op cit*, p. 160; Paul Auerbach, *Competition: the economics of industrial change*, Basil Blackwell, Oxford, 1988, pp 130–6; Neil Fligstein, *The transformation of corporate control*, Harvard University Press, Cambridge, 1990.
7 *Report of the Steering Committee for Efficiency Studies in Universities*, Committee of Vice-Chancellors and Principals of the United Kingdom (the Jarratt Committee), 1985, p. 26.
8 Council Committee report on top administrative structure (the McNeill Committee report), Monash University Council Meeting 9 September 1985, pp 5–12.
9 *ibid*, pp 12, 15; Council Meeting 19 December 1985.
10 *McNeill report, op cit*, p. 12.
11 *ibid*, pp 5–6.
12 Wade later became General Manager (see chapter 7).
13 Peter Greonewegen and Bruce McFarlane, *A history of Australian economic thought*, Routledge, London, 1990, p. 237.
14 Logan 22.11.1995, 20.12.1995.
15 Louis Waller 29.7.1996.
16 Logan 22.11.1995.
17 The other new members were Professor Di Yerbury of the University of NSW (later Vice-Chancellor of Macquarie University, the first woman to achieve this in Australia) and the publisher Hilary McPhee.
18 University Calendar; Council minutes for 1983–84; Logan, 22.11.1995, 12.12.1995.
19 Minutes of the Monash Council Search Committee of 1984, Council, 8 October 1984.
20 Logan, speech to farewell function, *op cit*.
21 Logan 22.11.1995.
22 Minutes of the Monash Council Search Committee of 1985, and the Council meeting of 19 December 1985; Peter Darvall, 29.4.1997.
23 Mal Logan, *Monash: toward 2000*, report to the University Council, June 1992; Logan, 'Occasional address', Gippsland campus graduation, 25 May 1996.

24 Mal Logan, speech to farewell function, Great Hall of the National Gallery of Victoria, 25 November 1996; Logan, *Monash: toward 2000, op cit*, pp 13–14; Logan 12.12.1995.
25 *ibid*; Logan, *Monash: toward 2000, op cit*; Mal Logan, *Address to TAFE Directors, op cit*.
26 Geoff Maslen and Fiona Whitlock, 'The view from the top', *The Age*, 10 October 1988; Logan 20.12.1995; Mal Logan, 'Economic and higher education linkages between Australia and Asian Pacific nations', *op cit*; Mal Logan, 'Directions for the future', paper to leadership and management group, 1 August 1995.
27 Tony Pritchard 7.11.1995; Porter 7.11.1995; Lauchlan Chipman 16.11.1995; Bob Baxt 12.8.1996.
28 Logan, *Towards 2000, op cit*, p. 11; Logan, 'Address to TAFE Directors', *op cit*; Logan, speech to farewell function, *op cit*; Mal Logan, 'Economic and higher education linkages between Australia and Asian Pacific nations', paper to the Pacific Rim University Presidents' Conference, Tamkang University, December 1990; Mal Logan, Address to the Multifunction Polis Investment Mission, Adelaide, 3 December 1991.
29 Angela Martinkus, 'The Monash makeover', *Melbourne Weekly*, 16 November 1997.
30 Porter 7.11.1995; Gary Spink, 'Logan's legacy', *Montage*, 8 November 1996, pp 4–5.
31 Logan, speech to farewell function, *op cit*; *1989 Annual Report*, p. 5; Maslen and Whitlock, *op cit*.
32 Michael Porter, *Competitive advantage*, The Free Press, New York, 1985.
33 Paul Auerbach, *Competition: the economics of industrial change*, Basil Blackwell, Oxford, 1988.
34 Micklethwait and Wooldridge, *op cit*, pp 162–74.
35 Logan 7.11.1995; Wade 19.10.1995.
36 Bellamy 19.6.1996.
37 Monash Archives files on Administrative Correspondence and Continuous Long Term Planning; Minutes of the Development Committee of the Professorial Board; Mal Logan, 'Longer term policies and planning', August 1986; Hore 23.7.1996.
38 Minutes of the Development Committee, *op cit*; Planning Working Group papers, Monash Archives.
39 *ibid*; Logan 7.11.1995 and 12.12.1995; Administrative Correspondence; Mal Logan, 'Planning at Monash: the current situation', from minutes of the Development Committee, *op cit*.
40 Mal Logan, 'Some general observations', paper to the Planning Working Group, 6 July 1987.
41 The written responses indicate that few sections of the University were critical: exceptions included the Department of Psychology, and the Manager of Occupational Health and Safety.
42 Council meeting, 14 December 1987; Monash University, *Strategy for the future*, March 1988; Logan 12.12.1995.
43 Baxt 12.8.1996; Monash University, *Resume of achievements 1988*; Stephen Matchett, 'A tale of two vice-chancellors', *The Australian*, 12 September 1992.
44 Wade 19.10.1995.
45 Robert Pargetter 2.9.1995.
46 Stuart Rintoul, 'The entrepreneur of education', *The Australian*, 9 September 1995; Logan, 12.12.1995.
47 Logan 7.11.1995; Pritchard 7.11.1995; Williams 9.7.1996.
48 Baxt 12.8.1996; Endersbee 26.6.1996; Darvall 16.7.1996; Williams 14.11.1995; David Aspin 19.6.1996.
49 Logan 7.11.1995.
50 Logan, *Monash: toward 2000, op cit*, p. 17.
51 *ibid*, p. 15; Monash University, *Quality portfolio 1993*, p. 23; Monash University, *Directions for the future*, pp 3–7; Mal Logan, 'Talk to leadership and management development group', *op cit*.

52 *Strategy for the future, op cit*, p. 5.
53 Peter Fensham, Dean of Education: 'I had begun to see good scholars being deflected from their most effective research because they were "needed" (as I observed in Britain) to bring in the large funds that were available for less significant (in the longer term) projects'—Monash University, *Annual Report 1988*, p. 15. See also *1987 Annual Report*, p. 16.
54 Logan, letter to the author, 28 March 1998.
55 Pritchard 7.11.95. Maslen and Whitlock, *op cit*.
56 Logan 7.11.1995; Porter 7.11.1995.
57 Logan 7.11.1995.
58 Committee for Quality Assurance in Higher Education, *Report on 1995 quality reviews*, Vol. 2, AGPS, Canberra, p. 145.
59 Logan, letter to the author, 28 March 1998.
60 Darvall 16.7.1996, 29.4.1997.
61 Rintoul, *op cit*.
62 Logan, *Monash: toward 2000, op cit*, pp 17–18.
63 Helen Trinca, 'Our Australians of the year: Penington and Logan', *The Australian*, 25 January 1996.
64 Logan, letter to the author, 28 March 1998.

5 Monash merges

1 Poynter and Rasmussen, *op cit*, pp 243–4; Martin, 1964, *op cit*, p. 54.
2 Logan, letter to the author, 28 March 1998.
3 Grant Harman and Lynn Meek, 'Introduction and overview', in Harman and Meek (eds), *Australian higher education reconstructed? Analysis of the proposals and assumptions of the Dawkins Green Paper*, Department of Administrative and Educational Studies, University of New England, Armidale, 1988.
4 Roy Lourens, *University management: tensions in a changing environment*, paper to AVCC Administrative Staff Conference, Hobart, 1990, p. 9.
5 Harman and Meek, *op cit*, p. 8; Grant Harman and Lynn Meek, 'Lessons from recent experience with mergers', in Harman and Meek (eds), *op cit*, p. 119.
6 *ibid*, p. 119.
7 Commonwealth Tertiary Education Commission, *Selected higher education statistics 1987*, CTEC, Canberra.
8 Bill Yeadon, 'Exporting success', *Chisholm Gazette*, vol. 7, no. 1, 1990, p. 8.
9 'Timeline', *Chisholm Gazette*, vol. 7, no. 1, 1990, p. 40; *Victorian Government Gazette*, no. 23, 3 March 1982, pp 630–6; Arthur O'Neil.
10 Arthur O'Neil.
11 John Hay 26.11.1996; Logan 7.11.1995.
12 Brian Costar 5.8.1996.
13 Paul Ramler 3.9.1996.
14 Logan remarked later that Vaughan probably found it easier to support the merger because he was a recent arrival at Chisholm. Logan 7.11.1995, 22.11.1995, 28.10.1996; Pritchard 7.11.1995; Peter Chandler 3.7.1996; Costar 5.8.1996; Ramler 3.9.1996.
15 Logan, letter to the author, 28 March 1998.
16 Ramler 3.9.1996.
17 Ramler 3.9.1996; Chandler 3.7.1996; 'New President a graduate of CIT', *Chisholm Gazette*, vol. 6, no. 2, 1989, p. 7; Geoff Smith 5.8.1996.
18 Smith 5.8.1996; Hay 26.11.1996; Dick Whyte 13.8.1996; Chandler 3.7.1996.

19 Council meeting, 11 April 1988. The account that follows is drawn partly from research by Arthur O'Neil.
20 Logan 22.11.1995.
21 *ibid*.
22 Monash Council, 3 April 1989.
23 'Lush greenery at Chisholm', *Chishlom Gazette*, vol. 7, no. 1, 1990, p. 4.
24 Whyte 13.8.1996; Costar 5.8.1996; Porter 7.11.1995.
25 Pritchard 7.11.1995; Darvall 29.4.1997; Costar 5.8.1996; Hay 26.11.1996; Ramler 3.9.1996.
26 Logan 7.11.1995.
27 Logan 28.10.1996.
28 Reflecting on SAMU's outlook in this period, the then Chisholm Political Scientist and academic union leader Brian Costar remarked in 1996 that 'they were exclusivists. None are so insistent on status as those whose own status is insecure'. If the respective unions had been able to work together they could have achieved more, he argued—Costar, 5.8.1996. After the merger a combined union branch was formed that embraced academic and general staff on all Monash campuses, and this functioned relatively harmoniously and effectively.
29 Monash Council, 18 September 1989.
30 Logan 7.11.1995.
31 Hay 26.11.1996.
32 Hay 26.11.1996.
33 See chapter 4. 'TRAG was really great, that was a wonderful organisation; unfortunately the war was over'—Costar 5.8.1996.
34 Richard Snedden 8.7.1996.
35 Academic Staff Association of the Chisholm Institute of Technology and Victorian Colleges and Universities Staff Association (Chisholm Branch), *Joint unions audit of the merger implementation arrangements between Chisholm Institute of Technology and Monash University*, March 1990.
36 Costar 5.8.1996.
37 Joan Kirner, Minister for Education, *Monash University (Chisholm and Gippsland) Bill 1990*, second reading speech, Parliament of Victoria, 1 May 1990.
38 Costar 5.8.1996.
39 Mal Logan, 'Vice-Chancellor's statement', *Annual Report 1990*, p. 1.
40 DEET, *National report on Australia's higher education sector, op cit*, p. 37.
41 Commonwealth Tertiary Education Commission, *Selected higher education statistics 1987*, CTEC, Canberra.
42 Dawkins, 1987, *op cit*, p. 32.
43 Logan 28.10.1996; Barry Dunstan 14.8.1996.
44 Dunstan 14.8.1996.
45 Data supplied by Arthur O'Neil.
46 Wade was to remark later that it may have been a mistake to postpone the merger with Gippsland until after the merger with Chisholm was achieved—Wade 6.3.1996.
47 Dunstan 14.8.1996.
48 Dunstan 14.8.1996; Mike Hall 14.8.1996.
49 Dunstan 14.8.1996.
50 Logan, 'Occasional address', Gippsland campus graduation, *op cit*.
51 Logan 28.10.1996; Chipman 16.11.1995, Logan, *Towards 2000, op cit*, pp 43–4.
52 Wade 25.3.1996.
53 Logan 7.11.1996.
54 Logan, letter to the author, 28 March 1998.
55 Victorian College of Pharmacy, *The search for a partner: a history of the amalgamation of the Victorian College of Pharmacy and Monash university*, March 1993.

ENDNOTES

56 Colin Chapman 9.7.1996.
57 Memo to members of the Affiliation Negotiating Committee from T.R. Watson, Victorian College of Pharmacy, 28 May 1990.
58 Serle, *op cit*, p. 97.
59 Wade 19.10.1996.
60 Bellamy 19.6.1996.
61 Monash University, *Annual Report 1987*, pp 29–30; *Annual Report 1988*, pp 28–9; *Statistics 1994*, p. 70; *Statistics 1995*, p. 81.
62 Matheson, *op cit*, p. 43.
63 Mal Logan, 'Vice-Chancellor's statement', *Annual Report 1991*, p. 3.
64 By 1995 the total cost of the three- and five-storey buildings at Caulfield had risen from an estimated $18.8 million to $22 million.
65 Monash University, *Annual Report 1992*, p. 17; 'Tis the season to be building', *Montage*, vol. 3, no. 8, November 1992, p. 5.
66 Monash University, *Annual Report 1994*, p. 27; *Budget* 1995, pp 18–20; *Budget* 1996, pp 28–9; *Annual Report 1995*, p. 19.
67 Though the policy of native planting at Peninsula dated from the Frankston Teachers' College days—Barry Bilham, 13.8.1996.
68 Conrad Hamann, 'Recollections of a plan: architecture at Monash', *Making Monash, op cit*, p. 36. Nevertheless, the problems of sustaining a consistent aesthetic in the construction of a university campus should not be underestimated. Not only does construction proceed through a series of incremental additions over time, offering a high degree of scope for variation, but a large number of people with often great differences in outlook might contribute to decision-making. For example, while some Monash people have expressed themselves as adamantly opposed to buildings of more than three or four storeys, Endersbee preferred a small number of high-rise buildings at the centre of the campus, surrounded by parkland—Endersbee 26.6.1996.
69 Dick White 31.7.1996; Marian Quartly 22.7.1996.
70 Hay 26.11.1996.
71 Chandler 3.7.1996; Darvall 16.7.1996; Costar 5.8.1996; Smith 5.8.1996.
72 Melbourne 9.11.1995; Darvall 16.7.1996; Smith 5.8.1996; Coldicutt 5.8.1996.
73 Snedden 8.7.1996; Melbourne 8.7.1996; Darvall 16.7.1996; Smith 5.8.1996.
74 Rae 15.7.1996. In support of this judgement Rae instanced Clayton staff in Mathematics and Physics.
75 Rae 15.7.1996.
76 Coldicutt 5.8.1996.
77 Rae 15.7.1996; Dunstan 14.8.1996.
78 Bellamy 19.6.1996.
79 Coldicutt 5.8.1996.
80 Coldicutt 5.8.1996; Costar 5.8.1996; Ramler 3.9.1996; Hay 26.11.1996.
81 Bellamy 19.6.1996.
82 Logan 11.3.1996; Bellamy 19.6.1996; Chandler 3.7.1996; Snedden 8.7.1996; Costar 5.8.1996.
83 Snedden 8.7.1996.
84 Snedden 8.7.1996.
85 Snedden 8.7.1996; Monash University, *Annual Report 1992*, p. 16.
86 Ian Walker 13.8.1996.
87 Costar 5.8.1996.
88 John Redmond 5.8.1996.
89 Logan 28.10.1996.
90 Chandler 1.7.1996, 3.7.1996; Ramler 3.9.1996.
91 Gus Sinclair 9.7.1996; Chandler 1.7.1996, 3.7.1996; Melbourne 8.7.1997.
92 Chandler 1.7.1996, 3.7.1996; Melbourne 8.7.1997; Williams 14.11.1995, 9.7.1996.

93 Costar 5.8.1996.
94 Meeting of David Syme Faculty of Business Advisory Board, 4 July 1990, Minute 10.
95 *Monash University Statistics, op cit*. Includes combined degree enrolments.
96 Sinclair 9.7.1996; Chandler 1.7.1996, 3.7.1996; Logan 28.10.1996.
97 Dunstan 14.8.1996.
98 For example, on 9 August 1991 the Clayton Accounting Department wrote to Logan, to tell him that it was strongly opposed to any relocation of Accounting headquarters to Syme at Caulfield (thanks to Arthur O'Neil).
99 Chandler 3.7.1996; Melbourne 8.7.1996; Costar 5.8.1996; Ramler 3.9.1996.
100 Symon Rubens 15.8.1996.
101 Chandler 3.7.1996; Council meetings, 6/92 and 7/92.
102 Council 3/95, 15 May 1995.
103 *Annual Report 1995*, p. 10.
104 *Budget 1996*, p. 50.
105 Chipman 16.11.1995.
106 Gary Spink, 'Logan's legacy', *Montage*, vol. 7, no. 8, November 1996, p. 5.
107 Harman and Meek, *op cit*, p. 120.
108 *ibid*, p. 120.
109 Waller 29.7.1996.
110 Logan, *Monash toward 2000, op cit*, p. 18, Logan, *Annual Report 1990*, Monash University, p. 1.
111 Costar 5.8.1996; Coldicutt 5.8.1996.
112 Hay 26.11.1997.
113 Logan, *Annual Report 1991*, Monash University, p. 2.
114 Ramler 3.9.1996; Costar 5.8.1996; Hay 26.11.1996.
115 Ramler 3.9.1996; Costar 5.8.1996.
116 Ramler 3.9.1996; Smith 5.8.1996; Whyte 13.8.1996; Coldicutt 5.8.1996.
117 Smith 5.8.1996; Whyte 13.8.1996; Coldicutt 5.8.1996; Snedden 8.7.1996.
118 Ramler 3.9.1996; Costar 5.8.1996; Chandler 3.7.1996; Smith 5.8.1996; Whyte 13.8.1996.

6 Gone global

1 Matheson, *op cit*, pp 12–13.
2 Data from research on the history of the Colombo Plan, by Alex Auletta, Monash Centre for Research in International Education.
3 Mal Logan, *Monash: toward 2000, op cit*, p. 2.
4 Arjun Appadurai, *Modernity at large: cultural dimensions of globalisation*, University of Minnesota Press, Minneapolis, 1996, p. 27.
5 Pacific Economic Cooperation Council (PECC), *Human resource development outlook 1994–1995*, PECC, Times Academic Press, Singapore, 1994, p. 83.
6 Appadurai, *op cit*, p. 31.
7 Maurie Daly and Mal Logan, *The brittle rim: finance, business and the Pacific region*, Penguin, Melbourne, 1989, pp 8, 23, 33, 215; Mal Logan, speech to OECD Conference, Melbourne, 20 November 1994.
8 Logan, *Monash: toward 2000, op cit*, p. 32.
9 Logan 1994, *op cit*.
10 Mal Logan, *Economic and higher education linkages between Australia and Asian Pacific nations*, speech to the Pacific Rim University Presidents Conference, Tamkang University, December 1990; Monash University, *Education and research policies*, p. 8; Logan, speech at farewell function, *op cit*, p. 5.

11 See the various contributions to *Asian Studies Review*, vol. 18, no. 1, 1994, published by the Asian Studies Association of Australia and edited at Monash.
12 Australian Pacific Economic Cooperation Committee, *6th report to the Australian Government, 1992,* Paragon Printers, 1993; 'Vice-Chancellor's statement', Monash University, *1995 Annual Report*, p. 2; Logan 20.12.1995.
13 'Vice-Chancellor's statement', Monash University, *1994 Annual Report*, p. 2; Georgie Allen, 'Setting the APEC agenda', *Montage*, vol. 6, no. 6 August 1995, p. 6.
14 Economic Planning Advisory Council (EPAC), *International trade in services*, Council Paper no. 28, EPAC, Canberra; DEET, 1993, *op cit*, pp 58–61; Marketing Australia Unit, Department of Foreign Affairs and Trade, *Australia through the eyes of Asia*, AGPS, Canberra, 1995.
15 Pacific Economic Cooperation Council (PECC), *Human resource development outlook 1992–1993*, PECC, 1992, p. 78.
16 Logan 20.12.1995.
17 Jolley, *op cit*, especially chapter 3.
18 DEET, 1993, *op cit*, pp 58–61.
19 Endersbee 26.6.1996.
20 DEET, 1993, *op cit*, p. 59.
21 Mal Logan, *Exporting education: responding to international quality expectations*, IIR conference, 23 November 1993.
22 Government of Malaysia, country report to the OECD conference on the transition from elite to mass education, Sydney, 1993.
23 PECC, 1992, *op cit*, p. 19.
24 Marketing Australia Unit, *op cit*; Department of Employment, Education and Training (DEET), 'Comparative costs of postgraduate courses for overseas students in Australia, New Zealand, the UK, Canada and the US', *Higher Education Series*, DEET Higher Education Division Occasional Paper no. 12, DEET, Canberra.
25 Australian Bureau of Statistics, *Education and training in Australia*, 1996, ABS Catalogue no. 4224.0, AGPS, Canberra, 1996, p. 11.
26 Monash University, *Quality portfolio 1993, vol. 2*, p. 85.
27 Logan 28.10.1996.
28 Logan 12.12.1995.
29 Auditor-General of Victoria, *International student programs in universities*, Special Report no. 29, Government Printer, Victoria, November 1993, pp 24, 35, 46.
30 Monash Council, 3 August 1992 and 14 December 1992; 'Fifth year of overseas graduation ceremonies', *Monash Asia Institute Newsletter*, vol. 7, no. 2, 1995, p. 4; Logan 20.12.1995.
31 Mal Logan, *Capitalising on the growth of education in Asia: overview of education opportunities in Southeast Asia*, Kuala Lumpur, 19–20 January 1994, p. 2; Geoff Maslen, ' . . . as VC signals shift to altruism in OS education', *Campus Review*, 13 October 1993.
32 Monash University, *Preliminary report on the establishment of the National University of Vietnam in Hanoi*, January 1994.
33 Logan 28.10.1996.
34 Monash University, *Annual Report 1991*, p. 19.
35 'Annual report of Directors, Monash International P-L', Monash University, *Annual Report 1994*; Monash University, *Budget 1996*, p. 14.
36 'Vice-Chancellor's statement', Monash University, *Annual report 1994*, p. 2.
37 Logan 20.12.1995.
38 Logan 20.12.1995; John Lahey, 'Journey's end', *The Age*, 7 September 1995.
39 Chapman 9.7.1996.
40 Wade 6.3.1996.
41 *Monash University statistics 1995*, p. 23.
42 Logan, *Talk to leadership and management development group, op cit*, p. 28.

43 *International activities at Monash University, op cit*; Monash University, *1996 Budget*, p. 15; Logan 12.12.1995.
44 'Honours for two distinguished Malaysians', *Monash Asia Institute Newsletter*, vol. 7, no. 2, 1995, p. 3.
45 Logan 11.3.1996.
46 Baxt 12.8.1988.
47 Mal Logan, *Capitalising on the growth of education in Asia*, speech in Kuala Lumpur, 19–20 January 1994, pp 8–10.
48 *Etcetera*, 23 January 1996. The application for a Monash Malaysian campus finally bore fruit in 1998, seven years after the Malaysian government had made the first guarded statement of support.
49 *International activities at Monash University, op cit*.
50 *International Business Asia*, 18 September 1995.
51 Mal Logan, *Economic and higher education linkages between Australia and Asian Pacific nations*, paper presented to the Pacific Rim University Presidents Conference, Tamkang University, December 1990, p. 6.
52 Logan 20.12.1995.
53 'New centre will be crucial test', *Monash Reporter*, no. 5, 6 July 1988.
54 John McKay, Monash Asia Institute Operating Plan 1992/93, June 1992; Monash Asia Institute Newsletter, vol. 7, no. 2, 1995, pp 5–7.
55 Wade 25.3.1996.
56 Memorandum from Ian Polmear to Mal Logan, 12 September 1988; letter from Anne Mennell, Academic Services Officer, to the Commonwealth Department of Employment, Education and Training, 8 November 1988; Memorandum from Anne Mennell to Mal Logan, 22 May 1989.
57 Council 14 December 1992; *Monash quality portfolio 1994*, p. 13.
58 Council, 13 December 1993.
59 Dean Ashenden and Sandra Milligan, *Good Universities Guide*, 1994.
60 Robert Pargetter, *A report on Monash University's links with Victoria's secondary schools*, Monash University, 1995.
61 Helen Trinca, 'Our Australians of the Year: Penington and Logan', *The Australian*, 25 January 1996; Logan 12.12.1995.
62 Logan speech to farewell function, *op cit*, pp 13–14.
63 Jolley, *op cit*, p. 3.41.
64 Gary Spink, 'Logan's legacy', *op cit*, p. 4.
65 Wade 25.3.1996; Logan 20.12.1995.
66 Rae 15.7.1995; Jenny Strauss 12.7.1996; Logan, talk to Leadership and Management Group, *op cit*, p. 30; Paul Bourke and Linda Butler, *International links in higher education research*, NBEET Commissioned Report no. 37, AGPS, Canberra, 1995.
67 NBEET, 1995, *op cit*, p. xviii.
68 *Directions for the future, op cit*, pp 15–16; Logan, *Speech to leadership and management group, op cit*; 'Logan's legacy', *Montage*, vol. 7, no. 8, 1996, p. 5.
69 Communication from Peter Spearritt, May 1999.
70 John S. Daniel, *The mega-universities and the knowledge media: implications of new technologies for large scale distance teaching universities*, MA (Educational Technology) thesis in the Department of Education, Concordia University, Montreal, November 1995, pp 2, 16; DEET, 1993, *op cit*, p. 178; Jolley, *op cit*.
71 Daniel, *op cit*, pp 11, 16.
72 'Report of the Chancellor', *Annual Report 1988*, p. 3.
73 Hall 14.8.1996; John Harris 14.8.1996.
74 Evans and Harris had together prepared the Monash–Gippsland submission for Distance Education Centre status in 1988.

75 Dunstan 14.8.1996; Harris 14.8.1996; Monash University, submission for the 1994 profile visit, *op cit*.
76 DEET, 1993, *op cit*, p. 180.
77 Hall 14.8.1996; Harris 14.8.1996.
78 Pargetter 2.9.1996; Logan 28.10.1996.
79 Pritchard 7.11.1995; Logan *Farewell speech, op cit*.
80 Monash University, *Distance education courses 1996*.
81 Harris 14.8.1996; Hall 14.8.1996.
82 DEET, 1993, *op cit*, pp 182–93.
83 Communication from Peter Spearritt, May 1999.
84 Council 8 August, 21 September and 14 December 1992; DEET, 1993, *op cit*; p. 183; ABS, 4224.0, *op cit*, p. 31.
85 Harris 14.8.1996; Monash University, *Budget 1996*, pp 12–13; Jolley, *op cit*.
86 Monash University, *Budget 1996*, p. 13; Hall 14.8.1996; John Harris 14.8.1996.
87 Pargetter 2.9.1996; Pritchard 7.11.1995; Mal Logan, *Speech to leadership and management group, op cit*, p. 13.

7 Greater Monash

1 Logan, *Monash: toward 2000, op cit*, p. 36.
2 Monash statistics 1995.
3 DEET, *Australia's higher education sector, op cit*, p. 382; DEET, *Selected higher education statistics, 1995*. Monash staff had more job security than the average. The casual ratio was 11 per cent in all Australian higher education institutions—*ibid*, pp 10–11.
4 DEETYA, *Selected higher education staff statistics, 1995*, DEETYA, Canberra, 1996, pp 9–12.
5 'Vice-Chancellor's statement', *Annual Report 1991*, pp 3–4; Monash Council meetings, 24 February 1992, 21 September 1992 and 13 December 1993; 'Budget statement by the Vice-Chancellor', *1995 Budget*, pp 8–9.
6 Monash University, *Annual Report 1995*, p. 9; *1996 Budget*, pp 11–12; 'Berwick's first academic school'. *Etcetera*, no. 37, 3 October 1995, p. 3.
7 Logan 28.10.1996.
8 *Annual report 1995*, p. 9; 'Linking up with the future', *Etcetera*, no. 4, 13 February 1996.
9 Chipman 16.11.1995; Pargetter 15.7.1996, 2.9.1996; Ramler 3.9.1996; Logan 28.10.1996.
10 Waller describes the Deans Committee as a great back-up for Matheson during his 'time of troubles' with the student revolt, Waller 29.7.1996.
11 Peter Fensham 2.7.1996; Melbourne 8.7.1996; Chapman 9.7.1996; Ramler 3.9.1996.
12 Simon Marginson and Mark Considine, *The enterprise university: governance, strategy, reinvention*, Cambridge University Press, Cambridge and Melbourne, 2000.
13 Williams 9.7.1996; Ramler 3.9.1996.
14 Logan, *Monash: toward 2000, op cit*, p. 9; Strauss 2.7.1996.
15 Logan, *Monash: toward 2000, op cit*, pp 28–9.
16 Rae 15.7.1996.
17 Rae 15.7.1996.
18 Melbourne 8.7.1996; Hay 26.11.1996.
19 Darvall 16.7.1996.
20 Academic Board, 10 March 1993.
21 Snedden 8.7.1996.
22 Williams 14.11.1995; Strauss 2.7.1996; Snedden 8.7.1996; Pargetter 15.7.1996, 2.9.1996; Darvall 16.7.1996; Hore 23.7.1996.

23 Chapman 9.7.1996; Rae 15.7.1996; Pargetter 2.9.1996.
24 Monash University, *Senior Women's Advancement Scheme*, October 1995, p. 17.
25 *Annual Report 1988*, pp 35–6.
26 Logan 7.11.1995.
27 Massaging the media had a long history at Monash. Plagued by negative publicity about the student revolt, Matheson called in his own professional media manager. 'It was essential . . . to have an office which would establish friendly relations with reporters and editors, and which would be available to answer enquiries. Such an office might perhaps have some influence on what appeared about Monash in the media'—Matheson, *op cit*, p. 152.
28 Gay Baldwin, 'The nature of universities: four elementary lessons', *Faculty of Arts Occasional Papers*, no. 1, 1997, p. 5.
29 Hore 23.7.1996.
30 Business/Higher Education Round Table, *Promoting partnerships*, Task Force Report no. 2, August, BHERT, Melbourne; *Educating for excellence*, Commissioned Report no. 2, September, BHERT, Melbourne.
31 Logan, *Monash: toward 2000*, *op cit*, p. 42; Logan, speech to farewell function, *op cit*, pp 11–12.
32 Pacific Basin Economic Council, *1995–1996 International membership directory*, PBEC, Honolulu.
33 Wade 25.3.1996; Waller 29.7.1996.
34 Logan 7.11.1995, 12.12.1995; Logan, *Monash: toward 2000*, *op cit*, p. 20; *Annual Report 1994*, pp 1, 27.
35 Monash university, *Directions for the future*, *op cit*, pp 21–2; Catherine Armitage, 'Monash operating surplus up by 21 per cent', *The Australian*, 19 June 1996. Mal Logan, *Talk to leadership and management development group*, 1 August 1995, pp 21–2.
36 Strauss 2.7.1996.
37 *ibid*.
38 Monash University, *Annual Report 1995*, p. 7; data supplied by Peter Wade; Monash University, *1996 Budget*, pp 22–3.
39 Stuart Rintoul, 'The entrepreneur of education', *The Australian*, 9 September 1995; *Budget 1996*, p. 30; DEET, *Selected higher education finance statistics 1995*, 1997, p. 8.
40 Excluding international students.
41 *ibid*, pp 8, 14; DEET, *Selected higher education statistics 1995*, 1996, pp 122–33; Monash University, *1995 Annual Report*, pp 52–5.
42 The DEET data on incomes are calculated on a different basis from the Monash data, so that the figure is 11 per cent in the Monash accounts and 10 per cent according to DEET.
43 Logan, *Monash: toward 2000*, *op cit*, pp 19, 42; Logan, 'Introduction', in Department of Business Management, Monash University, *Annual report and profile 1995*, p. 3.
44 Wade 19.10.1995, 6.3.1996, 25.3.1996.
45 Wade 25.3.1996; Williams 14.11.1995; Waller 29.7.1996.
46 Wade 19.10.1995, 25.3.1996; Monash University, *1996 Budget*, pp 4, 9–10.
47 Hore 23.7.1996.
48 Melbourne 8.7.1996; Chapman 9.7.1996.
49 Wade 19.10.1995.
50 Waller 29.7.1996.
51 Strauss 2.7.1996; Chapman 9.7.1996; Darvall 16.7.1996.
52 Logan at the Academic Board, 27 November 1991.
53 Monash Council meetings, 17 December 1990, 1 July 1991 and 23 September 1991.
54 Williams 14.11.1995.
55 Council, 16 December 1991; Academic Board, 17 November 1991 and 18 November 1992.

56 Bellamy 19.6.1996; Melbourne 8.7.1996; Sinclair 9.7.1996.
57 Wade 19.10.1995, 6.3.1996; Rae 15.7.1996; Pargetter 15.7.1996; James Warren 23.7.1996; Ramler 3.9.1996.
58 Pargetter 15.7.1996; Williams 14.11.1995; Hay 26.11.1996.
59 Williams 14.11.1995, 9.7.1996; Bellamy 19.6.1996; Fensham 2.7.1996; Aspen 19.6.1996; Snedden 8.7.1996; Sinclair, 9.7.1996; Warren 23.7.1996.
60 Williams 14.11.1995, 9.7.1996; Darvall 16.7.1996; Bellamy 19.6.1996.
61 Logan, *Monash: toward 2000, op cit*. p. 29.
62 *ibid*, early draft.
63 Melbourne 8.7.1996; Rae 15.7.1996.
64 For example at the Board meetings of 2 May 1990 and 24 October 1990.
65 Logan 7.11.1995, 12.12.1995.
66 Robin Middlehurst and George Gordon, *Leadership, quality and institutional effectiveness*, mimeo.
67 Commonwealth Committee for Quality Assurance in Higher Education (CQAHE), *Report on 1995 quality reviews, vol. 1*, AGPS, Canberra, pp 1–2.
68 Chipman 16.11.1995; Wade 25.3.1996; Hore 23.7.1996.
69 Communication from Gay Baldwin, 18 June 1998.
70 Monash University, *Monash: quality portfolio 1994*, 1994, p. 19.
71 *ibid*, pp 1, 19–20, 41–3.
72 CQAHE, *op cit*.
73 CQAHE, *op cit*, vol. 2, pp 144–50.
74 Logan 20.12.1995; Wade 25.3.1996.

8 The arts

1 John Monash in a letter dated 17 June 1930, in Serle, *op cit*, p. 477.
2 Professorial Board minutes, 29 March 1961, cited in Jenepher Duncan, 'Monash and art: the collection, commissions and gallery', *Making Monash*, p. 81. Duncan provides an admirable history of the collection and the Gallery, from the beginning to the transfer of the Gallery to its own premises in 1987.
3 The University of Melbourne did not begin to collect contemporary Australian art until 10 years after Monash.
4 Art Advisory Committee, *An art acquisition policy for Monash*, 1976.
5 Duncan, *op cit*, pp 104–5.
6 The amount raised at the auction was rather disappointing despite the good quality of the works donated for the purpose. Later the sum raised in bids was supplemented by gifts, securing what Andrew later estimated as a total of $150 000—Duncan, *op cit*, pp 105–6; letter from Rod Andrew to Mal Logan, 27 August 1991; conversation with Ray Marginson, one of the 'Friends', on 6.7.1998.
7 Jenepher Duncan 1.7.1996.
8 Duncan 1.7.1996.
9 Monash University, *Monash University collection—acquisition policy*, 1988.
10 Duncan 1.7.1996.
11 Annual reports by the Australian Centre for Contemporary Art, 1990–95; Duncan 1.7.1996.
12 Data from the annual report of the Director of the Monash University Gallery, and associated papers.
13 Celia Rosser was later awarded the Jill Smythies Prize for Botanical Illustration, presented annually by the Linnaean Society of London—'Award winning Banksias', *Etcetera*, issue 6, 25 February 1997, p. 2.

14 *ibid*; research by Isabelle Normand.
15 *ibid*.
16 *ibid*.
17 Monash University, *Sight and sound: visual and performing arts Monash University*, 1996; 'A Stelarc performance', *Etcetera*, issue 8, 12 March 1996, p. 4.
18 Margaret Kartomi 29.8.1996.
19 Monash University, *Annual Report 1987*, p. 33; RBH structure and management papers in Monash University Archives.
20 Letter from N.W. Murray, Chair of the Robert Blackwood Hall Management Committee, to David Hill, Managing Director of the ABC, 19 May 1988; reply by Hill, 24 June 1988; Logan to Hill, 5 October 1988; Hill to Logan, 11 October 1988.
21 Monash University, *Annual Report 1988*, pp 36–7; RBH structure and management papers in Monash University Archives; Interview with Margaret Kartomi, 29 August 1996.
22 RBH structure and management papers in Monash University Archives, including Minutes of the Management Committee, November 1993; Margaret Kartomi to Logan, 3 November 1993; Karpin to Logan, 17 December 1993.
23 Letter from Victoria de los Angeles to 'The Management, Robert Blackwood Hall', 25 April 1995.
24 David Bradley, 'Theatre at Monash: a personal view', in F.W. Kent and D.D. Cuthbert (eds), *Making Monash, op cit*, pp 77–8.
25 *ibid*, pp 67–78.
26 Alexander Theatre, *Annual report 1986*; Philip A'Vard 9.7.1996.
27 Memorandum from Philip A'Vard to Dr P.S. Lake, Chair of the Alexander Theatre Committee, 16 August 1988; A'Vard 9.7.1996.
28 Letter from Logan to all staff ('Dear Colleague'), 13 June 1989.
29 Philip A'Vard, *Report on 1989 Monash Play Season*.
30 A'Vard 9.7.1996; letter from Justin Macdonnell to Logan, 5 October 1990.
31 Memorandum from Geoff Vaughan to R.J. Cochrane, Finance Manager, 1 October 1991.
32 Monash University, *Quality portfolio 1995*, p. 33.
33 Terry Threadgold to Logan, 1 March 1995; A'Vard 9.7.1996.
34 See chapter 6.
35 A'Vard 9.7.1996; Kartomi 29.8.1996.
36 *Etcetera*, issue 8, 12 March 1996.
37 John Clark, 'New arts centre puts Monash in the spotlight', *Mosaic*, December 1995, p. 4; note from Peter Fitzpatrick to the author, 1998.
38 Monash University, *Sight and sound*, 1996, p. 15.
39 Kartomi 29.8.1996; Clark, *op cit*, pp 4–5.
40 *ibid*, p. 5.
41 Memoranda from Jenepher Duncan to Logan, 30 May 1996 and 20 June 1996; Duncan 1.7.1996, 22.8.1996; Redmond 5.8.1996.
42 'Reflections with Redmond', *The Scene*, issue 1, 1996, p. 18.

Chapter 9 Learning, teaching, research

1 Replaced later by Shane Lucas.
2 Jenny Munz 14.8.1996, David Strover 16.8.1996.
3 Monash University, *Annual report 1988*, p. 38; Dimitri Serghis 30.8.1996.
4 Monash University, *Annual report 1988*, pp 38–9; Serghis 30.8.1996.
5 Sean Stratton 13.8.1996.
6 See chapter 2.
7 For example views expressed in interview with Baxt 12.8.1996.

8 Peter Nugent 16.8.1996; Marian Quartly 22.7.1996; Edwina Hanlon 30.8.1996.
9 Strover 16.8.1996; Serghis 30.8.1996.
10 David Cody 16.8.1996; Hanlon 30.8.1996.
11 Munz 14.8.1996; Strover 16.8.1996; Economou 23.8.1996.
12 Ben Richards 21.8.1996.
13 Cody 16.8.1996; Hanlon 30.8.1996; Serghis 30.8.1996.
14 Cody 16.8.1996.
15 Symon Rubens 15.8.1996.
16 Rubens 15.8.1996.
17 Richards 21.8.1996.
18 Richards 21.8.1996.
19 Hanlon 30.8.1996.
20 Hanlon 30.8.1996.
21 Letter from Lieutenant Colonel D.G. Blackwell, Commanding Officer, Monash University Regiment, to Elizabeth Anderson, adviser to the Vice-Chancellor, 24 January 1996.
22 Munz 14.8.1996; Rubens 15.8.1996; Cody 16.8.1996.
23 'Underemployment' refers to graduates who were seeking full-time work and working part-time.
24 Statistics from Bob Birrell, Centre for Population and Urban Research, Monash University, using the GCCA data set.
25 Mark Lawson, 'Education by degrees: where the paper trail ends', *Financial Review*, 15 January 1996.
26 Monash University, *1996 graduate destination survey*, pp 37, 44, 65.
27 *ibid*, pp 14, 53.
28 DET, 1993, *op cit*, p. 237.
29 Monash University, *Quality portfolio 1993, op cit*, pp 45–6; Pheona Selby and Terry Hore, *Cohort 94: a longitudinal study of student characteristics and expectations*, Interim Report, Professional Development Centre, Monash University, 1996.
30 Logan 20.12.1995.
31 Sinclair 9.7.1996; Warren 23.7.1996; Aspin 19.6.1996; Williams 14.11.1995, 9.7.1996.
32 Munz, 14.8.1996.
33 Economou 23.8.1996.
34 Baldwin, *op cit*, p. 3; Monash Students Association, *Counter Faculty Handbook: student opinions of subjects on campus*, 1996.
35 Business/Higher Education Round Table (BHERT), *Educating for excellence*, BHERT, Melbourne, 1992, pp 10–12, 26–9, 38–9; *Financial Review*, 'Education: the real key to success', editorial, 15 January 1996; Phil Ruthven, 'A bountiful future if you know where to look, *Financial Review*, 17 January 1996.
36 Monash University, *Quality portfolio 1993, vol. 2*, p. 24; *Monash University Statistics*, various years.
37 Logan, *Monash: toward 2000, op cit*, p. 41.
38 DEET, *Diversity and performance of Australian universities*, Higher Education Series no. 22, DEET, Canberra.
39 At Pharmacy in 1995, 86 per cent of all 1995 entrants had tertiary entrants marks that placed them in the top 10 per cent of school-leavers in the State.
40 Monash University, *Monash University enrolled VTAC applicants by school, 1991–1995*, unpublished data.
41 Data from Andrew Stephanou, University of Melbourne.
42 *Enrolled VTAC applicants by school, op cit*; ABS, *Schools Australia*, Catalogue no. 4221.0.
43 *Enrolled VTAC applicants by school, op cit*.
44 The latter group includes Catholic independent schools such as Xavier and St Kevins.
45 Robert Pargetter, *A report on Monash University's links with Victoria's secondary schools*, pamphlet, Monash University, 1995.

46 Pargetter 2.9.1996.
47 Pargetter, *A report on Monash University's links with Victoria's secondary schools, op cit*; Mike Brisk 24.7.1996.
48 Pargetter, *A report on Monash University's links with Victoria's secondary schools, op cit*; Pargetter 2.9.1996.
49 Pargetter, *A report on Monash University's links with Victoria's secondary schools, op cit*; *Annual Report 1995*, p. 9; Pargetter 2.9.1996.
50 Guy Healy, 'Dean alleges Rhodes bias against Monash', *The Australian*, 18 September 1996.
51 Monash University, *Quality portfolio 1993*, vol. 2, pp 92–5; *Quality portfolio 1994*, pp 11–12; *Annual Report 1995*, pp 18–19.
52 See chapter 2.
53 DEET, *Equity in higher education: a summary report*, AGPS, Canberra, 1993, pp 83–4; Monash University, *Profile visit, op cit*.
54 Monash University, *Annual report 1995*, p. 18; Byrt, *op cit*.
55 For example, interviews with Justin Castelan and Karen Hermann, co-editors of *Lots Wife* in 1992, 2.9.1996.
56 The first research unit on learning and teaching, with a single research officer, was established in 1966. Monash was the fourth Australian university to create such a capacity. The change from HERU to HEARU took place in 1974—*Quality Portfolio 1993*, vol. 2, p. 56.
57 Hore, *op cit*.
58 As a young Engineering academic Darvall took out a Monash diploma in tertiary teaching in the early 1970s.
59 Hore 23.7.1996; Aspin 19.6.1996; Rae 15.7.1996; Williams 9.7.1996; Fensham 2.7.1996.
60 Mal Logan, *Address to TAFE Directors*, 29 April 1993.
61 *Quality portfolio 1993*, vol. 2, pp 48–59; Hore, *op cit*.
62 Hore 23.7.1996; Melbourne 8.7.1996; Rae 15.7.1996; Darvall 16.7.1996; Warren 23.7.1996; Brisk 24.7.1996.
63 Communication from Marian Quartly, 16 March 1999.
64 After Chubb's resignation a review chaired by Darvall led to the re-separation of the two staff development centres, but they continued to share premises in Blackburn Road.
65 *Quality portfolio 1993*, vol. 2, pp 52, 54; Monash University, *Education and research policies*, pp 9–13.
66 See chapter 5.
67 Pargetter 2.9.1996.
68 Marginson and Considine, *op cit*, chapter 6; CQAHE, *op cit*, vol. 1, pp 3–7.
69 Monash University Academic Board, *Report of the Research Review Committee*, April 1992.
70 Pargetter 15.7.1996.
71 Melbourne 8.7.1996.
72 *Annual report 1992*, pp 17–18.
73 Logan, *Monash: toward 2000, op cit*, p. 26 and Tables 5.1 to 6.4; the University of Western Australia, *Annual Report and accounts 1994*.
74 See chapters 2 and 4.
75 Peter Darvall, Speech to members of Monash staff being presented with their 25-Year service medals, 28 October 1994.
76 Darvall 16.7.1996.
77 University of Western Australia, *op cit*; *Quality portfolio 1995, op cit*, p. 15.
78 *Directions for the future, op cit*, p. 11; *Quality portfolio 1995, op cit*, p. 2.
79 *ibid*, p. 3; CQAHE, *op cit*, vol. 2, pp 145–6.
80 *ibid*, pp 30–2; vol. 2, pp 144–7; *Quality portfolio 1995*, p. 13.
81 *Quality portfolio 1995*, p. 4; *Budget 1996*, p. 39.

82 *ibid*, pp 8–9.
83 *Annual Report 1995*, pp 20–1; *Quality portfolio 1995, op cit*, p. 23.
84 *ibid*, pp 27–8.
85 *ibid*, pp 9–10; *Annual Report 1995*, pp 20–1.
86 Logan 20.12.1995.
87 After his retirement from the University in 1998 Porter took the post of Planning Dean of the new medical school at James Cook University of North Queensland, based at Townsville and Cairns.
88 Porter 31.7.1996.
89 Porter 31.7.1996.
90 Porter 31.7.1996
91 Porter 31.7.1996; *Budget 1996*, p. 65; *Quality portfolio 1995*, pp 23, 25.
92 Data collated by Isabelle Normand on the basis of information from Monash IVF.
93 Alan Trounson 19.2.1996.
94 Trounson 19.2.1996; Institute of Reproduction and Devlopment, *Annual Report 1994*.
95 *ibid*; Normand, *op cit*; David de Kretser 24.4.1996; Trounson 19.2.1996.
96 de Kretser 24.4.1996.
97 Monash University, *Eureka* 1995, pp 14–15, 18–19.
98 Tracey McDonald 13.8.1996.
99 Porter 31.7.1996; McDonald 13.8.1996; *Annual Report 1994*, pp 21–2.
100 Chapman 9.7.1996; *Annual Report 1995*, p. 16.
101 *Annual Report 1995*, pp 16–17.
102 *Budget 1996*, p. 68; *Quality portfolio 1995*, p. 23; *Annual Report 1994*, p. 23; *Eureka: 1994 research report*, p. 7.
103 William Muntz 12.8.1996; Rae 15.7.1996; Warren 23.7.1996; Ron Davies 17.7.1996.
104 Rae 15.7.1996.
105 'New mine detector a sound idea', *Eureka*, 1994, p. 12.
106 Rae 15.7.1996; *Quality Portfolio 1995*, p. 23.
107 *Quality Portfolio 1995*, pp 24–5; *Budget 1996*, pp 71–2.
108 Sam Lake 1996.
109 Andrew Prentice 1996.
110 Prentice 1996; Cotton, 'Cosmic number cruncher', *Age/Sydney Morning Herald Good Weekend*, 15 June 1996.
111 *ibid*.
112 Prentice 1996; Cotton, *op cit*; Tim Thwaites, 'Where no man has gone before', *Montage*, 7 (2), April 1996, pp 10–11.
113 Pat Vickers-Rich 1996.
114 *Etcetera*, 23 January 1996, p. 3.
115 Bruce Williams, committee chair (1988), *Review of the discipline of Engineering, vol. 2: Comparative review of Engineering schools*, AGPS, Canberra, p. 242.
116 Melbourne 8.7.1996.
117 *Budget 1996*, p. 59; Brisk 24.7.1996.
118 Darvall 16.7.1996; *Annual Report 1994*, p. 20; *Annual Report 1995*, p.13.
119 Darvall 16.7.1996; *Annual Report 1994*, p. 19; *Quality portfolio 1993, vol. 2*, p. 107.
120 Darvall 16.7.1996; Brisk 24.7.1996.
121 *Quality portfolio 1995*, p. 12.
122 Interview with Bill Melbourne, by Bridget Nettelbeck, 1996.
123 Darvall, 16.7.1996; Melbourne, interview by Bridget Nettelbeck.
124 Bellamy 19.6.1996.
125 Interview with Branko Cesnik, by Bridget Nettelbeck, 1996.
126 Cesnick, interview by Bridget Nettelbeck; Bellamy 19.6.1996.
127 Juliet Ryan, 'The country road to the information superhighway', *Montage*, vol. 7, no. 8, November 1996, p. 13.

128 *ibid*; *Annual Report 1994*, p. 17.
129 Bellamy 19.6.96; *Budget 1996*, pp 53–4.
130 *ibid*, *Annual Report 1997*, p. 13.
131 *Quality portfolio 1993*, p. 66.
132 Chandler 1.7.1996, 3.7.1996.
133 Williams 14.11.1995; Monash University Faculty of Law, *A profile of the Monash Law Faculty 1995*, Attachment 1.
134 *ibid*, p. 2.
135 Williams 9.7.1996.
136 Williams 9.7.1996; Craig McInnis and Simon Marginson, *Australian law schools after the 1987 Pearce Report*, Evaluations and Investigations Program, DEET, AGPS, 1994.
137 Williams 9.7.1996.
138 Faculty of Law, *A profile*, *op cit*, Attachment 6.
139 *ibid*, pp 10, 12.
140 Hay 26.11.1996; Quartly 22.7.1996.
141 de Kretser 24.4.1996.
142 Helga Kuhse 28.5.1996.
143 *Annual Report 1988*, p. 10; National Centre for Australian Studies brochure and reports.
144 Pargetter 15.7.1996.
145 Interview with Liz Grosz by Bridget Nettelbeck, 1996.
146 Interview with Kevin Hart by Bridget Nettelbeck, 1996.
147 Strauss 2.7.1996.
148 *ibid*.
149 Quartly, 22.7.1996.
150 *1996 Budget*, p. 39; Quartly 22.7.1996.
151 Pargetter 15.7.1996.
152 *1996 Budget*, pp 47–8.
153 Matheson, *op cit*, p. 18.
154 *Annual Report 1987*, p. 14; White 31.7.1996.
155 Fensham 2.7.1996.
156 *1996 Budget*, pp 39, 56–7.
157 White 31.7.1996; Walker 13.8.1996.
158 Matheson, *op cit*, pp 18–19.
159 Gary Spink, 'A head of his times', *Montage*, vol. 7, no. 2, April 1996, pp 1–2.
160 Quartly 22.7.1996.
161 Amanda Vanstone, Commonwealth Minister for Employment, Education, Training and Youth Affairs, budget statement on higher education, August 1996.
162 *ibid*, p. 1.
163 Spink, *op. cit*.

Afterword

1 Marginson and Considine, *op cit*.

Index

Academic Board (formerly Professorial Board), 92–3, 110, 116, 124, 128–9, 147, 179, 181, 182, 217, 220
academic freedom *see* scholarship and scholarly values
academic performance, 20, 65, 67, 155, 165, 211–20
academic staff and academic work, 20–1, 25, 26, 31, 34–5, 49, 53, 63, 65–7, 84, 89–93, 144–5, 163–4, chapter 9 *passim*, 211–20, 233, 237, 238, 247; *see also* academic performance, FAUSA, MUSA, research, scholarship and scholarly values, teaching, women at Monash
academic staff responses to the remaking of Monash, 68, 83, 87, 89–93, 104–7, 171, 250
access to and equity in higher education, 26, 39–40, 50, 59, 62, 64, 78, 89, 114, 164–5, 207–11, 220, 248
Accident Research Centre, 219, 231–2
administration and administrative staff of the University, 10, 17, 20, 30, 73–4, 141, 155–6, 177, 211, 216, 219, 238; integration of merged administrations, 113, 118
'a place apart' as an idea of the university, ix, 6–8, 48–50
Age, The, 79, 91, 147, 185
Aitkin, Don, 56, 65–6

Alexander Theatre, 92, 186, 190, 192–5
ALP *see* Labor Party
alumni, 32, 62, 102, 177
Anderson, Elizabeth, 80, 122, 146, 166–7
Andrew, Rod, 11, 187, 189
archives and archive management, ix–x, 122, 234
Art and Design sub-faculty/ Faculty, 108, 123–5, 196–7
Arts Faculty, 2, 9, 11–12, 30–1, 34, 38, 41, 48, 63, 66, 104, 123–5, 132, 147, 151, 152, 158, 160, 162–3, 169, 172, 174, 175–6, 184, 187, 203–47 *passim*
art collection of the University, 186–90
arts, the, 3, 28, 185; at Monash, 84, 113, chapter 8 *passim*, 249, Plates 9–15; *see also* Art and Design, galleries, music, theatre
Asia-Pacific region, 74–5, 84, 135–55 *passim*, 235; *see also* East Asia, Southeast Asia
Asia-Pacific Economic Cooperation (APEC), 139–40; APEC Study Centre, 141
'Asianisation' strategy of Australian government, 139–41
Aspin, David, 88, 124, 179, 244
Australian, The, 33, 64, 85, 94
Australian Broadcasting Corporation (ABC), 191–2, 226, Plate 13

Australian Centre for Contemporary Art, 188–90
Australian Centre for Jewish Civilisation, 173
Australian government policy *see* Commonwealth policy
Australian National University (ANU), 28, 29, 31, 56, 135, 141, 160, 183
Australian Research Council (ARC), 56, 65–6, 177, 215, 219, 223, 225, 231, 236, 244, 245
Australian Research Grants Council (ARGS), 37
Australian Science and Technology Council (ASTEC), 29
Australian studies centres, 152–3
Australian Vice-Chancellors' Committee, 40, 41, 64, 76
A'Vard, Philip, 192–5

Baldwin, Gay, 40, 172, 206
Baldwin, Peter, 64, 159
Baxt, Bob, 34, 85, 87, 150, 200, 238
Beilby, Peter, 82–3, 103
Bellamy, Cliff, ix, 36, 82, 122–3, 179, 181, 234
Berwick campus, viii, 98, 102, 164–5, 170, 208, 234, Plates 16–17
binary system, 26, chapter 3 *passim*, 54, 58–9
Blackwood, Robert, 8, 18–19
Bornstein, Joseph, 27, 28

Braudel, Fernand, x, 69, 74,
Brisk, Mike, 121
broadcast education, 157–60
Broken Hill Proprietary Ltd (BHP), 26, 34, 73, 146, 173, 231
Brown, Ron, 27, 34, 37
Brunt, Maureen, 34–5
buildings at Monash, 15–16, 18–20, 25, 118–20, 131–4, 186–96, 229, Plates 13–25; embellishment with art works, 186–7
Burma see Mynamar
business education, 7–9, 58, 69–70, 127, 143
Business and Economics Faculty, 63, 118, 125, 147, 155, 158, 160, 162–3, 164, 172, 175–6, 178, 179, 203, 205, 206, 209, 212, 218, 224, 233–4, 235–7, 245; problems of merger, 88, 103, 108, 125–31, 133, 146, 152, 169, 197, 235
Butchardt, Jim, 15, 17, 20, 26, 74, 86
Button, John, 52, 54–5, 139–40, 146

Cambodia, 145
Cambridge University, 28, 29, 32
Campbell, Enid, 34, 93, 238–9
Canada, 136, 142, 155, 220
Catholic schools, 208–10
Caulfield campus, 9–10, 100, 118–19, 120–34 passim, 147, 155, 158, 161–2, 189, 196–7, 199, 200, 208, 219, 230, Plates 20–21
Caulfield Institute of Technology (later part of Chisholm), 12, 97, 100
Centre for Human Bioethics, 35, 36, 158, 240–1
Centre of Policy Studies, 23, 35, 37, 141, 235
chancellorship, 33–4, 88, 95, 106
Chandler, Peter, 127–9, 133, 146, 159, 235
Chemistry department, 20, 29, 31, 91, 122, 212, 224–5
children's theatre, 190, 193–4
China and Chinese studies, 38, 64, 75, 135–55 passim, 157, 228, 230, 236
Chipman, Lauchlan, 168, 170
Chisholm Institute of Technology, 61, 97–110, 133–4, 144, 163; unions, 103, 107–10, 149, 188, 211
Chisholm merger, 36, 80, 85–7, 91, 100–10, 217, 235
Chubb, Ian, 80, 130, 166, 169–70, 180, 181, 183–4, 212–13
City campus (30 Collins Street), 10, 85, 98, 120, 174, 188, Plate 23
Clayton campus, 9, 120, 147, 160, 161–2, 165, 172, 183–4, 198–203, 208, 230, 235–6, Plates 14–15 and 24–26
Clayton, the suburb, 9–10, 155
coat of arms of the University, 10, 171–2
Cochrane, Donald, 11, 26, 136
colleges of advanced education (CAEs), 24, 26, chapter 3 passim, 58–61, 67, 87, 90, 107, 127, 133–4, 211, 215, 223
Colombo Plan, 17, 135–6, 143
combined courses, 152, 206–7, 244
Committee of Deans see deans and the deanship
Commonwealth government, chapter 3 passim, 135–6, 138–41
Commonwealth policy on higher education, 6–9, 22–7, 28, 35, 41–2, chapter 3 passim, 112, 141–2, 154–5, 158–9, 164–5, 179, 182–4, 198–202, 215, 218, 228–9; see also Dawkins reforms, government funding
Commonwealth Scientific and Industrial Research Organisation (CSIRO), 5, 9, 14, 26, 65, 224, 232
Commonwealth Tertiary Education Commission (CTEC), 24, 26, 40, 53–6, 59
communications, 114, 136–9, 155–60, 164–5, 234, 240, 250
competition and competitive strategies, 3–4, 49, 51, 81, 236; between universities, 20, 23, 31, 53–4, 56, 64, 89, 94, 182–4, 204, 207–11, 215, 218–19, 233, 237–8, 245, 249; see also markets
computers in education, 36, 155–7, 230–1, Plate 8
Computing Faculty, ix, 108, 118–19, 122–5, 144, 147, 155, 158, 160, 162–3, 175–6, 179, 205, 209, 224, 233–4, 245
consulting see funding and fund-raising
context (economic, social and cultural), ix, chapters 1–3 passim, 72, 78–9, 154, 249–50
continuing professional education, 38, 62–3, 84, 156, 247
Cooperative Research Centres (CRCs), 65, 90, 175, 218–19, 225, 227, 232–3
corporate (company) activity at Monash, 96, 146–8, 165, 173
Costar, Brian, 127
Council of Chisholm Institute of Technology, 101–9
Council of Monash University, 8, 15, 26, 33–4, 40–2, 45, 67, 72–4, 75, 82, 84, 86, 88, 92, 103–9, 116, 121, 144, 153, 166, 173
Council of Gippsland Institute of Advanced Education, 112–13
counter-culture, 16, 42, 46
cultural change in the University see remaking
cultural difference and diversity, 38, 42, 89, chapter 6 passim, 147–8, 150, 151, 155, 220, 244–5

Darvall, Peter, 72, 87, 120–1, 146, 166, 168–70, 180, 184, 214–19, 228–33
David Syme Business School, 83, 102–9, 125–31, 144, 235
Dawkins, John and the Dawkins reforms, viii, chapter 3 passim, 48, 53–6, 67–8, 75, 79, 81, 87, 92–3, 97, 101, 107, 112, 146, 167, 182, 233, 249
de Kretser, David, 219, 221–3, 240

INDEX

Deakin University, 32, 94, 106, 110–12, 115, 158, 159, 205, 208, 235, 238
deans and the deanship at Monash, 15, 33–4, 75, 79–80, 84, 87–8, 92, 95, 103–4, 106, 111, 121, 166–70, 177–82, 212, 213, 220, 244
Department of Employment, Education and Training, 54, 59
Department of Prime Minister and Cabinet, 29, 53–4
Deputy Vice-Chancellors (DVCs), 73–4, 80, 165–70, 180–1
Derham, David, 11–12
devolution, 5, 12, 15, 33, 53, 70, 79, 92, 179–82, 184, 214–19, 245, 247
disabled students, 42, 210–11
distance education, 93, 110–12, 119, 131, 147, 155–60 *passim*, 162, 207, 248
distinctive Monash strategy for development, viii, 13, 32, 81–9, 94, 96, 136, 249–50; *see also* State university model
diversity in higher education, 60, 94; within Monash, 89, 93–4, Plates 23–25
Drucker, Peter, 69–70, 72, 79
Duncan, Jenepher, 187–90, 197
Dunstan, Barry, 111

East Asia, viii, 38, 135–55 *passim*, 220, 250, Plate 26
economic role of education, 6, 22–3, 49–53
Economics and Politics Faculty, later Economics and Management, Business and Economics, 9, 11–12, 13, 30–1, 42, 87, 104, 106, 125–31, 162–3, 175–6, 194
Economou, Nick, 32, 44, 206
education–business/industry relationships, 5–8, 26, 32, 37, chapter 3 *passim*, 49–53, 75, 82, 84, 95, 172–3, 205–6, 217–18, 224–5, 228–33, 237–8; Business-Higher Education Round Table, 52–3, 77
Education Committee, 169, 183–4, 213

Education Faculty, 11–12, 30–1, 34, 98, 104, 114, 124–5, 158, 162–3, 169, 175–6, 178, 179, 184, 205, 212, 218, 243–5, 247
Eggleston, Richard, 27, 33–4
Endersbee, Lance, 26, 31, 34, 36, 37, 41, 42, 87, 88, 142, 167, 216, 217, 229
engagement of Monash in the larger context, ix, 4, 21, chapters 3 and 4 *passim*, 48–53, 78–9, 136, 171, 249–50; *see also* education–business
Engineering Faculty, 2, 9, 11–12, 17, 20, 26, 30–1, 37–8, 39, 41–2, 87, 89, 104, 106, 118, 120–2, 132, 146, 152, 158, 160, 162–3, 172, 175–6, 179, 197, 203, 205, 206, 208, 212–13, 216–17, 218, 219, 229–33, 243, 245
Evans, Gareth, 139–40
equity *see* access
executive group of leaders, 33, 73–4, 88, 96, 165–70, 171, 181, 186–7, 197

faculties, role and structure at Monash, 13, 15, 33–4, 75, 93, 106, 107–8, 131, 158, 165–70, 174–82, 183, 207, 212–19, 243, 245, 247, 250
'Farm Week' (later 'Green Week'), 42, 199
Federation of Australian University Staff Associations (FAUSA), 25, 35, 39, 41, 92, 216–17
fee-charging of students, 23, 42, 53–4, 62–3, 141, 142–6, 159, 174–7, 198–9, 234, 247
Fels, Alan, 36, 83, 95
feminism *see* gender
Fensham, Peter, 34, 87, 90, 124, 243–4
financial management *see* management
foundation of Monash, viii, chapter 1 *passim*, 6–10
Frankston campus *see* Peninsula campus

Fraser (1975–83 Liberal–National) government, 22–6
Friends of Russell Drysdale, 25, 187, 189
funding and fund-raising at Monash, 35, 91–2, 174–9, 220, 222–3, 245–50; capital funding, 81, 117, 129, 131, 164, 186; consulting work, 35, 236; distribution of funds inside the University, 15, 84, 165, 167, 177–9, 214–15, 218–19, 237; 'outside' (non-government) earnings, 25, 26, 32, 37, 81, 85, 87–8, 91, 131, 144–5, 153–4, 174–7, 219, 222–3, 224, 228–33, 234, 235, 243, 244
funding of universities, chapters 1–3 *passim*, chapter 7 *passim*; capital funding, 17, 24, 60, 62, 64, 101, 118–19; government funding, 4–5, 17, 20, 22–7, 28, 32, 50–1, 56, 58, 62–3, 118–19, 174, 207, 242–3, 244, 245–9; non-government funding, 48–56, 62–3; relative funding model, 62, 179; research quantum, 215, 218

galleries at Monash, 178, 186–90, 196; Clayton Gallery and Gallery Building, 25, 118, 186–90, Plate 25
gender, 5, 16; in education, 24, 58; *see also* women at Monash, men at Monash
general staff *see* administrative staff
Gippsland campus, 55, 118, 120–34 *passim*, 146, 147, 157, 157–60, 161–2, 164–5, 170, 188–90, 196–7, 199, 205, 208, 213, 219, 234, 244, Plate 22
Gippsland Institute of Advanced Education, 2, 61, 98, 103, 110–14, 133, 144, 149, 163, 211
Gippsland merger, 85–6, 110–14, 217
global role of Monash, Foreword *passim*, viii, 89, 93, 114,

275

chapter 6 *passim*, 171, 249–50, Plates 5–6
globalisation and globalisation of education, 49, 52, 74–6, 79, 114, chapter 6 *passim*, 136–9, 234, 246, 249
governance of Monash, 13, 15, 75–6, 96, 147, chapter 7 *passim*, 217, 245, 247, 250
government funding of universities *see* funding
government schools, 39, 208–10
government university relations, 7–8, 26, 31, 39–40, chapter 3 *passim*, 48–53, 56, 62–4, 78–9; at Monash, chapters 3 and 4 *passim*, 54–6, 64, 68, 81, 94–5, 112, 137, 191, 247–8, 250
graduate labour markets, 6–8, 42, 48, 52, 57, 132, 138–9, 203–7
graduation off-shore, 145, 147
Green Paper on higher education (1987), 55, 56–67, 84, 87, 91, 101, 107, 110, 115
Grosz, Elizabeth, 240
grounds and plantings at Monash, 15–16, 133–4, 186, Plates 14–15, 18–19 and 26
growth of higher education, chapter 1 *passim*, 23, 26, chapter 3 *passim*, 59–62
growth of the University and its absence, and their effects, viii, 11–12, 20–1, 22–7, 32, 47, 59–62, 81, 87, 89, 91, chapter 5 *passim*, 131–2, chapter 7 *passim*, 217, 229–30, 237

Halls of Residence, 200, 202–3
Harman, Grant, and Meek, Lyn, 48, 99–100, 131
Hart, Kevin, 241–2
Hawke (1983–92 Labor) government, 22, 23–6, 37, 39–40, chapter 3 *passim*, 51–6
Hay, John, 80, 82, 85, 87, 91, 94, 95, 101, 106–8, 120, 132, 168, 173, 180, 237, 239–40
Higher Education Advisory and Research Unit (HEARU), 24, 40, 42, 212–13
Higher Education Contribution Scheme, 62–3, 199, 202
Higher Education Council, 56, 169
Holman, Mollie, 34, 220
Hong Kong, 17, 41, 111, 135–55 *passim*
Hore, Terry, 12, 24, 39, 83, 95, 172
Howard (1996– Liberal–National) government, 154–5, 247
Hunt, Ken, 11, 216

India, 135, 145, 148, 154, 228
Indonesia, 135–55 *passim*, 196
independent private (non-government) schools, 39, 207–10
indigenous education and indigenous studies, 35, 38, 40–1, 64, 196, 200, 202, 211, Plate 1
industrial relations, 34–5, 54, 92, 103, 109–110, 123
institutional size in higher education, 59–61, 101, 110, 115
intellectual property, 37, 63, 65, 67, 157, 238–9
international education and international students, 17, 38–9, 41–2, 74, 89, 90, 93–4, chapter 6 *passim*, 247–8, Plates 5–6; international education as a field of study, 244–5
international marketing of education, 23, 51–2, 53, 62–3, 67, 126–8, 135–55 *passim*, 142–8, 171–2, 174–7, 234, 235
international trade, 51–2, 137–43
internationalisation as a University strategy, 136–55 *passim*; of the curriculum, 138, 143, 151, 153, 154; impact of internationalisation on Anglo-Australian students, 38, 136, 152
internationalism, 4, 38–9, 41, 74–80
in-vitro fertilisation (IVF), 36, 74, 174, 178, 219, 221–3, 240–1

Jackson report, 42
Japan and Japanese studies, 38, 50, 75, 76, 135–55 *passim*, 196, 238, Plate 26
Jarvis, Ray, 230–1
Johnson, Frank, 15, 17, 20, 26

Kartomi, Margaret, 196
Keating (1992–96 Labor) government, chapter 6 *passim*
Keating, Paul, 52, 150
Kemp, David, 37, 45
Kennedy, Tom, 111–13
Korea *see* South Korea

La Trobe University, 12, 13, 16, 32, 61–2, 97, 98, 101, 208, 238
La Trobe Valley, 2, 110–14, 133, 161–2, Plate 22
Labor Party, 17, 43–4, 55, 75, 79, 200; *see also* Button, Commonwealth policy, Dawkins, Evans, Hawke, Keating, Ryan
Langer, Albert, 16, 43, 199
language and languages, 135–55 *passim*, 242–3
Laos, 145, 150, 152
Law Faculty, 9, 11–12, 17, 30–1, 35, 38, 41, 118–19, 162–3, 175–6, 203, 206, 207, 210, 211, 212, 214, 218, 237–9, 243–4, 245, 247
leadership, in business, 69–72; in universities, 31–2, chapter 4 *passim*, 69–74, 79, 165–70, 179–82, 186–7, 216
Legge, John, 9, 12, 27, 47
Liberal and National Parties, 37, 44, 75, 199–200; *see also* Commonwealth policy, Fraser government, Howard government

libraries and librarianship, ix, 25–6, 31, 35, 108, 118–19, 122, 123–4, 151, 218, 234, 238
Logan, Mal, 29, 31, 33, 44, 54–5, 60, 67–8, chapter 4 *passim*, 73–81, 94–6, 98–116 *passim*, 120, 125, 128–9, 131–2, 135–55 *passim*, 158, 160, 165–73, 177, 179–81, 183–4, chapter 8 *passim*, 205, 207–8, 212, 215–16, 219, 228–9, 237, 245, 248, 250
Lots Wife, 25, 32, 38, 41–6, 198–203, 206
Lush, George, 33, 88, 95, 105–6

Malaysia and Malaysian studies, 17, 41, 75, 127–9, 135–55 *passim*, 177, 245
Malaysian (Kuala Lumpur) campus of Monash, 150, 152
management of universities, including Monash, 5, 49, 53, 56, 59, 60, 67, chapter 4 *passim*, 71–2, 79, 92, chapter 7 *passim*, 186–7, 211–19, 243, 247; financial management, 53, chapter 7 *passim*, 229; *see also* administration, leadership
market competition *see* competition
marketing of Monash, viii, 84, 90, 113, 153–4, 155, 165, 170–3, 247
markets, 23; in education, 48–54, 56, 62–3, 64–5, 81, 94, 138–55 *passim*, 157–9
Marshall, Jock, 10, 11, 16, 186
Martin, Ray, chapter 2 *passim*, 28–30, 31, 33, 62, 74–5, 77, 80–2, 90–1, 97, 150, 166, 177, 233, 250
Martin report (1964), 67, 97
mass higher education, 4, 7, 16, 48, 50
Mathematics departments, 122, 212, 219, 225, 233
Matheson, Louis, chapter 1 *passim*, 14, 17–18, 26, 29, 33, 37, 62, 76, 90, 96–7, 166, 177, 186, 212, 233, 250
McCaughey, Patrick, 186–7
McNeill, James and McNeill Committee (1985), 34, 72–4, 77, 176, 178
medical education, 6, 13, 220
Medicine Faculty, 9, 11–13, 15, 17, 20, 30–1, 35, 38–9, 89, 116, 119, 162–3, 175–6, 179, 197, 203, 205, 207, 210, 212–13, 220–4, 225, 232–4, 243, 245, 247, Plate 2
men at Monash, 11, 42, 162, 199
Melbourne, Bill, 31, 129, 231–3
Menzies, Douglas, 14, 33
Menzies building, 16, 18–19, 43, 119, 187, 192, 201, 242
mergers, in business, 70–2; in higher education, chapter 3 *passim*, 53, 56, 58–62, 67, 98–9, 248
mergers at Monash, viii, 87, 89–90, 95–6, chapter 5 *passim*, 136, 171, 183, 188, 215, 244, 250; outcomes, 131–4; *see also* Chisholm merger, Gippsland merger, Pharmacy merger, Faculties
Micklethwait, John, and Woolridge, Adrian, 69, 70
Middle East, 44, 145, 198
modernisation, 6–7; of universities, 13, 21, 82, 95–6, 132, 136, 171, 177, 216, 220, 248
modernism, 4–5, 13, 16, 18–19, 44–5, 54, 69, 78, 134, 186
Monash, City of, 161
Monash, John, 1–6 *passim*, 110, 117, 161, 185–6, 203, 217, 233, Plates 9–10
Monash Association of Students (MAS) *see* students
Monash Gallery *see* galleries
Monash International, 102, 146–8, 158–9, 165, 174, 178, 245
Monash Jewish Students Society (MONJSS), 44, 198
Monash Orientation Scheme for Aborigines (MOSA), 40–1, 211, Plate 1

Monash University Act 1958, viii, 1, 8–9, 13, 81, 86, 158
Monash University (Chisholm and Gippsland) Act 1990, 86, 108
Monash University Foundation, 25, 26, 73, 120, 165, 175–8
Monash University Foundation Year (MUFY), 148–9, 154
Monash University Staff Association (MUSA), formerly SAMU, 25, 35, 40, 66, 91, 104–8, 110, 115, 169
motto of the University, 10, 136, 171
Mount Eliza Business School, 130, 132, 150, 169, 175
'multiversity', the, 78, 97; *see also* State university model
Murray, Noel, 191–2, 194
Murray Committee (1957), 7–9, 67
Music department and music at Monash, 186, 191–2, 195–6, 209, 242, Plates 11–13
Mynamar, 136, 153

naming of the University, 1, 8, 129
National Centre for Australian Studies, 95, 239–40, 243
National Health and Medical Research Council, 37, 215, 219, 223
national identity and nationalism, 5, 13, 16, 74, 76, 186–8; in a global environment, 136–41, 249–50
Neat, Gary, 95, 153, 166–7, 170–3
Neave, Marcia, 238–9
neo-liberalism in politics and economics, 23, 49, 54, 58
New Zealand, 135, 149, 228
Newman, John and his idea of the university, 48–50, 59, 67, 77–8
Nottinghill Hotel ('the Nott'), 9–10, 42, 200
Nursing education at Monash, 108, 118–19, 123–4, 132, 147, 158, 205, 223–4, 233–4, Plate 18

on-line education and 'virtual universities', 155–60, 164–5
Open Learning, 64, 88, 93, 158, 159–60, 170, 175, 177–8, 247–8
Organisation for Economic Cooperation and Development (OECD), 49, 50, 52, 57–8, 63, 65, 76, 82, 135, 138, 235

Pacific Economic Cooperation Council (PECC), 140–1
Pakistan, 136
Pargetter, Robert, 86, 87, 91, 113, 166, 168–70, 182, 184, 195, 208, 241–3
Parkville campus *see* Pharmacy
participation and participation rates in education, 24, 50, 56, 57–8, 84, 161–2, 200, 211, 248
Penington, David, 67, 77, 87, 94
Peninsula campus, 100, 105, 118–34 *passim*, 147, 162, 165, 194, 196, 199, 205, 208, 219, 224, 233, 244, Plates 18–19
Performing Arts Building, 119, 186, 195–6, Plates 11–15
Peters and Waterman, 69–70
Pharmaceutical Society of Victoria, 115–17, 224
Pharmacy campus and Faculty, 10, 62, 98, 118–19, 132, 133, 147, 162–3, 175–6, 199, 205, 208, 219, 224, 245, 247
Pharmacy merger, 115–17, 218
Physics department, 20, 31, 38, 122, 212, 225
planning, 3, 5, 53, 182; planning at Monash, viii, 17, 34, chapter 4 *passim*, 73, 81–5, 170, 182–4, 218
Playbox Theatre, 77, 178, 193–4
Polmear, Ian, 83, 104, 167
Porter, Michael (Harvard), 49, 81
Porter, Michael (Monash), 23, 235
Porter, Robert, 31, 77, 80, 87–8, 91, 106, 116, 168–70, 214, 220
postgraduate students and postgraduate education, 20, 35, 57, 58, 100, 110, 123–4, 127, 154, 162, 174, 179, 183, 188, 218–19, 224–5, 234, 235, 237–8, 242–4
Prentice, Andrew, 226–8
Pritchard, Tony, 74, 79, 82–3, 85–6, 91, 95, 98, 111, 159, 177–8
private universities, 54, 58, 60, 150
Pro-Vice-Chancellors (PVCs), 73, 165–70, 180
Professional Development Centre, 172, 213
Professional Studies Faculty, 108–9, 122–4, 234
Professorial Board (later Academic Board), 15, 36, 40, 41–2, 82–4, 86, 88, 92, 98, 105–7, 110, 112, 121, 144, 166
Psychology, 47, 92, 122, 123–4
public good and public service, 3, 5, 7–8, 21, 185–9, 221–3, 239
public image of the University, 16–17, 31, 170–3; *see also* marketing
Pugh, Clifton, 95, 186
'Purple Circle', 55–6, 75, 79

quality of education, 50, 78, 89–90, 107, 182–4, 237, 247–8; quality assurance systems, 53, 56, 170; Commonwealth Committee on Quality Assurance in Higher Education, 86, 93, 182–4, 201, 211, 218
Quartly, Marian, 19, 80, 87, 243

racism and ethnocentrism, 5, 16, 41–2, 136, 140, 154–5
Rae, Ian, 66, 122, 168, 212, 225
Ramler, Paul, 101–6, 126, 133, 146
Redmond, John, 197
reinforced concrete technique in engineering, 2, 217
re-engineering of universities, chapter 3 *passim*, 60, 62, 63–5
remaking ('re-engineering') of Monash University, Foreword *passim*, viii–ix, 21, 26, 31–3, 49–53, 56, 68, chapter 4 *passim*, 74, 78–81, 89–90, 93–6, 131, 170–3; consent building, 79–84, 87, 91–3, 101, 104–8, 167, 181, 245–50; *see also* academic staff responses, American State university model, distinctive Monash strategy for development
research and research at Monash, viii, 29–30, 31, 36–7, 49, 74, 77, 82, 84, 90, 94, 115, 125, 137, 151, 155, 175, 177, 180, 182–4, chapter 9 *passim*, 211, 213–19, 249–50; entrepreneurial science, 51–3, 59, 65–7; research management and organisation, 35, 51, 53, 56, 59, 64, 213–19; research policy and funding, 20, 51–2, 59, 62, 64–7, 213–14; research–teaching nexus, 65–7
Research Committee, 214–19
Rickard, John, 130, 235–6
Rizvi, Fazal, 244–5
(Sir) Robert Blackwood Hall, 16, 186, 190–2, 194–6, Plate 24
Robinson, David, 132, 216, 246–8
Rodan, Paul, 122, 133
Rogers, Bill, 95
Royal Melbourne Institute of Technology (RMIT), 8, 56, 61–2, 100–1, 154, 160–1, 200, 208
Rusden campus of Victoria College, 62, 97, 98, 103, 115
Ryan, Susan, 26, 35, 39–40, 41, 53

salaries of staff, 35, 123, 248–9
Schofield, Graeme, 27, 35, 87
scholarship and scholarly values, 4, 20, 28, 31, 35, 48–53, 67–72, 75, 78–80, 89–93, 170–3, 181–2, chapter 9 *passim*, 206, 209–17, 250

school–university transition and schools liaison, 13, 57, 89, 170, 171, 190–5, 207–11, 228–30
schools *see* Catholic schools, government schools, independent private schools
science, 4, 5, 6–8, 13, 49, 51
Science Faculty, 8, 10, 11–12, 15, 25, 30–1, 37–8, 48, 63, 66, 89, 91, 104, 106, 121–2, 132, 158, 160, 162–3, 168–9, 175–6, 179, 184, 203, 205–6, 209, 212–13, 218, 220, 224–9, 232–3, 243, 245, 247
Scott, Bill, 11, 26, 33
Selby-Smith, Richard, 11, 124, 244
selection of students, 26, 39–40, 220
Serle, Geoffrey and his biography of Monash, 2–3, 36
Sinclair, Gus, 25, 38, 83, 87, 126–7, 180, 206
Singer, Peter, 36, 236, 240–1
Singapore, 41, 111, 135–55 *passim*, 190
siting of the University at Clayton, 9–10, 45, 84, 165, Plates 20–21
Snedden, Richard, 123–4, 133
Social Work, 108, 123–4, 158, 205
South Africa, 150
South Asia, 136, 151–2
Southeast Asia, viii, 38, 41–2, 84, 111, 114, 126, 135–55 *passim*, 171, 228, 243, 250, Plate 26
Southeast Asian studies, 35, 196, Plate 26
South Korea, 135–55 *passim*, 157
Spearritt, Peter, 95, 159, 240
Sports and Recreation Association, 43, 45, 203
Sri Lanka (formerly Ceylon), 135, 145, 148
Staff Association of Monash University (SAMU) *see* Monash University Staff Association
State College of Victoria (SCV) Frankston, 97, 100
State Electricity Commission of Victoria (SECV), 1, 110, 113, 120, 233, Plate 22

State university model, 59, 78, 87, 101, 136, 161–2, 207, 249
Steedman, Peter, 43
strategic management *see* management
strategic planning *see* planning
Strauss, Jenny, 25, 174, 242
students, 10–12, 30–1, 39–47, 131–3, 146–7, 161–3, 193, 195, 197, 198–211 *passim*, 235, 238, 245, 249; as consumers, 53, 131, 156, 207; financial assistance, 24, 26; mature aged students, 24, 57, 207; political activism, 16–17, 20, 23, 32, 43–4, 128, 130, 185, 198–202; student theatre, 185–6, 192; student unions and activities, 4, 42–6, 102, 108, 119, 132, 169, 198–203, 211
Sullivan, Martin, 25, 40
Sungwei Group of companies, 149–50
Sunway College, 85, 149–50
Swan, John, 1, 33
Swinburne Institute/University, 61–2, 94, 98, 101–3, 114–15

Taiwan, 135–55 *passim*
teaching and learning, viii, 155–60, 169–70, 182–4, chapter 9 *passim*, 211–13, 250; status of teaching, 65, 67, 212–13; *see also* academic staff and academic work, students
Teaching and Research Action Group (TRAG), 91–4, 108, 171
Technical and Further Education (TAFE), 24, 53, 54, 56–9, 69, 88, 93, 100, 102, 164–5, 170, 207
technologies in education and administration, 56, 155–60 *passim*, 164–5, 212, 220, 234, 238
tenure, 35, 242
Tertiary Education Commission (later Commonwealth Tertiary Education Commission), 19

Thailand, 17, 41, 135–55 *passim*
theatre at Monash, 185–6, 190, 192–5, 242
transport to Monash *see* siting of the University
Trounson, Alan, 219, 222–3

Unified National System, chapter 3 *passim*
United Kingdom, chapter 1 *passim*, 51, 71–2, 135, 138, 142, 148–9, 155, 157, 243
United States of America, 50–1, 65, 76, 86, 135–55 *passim*, 224, 226–7, 232, 241, 243, 250; *see also* State university model of university
universities in Australia, 1, 6–8, 13, 16, 20, 22–4, 26, 30–1, 35, chapter 3 *passim*, 48–53, 159–60, 182–4, 220, 249–50
universities, international, 28, 35, 37, 50–2, 97, 143, 152–3, 169, 220, 223, 231, 249–50
University of Adelaide, 31, 183, 215, 238–9
University of California, 38, 97–8, 152, 223, 249
University of Melbourne, viii, chapter 1 *passim*, 6–8, 28–32, 61–2, 80–2, 86, 94, 97, 101, 115–17, 133, 135, 161, 174, 179, 183, 200, 207–10, 215, 218–21, 233, 236–8, 250
University of NSW, 8, 29, 30–1, 94, 135, 141, 144, 146, 154, 183, 215, 219
University of Queensland, 30–1, 94, 160, 179, 183, 215, 218–19, 220, 244
University of Sydney, 6, 30–1, 76, 101, 135, 174, 183, 200, 215, 219, 220, 233
University of Western Australia, 31, 56, 183, 215, 219
utilitarianism in education, chapter 3 *passim*, 48–53, 56, 67–8

Vaizey, John, 27
Vaughan, Geoff, 101–6, 109, 114, 116, 126, 133

279

vice-chancellorship, 15, 26, 29, 35, 71–4, 88, 94–6, 147, 166, 170, 178, 180, 250
Vickers-Rich, Pat, 228–9
Victoria, State government and parliament, 1, 6, 8, 37, 62, 97, 105, 109–10, 126, 164, 178, 202, 231–2, 239
Victoria College, 85, 97, 98, 100, 101, 114
Victorian Post-Secondary Education Commission, 98, 101
Vietnam, 145–6, 152, 153
'virtual universities' *see* on-line education

vocationalism, 42, 48, 52–3, 61, 77–8, 138, 197, 203–7, 238, Plates 7–8

Wade, Peter, 43, 74, 82–3, 85–6, 95, 102–3, 116–17, 125, 133, 146, 152, 166–8, 170, 172, 174–9, 181, 187, 189, 193, 216, 222, 232
Waller, Louis, 12, 17, 36, 77, 95, 214–15
Watts, Don, 55–6, 60, 77
West, Bruce, 27, 33
West, Leo, 39, 83, 95, 146, 153, 166, 168

Westfold, Kevin, 11, 20, 33, 35–6, 39, 73–4, 82, 167
White, John, 103, 133
White Paper on higher education (1988), 56–67, 115
White, Richard, 243
Whyte, Richard, 133–4
Williams, Bob, 20, 87–8, 106, 170, 179–80, 206, 210, 237–8
women at Monash, 11, 21, 26, 30, 34, 40, 42, 58, 80, 147, 162–4, 170, 190, 203, 206, 217, 220, 238–43, Plates 2–4; childcare, 40
Wood, Carl, 27, 36, 222–3